TURKISH ECONOMY
AT THE
CROSSROADS

Facing the Challenges Ahead

Highly Recommended Titles

Economics of the Middle East: Development Challenges
by Julia C Devlin
ISBN: 978-981-4675-18-5 (hardcover)
ISBN: 978-981-4675-19-2 (paperback)

Abu Dhabi's Vision 2030: An Ongoing Journey of
Economic Development
by Linda Low
ISBN: 978-981-4383-92-9

Women, Work and Welfare in the Middle East and North Africa:
The Role of Socio-demographics, Entrepreneurship and Public Policies
edited by Nadereh Chamlou and Massoud Karshenas
ISBN: 978-1-78326-733-0

Understanding the Political Economy of the Arab Uprisings
edited by Ishac Diwan
ISBN: 978-981-4596-00-8

The Economics of the Middle East and North Africa (MENA)
by Joseph Pelzman
ISBN: 978-981-4327-51-0

TURKISH ECONOMY
AT THE
CROSSROADS

Facing the Challenges Ahead

editors

Asaf Savaş Akat
Istanbul Bilgi University, Turkey

Seyfettin Gürsel
Bahçeşehir University, Turkey

 **World Scientific**

NEW JERSEY · LONDON · SINGAPORE · BEIJING · SHANGHAI · HONG KONG · TAIPEI · CHENNAI

Published by

World Scientific Publishing Co. Pte. Ltd.

5 Toh Tuck Link, Singapore 596224

USA office: 27 Warren Street, Suite 401-402, Hackensack, NJ 07601

UK office: 57 Shelton Street, Covent Garden, London WC2H 9HE

Library of Congress Cataloging-in-Publication Data
Names: Akat, Asaf Savaş, 1943–   editor. | Gürsel, Seyfettin, editor.
Title: Turkish economy at the crossroads : facing the challenges ahead /
    editors, Asaf Savaş Akat, Seyfettin Gürsel.
Description: Hackensack : World Scientific, 2020. |
    Includes bibliographical references and index.
Identifiers: LCCN 2020012149 | ISBN 9789811214882 (hardcover) |
    ISBN 9789811214899 (epub) | ISBN 9789811214905 (ebook other)
Subjects: LCSH: Turkey--Economic conditions--1960- | Turkey--Economic policy.
Classification: LCC HC492 .T876 2020 | DDC 330.9561--dc23
LC record available at https://lccn.loc.gov/2020012149

British Library Cataloguing-in-Publication Data
A catalogue record for this book is available from the British Library.

For any available supplementary material, please visit
https://www.worldscientific.com/worldscibooks/10.1142/11682#t=suppl

Desk Editor: Yulin Jiang

Typeset by Stallion Press
Email: enquiries@stallionpress.com

Printed in Singapore

Important Note from the Editors

The authors finalized the chapters of this book in December 2019, only months before the Covid-19 pandemic hit Turkey, along with the rest of the globe. By the time the book went into print in the summer of 2020, the world had become a radically different place compared to only a few months ago. Yet, from Turkey's perspective, we believe that the themes and the analyses of the book remain just as relevant post-Covid, as they were pre-Covid. If anything, in fact, the pandemic has increased the urgency of the policy choices to be made in order to remedy the structural weaknesses and imbalances of the Turkish economy, and perhaps even to avoid another round of financial turmoil. We believe vulnerabilities have markedly intensified since the epidemic because of, *inter alia*, growing fiscal deficits, a higher reliance on monetary financing, inadequate foreign currency reserves, an acute lack of policy visibility and more broadly, drifting further away from a well-functioning market economy. We think these developments further validate our choice of the "Crossroads" metaphor.

About the Editors

Professor Asaf Savaş Akat, currently at Istanbul Bilgi University, is a well-known and highly respected Turkish economist, with a distinguished career in academia, media, business and public life. In addition to his extensive teaching and lecturing activities, he wrote op-ed columns for newspapers (*Sabah, Vatan*) and magazines (*Para, Fortune*), edited scholarly journals (*Toplum ve Bilim*), co-hosted a popular prime-time television program on current economic issues (NTV), co-founded and became the first Rector of the private Istanbul Bilgi University, co-founded a liberal political party (New Democracy Movement — YDH), worked in private industry (Kavala, Eczacıbaşı), and has been active in non-governmental organizations in education, social research, etc. as well as charities. He authored many books, several articles and received prestigious awards for his contributions (Simavi Foundation, Turkish Economic Association, etc.). He obtained his BA and PhD from Istanbul University, MA from University of East Anglia (UK) and did post-doctoral work at London School of Economics (both with a grant from the Organisation for Economic Co-operation and Development).

Seyfettin Gürsel is a Professor of Economics at Bahçeşehir University in Istanbul and the Founding Director of its Center for Economic and Social Research (BETAM), one of Turkey's most highly respected think tanks since its foundation in 2008. Under Professor Gürsel's leadership, BETAM publishes regular research briefings, working papers on current issues concerning the Turkish economy and produces special reports commissioned by public and private organizations. After receiving his PhD in economics at the University of Paris X-Nanterre, Professor Gürsel worked as a lecturer at Istanbul University and Galatasaray University, where he chaired the Department of Economics, and as visiting professor at the universities of Paris-Sorbonne and Dauphine. In addition to teaching and conducting research, Professor Gürsel has written op-ed columns for national newspapers, produced television programs on current economic issues and served on the board of several private enterprises. He has also published books, articles and studies on Turkish economic history (such as *L'empire Ottoman face au capitalisme*, L'Harmattan, 1987), labor economics (such as *Employment and Unemployment in Turkey*, YKY, 1999), income inequality and poverty. He is the recipient of the Turkish Economic Association 2018 Academic Merit Award.

About the Contributors

Daron Acemoglu is an Institute Professor at the Massachusetts Institute of Technology. He is an elected fellow of the National Academy of Sciences, the Turkish Academy of Sciences, the American Academy of Arts and Sciences, the Econometric Society, the European Economic Association, and the Society of Labor Economists. Daron Acemoglu has received a B.A. in economics at the University of York, 1989, M.Sc. in mathematical economics and econometrics at the London School of Economics, 1990, and Ph.D. in economics at the London School of Economics in 1992. He is the author of four books, *Economic Origins of Dictatorship and Democracy* (with James A. Robinson), *Introduction to Modern Economic Growth, Why Nations Fail: The Origins of Power, Prosperity and Poverty* (with James A. Robinson), *Principles of Economics* (with David Laibson and John List), and *The Narrow Corridor: States, Societies, and the Fate of Liberty* (with James A. Robinson). Daron Acemoglu has received numerous awards and fellowships, including the inaugural T. W. Shultz Prize from the University of Chicago in 2004, and the inaugural Sherwin Rosen Award for outstanding contribution to labor economics in 2004, Distinguished Science Award from the Turkish Sciences Association in 2006, the John von Neumann Award, Rajk College, Budapest in 2007, and the Carnegie Fellowship in 2017. He was also awarded the John Bates Clark Medal in 2005, given every two years to the best economist in the United States under the age of 40 by the American Economic Association, the Erwin Plein Nemmers prize awarded every two years for work of lasting significance in economics, and the

2016 BBVA Frontiers of Knowledge award in economics. His book (with James A. Robinson) *Economic Origins of Dictatorship and Democracy* received the Association of American Publishers Award for Excellence in Professional, the William Riker Prize for Best Book Published in Political Economy, and the Woodrow Wilson Foundation Award for Best Book Published on Government, Politics or International Affairs. *Why Nations Fail* also received several prizes and awards, and was a New York Times bestseller in 2012.

Cengiz Aktar, is an adjunct professor of political science at the University of Athens. He is a former director at the United Nations specializing in asylum policies. He is known to be one of the leading advocates of Turkey's integration into the EU. He was the Chair of European Studies at Bahçeşehir University-Istanbul. In 1999, he initiated a civil initiative for Istanbul's candidacy for the title of European Capital of Culture. Istanbul successfully held the title in 2010. He also headed the initiative called "European Movement 2002" which aimed at putting pressure on the lawmaker to speed up political reforms necessary to begin the negotiation phase with the EU. In addition to EU integration policies his research focuses on politics of memory regarding ethnic and religious minorities, on history of political centralism and on international refugee law.

Izak Atiyas is a research associate at the TUSIAD-Sabancı Üniversity Competitiveness Forum in Istanbul and a research fellow at the Economic Research Forum in Cairo. He retired from Sabancı Üniversity in 2019, where he was an associate professor of economics (since 1998) and the director of the Competitiveness Forum (since 2011). He received his Ph.D. in economics from New York University in 1988. He worked at the World Bank between 1988–1995. He currently works as a consultant. His research areas include productivity, political economy, industrial policy, competition policy, regulation of network industries and privatization.

Ozan Bakış received his Ph.D. in Economics from University of Paris 1 Pantheon-Sorbonne in 2006. Before joining BETAM as senior researcher in 2016 he worked, respectively, at Galatasaray University and Sabancı

University. He did his postdoc at University of Montreal in 2011. His early research interests are in macroeconomic modeling, economic growth and optimal taxation. His recent research has focused on applied economics, short-run economic forecasting, and firm dynamics with a particular focus on innovation, productivity, and job creation.

Ayşe Aylin Bayar is an Associate Professor of Economics at Istanbul Technical University. Her main areas of research are Economic Development and Labor Economics, in particular inequalities in the labor market, poverty and income distribution. Bayar holds M.A. in Economics and a Ph.D. degree in Management Engineering from ITU. She worked as researcher in EU Project Increasing the Institutional Capacity of the Ministry of Family and Social Policies in the Field of Social Inclusion Policies and in other Erasmus+ Program projects. In addition to her research experiences at ITU, she also strengthened her research skills through two visiting scholarship positions at University of Laval and University of Sussex.

Öner Günçavdı is Professor of Economic Development at the Faculty of Management, Istanbul Technical University (ITU). He holds a BSc. degree from ITU, MSc. degrees from ITU and the University of Warwick, and finally Ph.D. degree from the University of Nottingham. He is the author of two books, *From Dream to Reality: Elginkan Holding Group in the Process of Turkish Industrialisation* (2009, Istanbul: Turkish History Foundation) and *The End of the Road: Growth, Interest Rate, Distribution and Discourse of New Turkey* (2015, Ankara: Efil Publishing Company). He published various research papers in domestic and international academic journals such as the *Journal of Development Economics*, the *Journal of International Development*, *Applied Economics*, the *Journal of Policy Modelling*, *Turkish Studies*, and *Empirical Economics*. He is also the author of various chapters in international book projects. He widely writes about international trade, business history of the Turkish corporate sector, income distribution and poverty.

Hande Paker is a political sociologist who works on civil society, state, cosmopolitan citizenship, and political ecology. She has carried out research and published on modes of civil society–state relations, politics of the environment at the local–global nexus and grounded cosmopolitan citizenship with a particular focus on environmental struggles and women's rights. Hande Paker received her M.A. and Ph.D. from McGill University. She has held the Mercator-IPC fellowship at Istanbul Policy Center, Sabancı University and has been a visiting fellow at CliSAP, Hamburg University. She is based at the Faculty of Economics, Administrative and Social Sciences at Bahçeşehir University.

Şevket Pamuk is Professor of Economics and Economic History at the Ataturk Institute for Modern Turkish History at Bogaziçi University, Istanbul. He graduated from Yale University and obtained his Ph.D. in Economics from University of California, Berkeley (1978). He is a leading economic historian and the author of many books and articles on Ottoman, Middle East and European economic history, most recently of *Uneven Centuries: Economic History of Turkey since 1820* published by Princeton University Press in 2018. Pamuk was Professor and Chair in Contemporary Turkish Studies at the London School of Economics from 2008 through 2013. He was the President of European Historical Economics Society (2003–2005), the President of Asian Historical Economics Society (2012–2014), Editor of *European Economic History Review* (2011–2014) and a member of Academia Europea and Science Academy, Istanbul.

Selin Pelek currently works at the Department of Economics at Galatasaray University. Her research interests include minimum wage, wage structure, informal employment and social assistance benefits. She holds a Ph.D. from University of Paris Sorbonne-Cité, an M.A. in Macroeconomic Politics and Quantitative Analysis from University of Paris 1 Panthéon-Sorbonne, and a B.A. in Economics from Galatasaray University.

E. Murat Üçer is Global Source's macro consultant in Turkey, is co-founder of Turkey Data Monitor, and a senior lecturer at Koç University in Istanbul. As a consultant, he provides macroeconomic expertise to commercial banks, multinational corporations and public sector organizations, and gives training programs and seminars on Turkish as well as global macroeconomic developments. Formerly, he worked as an economist at the Institute of International Finance, Credit Suisse and the International Monetary Fund and was an advisor to the Minister of Treasury at the Turkish Treasury in 2001 and the Governor of the Central Bank of Turkey in 1997. Üçer received his B.A. and Ph.D. in Economics from Boğazici University and Boston College, respectively, and has authored various articles on the Turkish economy, including a book on the 2001 Turkish crisis.

Gökçe Uysal is an associate professor of economics and the deputy director of Betam, Bahçeşehir University Center for Economic and Social Research. Her work focuses on economics of gender and labor markets, with a special focus on Turkey. Recently, she has carried out research on the Syrians in the labor market in Turkey and how their access can be facilitated. Gokce Uysal holds a Ph.D. from University of Rochester. She is currently based in BETAM, Bahcesehir University, and a Mercator-IPC Fellow 2019/20 at the Istanbul Policy Center of Sabancı University.

M. Ege Yazgan currently is a professor of economics and the director of center for financial studies at Istanbul Bilgi University. His research interests include applied macro-economics, macro-finance, international finance and economic growth. He is the former rector of Istanbul Bilgi University, where he has also served as the vice-rector and the dean of faculty of economics and administrative sciences. He holds a Ph.D. in Economics from the University of Sussex and a B.A. and M.A. from the University of Istanbul.

Atilla Yeşilada currently advises GlobalSource Partners as Turkey country consultant on economic and political affairs. Mr. Atilla Yeşilada received his B.A. in Business Administration from Eastern Illinois University. He holds an M.A. in economics from the University of California, Santa Barbara and has done doctoral work at Rennselear Polytechnic University, Troy-New York. During his studies in the United States, Mr. Yeşilada taught economics and finance in various universities. He also held a research fellowship at the New York-based liberal think-tank Jerome Levy Institute, where he specialized on banking crisis. Yesilada authored four economics books.

Contents

Introduction

Asaf Savaş Akat and Seyfettin Gürsel

Why "Crossroads"?

Probably you ask yourself: "Do we need another book on Turkey?" Our answer is yes; we do. One reason, Turkey has a mysteriously low profile in international economic literature compared to its size and level of development. The small number of books on the market are neither comprehensive nor up-to-date. More importantly, they usually lack a clear perspective and a unifying theme. We hope this to be the distinguishing feature of our book, already implicit in the two key concepts of its title: Crossroads and Challenges. These reflect a shared preoccupation, not only by the editors and contributors of this book but also by a large community of economists, intellectuals, and politicians that the country is at a critical juncture of history. To put it very bluntly: Will Turkey's journey toward a mature market economy proceed smoothly, or will there be economic, political, and societal reversals and discontinuities, delaying, even arresting further material and human progress?

The transformation of pre-industrial societies of peasants and traditional agriculture into open market economies based on high-productivity industrial and service sectors has been the biggest challenge of the last century. It is a tricky and complicated process. History shows that it entails many wrong turns, *cul-de-sac*, failures, and much unnecessary sufferings, as well as remarkable successes. An impressive intellectual effort by many great minds accompanied it, to understand and to tame the forces at stake during this civilizational upheaval. Hobbes, Smith, Marx, Weber, Walras, Polanyi, and others made groundbreaking contributions toward a theory of society, economy, and state. A new paradigm, part of this historical chain, gained acceptance recently: institutional economics, from the pioneering work of Douglass North, further elaborated by Daron Acemoğlu (one of our contributors) and James Robinson.

Institutions are the norms and the organizations sustaining human social interaction; they matter enormously for the performance and the evolution of human societies. They can be "inclusive" or "exclusive", "complementary" or "contradictory", orienting actors toward "wealth-creation" or "rent-seeking", creating a political environment of "liberty" or "dictatorship". Any existing society and economy reflect the outcome of the combinations and differences in institutions. In other words, an in-depth analysis of the institutional setup brings a new dimension to the usual discussions on economic performance and policy; therefore, a superior take on the past, current, and future economic trends and issues.

In a sense, this book can be considered as part of the growing litera-ture on the applications of the theoretical tools of institutional econom-ics to actually existing economies. The reader will encounter again and again similar efforts to establish the close casual links between institu-tional developments and the economic performance of Turkey today and in the recent past. The preoccupations behind the "crossroads" corre-spond to several indicators about the onset of institutional degradation in Turkey. This is a relatively recent phenomenon, coming after a period of visible improvements in the institutional setup. Identifying and dat-ing the infliction point is not straightforward, with early signs going back to the beginning of the decade (2010s) and rapid acceleration toward the end.

What is at stake? Turkey seemed to have made an irreversible choice since the 1980s, by gradually adapting its institutions through a long series of reforms to the requirements of an open market economy with a high degree of integration into the global system coupled with a pluralistic political regime. Progress rarely happens on a smooth straight line. Turkey also faced many road accidents: macroeconomic imbalances, financial crises, political instability, internal strife, etc. Nevertheless, the overall orientation of Turkish society never wavered. Turkey's determination to reform was crowned in 1995 with a Customs Union agreement with the European Union (EU), thus inserting Turkey into the European single market. A decade later, in October 2005, the Justice and Development Party (AK Parti) and its incontestable leader Recep Tayyip Erdoğan (now the President of Turkey), in power since November 2002, gave the final push to Turkey's civilizational project by starting the formal accession negotiations with the EU for full membership.

Unfortunately, it did not take long for little dark spots to spoil this rosy picture. Early signs, barely noticeable, appeared after the Global Financial Crisis of 2008; over time they have grown larger and darker. All have its origins in politics, especially in Erdoğan's political agenda. In retrospect, it is easy to extract its roots in Erdoğan's understanding of power and democracy, which is very similar to those of other contemporary "strongmen" (Victor Orban of Hungary, Vladimir Putin of Russia, among others). His early interventions were piecemeal modifications in the rules of the game, as elsewhere: strengthen the Executive Branch, curb civil liberties, take over the Judiciary, get rid of the "checks and balances". The constitutional referendum in April 2017, which abolished Turkey's traditional Parliamentary system of government and replaced it with a Presidential system dominated by the Executive branch, supplied him with the opportunity to formalize and consolidate his powers further. The aforementioned institutional degradation is the consequence of these new rules of the game.

Erdoğan was elected as the first president of the new regime in June 2018. Less than two months later, early August 2018, the Turkish Lira (TL) faced a massive sell-off in the global financial markets, shedding over 30% of its value in just a few days, the worst ever. It was a devastating shock to the economy. The steep fall in consumption and investment spending hit hard on domestic demand, imports, and the production of non-tradable activities. The limited increase in exports could not make up for the fall in demand; therefore, output fell for two consecutive quarters, the official definition of recession, and unemployment reached record levels. The exchange rate shock aggravated the currency mismatches in the highly leveraged balance sheets of both real sector firms and banks, leading to a severe credit crunch, as banks tried to deleverage. Meanwhile, high pass-through effects from the exchange rate caused a big jump in inflation. The only good news was the correction in the external balance, which moved from a large deficit (above 6% of GDP) to a small surplus.

The reaction of Erdoğan and his administration to this dire economic situation was typical of such regimes when faced with economic hardships: "conspiracy theories", denial, confusion, voodoo-economics, lack of focus and coordination, and search for administrative measures to replace the markets. These constitute the economic part of the "crossroads". Will the regime continue respecting the rules of the game in the economic sphere, or will it try to modify them, as in politics, toward protectionism, capital controls, fixed exchange rates, discrimination among firms, etc.? If this happens, Turkey's drift toward an economic environment which is less open, less market oriented, and where the playing field is much less level will make the next stage of the transition to a mature open economy and society even more challenging. From the perspective of Turkey's long-term historical trends and evolution, such an outcome seems a not negligible probability event. Nevertheless, it imposes new critical challenges to politics as well as economic policymaking.

Basic Economic Indicators

Before proceeding further, we must ease the task of readers unfamiliar with Turkey by providing some basic indicators. Turkey is a relatively large, populous, open economy, with a GDP per capita at market exchange rates in the Upper Middle-Income Countries (UMC) range of the World Bank. In a nutshell, it is neither a continent nor a small country, neither an export engine nor inward-looking; it has competitive industrial and service sectors but is not a fully developed (mature) economy. The following table shows the values as well as Turkey's ranking in the world for each indicator.

TURKEY: Basic Indicators

Indicator	Unit	Value	Rank
Area	Thousand sq.km	**770**	35
Population	Million	**82**	18
GDP	Billion (current US$)	**767**	19
GDP	Billion (PPP-current US$)	**2,300**	13
GDP per capita	Thousand (Current US$)	**9.3**	71
GDP per capita	Thousand (PPP-current US$)	**27.9**	50
Exports (goods+services)	Billion US$	**235**	30
Urban Population	% of total population	**75**	70

Data: World Development Indicators (all for 2018), https://databank.worldbank.org/source/world-development-indicators#

Turkey's overall development performance during the last half-century is neither a miracle (e.g., Korea, Singapore, later China) nor a failure (e.g., Argentina, Venezuela). For the period 1970–2018, average annual growth of GDP per capita has been at 2.7%, above the average for both the world at 1.6% and high-income countries (HIC) at 1.9%, but below that of UMC at 3.2%. Turkey has converged with the HIC at 0.8 pts, a reasonable but not impressive pace, while it underperformed the UMC by 0.5 pts, not a negligible figure. Turkey's relative performance improves somewhat when based on total GDP, due to higher population growth in Turkey compared to the world (0.1 pts) and the UMC (0.3 pts).

To get a better picture, we constructed a "peer group" for the period 1970–2018 consisting of 14 countries[1] on the following criteria: population above 20 million in 2018, GDP per capita growth rate above that of the HIC (1.9%) for the period, GDP per capita level in 1970 between 100 and 1,000 current US dollar. Turkey satisfies these criteria.[2] The "peer group" plus Turkey represented 49% of the world population in 2018.

---

[1] Bangladesh, Chile, China, Columbia, Egypt, India, Korea, Malaysia, Morocco, Pakistan, Philippines, Sri Lanka, Thailand, Uganda.

[2] Data: consumer price inflation from IMF Financial Statistics, the rest from the World Development Indicators.

The weighted average growth[3] of GDP per capita in the "peer group", at 5.3%, is double of that of Turkey, at 2.7%. The difference is driven especially by high performance of two populous countries, China and India. Turkey ranks 8th among the 15 countries, right in the middle. This confirms that Turkey's secular growth performance has been decent, but also mediocre.

Economic growth, a purely quantitative indicator, may give an inadequate image as it hides essential qualitative aspects of the development process. Price stability is one such indicator, it signals to the coherence of the macroeconomic policies sustaining economic growth. The "peer group" has an average annual consumer price inflation of 7.2%. Turkey is a big outlier compared to the "peer group", with average annual inflation of 35.4% over the last half-century. Only three countries in the "peer group" have consumer inflation rates in double-digits: two from Latin America (Chile 27.5%, Columbia 15.1%) and one from Africa (Egypt 11.1%). The remaining 11 countries all have inflation at single digits. Very high inflation rates have been one of the idiosyncrasies of Turkey's development experience. Price instability may go a long way in explaining Turkey's relative underperformance compared to the "peer group".

The external account is the other critical qualitative indicator; it is a meaningful measure of the domestic effort and mobilization for economic development. The "peer group" has an average annual current account surplus of 0.3% of GDP, compared to a current account deficit of 2.7% for Turkey. Three countries (Malaysia, China, Korea) produce the surpluses which dominate the group average. Eleven countries have deficits. Turkey's place is below the middle among deficit countries; six have smaller deficits (Columbia, Egypt, Philippines, India, Bangladesh, Thailand), from 2.2% to 0.3%, and five have bigger deficits (Chile, Pakistan, Morocco, Uganda, Sri Lanka), between 2.9% and 4.4%. The size and persistence of current account deficits has been another critical characteristic of Turkey's development process. Recurrent foreign exchange crises increased the volatility of economic growth, contributing to the mediocre development performance.

---

[3] The weights for this and all other averages below are mid-period (1995) GDP values of the 14 countries.

At this point, a few words are warranted about the natural environment. Turkey's vast landmass is not endowed generously in natural resources. Overall, we can confidently claim Turkey to be a resource-poor country. Anatolia is a high, mountainous, and arid plateau where fertile agricultural land is limited to coastal areas. Production barely meets domestic needs; the exportable agricultural surplus is negligible. Of higher significance, Turkey has no reserves of fossil fuels worth mentioning: a geological puzzle in terms of its location (eastern neighbors Iran, Iraq, Syria, Azerbaijan are major oil/gas producers). It also lacks large deposits of essential minerals for commercialization.[4] This resource base has critical implications. First, Turkey did not have the sizable natural resource surpluses to finance the early phases of industrialization. Second, for resource-poor countries, economic growth and development necessitates, by definition, ever-larger trade deficits in primary commodities (energy, raw materials).

Brief Historical Background

The Republic of Turkey, a nation-state founded in 1923, is the successor to the Ottoman State, a multiethnic, multireligious empire ruling over Southeast Europe and the Middle East from the 14th century until its defeat in WWI. This continuity from Empire to Republic and the absence of a history (and experience) of direct colonial rule by imperialist powers is a distinguishing feature of Turkey among its peers. The Ottoman legacy manifests decisively on the institutional evolution of the Republic. Other sources of the heritage emerge from the repercussions (often unintended) of the sequence of events leading to the disintegration of the Empire in the first two decades of the 20th century. Both these threads allow precious insights into the history of the Republic.

The Empire suffered from the economic and military superiority of the rising Occident long before others. However, it failed to undertake the necessary transformations to meet the challenge of the West. By the beginning of the 20th century, it was evident the Ottomans had missed

---

[4]Turkey's only abundant "natural" resource is the rich history of Anatolia and its sunny beaches. But tourism is a very competitive modern service industry.

the opportunity even to imitate the institutional framework necessary to replicate the Industrial Revolution. The contrast with the 19th century Japan, late in the contact but prompt in responding to the challenge is striking. From the 1830s onward, Ottomans initiated institutional reforms to reverse the decline, often to appease Big Powers. Early timid experiments with the rule of law and constitutional monarchy (1876 and 1908) were too little, too late, and could not prevent the disintegration of the Empire.

The distinct institutional characteristic of the Empire was the heavily centralized structure of power, the dominant form of government in Asia in the past. The mighty state bureaucracy, with the Sultan at the top, firmly kept the whole society under its iron grip, making sure to destroy all potential centers of political power at the source. The land belonged to the State; state regulatory institutions controlled most economic transactions and severely constrained any private property on productive assets. Centrifugal tendencies intensified in the 19th century, along with the integration of the economy into the global markets and the rise of nationalism among Christian minorities. Still, the Empire managed to protect its essence of a strong centralized state, and pass it onto the new Republic. We also note that the Ottomans had already dissolved local tribal–kinship identities (and the corresponding elites) in Anatolia, except for the Kurdish populated Southeast.

This continuity has critical consequences. Positively, the existence of a strong state tradition (backed by the military), internalized by the elites as well as the general public, reduces the probability of falling into anarchy and social violence; i.e., Turkey faces no risk of turning into a failed state. Negatively, this strength is a hindrance to the emergence of private property and markets, of civil society, of "inclusive" institutions, which in turn delays economic and societal development. Deeply entrenched *Etatism* of the republican elite has been a serious brake on Turkey's economic performance. Also, by suppressing civil society and eulogizing authority, the tradition of a strong state clears the ground for the rise of popular authoritarian regimes. Current trends in Turkish politics bear witness.

The transition from the Empire to a modern nation state in the early 20th century was not exactly a smooth process. The Republic was preceded by a period of intense trauma and enormous human suffering and tragedies. These are beyond our scope, but their impact on the economy was a substantial contraction in the human capital stock of Republic. The cause is the evolution of a peculiar ethnic/religious division of labor in the Empire, more pronounced after the 19th century. Muslim subjects (mainly Turks) concentrated in farming and the public administration; non-Muslims (Greeks, Armenians, Jews) dominated commerce and urban trades (artisanal manufacture). Before 1923, first the Armenians, then the Greeks were expulsed from Anatolia, only in small part replaced by Turkish farmer refugees from the Balkans. This was a big blow to commerce in general, to urban trades and commercial agriculture, reducing output for at least a generation. On the other hand, the depopulation of Anatolia reversed the relative factor scarcity many societies faced in the early stages of development, by making land, not labor, the abundant factor of production.

The disappearance of commercial and urban Christian bourgeoisie, combined with the Ottoman legacy of small landholdings in agriculture (mainly subsistence farmers) had an important corollary for the young Republic. Large landowners were the exception rather than the rule in Turkey; limited to commercial farming in few coastal plains and to Kurdish areas in the Southeast where bondage relations still prevailed. Therefore, in contrast to most countries at the onset of development, Turkey did not have to overcome the resistance of a politically powerful landowning oligarchy for the institutional reforms required by development. This also implied a more equal initial wealth distribution, despite the widespread poverty due to low productivity in subsistence farming.

The Republic was founded by nationalist officers of the Imperial Army, issued directly from and with organic links to the reformist "Young Turks", who held power through the Union and Progress Party in the last decade of the Empire. Civilians provided support, but their decision-making power was limited. The founders, led by Mustafa Kemal Pasha — later Atatürk (father of Turks) — consolidated their power in 1923. Facing grave security challenges from abroad and determined to transform the pre-modern society they inherited, they opted for an authoritarian "single-party regime" (in the official terminology), in order to accelerate the top-down project of nation-building and "westernization". The project's blueprint had a rich civilizational content, but was vague and deficient on economic issues.

A set of cultural, legal, administrative reforms attempted to reorient society toward "Civilization" by adopting Western calendar, metrics, dress code, laws, legal procedures, etc. In parallel, to tighten its grip over an essential part of the civil society, the Republic banned all Muslim religious organizations and transferred their functions to the state. The nationalization of religion is still called, bizarrely, the separation of the state and religion or "laicity" (after the French *"laïcité"*[5]). The hostility of large segments of the population to the civilizational reforms had economic consequences. The reforms exhausted the political capital of the founders and decreased the political feasibility of enforcing on the public the hardship required by the massive economic mobilization that rapid industrialization entails; the state left the economy on its own.

WWII and its political and geostrategic implications triggered a new period of transformation in Turkey. Multiparty elections in 1950 permitted the peaceful transition of power to the opposition, kick-starting the slow process of democratization, although the tutelage of the army persisted for half a century, with three overt and several aborted or implicit military interventions. The Cold War put Turkey in a valuable geostrategic position, securing a special status within the US-led Western military alliance, permitting membership in the North Atlantic Treaty Organization (NATO), along with the Council of Europe, Organisation for Economic Co-operation and Development (OECD), and an association agreement (in 1963) with European Economic Community (EEC), the forerunner of EU. Turkey's insertion into the Western civilization outlived the end of the Cold War, and remains a work-in-progress, with mounting stress lately.

The period after WWII has been one of rapid economic and social transformation. Competitive elections refocused the political agenda from civilizational to economic issues. Populism, in the positive sense of destroying the privileges of the old elite revolutionized the political discourse, elevating concepts like "economic development", "free enterprise",

---

[5] Please note: "laïcité" when translated into English as "secularism" increases further the conceptual confusion. Secularism means taking the state out of the religion and the religion out of the state; the exact opposite of the situation in Turkey.

"investment in infrastructure" to positions of domination. The alliance with the West, in turn, created an opportunity in the form of substantial military and economic aid. These external subsidies permitted rapid industrialization without the large-scale mobilization of domestic resources, thus alleviating its hardships and political handicaps. Turkey discovered its distinct model of "development with external resources" in such circumstances.

Turkey was basically a private property economy. Even during the official *Etatism* of the 1930s, state-owned enterprises (SOEs) existed only in the utilities and a limited number of sectors, either monopolies for tax purposes or suppliers to the administration and the bureaucratic elite. Their quantitative impact on the rest of the economy was negligible; their contribution controversial. Private enterprises dominated agriculture, domestic and foreign trade, small-scale manufacturing, and most services. From the perspective of property relations, Turkish *Etatism* never went anywhere near socialism; its origins lay either in pragmatism or the bureaucratic reaction to private business. First, the rapid rise of the private industry after the 1950s, then the waves of privatization since the 2000s decreased the share of the SOEs in output to practically nil.

In turn, very heavy state intervention in the markets has been the trademark of the Turkish economy. A complex system of administrative controls over markets, prices, and quantities, erected during the WWII evolved into a full-scale "command economy" with industrialization in the 1950s. Its advantages outweighed its inefficiencies and the corruption in its implementation. The rents created and distributed by state intervention constituted the main instrument for the first phase of the accumulation of private capital. It also projected the power of the state (politics) over the economy, in perfect harmony with the heritage of the strong state. Its inability to generate foreign exchange through manufacture exports led to its demise at the end of the 1970s. Although the transition to an open market economy after the 1980s was successful, the re-emergence of heavy state intervention — should things get tough in the future — cannot be ruled out.

One final general observation is needed before moving to the topics covered in the book. Despite early institution building, multiparty politics, and a poor resource base, Turkey failed to develop its critical asset, i.e., to invest adequately in education and human capital. The Republic inherited a population with a tiny minority able to read and write, plus extremely low enrollment ratios. Unfortunately, large-scale mobilization for education was neglected over several decades. Primary school student enrollment ratio reached 100% only in the late 1970s; compulsory education was increased to eight years (from five) in the late 1990s and to 12 only in 2012, which places Turkey well below its peers in terms of educational attainment. Education, especially quality issues, will remain a controversial yet vitally important topic in the foreseeable future.

Range of Topics

The first chapter, "Economic Policies, Institutional Change, and Economic Growth since 1980" examines the evolution of the new economic policies and institutions after 1980. Şevket Pamuk is an eminent economic historian with expert knowledge of the late Ottoman Empire as well as the Republican period. Why 1980? Because it corresponds to a historical turning point in Turkey's post-WWII development strategy, the beginning of a transition from the previous inward-looking import substitution regime to an open economy where exports play a more significant role. He distinguishes two long-run cycles: the first starts in 1980, the second in 2001. Severe economic and political crises precede both dates. His analysis highlights the reciprocal interactions and interdependencies between the economic and political spheres in recent Turkish history. He makes a note of the troubling inconsistencies between the intentions of the "new economic policies" and what actually happened in practice. The role of the state in the economy is of particular importance in this evolution. Pamuk agrees that the Turkish economy has achieved, step by step, full integration with the global economy. However, the theoretical model behind the policies had predicted a smaller role for the state, which simply did not materialize. Turkish state remained unchallenged *vis-à-vis* the private sector; thus, "the government continued to have a great deal of power and discretion to decide the winners in the economy."

The second chapter, "High-Quality Versus Low-Quality Growth in Turkey: Causes and Consequences", covers the relations between institutional development and the quality and sustainability of Turkey's growth in the long run, within a comparative perspective. We already referred earlier to Daron Acemoğlu's pioneering work in institutional economics; E. Murat Üçer is a macroeconomist of global reputation, one the best analysts of Turkish economy. Low-quality growth is a process driven by consumption, credit, and government spending, without sufficient investment that enhances significant productivity and technological improvements. This type of economic growth, to paraphrase the authors, "tends to run out of steam more rapidly and may even prepare conditions for subsequent economic crashes." In contrast, "high-quality" and "shared growth", defined as a "growth driven by productivity improvements" and as "growth from which the population at large benefits" is faster and as well as sustainable over the long run. The success of the growth process, in turn, depends on the quality of the economic and political institutions. The chapter investigates and discusses in detail the causes of successes in some periods and failures at others, as well as the challenges faced by Turkey in institution building to generate the kind of high quality and shared growth.

The third chapter, "Productivity, Reallocation, and Structural Change: An Assessment" supports and complements the analysis of the second chapter, by further elaborating on the technical issues of measuring productivity. Izak Atiyas and Ozan Bakış are top academic experts on growth accounting in Turkey. Rapid increases in productivity constitute the foundation of sustainable economic development. The authors renew and update total factor productivity (TFP) estimates, extending these to sub-periods and the four major productive sectors (agriculture, industry, construction, services). This new research, published for the first time, provides several valuable insights on the possible causes of the low-quality growth for sub-periods and sectors. Typically, the use of growth accounting method for the analysis of the construction sector, which lost one-third of its employment over the last six quarters, points to its impact on the severe recession in the second half of 2018 and the abrupt rise of unemployment ratio in Turkey. Another important finding relates to the slowdown in the quality of Turkey's exports in recent years, a serious challenge to the search for sustainable growth.

The fourth chapter, "Financial Cycles of the Turkish Economy: How Will It End This Time?" focuses on a crucial aspect of the modern economies, namely the identification and analysis of the financial cycles in

Turkey, especially in the last two decades. M. Ege Yazgan is an excellent financial and macroeconomist, as well as econometrician. In opposition to business cycles, measured using output data, financial cycles are complex phenomenon involving the formation of bubbles in credit and asset prices, which attracted the attention of economists recently, in the wake of the financial crisis of 2008. His pioneering research, published for the first time, establishes the causes and the lifespan of the last financial cycle in Turkey through state-of-the-art econometric methods. He is especially interested in the interaction of the financial cycle with the business cycle in order to assess more realistically the causes and consequences of the recession in the second half of 2018. His findings point to the possibility of a slower and longer recovery this time, due to deleveraging by banks and the corporates, compared to similar events in the past.

The fifth chapter, titled "Structural Transformation and Income Distribution in Turkey", focuses on two critical challenges of Turkey's economy, not covered in the previous chapters, namely the transformation of the economic structure and its impact on the distribution of income. Öner Günçavdı and Ayşe Aylin Bayar are pioneers of the field in Turkey. The chapter shares with the first chapter the observation that structural transformation can be traced back to the 1980s, when Turkey changed direction, from a closed command economy toward integration with the global system. The authors' contribution is based on two key concepts: "tradable and non-tradable dichotomy" and "de-industrialization". They find a new intentional orientation after 2003 "partly due to deteriorations in relative prices between tradable and non-tradable goods and partly because of a change in sectoral preferences of the government in favor of non-tradable economic activities such as construction, trade, and banking." They interpret this as the eagerness of the new government to obtain electoral approval, while de-industrialization is an unintended outcome of these policies. Finally, the chapter looks into income distribution and inequality, the worst in Europe, establishing improvements in periods of high growth and a reversal lately.

The sixth chapter, "Labor Market Challenges in Turkey", completes the macroeconomic and structural analyses of the preceding chapters, by looking at Turkey's labor market. Gökçe Uysal, Hande Paker and Selin Pelek are well-known academic experts on the labor market, social policy, and gender studies. The volatility of growth in the last two decades implied an unstable path in employment, characterized by large fluctuations in unemployment. The authors examine in great detail the complex dynamics governing unemployment cycles, with differences in the behavior of the leading labor market indicators, namely the labor force participation ratio, employment ratio, and the growth elasticity of employment, as well as "labor market flexibility". Meager rates of female participation and employment ratios get special attention, with an original analysis of the gender gap. To paraphrase the authors, "increasing women's labor force participation is the main challenge that Turkey faces today." Finally, the authors tackle the burning issue of integrating into the labor market the millions of Syrian refugees painfully trying to survive under miserable conditions.

The seventh chapter, "European Union and Turkey: Why It Failed? What is Next?" is the compact and analytical history of Turkey's difficult relations with the EU. Cengiz Aktar is one of the best specialists on the subject, with hands-on experience of the lengthy process. Although Turkey's first attempt to join the Club was initiated in 1963; as mentioned earlier, relations were kept in the freezer until the late 1980s. They rewarmed in the early 1990s, resulting in the Customs Agreement of 1995, followed by membership negotiations in 2005. The last two events, especially the second, made a sizable contribution to Turkey's growth performance in that period. Lower risk premia due to confidence in policymaking, a big jump in the inflows of foreign direct investment (FDI), series of democratic and legal reforms improving the institutional framework were the multiple channels that benefited the economy. Aktar explains how both Turkey and the EU missed on that historical opportunity and why the membership negotiations turned into a deadlock. With this failure, the risk of divergence between the two parties are now bigger, further amplifying Turkey's challenges, especially by driving the country "towards uncharted waters".

The eighth and final chapter, "Turkey's Development Conundrum: Three Scenarios for the Next 10 Years" is a courageous effort to predict how Turkey will evolve in the next 10 years from a perspective of economic and societal development, in line with the major themes of this book. Atilla Yeşilada is an influential analyst and media commentator, respected for his opinions both in Turkey and abroad. He starts with the observation that Turkey went through an unfortunate political and institutional decline in the last decade, especially after the move to the executive-dominated Presidential system, leading to substantial loss of momentum in the development process. He summarizes his forecasts at the crossroads by depicting three distinct development scenarios, attaching each a different probability. These will help the interested reader to concretize the "crossroads" and "challenges" facing Turkey in the near future.

Chapter 1

Economic Policies, Institutional Change, and Economic Growth since 1980

Şevket Pamuk*

1.1. Introduction

From the early 1960s through the 1970s, the basic strategy for economic development in Turkey was import substitution industrialization (ISI). As was the case in most developing countries at the time, Turkey's large domestic market remained strongly protected from international competition. The agricultural sector which provided employment and incomes to a large part of the labor force was based mostly on the family farm. In the urban areas, the public sector played an important role in infrastructure investment and industrialization but the private sector based mostly in the Istanbul region gradually took control of the economy. The State Planning Organization at Ankara was responsible for the distribution of various subsidies, foreign exchange allocations, and other privileges especially to well-connected firms. The industrial sector remained focused on the domestic market. While rates of industrialization were high, total exports

*The author would like to thank the editors of the volume, Asaf Savaş Akat and Seyfettin Gürsel, for their useful comments on an earlier draft and Murat Üçer for his help with the data.

1

remained below 5% of GDP and the share of manufactures in total exports remained below 40% until 1980. Nonetheless, increases in GDP per capita averaged close to 3% per annum in this earlier period.

Turkey's encounter with neoliberal policies and institutions began with a new policy package launched in January 1980 with the support of the International Monetary Fund (IMF) and in response to the severe economic crisis at the end of the 1970s. As was the case in many other developing countries at the time, the ISI strategy was abandoned with the adoption of the more market-oriented policies and Turkey's economy entered a new era. The most important policy changes in the new era were trade liberalization, emphasis on exports of manufactures, lifting of restrictions on global capital flows, and privatization of the state economic enterprises. The signing of the Customs Union agreement with the European Union (EU) in 1995 and beginning of its implementation in the following year provided further support for exports of manufactures (Chapter 7 in this volume by Cengiz Aktar).

This chapter examines the evolution of the new economic policies and institutions and the interaction between the economy and politics in Turkey since 1980. It will argue that the adoption of new economic policies and the new institutions were only the beginning of the story. Their adoption did not mean that they would remain unchanged. As has been the case in most developing countries while embracing the new policies and institutions, Turkey's politics too have interacted with them and with the economic outcomes in many ways. The new policies and the performance of the economy had important consequences for domestic politics. In turn, the cycles of stability and instability in domestic politics not only determined the timing and extent of the new economic policies but also influenced the performance of the economy.

The chapter will also show that governments in Turkey have adopted neoliberal or market-oriented economic policies and institutions in two cycles, the first began in 1980 and the second in 2001, both during periods of economic and political crises and with the input of IMF and other international agencies. The chapter will argue that of the new economic policies and institutions, those that concerned relations with the global economy — most importantly trade liberalization, the emphasis on exports and the lifting of restrictions on international capital flows — have remained intact since 1980. Along with the Customs Union, these policies opened Turkey's economy to greater integration with the world economy.

In contrast, many of the new policies and institutions that concerned with the workings of the domestic economy, were later changed. In many of these latter areas, longer term results thus turned out to be quite different than what the new economic policies and institutions were supposed to achieve. Perhaps the most important area where major differences emerged between what the new economic policies intended in theory and what actually happened in practice concerned the role of the state in the economy.

In the interventionist model of the ISI era, the state had played a central role in the economy, allocating scarce resources such as foreign exchange and often deciding on the winners. With the adoption of the Washington Consensus policies in 1980, it was claimed that the role of the state in the economy would shrink and its old interventionist role would disappear. Under the new model, most of the measures of support for industrial activity including sector-based policies were in fact scaled down and dismantled. Obstacles to foreign trade and controls over international movements of capital were lifted to a large extent. Almost four decades later, however, the role of the state in the economy remained strong. The chapter will show that while some important changes occurred in the relationship between the state and the private sector, the government continued to have great deal of power and discretion to decide the winners in the economy.

1.2. Two Cycles since 1980

Turkey's population increased from 44 million in 1980 to 82 million in 2018. Per capita incomes increased approximately three-fold at average annual rates around 2.7% during the same period from $5,000 to $15,000, both in purchasing power parity-adjusted 2010 US dollars (Table 1.1). This average growth rate since 1980 has been higher than the average growth rate for the developed countries as a whole and close to but lower than the average for the developing countries. It has been higher than those of Latin America, Africa, and the Middle East but lagged well

Table 1.1. A periodization of economic trends for Turkey, 1980–2018

Sub-Period	Average Annual Growth Rates for Each Sub-Period					Level of GDP per Cap. at the End of Period 1980 = 100
	Population	GDP	Agricult.	Manufact.	GDP per Cap.	
First Cycle						
1980–1987	2.4	5.6	0.7	8.7	3.1	124
1988–2002	1.7	3.2	1.4	4.0	1.5	155
Second Cycle						
2003–2007 (Old Series)	1.4	6.9	0.4	8.1	5.4	202
2003–2007 (New Series)	1.4	7.3	1.0	9.8	6.5	214
2008–2016 (Old Series)	1.6	3.3	2.5	2.8	1.7	240
2008–2018 (New Series)	1.6	4.8	3.5	5.1	3.2	302
Overall since 1980						
1980–2016 (Old Series)	1.6	4.1	1.1	5.6	2.5	240
1980–2018 (New Series for the period after 1998)	1.6	4.5	1.4	6.3	2.9	302

Note: Turkey's official national income accounts began to be revised and updated rather frequently in recent years raising concerns about their quality and reliability. The most recent revision announced at the end of 2016 and covering the years since 1998 has been criticized, among other things, for raising the weights of the more rapidly growing sectors such as construction and providing a more optimistic picture for the later years of the AK Parti era. For this reason, both the old and the new series are included in the table for the period since 2008.

Source: Turkey, TurkStat (Turkish Statistical Institute), national income accounts, various years.

behind those growth of East, Southeast, and South Asia, most importantly China, South Korea, and India.

A comparison with four countries with similar populations, two in southern Europe and two in the Middle East may provide additional insights into Turkey's trajectory since 1980. Italy and Spain had experienced high rates of economic growth and were able to converge significantly to the level of the developed countries during the decades after World War II. Turkey's GDP per capita increased at higher rates than those of developed countries as a whole since 1980. Nonetheless, GDP per capita levels in Turkey remained well below those of Italy and Spain. Turkey's GDP per capita also increased at higher rates than those of Egypt and Iran since 1980. As a result, the GDP per capita gap between Turkey and Egypt continued to widen. With the support of oil revenues, Iran's GDP per capita had remained above that of Turkey during the decades after World War II but has fallen behind that of Turkey since 1980 (Figure 1.1).

One basic cause of the productivity and per capita income increases is investment in plant and equipment and capital deepening. In the decades after World War II, Turkey had attained rates of increase in GDP per capita that approached 3% per year by raising its savings and investment rates from around 11% of GDP in the early 1950s to 22% of GDP in the late 1970s. Investments in plant and equipment as well as

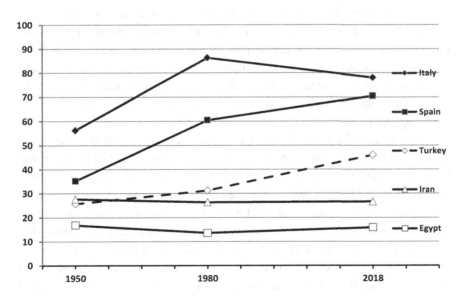

Figure 1.1. GDP per capita in four countries and in Turkey, 1950–2018 (PPP adjusted and as % of Western Europe and the United States)

Source: Pamuk (2018), p. 277 and Bolt and Van Zanden (2014).

education were financed primarily by domestic savings in this earlier period. Even though per capita incomes continued to rise, the savings rate fluctuated mostly between 18% and 24% since 1980. As a result, a significant part of fixed investment in recent decades has been financed by borrowing from abroad. The growing dependence on short-term foreign capital inflows caused a significant increase in macroeconomic instability since 1980.

Secondly, urbanization and the shift of the labor force from the agricultural sector where they worked with lower productivity to the urban economy where they worked with higher levels of physical capital has been one of the leading causes of productivity increases and economic growth in Turkey. Share of agriculture in total employment declined from 75% to 80% in 1950 to 50% in 1980 to less than 20% in 2015, while share of the urban economy in employment increased from 20% to 25% in 1950 to more than 80% in 2015. The share of the urban economy in GDP also increased from about 58% in 1950 to 75% in 1980 and to 92% in 2015. It is estimated that as much as a third of the growth rate since 1980 has been due to this shift effect. In contrast, increases in total factor productivity averaged less than 1% per annum. In other words, most of the total increase and increase in per capita production was achieved not by increasing production per unit of input but through new investments and the accumulation of inputs as has been the case in most developing countries (also Chapter 3 in this volume by Atiyas and Bakış; Altuğ *et al.*, 2008, pp. 393–430).

Low rates of total productivity growth during recent decades have gone hand in hand with the relatively low education and skill levels of the labor force and the low technology content of the manufactures. Turkey continues to lag behind world averages and the averages of countries with similar GDP per capita levels in terms of years of schooling as well as skills. The shortcomings of the education system have caused serious difficulties in the transition to an economy that can use and develop more advanced technologies. The manufacturing industry has been reluctant to invest in branches of production that involve higher technology and require higher skills as they turned to export markets after 1980. As a result, manufactures with standard technologies dominated the exports in the new era (Taymaz and Voyvoda, 2012, pp. 83–111).

The rest of the chapter will emphasize that Turkey's encounter with the new economic policies, globalization, and economic growth since 1980 did not follow a linear path. Global economic developments and forces have certainly played some role in Turkey's economic fluctuations. Much more important in the trajectory of the new policies and as well as the medium-term fluctuations of the economy, however, have been Turkey's domestic politics. The rest of the chapter will examine the evolution of Turkey's economy and its interaction with domestic politics since 1980 in two cycles and four sub-periods.

Turkey's first cycle with the new economic policies and institutions began in 1980. In the first phase until 1987, the aim was to replace the interventionist and inward-oriented model that prevailed since the 1930s with one that relied more on markets and was more open to international trade and capital flows. With the help of the military regime which reduced wages and agricultural incomes, significant increases were achieved in exports of manufactures during this period. The achievements of the new policies in other areas such as privatization were limited, however. The second phase of the first cycle covering the years 1988–2002 was characterized by rising political and economic instability. The repression of domestic politics during the military regime of the early 1980s had led to fragmentation on both the right and left of the political spectrum. As a result, the 1990s witnessed growing rivalries between large numbers of parties and series of short-lived coalitions. One important outcome of the political instability was the loss of fiscal discipline. After the decision in 1989 to fully liberalize the capital account, the growing budget deficits were financed not only by high rates monetary expansion and domestic borrowing but also by external borrowing. Large fiscal deficits combined with financial globalization resulted in stop-go cycles of short-term international capital flows that culminated in the banking crisis of 2001. The average growth rate during this second phase of the first cycle was distinctly lower than the growth rate during the first phase, as can be seen from Table 1.1.

Turkey's experience with neoliberal policies entered the second cycle with the economic program of 2001 and the rise to power of the Islamist Justice and Development Party or the AK Parti after the national elections in the following year. The new economic program recognized the role played by institutions and independent regulating agencies and was supported by a series of reforms and new legislation. It also placed a great deal of emphasis on fiscal discipline and macroeconomic stability which was embraced by the AK Parti. It would however be best to divide the AK Parti era into two phases. The first phase through 2007 was characterized by improvements in both political and economic institutions supported by Turkey's candidacy for EU membership as well as growing liquidity and low interest rates in global financial markets (Chapter 7 in this volume by Aktar). As a result, the early impact of the global crisis of 2008–2009 on Turkey's economy remained limited. In the second phase since, in contrast, the AK Parti and its leader Recep Tayyip Erdoğan moved to establish a new and increasingly authoritarian regime. Along with growing political polarization, political as well as economic institutions deteriorated steadily (Chapter 2 in this volume by Acemoğlu and Üçer). To compensate for the ensuing decline in both domestic and international investments, AK Parti governments kept interest rates low and let the banks and the private sector borrow large amounts from abroad. As the era of high global liquidity and low interest rates created by the leading central banks began to end, however, it became difficult to sustain these pro-growth policies. As can be seen again from Table 1.1, the average growth rate during this second phase of the second cycle since 2008 has been distinctly lower than the growth rate during its first phase.

1.3. First Phase of the First Cycle: Adoption of Washington Consensus Policies (1980–1987)

Turkey's democracy and political institutions have remained under pressure ever since the shift to a multiparty political system in 1950. The military coups in 1960 and 1971 gave the armed forces significant power over the regime and veto power on many issues. At the same time, tensions between the right and the left and between the secularists and the emerging Islamists persisted. The coup of 1980 further boosted the power of the military. The 1982 Constitution prepared by the military regime brought in broad restrictions on freedom of thought and association and cast a long shadow on the political system that would last for decades.

The 1970s was a period of political instability. The short-lived coalition governments following the military coup of 1971 tried to avoid dealing with the root causes of the economic problems by relying on the remittances from workers in western Europe and short-term borrowing under unfavorable terms. As military expenditures increased during and after Turkey's intervention in Cyprus, they were also willing to print money to finance part of the budget deficits. As a result, the rate of inflation rose sharply during the 1970s (Figure 1.2). Political difficulties, large budget deficits, high rates of inflation, rising oil prices, and growing external debt then resulted in a severe economic crisis at the end of the decade.

Against the background of import and output contraction, commodity shortages, rate of inflation approaching 100%, and strained relations with the IMF and international banks, the newly installed center-right minority government of Süleyman Demirel announced a comprehensive and unexpectedly radical policy package of stabilization and liberalization in January 1980. Turgut Özal, a former Chief of the State Planning Organization, was to oversee the implementation of the new package.

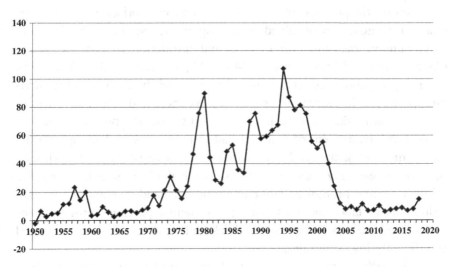

Figure 1.2.   Annual rate of inflation in Turkey, 1950–2018 (in %)

Source: TurkStat, official statistics.

While the Demirel government lacked the political support necessary for the implementation of the package, the military regime that came to power after the coup in September of the same year endorsed the new program and made a point of appointing Özal as Deputy Prime Minister responsible for the economy. Özal thus made his mark on Turkey's economy during the 1980s, first as the architect of the January 24 decisions, later as Deputy Prime Minister during military rule, and as Prime Minister after his party won the elections in 1983. With the experience he had acquired at the World Bank during the 1970s, he had first-hand knowledge of the new economic policies and, once in power, made radical decisions toward opening the economy.

The aims of the new policy package were three-fold: to improve the balance of payment and to reduce the rate of inflation in the short term and to create a market-based, export-oriented economy in the longer term thus putting the economy on an outwardly oriented course, a sharp turn from the previous ISI era. The package began with a major devaluation of the lira from 47 to 70 to the dollar followed by continued depreciation of the currency in line with the rate of inflation, greater liberalization of trade and payments regimes, elimination of price controls, substantial price increases for the products of the state economic enterprises, elimination of many of the government subsidies, freeing of interest rates, subsidies, and other support measures for exports and promotion of foreign capital (Aricanli and Rodrik, 1990a, pp. 1343–1350; Aricanli and Rodrik, 1990b).

Bringing about reductions in real wages and the incomes of agricultural producers in order to improve fiscal balances and competitiveness in international markets was an important part of the new policies. The parliamentary government of Demirel had little success in dealing with the labor unions as strikes and other forms of labor resistance, often violent, became increasingly common in the summer of 1980. After the coup, the military regime prohibited labor union activity and brought about large reductions in labor incomes. The government's purchase programs for agricultural crops were also scaled back and agricultural prices remained significantly lower during military rule.

In its early years, the January 1980 program benefited from the close cooperation and goodwill of the international agencies, especially the IMF and the World Bank as well as the international banks. One reason for this key support was the increasingly strategic place accorded to Turkey in the aftermath of the Iranian Revolution. Another reason was the close relations between Özal and the international agencies and the special status accorded to Turkey. For most of the decade Turkey was portrayed by these agencies as a shining example of the validity of the stabilization and structural adjustment programs they promoted and enjoyed their goodwill. In economic terms this support translated into better terms in the rescheduling of the external debt and substantial amounts of new credit.

After the shift to a restricted parliamentary regime in 1983, Özal was elected Prime Minister and as the leader of the new Motherland Party (ANAP) he had formed. He launched a new wave of liberalization of trade and payments regimes including reductions of tariffs and quantity restrictions on imports. These measures opened domestic industry further to the competition from imports especially in consumer goods. However, the frequent revisions in the liberalization lists, the arbitrary manner in which these were made and the favors provided to groups close to the government created a good deal of uncertainty regarding the stability and durability of these changes. The response of the private sector to import liberalization was mixed. While export-oriented groups and sectors supported the new measures, the domestic market-oriented sectors, especially the large-scale conglomerates whose products included consumer durables and automotives, continued to lobby for protection of their industries. The new regime gained permanence and the protectionism of the earlier era was dismantled in the following years; however, industry turned increasingly toward exports.

One of the more important new policies was the liberalization of the financial sector and opening it to the outside world. The exchange regime underwent fundamental changes and many transactions involving foreign exchange that were earlier the monopoly of the Central Bank were opened to commercial banks. With the flexibility provided by the new exchange rate regime, private banks were able to secure new credit from international sources, both private and public. These innovations created important opportunities but also brought on new risks. In addition, the government allowed all citizens to open and maintain accounts in foreign currency in the domestic banks. This new policy aimed at and succeeded in drawing the large foreign currency balances of the public from "under the mattress" into the banking system. In the longer term, however, it made currency substitution away from the lira or "dollarization" easier. Because of the decline in the effectiveness of monetary policy, it became harder to deal with inflation in later years (Aricanli and Rodrik, 1990a, pp. 1343–1350).

The most notable success of the new policies was the increase in exports. From very low levels of US\$2.3 billion and 2.6% ratio of GDP in 1979, export revenues rose to US\$8 billion in 1985 and US\$13 billion or 8.6% of GDP in 1990 (Figures 1.2 and 1.3). Most of the increases were due to the rise in exports of manufactures whose share in total exports rose from 36% in 1979 to 80% in 1990. Textiles, clothing, and iron and steel products ranked at the top of the list of exports. The growth in exports was achieved primarily by reorienting the existing capacity of existing ISI industries toward external markets. In the early years, the exporters were supported by a steady policy of exchange rate depreciation, by credits at preferential rates, tax rebates, and foreign exchange allocation schemes. The latter mechanisms amounted to 20–30% subsidy on unit value

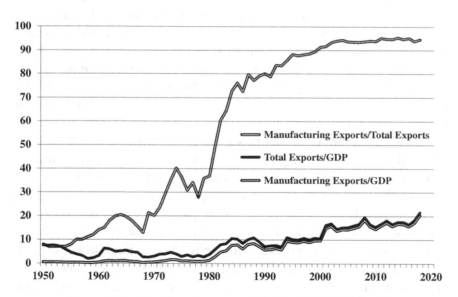

Figure 1.3.   Manufacturing exports in Turkey, 1950–2018 (in %)

Source: TurkStat, official statistics.

although their magnitudes gradually declined during the second half of the decade (Barlow and Şenses, 1995, pp. 111–133).

Aside from the export performance, however, the impact of the new policies on the real economy was rather mixed. Most importantly, the new policies were not able to mobilize high levels of private investment. In manufacturing industry, high interest rates, steady depreciation of the currency which raised the cost of imported capital and the unstable political environment were the most important impediments. Most of the increase in exports of manufactures was achieved with the existing industrial capacity. The same concerns adversely affected foreign direct investment as well. Some foreign capital flowed into the banking sector thanks to the liberalization of banking and finance, but in other areas, foreign direct investments remained limited, as was the case in earlier periods (Aricanli and Rodrik, 1990a, pp. 1347–1348; Boratav *et al.*, 1996, pp. 373–393).

Politics largely determined in which sectors, and to what extent, the new economic policies would be implemented. After military rule ended and a new multiparty political regime was established, albeit with many restrictions, the government decided to pursue policies that were politically beneficial or less costly, while staying away from policies or measures that appeared politically more difficult. For example, one of the priorities of the 1980 program was the privatization of state economic enterprises. Many of these companies had accumulated large losses during the 1970s. Initially, it was decided that they would be privatized after their balance sheets were improved. The privatization process however was strewn with technical, legal, and political obstacles. Those standing again privatization did not just include the workers but also the politicians who had no intention of abandoning the control they exercised over these firms (Öniş, 2004, pp. 113–134).

Reducing labor and agricultural incomes was one of the most fundamental elements of the January 1980 program. Both the military regime and the ANAP until 1987 followed policies that kept increases in wages and agricultural prices below rates of inflation. The closure of the unions by the military government and the introduction of new laws that eroded their power played important roles in the decline of real wages. The agricultural sector which provided employment and income to about half of the labor force was all but ignored by the ANAP. As a result, agricultural output increased at only 1.4% per year for the decade and failed to keep pace with population growth for the first time since the end of World War II. Despite the decline in wages and the agricultural prices paid by the government, public sector deficits, high rates of monetary expansion, and inflation continued. Annual rate of inflation declined from 90% in 1980 to 30% in 1983, but remained around 40% in the following years (Figure 1.2).

1.4. Second Phase of the First Cycle: Return of Political and Economic Instability (1988–2002)

The new constitution prepared by the military regime in 1982 introduced many restrictions on freedom of thought and association. By prohibiting the prominent politicians of the 1970s from returning to politics, the military regime also caused a great deal political instability. As a result, the 1990s witnessed a series of short-lived coalition governments in which both center-right and center-left parties competed primarily against parties occupying the same positions on the political spectrum rather than against those across the spectrum. The repeated dismantling of the main political parties by the military helped the rise of the Islamist parties and resulted after 2002 in the consolidation of the rule of the AK Parti with Islamist roots.

The restrictions placed by the military regime on the politicians of the 1970s were lifted after a referendum and they returned to active politics in 1987. With the transition to a more open electoral regime, the opposition began to criticize, both the deterioration of income distribution and the arbitrary manner in which Özal and the ANAP implemented the new policies. The protests and resistance movements that began among public-sector workers and continued with the miners of Zonguldak in 1989 showed that the period of repression imposed by the military government was being left behind. Workers' protests resulted in increases in their wages which made up for most of the decline in their purchasing power during the 1980s but real wages would decline once again during the following decade under high inflation. In the longer term, the fragmentation on both the center-right and center-left of the political spectrum between the old and new politicians fueled a good deal of instability.

Under short-lived coalition governments, budget deficits soared and public-sector debt accumulated. Between 1987 and 2002, Turkey thus went through a very difficult period, marked by intertwined political and economic crises. Like the other military coups that were launched ostensibly to restore political stability, the 1980 coup also became the cause of long-lasting political and economic instability.

In response to the more competitive political conditions after 1987, the ANAP government and the coalition governments that replaced it in early 1991 responded with populist policies. They sharply raised wages in the public sector as well as the prices of agricultural products and broadened the scope of the state's purchase programs for agricultural crops. Through public banks, they extended cheap credits to small businesses as well as agricultural producers. In addition, the prices of products sold by state economic enterprises began to lag behind inflation. These policies rapidly widened the budget deficit. In addition, state economic enterprises including public banks began to record huge losses. The expanding war with the Kurdish Workers' Party (PKK) which began in 1984 in the southeast continued to place new burdens on the budget.

In August 1989, as macroeconomic balances began to deteriorate, Özal and the ANAP decided to further liberalize the exchange rate regime and remove the restrictions on inflows and outflows of capital including foreign borrowing by the Treasury. With the infamous decree number 38, financial globalization acquired a legal framework. The basic aim of the decree was to ease the difficulties that the public sector was facing with financing its budget deficits, even if only in the short term, and to widen the room for maneuver of the government. After the decree, high domestic interest rates and a pegged exchange rate regime attracted large amounts of short-term capital inflows. Private banks rushed to borrow from abroad in order to lend to the government at high rates of interest. Public-sector banks were directed by the governments to finance part of the deficits.

In the longer term, the decision to liberalize the capital account without achieving macroeconomic stability and creating a strong regulatory infrastructure for the financial sector proved to be very costly. As the economy became increasingly vulnerable to external shocks and sudden outflows of capital, the 1990s turned into the most difficult period in the post-World War II era. Turkey's economy continued to struggle with large current account deficits and macroeconomic instability in later years as well. In fact, one can argue that full liberalization of the capital account or financial globalization has not interacted very well with Turkey's domestic institutions (Akyüz and Boratav, 2003, pp. 1549–1566; Gemici, 2012, pp. 33–55; Rodrik, 1990).

Another method used to finance the rapidly widening budget deficit, as was the case in earlier periods, was printing money. As the money supply began to increase, inflation, which was brought under control only partially during the 1980s, began to pick up pace again. Annual rates of inflation rose at the end of the 1980s and fluctuated between 50% and 100% during the 1990s (Figure 1.2). One important factor that reinforced the link between public-sector deficits and inflation was the introduction of foreign exchange deposit accounts in 1984 as part of the policies of financial liberalization. By reducing the demand for domestic money, this measure increased the inflationary impact of the public-sector deficits.

It was not easy to follow the rise of public-sector deficits and outstanding debt from the official series at the time since large parts of the deficits and losses were transferred to the balance sheets of the public-sector enterprises during this period. Moreover, the full cost to the public of the pillaging of the assets of the public banks could be estimated only after the 2001 crisis. It is now possible to put together an approximate account of the rise of the outstanding debt of the public sector in relation to the size economy. Figure 1.4 shows that the total domestic and foreign debt of the public sector rose dramatically from about 40% of GDP in 1990 to 90% in 2001.

Along the way, measures that would have increased the resilience of the economy to internal and external shocks were pushed aside. Virtually no progress was made in the privatization of the state economic enterprises. Both workers and politicians remained opposed to privatization. Moreover, attempts to sell some of the large state enterprises were accompanied by scandals involving leading politicians. The sale of some of the smaller public sector banks resulted in large losses for the state sector as these banks were stripped of their assets by the well-connected buyers, and the full guarantees on bank deposits made the public sector responsible for their large losses. These large losses were all added to outstanding public debt after 2001 (Tükel *et al.*, 2006, pp. 276–303).

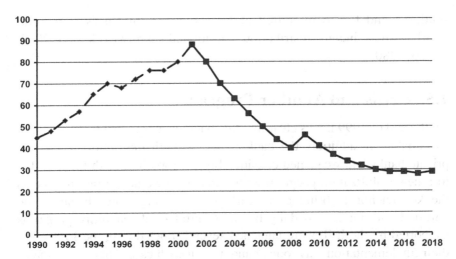

Figure 1.4.   Public Sector Debt Stock/GDP, 1990–2018 (%)

Source: Turkey, Ministry of Development.

The large public-sector deficit and the rapidly rising public-sector debt made the economy very vulnerable to external as well as internal shocks. A negative event in the global economy or politics or the perception that the public-sector deficit was becoming unsustainable could trigger large outflows of short-term capital, raise interest rates, depreciate the currency, and lead to a recession. These stop-go cycles of capital flows were repeated four times, in 1991, 1994, 1998, and 2000–2001, the last of which was the most severe. Even though GDP per capita continued to rise during these years, the trend rate was significantly lower than those in the earlier and later periods (Table 1.1).

High rates of inflation and high real-interest rates made income distribution increasingly more unequal during the 1990s. The more organized groups were able to develop some protection and shield themselves to some extent. Organized workers benefited from collective wage agreements, agricultural producers from support purchases, and small business owners from low interest credit. Middle classes relied on bank accounts in foreign currency and those with larger cash assets lent to the government at high rates of interest. However, not all sections of society were equally successful against inflation. With the added impact of the war in the

southeast and forced migration of large numbers of Kurds from rural
to urban areas, income distribution deteriorated sharply (Yükseker, 2009,
pp. 262–280).

1.5. Crisis and Another Program

By the end of 1999 it was clear that the macroeconomic balances were not
sustainable. In addition, the banking sector, both the public sector and
private banks had weakened considerably. Negotiations with the IMF led
to a new stabilization program with a managed exchange rate regime as
the key anchor to bring down inflation. Exchange rates began to be
adjusted and announced daily by the Central Bank. Stability programs
supported by the IMF were launched several times during the 1990s, but
their implementation was soon abandoned in each case. There were major
questions about the design and implementation of the new program. While
the program included a plan to reduce the large deficits in public finances
and deal with the large losses accumulated by public banks as well as the
problems of the private banks, it remained to be seen whether these measures would be adopted by the government.

Even though some progress was made toward reducing the budget
deficit, many of the measures envisaged in the program could not be implemented because the coalition government led by Bülent Ecevit could not
muster the necessary political will. Economic policy mistakes as well as
the IMF's insistence on managed rather than floating exchange rate policies also contributed to the problems. As the economy heated up, inflation
rose and the managed exchange rate of the lira began to appreciate. The
large deficits of the private and public banks also contributed to a major
crisis early in 2001. The government was forced to abandon the exchange
rate anchor after watching outflows of approximately US$20 billion within
a few days. The lira was then allowed to float and lost half of its value
against major currencies. As interest rates rose and the banking sector
collapsed, GDP declined by 6% in 2001 and unemployment and urban
poverty increased sharply (Akyüz and Boratav, 2003, pp. 1549–1566;
Özatay, 2009, pp. 80–100; Van Rijckeghem and Üçer, 2005, pp. 7–126).

Kemal Derviş who was a Senior Executive at the World Bank was
invited to Turkey soon after the crisis began to prepare a new program and

secure international support for it as minister in charge of the economy. The new program, prepared with the support of the IMF, contained stabilization measures as well as long-term structural and institutional reforms. For long-term macroeconomic stability, the program aimed to build large budget surpluses before debt payments for years to come in order to reduce the large outstanding public-sector debt. It also aimed to insulate the public-sector enterprises and especially the banks, legally and administratively, against the encroachment of the governments. Furthermore, instead of trying to control the inflation by managing the exchange rate and limiting the depreciation of the lira, a strategy that turned out to be very costly in the previous period, the new program adopted a floating exchange rate regime.

The 2001 program also contained elements that differed significantly from those in the previous programs prepared with IMF support after 1980. In fact, it has been argued that the program reflected the post-Washington Consensus principles (Öniş and Şenses, 2005, pp. 263–290). Instead of establishing the macro balances and leaving the rest to the markets, it accepted that the markets, left to their own devices, could produce undesirable outcomes and needed to be regulated. The program thus envisaged a new division of labor between markets and the state, at least in theory. The regulation and supervision of specific markets was being delegated to newly established institutions, which were intended to be independent from the government. For this reason, the program was needed to be supported by a series of structural reforms and new laws. Some of the other legislative changes were designed to prevent governments from using it for its short-term goals in the public sector, particularly the public banks, and more generally increase the autonomy of the Central Bank. To what extent these regulations would be effective and whether and to what extent the new institutions would be independent from the political authorities would be determined more by how the laws would be implemented over time, rather than by the laws themselves (Sönmez, 2011, pp. 145–230).

The new program also sought to restructure the banking sector after all the turbulence it went through during the 1990s. Both public and private-sector banks that had gone bankrupt would be dismantled and the outstanding debts of the public banks would be assumed by public sector and spread out over time. In addition, contrary to the lax practices of the 1990s, the program envisaged closer supervision of the banking sector. A Banking Regulation and Supervision Agency which was to function independently of the government was set up for this purpose. After the AK Parti came to power on its own following the elections of 2002, it decided to continue to implement the new program with the support of IMF.

1.6. Customs Union and the EU Candidacy

The Common Market and later the European Community was Turkey's most important trading partner, accounting for approximately 50% of its exports and more than 60% of its imports since the 1960s. During the military regime and its aftermath, Turkey remained far from fulfilling the political criteria for membership and little progress was made toward membership. The coalition governments of the 1990s thus sought to at least take economic relations one step closer by signing the Customs Union agreement in 1994. With the agreement, the two sides eliminated the customs duties in the trade of manufactured goods between Turkey and the EU, and aligned customs tariffs on imports from third countries with the levels applied by the EU. Trade in agricultural goods was left outside the Customs Union. While it is true that Prime Minister Tansu Çiller was trying hard to secure the agreement, it is not clear whether a better deal could have been obtained at the time.

The elimination of tariffs at the beginning did not come as a shock to domestic producers and the EU's share in Turkey's foreign trade did not increase after the Customs Union went into effect in 1996 because the tariff levels between Turkey and the EU had been declining since the 1980s. Nonetheless, the EU remained Turkey's largest trading partner by a large margin. With the return of economic stability after 2001, Turkey began to expand its external trade including trade with the EU. Turkey's exports to the EU began to rise rapidly and multinational companies producing in Turkey, especially in the automotive industry, started to use Turkey as a production base for export to the EU and to other countries. In the more labor-intensive sectors such as textiles, exports to the EU also increased initially but they declined after the EU lifted restrictions imposed on China.

The Customs Union with the EU brought important benefits to Turkey's economy and especially to its manufacturing sector. At the time the agreement was signed, the government and the political establishment thought that Turkey would soon become a member of the EU and would be included in the decision making (Chapter 7 in this volume by Aktar). However, as Turkey continued to remain outside the decision-making structures of the EU in later years, the inability to influence tariffs related to imports from third countries, especially those from East Asia began to impose costs and reduce the benefits of the Customs Union (Yılmaz, 2011, pp. 235–249).

1.7. First Phase of the Second Cycle: Early AK Parti Years (2003–2007)

While the secular parties struggled with the rising political and macroeconomic instability as well as the many demands of a rapidly urbanizing society during the 1990s, the Islamist political parties focused on local organization and local government delivering urban services. They were often set back by the military and the judiciary but came back with perseverance. In the process, they moderated their policies and improved their political skills. The emergence of a conservative bourgeoisie seeking economic integration with the West also helped them reshape their political goals and ideology.

The depth of the economic crisis in 2001 generated strong reactions from the public, not only against the political parties in power but also all the parties that had been in charge of the economy during the previous decade. In the general elections held in 2002, none of them could reach the 10% threshold imposed by the military regime in the early 1980s. As a result, they were not able to enter the parliament. While the center-right and center-left parties paid dearly for more than a decade of political and economic instability, the AK Parti, formed by a group of politicians who had split from the Islamist Virtue Party was able to exploit this opportunity and came to power by itself with only 34% of the national vote. The weaknesses of the secularists and the strengths of the Islamist movement thus precipitated the AK Parti's ascent to government.

At the time the AK Parti won the elections, Turkey's relations with the EU were making significant progress. The new party had been established by politicians who had pursued Islamist policies and opposed Turkey's membership in the EU for many years. Before the elections of 2002, however, the AK Parti began to distance themselves from their earlier positions. Once in power, it continued to support Turkey's membership in the EU and the political reforms. Turkey was formally accepted by the EU as a candidate for membership in 2004. The IMF and the EU emerged in this period as the two external anchors reinforcing the stabilization of the economy and the long-term transformation of the institutional framework (Öniş and Bakır, 2007, pp. 1–29; Yılmaz, 2011, pp. 235–249).

In its early years in power, the AK Parti appeared to pursue democratization and the Westward-oriented goals of Republican modernization. The party hoped to expand the room for Islam and more generally religious freedoms with its goals of democratization and EU membership. With this agenda, it was able to build a broad coalition. In its first five years in power, the AK Parti also pursued policies that were more pro-private sector than any of the earlier governments. As a result, it received the support of major businesses and industrialists in Istanbul as well as the more conservative businesses and industrialists across the country.

By the time the AK Parti came to power, most of the political costs of the severe recession as well as the austerity measures associated with the 2001 program had already been borne by the previous government. The AK Parti government was then able to continue with the program without much hesitation. The AK Parti also embraced fiscal discipline which was a key element of that program for achieving macroeconomic stability. Indirect taxes on gasoline and consumer goods were raised sharply. Another important contribution to lowering the public-sector deficits came from privatizations. Earlier attempts at privatization had not made much progress because of legal and political obstacles but the AK Parti pursued privatization even at the cost of abandoning goals such as long-term productivity, efficiency, competition, or protecting the interests of the consumer. As a result, the AK Parti government was able to maintain large public-sector surpluses before debt payments until the global crisis of 2008–2009. Thanks to these surpluses, the ratio of public sector debt to GDP was reduced from approximately 80% in 2002 to 40% in 2008

(Figure 1.5; also Chapter 2 in this volume by Acemoğlu and Üçer; Chapter 3 in this volume by Atiyas and Bakış).

The large budget surpluses before debt payments also enabled the AK Parti government to bring inflation under control and below 10% per annum for the first time since the 1960s (Figure 1.2). The restoration of macroeconomic balances and the start of accession negotiations with the EU also paved the way for significantly higher levels of foreign direct investment. Supported by growing global liquidity, foreign direct investments, which had remained below US$3 billion per annum before 2004, rose to US$20 billion annually during 2005–2007. Because an important share of these investments took the form of acquisitions of existing local companies, their contribution to job creation remained limited.

Macroeconomic stability combined with strong increases in exports as well as the favorable global economic environment of low interest rates and greater availability of credit led to large increases in GDP per capita. The accumulation of unused industrial capacity and pent up demand during the previous 15 years of low economic growth also helped economic performance during the early AK Parti years. From 2003 through 2007, GDP per capita increased at an annual rate above 5% and by a total of about 30% (Table 1.1). These annual rates were well above the long-term trend rates for Turkey. Economic growth and lower debt payments thanks to declining public-sector debt soon enabled the government to raise spending on infrastructure investment, healthcare, and education. AK Parti was thus able to deliver significant material benefits to its constituents not only through the increases in incomes but also higher levels of government spending in these areas. These benefits supported the AK Parti at election time in later years.

After the political instability of the 1990s, the elimination of government support programs and more generally government interventionism in agriculture also gained momentum during the AK Parti era. The agreements signed with the IMF and the World Bank after the crisis of 2001, Turkey's candidacy for EU membership and the commitments made by the government for World Trade Organization membership played key roles in this shift. As a result, agricultural support policies for many commodities were largely discontinued, subsidies for agricultural inputs and credits were generally removed, most of the state agricultural enterprises were privatized, and the trade regime in agriculture was liberalized to a significant degree. This restructuring and deregulation increased the profile and power of the large international companies in domestic markets (Aydın, 2010, pp. 149–187; Keyder and Yenal, 2011, pp. 60–86).

While the economy recovered and incomes increased, economic policies of the AK Parti's did not evolve beyond the institutional regulations and the fiscal discipline included in the 2001 program. The AK Parti governments did not develop their own long-term perspective on industrialization, growth, and employment creation (Taymaz and Voyvoda, 2012, pp. 83–111). Nonetheless, the economic recovery and growth achieved in its first five years in power enabled the party to increase its share of the vote to 47% and secure a larger majority in parliament in the 2007 elections.

1.8. Second Phase of the Second Cycle: Political and Economic Deterioration (2008–2018)

The early impact of the global crisis of 2008–2009 was severe because the memories of the previous crises were still fresh. In the initial months, large declines were recorded not just in exports but also in investments and consumption. However, the banking sector had behaved more cautiously after the 2001 crisis, and the supervision and monitoring of the sector had been well managed. As a result, the banks remained resilient and the impact of the crisis was short lived. In addition, the tight fiscal policies followed in the previous years had brought down the public-sector debt ratio. In addition to lower interest rates, government spending was raised for a few years to soften the impact of the crisis, an option not available to many other countries. By 2010, production and employment had returned to their pre-crisis levels. However, as the economic problems faced by the EU, which accounted for 50% of Turkey's exports, and the problems in the Middle East deepened in the following years, Turkey's exports continued to stagnate.

Even more important were the political problems. The formal negotiations for Turkey's membership in the EU began in 2005. At about the same time, however, center-right governments came to power in Germany and France and they soon began to openly oppose Turkey's membership. This shift in the positions of the two key countries was an important turning point in Turkey's relations with the EU (Chapter 7 in this volume by Aktar). The EU anchor not only underpinned the political reforms but also contributed to the economic recovery after 2001. As that anchor began to weaken and the goal of EU membership became increasingly uncertain, the AK Parti's willingness to continue with the political reforms as well as long-term changes in economic institutions began to wane.

Growing domestic political difficulties, rising tensions, and the gradual slide toward authoritarian rule also hurt the economy after the early AK Parti years. The secular elites in the judiciary and the military attempted to close down the party in 2007 at a time when it was actually in government. After the national elections in 2007, defeating the rivals and consolidating power became the single most important goal for the AK Parti and its leader Erdoğan. Turkey's slide toward authoritarianism continued after Erdoğan was elected President by popular vote in 2014. As he struggled to change the constitution and move from a parliamentary to a presidential system, the civil war in Syria and the return of military conflict in the Kurdish areas added to the political and economic difficulties (Chapter 8 in this volume by Yeşilada).

As the AK Parti moved to control the economy more closely after 2007, many of the institutions and policies that were installed with the IMF to support the 2001 program began to be eliminated and the business environment began to deteriorate. The regulatory agencies established as part of the 2001 program came under increasing pressure. Similarly, the Central Bank was forced to adjust its stance under pressure from the government. It soon abandoned its goal of lowering the inflation rate further and began to lower interest rates and expand credit. Annual rate of inflation which had declined to 6% in the aftermath of the global crisis began to rise toward 10% in later years (Figure 1.2; also Gürkaynak and Sayek-Böke, 2012, pp. 64–69; Acemoglu and Üçer, 2015). At the same time, government interventionism in the economy became increasingly more partisan. Firms and individuals close to the AK Parti and Erdoğan were consistently favored in public-sector projects. In addition, the fight by the AK Parti leadership and the government against the rival Islamist Gülen network, especially after their coup attempt in 2016, has led to the wholesale confiscation of the assets of many individuals and firms without sufficient or proper scrutiny by the judicial system.

Rising political tensions, steady deterioration of the institutional environment and growing macroeconomic instability sharply reduced private investment in the later AK Parti era. The stagnation in European markets, the civil war in Syria, terrorism by the Islamic State of Iraq and Syria (ISIS) and the PKK and the sharp decline in tourism revenues also contributed to the economic slowdown. As a result, average annual growth rates were distinctly lower in the second phase of second cycle in comparison to the first phase (Table 1.1). The unemployment rate in the urban economy increased from 10.5% at the end of 2011 to more than 14% at the end of 2018.

Another long-term problem has been the steady decline in the savings rate. As a result, current account deficits widened and the private sector had to secure large sums from abroad every year in order to finance its investments (Figure 1.5). Foreign direct investments most of which came from the EU countries could finance only a fraction of the deficits. During the difficult 1990s, the large public-sector deficits had been the major problem for the economy. The emphasis on fiscal discipline during the

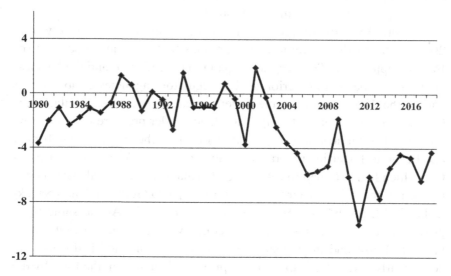

Figure 1.5.   Current account balance as % of GDP, 1980–2018

Source: Central Bank of Turkey.

early AK Parti years eliminated the public-sector deficits but shifted them, in effect, to the private sector. Thanks to the growth global liquidity created by the central banks of the United States, the EU, and Japan after the global financial crisis of 2008, the financing of the large current account deficits did not create serious difficulties in the early years. The banking sector was able to borrow record amounts from the international banks and direct most of these funds to the private sector and use the rest to finance private consumption.

As Erdoğan consolidated his power within the AK Parti and eliminated political rivals, the earlier competence in managing the economy began to disappear. While the independence of many of the economic institutions declined, the economic ministers and advisors became more dependent on the idiosyncratic views of the leader. Those most willing to please him were the ones that stayed in office. In addition, as the risks associated with losing power rose, Erdoğan's willingness to pursue growth policies increased. In response to lower rates of growth and rising unemployment, he put pressure on the central bank to keep interest rates low and expand credit. Given the high rates of urbanization and growing demand for real estate, the construction sector appeared especially attractive to the government for boosting the economy and creating employment. In addition, changing the existing rules on urban plans and allowing higher densities of construction was usually a safe and low-tech method for ensuring that firms and individuals close to the government would benefit directly and quickly. Large infrastructure projects such as roads, bridges, and airports also became increasingly popular with the government in the later years. The shopping malls rising in big cities, growing number of housing and office building projects, and large infrastructure projects by the government thus became symbols of an economic model based on construction and consumption.

Erdoğan and the AK Parti leadership pushed the pro-growth policies even further in advance of the national elections in 2015, the critical referendum for the transition to the presidential system supported by Erdoğan in 2017 and the first elections under the new presidential regime in 2018. While interest rates were kept low, government spending was increased during this period. Public sector banks and private banks were encouraged and in 2018 were even required to expand credit. As a result, after coming down in the early AK Parti years, the inflation rate began to rise after 2012 and exceeded 20% according to some measures in 2018. In addition, the current account deficit and the need to secure external finance kept growing. The banking sector had been able to borrow from abroad at low interest rates in the earlier years. As the era of low interest rates and high liquidity created by the leading central banks began to end, Turkey's economy looked increasingly vulnerable.

After the referendum in 2017 and the first presidential election in 2018, Turkey entered yet another difficult period full of political and economic uncertainties. Decline in the rule of law and a deterioration of the economic environment during the last decade have reduced the willingness of the private sector to undertake long-term investments in plant and equipment. After a long period of expansionary fiscal and monetary policies, the sharp decline in the exchange rate of the lira in 2018 in response to both economic and political developments was contained by the Central Bank only with a sharp increase in interest rates to 24%. The ensuing recession spilled into 2019. Public finances have also been deteriorating. Large-scale construction projects and consumption financed with funds borrowed from abroad that have sustained the economy in the second phase of the second cycle cannot be repeated in the new environment. As the confidence of the private sector and international investors in the one-man regime faded, chances of rapid economic recovery declined as well.

Disappearance of the rule of law, rising authoritarianism and growing polarization in the later AK Parti years inflicted long-term damage to the economy through other channels as well. Paralleling the decline in private-sector investment, capital flight and brain drain accelerated after 2010. Many companies and wealthy individuals in Turkey have always tended to keep a part of their wealth abroad. In recent years, however, capital flight has increased significantly. According to a recent report that aims to track the movements of wealth around the world, Turkey has experienced the most intense outflows of wealth and wealthy individuals anywhere in the world in 2016 and 2017. The same source lists Istanbul at the top of world cities experiencing highest levels of capital flight. Among the destinations of the fund outflows have been the countries in the Gulf suggesting that many of those who accumulated wealth in the AK Parti era have also been transferring their funds abroad (Global Wealth Migration Review, 2018).

Turkey has also been experiencing brain drain in recent years. Many young and better educated professionals have been leaving for employment opportunities abroad. In addition, many young people who have recently completed their higher education or advanced degrees abroad have been staying abroad rather than returning to Turkey.

The best years of the economy under the AK Parti are now well in the past. With the dismantling of the main political and economic institutions of the previous era, the disappearance of the independence of the judiciary, and the decline in the confidence of large segments of the private sector as well as the international investors, it will not be easy to reverse the recent economic trends. A strong recovery from the current recession appears unlikely. In the medium term, the economic outcomes will depend on the global environment as well as developments in Turkey. In the absence of a crisis, the current trends of low growth and high unemployment are likely to continue in the foreseeable future.

1.9. Conclusion

Turkey's encounter with neoliberal policies and institutions began with the new policy package launched in 1980 with the support of the IMF. As was the case in many other developing countries, the adoption of the Washington Consensus policies and institutions was only the beginning of the story. The adoption of the new policies and institutions did not mean they would remain unchanged. As has been the case in most countries embracing the new policies and institutions, Turkey's politics has interacted with them and with the economic outcomes in many ways. Just as the new policies and institutions influenced the economic and political outcomes, domestic politics, in turn, shaped the timing and extent of the new economic policies and influenced the performance of the economy.

This chapter has also emphasized that of the new economic policies and institutions, those that concerned relations with the global economy — most importantly trade liberalization, the emphasis on exports and the lifting of restrictions on international capital flows — have remained intact since 1980. In contrast, many of the new policies and institutions that concerned the workings of the domestic economy, were later changed by governments. In many of these latter areas related to the workings of the domestic economy, longer term results turned out to be quite different than what the new economic policies and institutions were supposed to achieve.

Turkey's encounter with the new economic policies, globalization, and economic growth since 1980 did not follow a linear path. Global economic developments and forces have certainly played some role in Turkey's economic fluctuations. Much more important in the trajectory of the new policies and as well as the medium-term fluctuations of the economy have been domestic politics. Turkey's democracy and political institutions have remained under pressure ever since the shift to a multi-party political system in 1950. The interaction between the new economic policies and institutions with domestic politics in Turkey unfolded in two cycles since 1980. In the first phase of each cycle new policies and institutions were adopted. In the second phase of each cycle, domestic politics dominated and many of the policies and institutions concerning the internal functioning of the economy were changed.

In countries which adopted the neoliberal policies in recent decades, their distributional consequences and popular discontent with them have often been the most important reasons for the subsequent changes in these policies. In Turkey, too, growing inequalities in income distribution during the 1980s played a key role in the movement away from these policies during the second phase of the first cycle after 1987. In the second cycle after 2002, however, strong economic growth and policies that paid attention to the welfare of low-income groups in the first phase took away distribution as a leading political issue. As a result, the main reason for the move away from the market-oriented policies during the second phase of the second cycle after 2007 was not popular discontent with them. Instead, the movement away from the neoliberal policies and institutions was due to the decision by the AK Parti and its leader Erdoğan to establish an authoritarian regime with a more centralized economy.

The most important area where major differences emerged between what the new economic policies intended in theory and what actually happened in practice concerned the role of the state in the economy. With the adoption of the Washington Consensus policies, it was claimed that the role of the state in the economy would shrink and its earlier interventionist role would also shrink if not disappear altogether. While protectionism and allocation of scarce foreign exchange, the much sought after benefits of government largesse in the previous era, disappeared, many other forms of government intervention and discretion continued and even expanded. Low interest credit from public-sector banks, various tax exemptions and subsidies continued. Privatization auctions and winning infrastructure and public procurement contracts from the government, both national and local, remained key mechanisms in the new era. Role of the government in the economy expanded further during the last decade.

Preferential treatment from political parties in power toward selected individuals and firms and reciprocal support from the latter toward the political parties have always been common in Turkey and played key roles in the rise of many individuals, families, and business groups. In the AK Parti era, these mechanisms were also used to create a new layer of conservative businessmen that would support the Islamist political project of the AK Parti and its leader. Moreover, because the party remained in power longer than any other party since the end of World War II and because it made efforts to change the legal framework for government–private sector relations, the role of government in the rise of business groups, and in turn, favors from the business groups toward the party in power were much more extensive in the AK Parti era. The political and economic institutions in Turkey were not particularly strong in the earlier periods but they have declined further during the latter years of the AK Parti era.

Moreover, in the era of neoliberal policies when state interventionism was expected to become more limited, the capacity of the national and local governments to decide who would win and who would lose in the economy actually increased in Turkey. In an environment of growing authoritarianism, partisanship in bureaucratic appointments, and the awarding of increasing number of government contracts and other forms of support on the basis of political affiliations made clear to all that remaining close to the government mattered. The AK Parti prepared the legal basis for these practices by introducing new legislation at each stage. New laws not only eliminated the independence of the regulatory agencies but also expanded the ability of the government to make decisions with greater flexibility and less accountability. The legal changes were not intended to create "a level playing field" for all the firms in the private sector. They were designed, instead, to facilitate the rise of a new stratum of conservative businessmen who were close to the party and especially to the party's leader by making it easier for national and local governments to award contracts to the favored individuals and companies. The AK Parti also opened new areas of the economy to the private sector under more flexible laws, allowing greater discretion to the government. The environmental laws and regulations were changed in order to expand the operations of the private companies in these sectors. The growing control of the judiciary by the executive branch in later years of the AK Parti era ensured that increasing government control over the economy was supported by the courts (Atiyas, 2012, pp. 57–81; Buğra and Savaşkan, 2014, pp. 76–176).

Not all sectors of the economy were equally influenced by these changes. In fact, the legislative changes and government favoritism at both the national and local levels, focused more on the areas and sectors that can be influenced most easily and most effectively by government decisions and interventionism such as energy, mining, tourism, and construction. One important instrument for increasing the ability of the government to decide which companies or individuals would be the winners was the changes made in the public procurement law. Because of rapid urbanization and economic growth, the government was involved in large-scale investment projects in energy, communications, transportation, and other areas. A new public procurement law which sought transparency and competitiveness was legislated and a Public Procurement Agency was established as part of the 2001 program. However, the new law was amended more than 150 times during the AK Parti era in order to give the government greater flexibility regarding how the public tenders were managed and how the winners were decided. In addition, large areas of the public sector and increasing number of industries and activities were exempted from the law. As a result, business groups close to the AK Parti were increasingly favored in tenders launched by the central government as well as the local governments, in large-scale energy, infrastructure and housing projects, in the allocation of credit by public and private banks and other areas (Çeviker Gürakar, 2016; Buğra and Savaşkan, 2014, pp. 76–81).

Another important mechanism in the emergence of new business groups close to the government was privatization of state economic enterprises. Major legal obstacles existed in the way of privatization until the AK Parti era. Higher administrative courts continued to intervene in the privatization process to overrule the political decisions made by the parliament and the executive branch. The AK Parti eliminated these difficulties by changing the laws and increasing government control over the Privatization Agency. Role of the administrative courts over the privatization process declined but continued until the referendum of 2010 when the independence of the judiciary was eliminated.

Urban construction emerged as another popular mechanism for enriching the business groups close to the government. The AK Parti carried the organization and distribution of urban rents to a new level by expanding the powers and operations of TOKİ, the Mass Housing Administration. The agency was connected directly to the Office of the Prime Minister during the AK Parti era and its control over state lands and its ability to enter partnerships with both large and small private companies and transfer ownership of state lands to private companies was expanded with new legislation. However, new legislation also exempted the agency from many of the financial disclosure requirements that had applied to the public-sector companies. The agency's operations thus became more opaque as it expanded cooperation with large and medium-sized construction groups close to the government. Extensive networks of patronage relations characterized the relations between the government and the construction companies. Business groups not well connected to the government were excluded from these projects (Kuyucu and Ünsal, 2010, pp. 1479–1499).

In contrast, government favoritism and interventionism played a more limited role in the tradables or internationally competitive sectors of the economy such as automotives, steel, textiles, and others. This is why some of the largest conglomerates which were not among the favorites of the government could concentrate their activities in these sectors and survive during the later years of the AK Parti era. Even these latter sectors were not immune from the effects of the favoritism of AK Parti and its mismanagement of the economy, however. After the public-sector and private-sector banks were pressured by the government and the banking authority to expand credit in advance of the elections, for example, the resulting weaknesses of the banking sector impacted the private sector across all sectors.

One of the key areas which tended to lose from this pattern of favoritism was technology and industries with higher technological component. Rather investing in education, skills, and technology to improve competitiveness in domestic and international markets was prioritized. Individuals and firms both well connected and not so well connected to the AK Parti networks often found it more expedient to use their resources to stay close to and seek favors from the government. Those that could not receive favors from the government often decided not to invest in long-term projects or carry their investments to locations abroad. There was some economic growth but there were significant limitations both to the level and type of economic growth created in such an environment.

References

Acemoglu, D. and Üçer, M. (2015). "The Ups and Downs of Turkish Growth, 2002–2015: Political Dynamics, The European Union and the Institutional Slide", NBER Working Papers, No. 21608, 2015, Cambridge, Mass.

Akyüz, Y. and Boratav, K. (2003). "The Making of the Turkish Financial Crisis", *World Development*, Vol. 31, pp. 1549–1566.

Altuğ, S., Filiztekin, A. and Pamuk, Ş. (2008). "Sources of Long-Term Economic Growth for Turkey, 1880–2005", *European Review of Economic History*, Vol. 12, pp. 393–430.

Aricanli, T. and Rodrik, D. (1990a). "An Overview of Turkey's Experience with Economic Liberalization and Structural Adjustment", *World Development*, Vol. 18, pp. 1343–1350.

Aricanli, T. and Rodrik, D. (eds.) (1990b). *The Political Economy of Turkey: Debt, Adjustment and Sustainability*, St. Martin's Press.

Atiyas, İ. (2009). "Recent Privatization Experience of Turkey: A Reappraisal", Ziya Öniş and Fikret Şenses (eds.), *Turkey and the Global Economy: Neo-Liberal Restructuring and Integration in the Post-crisis Era*, Routledge, pp. 101–122.

Atiyas, İ. (2012). "Economic Institutions and Institutional Change in Turkey during the Neoliberal Era", *New Perspectives on Turkey*, Vol. 47, pp. 57–81.

Aydın, Z. (2010). "Neo-Liberal Transformation of Turkish Agriculture", *Journal of Agrarian Change*, Vol. 10, No. 2, pp. 149–187.

Barlow, R. and Şenses, F. (1995). "The Turkish Export Boom: Just Reward or Just Lucky?", *Journal of Development Economics*, Vol. 48, pp. 111–133.

Bolt, J. and Van Zanden, J. L. (2014). "The Maddison Project. Collaborative Research on Historical National Accounts", *The Economic History Review*, Vol. 67, No. 3, pp. 27–651.

Boratav, K., Türel, O. and Yeldan, E. (1996). "Dilemmas of Structural Adjustment and Environmental Policies under Instability: Post-1980 Turkey", *World Development*, Vol. 24, pp. 373–393.

Buğra, A. and Savaşkan, O. (2014). *New Capitalism in Turkey: The Relationship Between Politics, Religion and Business*, Edward Elgar Pub. Ltd., pp. 76–176.

Çeviker Gürakar, E. (2016). *Politics of Favoritism in Public Procurement in Turkey, Reconfigurations of Dependency Networks in the AKP Era*, Palgrave Macmillan.

Gemici, K. (2012). "Rushing toward Currency Convertibility", *New Perspectives on Turkey*, Vol. 47, pp. 33–55.

Global Wealth Migration Review (2018). Worldwide Wealth and Wealth Migration Trends, February, https://samnytt.se/wp-content/uploads/2018/02/GWMR-2018.pdf.

Gürkaynak, R. and Sayek-Böke, S. (2012). "AKP Döneminde Türkiye Ekonomisi", *Birikim*, Istanbul, Vol. 296, pp. 64–69.

Keyder, Ç. and Yenal, Z. (2011). "Agrarian Change under Globalization: Markets and Insecurity in Turkish Agriculture", *Journal of Agrarian Change*, Vol. 11, pp. 60–86.

Kuyucu, T. and Ünsal, Ö. (2010). "Urban Transformation as State-Led Property Transfer: An Analysis of Two Cases of Urban Renewal in Istanbul", *Urban Studies*, Vol. 47, No. 7, pp. 1479–1499.

Öniş, Z. (2004). "Turgut Özal and His Economic Legacy: Turkish Neo-Liberalism in Critical Perspective", *Middle Eastern Studies*, Vol. 40, No. 4, pp. 113–134.

Öniş, Z. and Bakır, C. (2007). "Turkey's Political Economy in the Age of Financial Globalization: The Significance of the EU Anchor", *South European Society and Politics*, Vol. 12, pp. 10–29.

Öniş, Z. and Şenses, F. (2005). "Rethinking the Emerging Post-Washington Consensus", *Development and Change*, Vol. 36, No. 2, pp. 263–290.

Özatay, F. (2009). *Finansal Krizler ve Türkiye*, Doğan Kitap.

Pamuk, Ş. (2018). *Uneven Centuries, Economic Development of Turkey since 1820*, Princeton University Press.

Rodrik, D. (1990). "Premature Liberalization, Incomplete Stabilization", in Michael Bruno, Stanley Fischer and Elhanan Helpman (eds.), *Lessons of Economic Stabilization and Its Aftermath*, MIT Press, pp. 323–353.

Sönmez, Ü. (2011). *Piyasanın İdaresi, Neoliberalizm ve Bağımsız Düzenleyici Kurumların Anatomisi*, İletişim Yayınları.

Taymaz, E. and Voyvoda, E. (2012). "Marching to the Beat of a Late Drummer: Turkey's Experience of Neoliberal Industrialization since 1980", *New Perspectives on Turkey*, Vol. 47, pp. 83–111.

Tükel, A., Üçer, M. and Van Rijckeghem, C. (2006). "The Banking Sector, From Crisis to Maturation", in Sumru Altuğ and Alpay Filiztekin (eds.), *The Turkish Economy: The Real Economy, Corporate Governance and Reform*, Routledge, pp. 276–303.

Van Rijckeghem, C. and Üçer, M. (2005). *Chronicle of the Turkish Financial Crisis of 2000–2001*, Boğaziçi University Press.

Yılmaz, K. (2011). "The EU–Turkey Customs Union Fifteen Years Later: Better, Yet Not the Best Alternative", *South European Society and Politics*, Vol. 16, pp. 235–249.

Yükseker, D. (2009). "Neoliberal Restructuring and Social Exclusion in Turkey", in Ziya Öniş and Fikret Şenses (eds.), *Turkey and the Global Economy: Neo-liberal Restructuring and Integration in the Post-crisis Era*, Routledge, pp. 262–280.

Chapter 2

High-Quality Versus Low-Quality Growth in Turkey: Causes and Consequences

Daron Acemoğlu and E. Murat Üçer*

2.1. Introduction

Much of the emerging world has returned to rapid growth following the global financial crisis of 2007–2009. Figure 2.1 shows GDP per capita (in purchasing power parity, PPP) in a sample of selected emerging economies over the last two decades, where rapid growth in China, Turkey, Malaysia, and Mexico since 2009 is visible. However, much of this growth may be less sustainable than first meets the eye. Growth driven by consumption, credit, and government spending, without sufficient investment and productivity growth, tends to run out of steam more rapidly and may even prepare conditions for subsequent economic crashes.

Put simply, the key question is whether emerging economy growth during this period is "low-quality", meaning that it is not associated with significant productivity and technological improvements.

*The authors are grateful to Merve Aksoylar for the growth accounting calculations, Derya Karakaya for help with the data and figures, and to Dani Rodrik, Cihat Tokgöz and the editors of this volume, Asaf Savaş Akat and Seyfettin Gürsel, for useful comments and suggestions. The usual caveat applies.

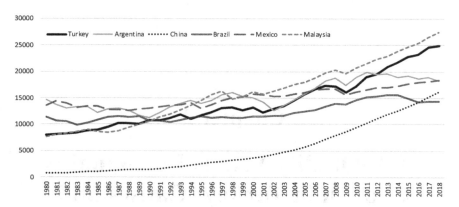

Figure 2.1. GDP per capita (in purchasing power parity, PPP, constant prices, 2011 international dollar)

Note: The figure shows purchasing power parity-based GDP, expressed in constant international dollars, divided by total population.

Source: International Monetary Fund (IMF), World Economic Outlook Database.

Figure 2.2 depicts total factor productivity (TFP) growth in the same economies. With the exception of China, TFP growth in these economies has been disappointing over the last 10 years, and in all cases TFP growth is significantly slower than in the previous two decades.[1] Figure 2.3 shows one potential reason for this: in these same economies, there has also been a sizable expansion of credit as a percent of GDP.

Moreover, much of this growth has not been broadly shared within the population, raising another set of concerns about its social desirability and its sustainability. The average Gini coefficient in China over the last 10–15 years is around 0.41, in Argentina it is 0.43, in Mexico it is 0.45, and in Brazil, it is even higher, 0.53 (although it has been declining from its yet higher levels, near 0.60, in the late 1980s).[2] These levels of inequality are

---

[1] However, as the figure shows, Conference Board's alternative estimates for China that do not rely on the official statistics paint a much less rosy TFP picture for this country as well.
[2] Roughly speaking, the Gini coefficient represents the differential income shares of the high percentiles of the income distribution relative to the rest of the distribution so that a Gini of zero implies a perfectly equal distribution, while a Gini of one means that the very few rich

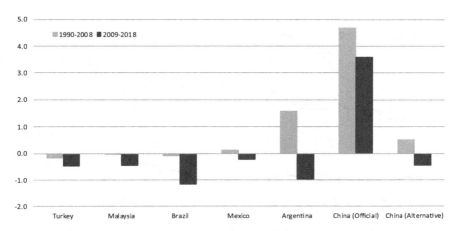

Figure 2.2.   Pre and post crisis TFP growth

Note: Simple period averages. For definition of TFP, see footnote 10. The figure also reports the Conference Board's alternative, much lower estimate for TFP growth in China, which eschews official growth figures. For Turkey, our own calculations, which we discuss in subsequent sections, show a more dramatic drop in TFP between the two periods, but for consistency, we have used Conference Board data for all countries in this figure.

Source: The Conference Board.

damaging to sustainable growth because they raise political tensions and conflict and encourage ultimately self-defeating "populist" policies.

In this chapter, we investigate the challenges of generating high-quality and shared growth in one emerging economy, Turkey. By *high-quality growth* we refer to economic growth driven by productivity improvements and technological upgrading. This sort of growth also typically entails improvements in the human capital and skills of the workforce. By *shared growth*, we mean growth from which the population at large benefits.

Though there are no universal recipes for achieving high-quality and/ or shared growth, recent research has emphasized the role of institutional

households capture all of the income. We present a more formal and detailed discussion in the following text. More directly, the income share of the top 1% of households is 13.9% in China, 23.6% in Brazil, 23.4% in Turkey, and 17% in Argentina (according to the World Inequality Database, where there are no data available for Mexico).

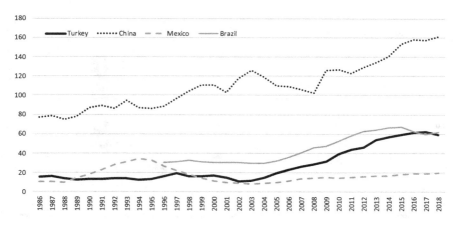

Figure 2.3. Bank credit to the private non-financial sector (as % of GDP)

Note: The figure shows bank credit to the private non-financial sector, as a percent of GDP. The private non-financial sector includes non-financial corporations (both private owned and public owned), households and non-profit institutions serving households, as defined in the 2008 System of National Accounts.

Source: Bank for International Settlements.

factors.[3] Of primary importance is the complex of economic institutions that Acemoğlu and Robinson (2012) refer to as "inclusive economic institutions". These are based on secure property rights, lack of coercion, and systematic discrimination in the labor market, a functioning legal system, public services, health and education investments, and a basic social safety net creating a level-playing field. These institutions, undergirded by political institutions that distribute political voice and power broadly in society and introduce basic checks on the exercise of political authority, appear to predict long-run, shared economic prosperity.[4]

Recent research also suggests that changes in economic and political institutions can have a major impact on the extent and nature of economic growth even in relatively short periods of time. Acemoğlu *et al.* (2019)

---

[3] See the discussion in World Bank (2008). Dollar *et al.* (2013) document that growth is good for the poor on average, but this average decline of poverty masks considerable heterogeneity and is not entirely undisputed.

[4] See, for example, Acemoğlu *et al.* (2001, 2005).

studied the economic implications of a transition from a non-democratic to a democratic regime and found that democratization increases economic growth substantially in the next 20 years (causing approximately a 20% rise in GDP per capita). Moreover, this growth boost tends to be high quality and shared: it is accompanied with higher taxes, more spending and better outcomes in education and health, and greater investments. Consistent with the institutional emphasis in Acemoğlu and Robinson (2012), this political change goes hand-in-hand with improvements in economic institutions, such as economic reforms in product, labor, and financial markets.

Another important argument in this literature is worth mentioning. Even though inclusive economic institutions, founded on inclusive political institutions, are conducive to faster growth, there should be no presumption that they emerge swiftly. Institutions are shaped by distributional conflicts and the relative powers of competing groups and individuals in society. Institutional reform follows either the collapse of existing political balances or results from new political coalitions in favor of reform coming together. Neither of these two paths works smoothly or rapidly, if at all.

Our basic premise in this chapter, building on our prior work, Acemoğlu and Üçer (2015), is that the recent Turkish macroeconomic experience confirms the role of institutions in shaping the extent and nature of economic growth. While Turkey has achieved considerable economic modernization and growth over the last three decades, much of this has been of low quality and the gains have been distributed rather unequally. These problems are rooted in the institutional structure of the Turkish economy. In fact, the short five years between 2002 and 2006, during which growth took a higher-quality form, accompanied with productivity improvements and technological upgrading, took place in the context of major improvements in economic and political institutions. When these improvements were reversed in the subsequent years, the quality of growth declined and inequality rose.

In the next section, we introduce our definitions for high-quality growth and shared growth, and discuss their institutional foundations. Section 2.3 is the heart of the chapter and develops our narrative on the extent and nature of economic growth in Turkey since the early 1990s. We document the limited extent of productivity improvements and technological upgrading in this growth process. This is visible in the lack of productivity growth and the types of goods the Turkish economy exports. It has also generally been unshared prosperity. Inequality in Turkey has remained high and appears to have increased further since 2006. The Turkish economy has continued to generate jobs during this time period, but much of this growth has come from services, and has likely been driven at least in part by government subsidies, rather than by productivity growth and private-sector investment.

Section 2.4 provides a brief discussion of the evolution of Turkish economic and political institutions and their impact on the nature of growth. We highlight how changes in the nature of Turkish growth are linked to the ups and downs of Turkish economic institutions, and how economic and political institutions are tightly connected.

Section 2.5 concludes by linking the current macroeconomic ills to the economic and institutional developments of the last two decades and stresses the extent to which many of these problems are consequences of recent low-quality growth. Looking forward, it also outlines reforms that look most promising for tackling both the short-run and the medium-run economic problems confronting the country.

2.2. High-Quality Growth: A Conceptual Framework

Saudi Arabia grew at a pace of almost 15% per annum in the 1970s.[5] This turbo-charged growth rate was not achieved by technological improvements, innovation, or even improved efficiency in the allocation of resources, but by oil exports in a period during which energy prices rose by six-fold.[6] During this period, the content of educational curricula deteriorated, however, turning increasingly toward religious indoctrination, and in part as a result, economic opportunities for Saudi workers dwindled. Four out of five workers employed in the private sector in Saudi Arabia are now foreigners.[7]

---

[5] Simple averages, OECD data.

[6] Inflation-adjusted oil price data from macrotrends.net.

[7] See, for example, International Monetary Fund (2019a).

Though Saudi Arabia is an extreme case, it vividly illustrates why the growth rate alone is not a sufficient gauge for measuring the success of an economy. Two problematic aspects of this type of growth are clear in the Saudi case. First, growth was not driven by productivity and technological improvements. This is an indication that the economy is not upgrading its productive potential (advanced economies during this period experienced steady productivity improvements, even if at a slower rate than in the 1950s and 1960s; see, e.g., Gordon, 2017). It is also often associated with a less sustainable type of growth. In the Saudi case, this lack of sustainability was rooted in the economy's dependence on international energy prices. Since 2014, for instance, as oil prices declined sharply, Saudi growth fell to a paltry 1.8%.[8]

Second, given the repressive and non-representative political system in Saudi Arabia, the gains which at first accrued to the national oil company, Aramco, were controlled and captured by the extended royal family and its cronies. As a result, Saudi Arabia remains a highly unequal country. We do not have Gini coefficients for Saudi Arabia, but World Inequality Database shows very high levels of inequality. For example, the bottom 50% in the Saudi economy gets 8% of national income, while the top 1% receives 20%.

Both productivity/technological improvements and shared prosperity are socially desirable, even if sharply missing from the Saudi experience. The first refers to whether growth is "high-quality", and the second to how broadly shared its gains are.

High-quality growth is first and foremost about whether growth is driven by productivity improvements and technological upgrading.[9] The standard measure of productivity in economics is TFP (also sometimes called multi-factor productivity). TFP growth looks at how much of growth in incomes (or gross domestic product, GDP) is due to

---

[8] In other cases, unsustainability may result because of excessive credit growth (often fueling rapid consumption or unproductive investment growth). On the link between credit and crises, see Schularick and Taylor (2012), who document a strong correlation between credit growth and financial crises in a sample of 14 countries between 1870 and 2008.

[9] We use the term high-quality growth rather than "sustainable growth" both to emphasize the critical role of productivity growth and technological upgrading and to highlight that sustainability is one possible consequence of the quality of economic growth.

improvements in technology and more efficient allocation of resources as opposed to increasing the labor force or the capital stock of the economy.[10]

Its interpretation is simple and powerful: a TFP growth of zero would imply that if an economy had the same level of capital stock and the same labor force (with exactly the same skills) the following year as this year, then its GDP would remain the same. In contrast, a TFP growth of 2% would imply that such an economy would have 2% higher GDP. Therefore, TFP growth is a boon to the economy. In addition, it captures the extent to which an economy is improving its productive potential. When focusing on advanced economies at the world technological frontier, TFP growth also represents how successful they are in inventing and introducing new production processes or products. For developing economies, which are typically behind the technology frontier, TFP growth captures how well they are able to import and adopt existing technologies and remove prevailing productive inefficiencies.[11] Thus, the failure to achieve high TFP growth for developing economies is also a failure to benefit from existing technological opportunities.

Because TFP is measured as a residual and is subject to considerable error,[12] it is useful to look at other proxies of the technological capabilities of an economy. One useful set of measures come from the content of exports. As economies adopt new technologies, they move up in the value chain and the content of their exports tends to change toward higher-tech and higher value-added products (see Hidalgo and Hausmann, 2009).

---

[10] TFP growth is computed as a residual from GDP growth such that,

$$\text{TFP growth} = \text{GDP growth} - \text{contribution of physical capital} - \text{contribution of human capital,}$$

where the contributions of physical and human capital are computed from the growth of the relevant capital stock and human capital measures multiplied by their (average) factor shares.

[11] See Acemoğlu *et al.* (2006) on distance to the frontier and growth among follower countries. See Acemoğlu (2009) for a broad discussion of structural transformation and changes in the efficiency of production process among developing countries.

[12] Most importantly, it is difficult to fully accommodate capacity utilization and quality of education and equipment into TFP calculations. See Acemoğlu (2009) for a discussion.

Motivated by this observation, we look at export composition as an additional measure of the productive and technological capabilities of an economy.[13]

Productivity improvements and technological upgrading often necessitate the upgrading of the skills of the workforce. Hence, it is also useful to track how the amount of educational investments and the skills of the workforce change over time. TFP growth and export content matter not just because of their direct impact on GDP and as measures of how efficiently the economy is growing but also because TFP-driven growth tends to be more durable. In contrast, growth unaccompanied by productivity improvements or growth fueled by commodity price booms or expansion in a few traditional sectors tends to be less sustainable, and often ends with sharp recessions and crashes.

It is equally clear why we should care about how shared growth is. In addition to normative concerns about the undesirability of growth accompanied with increasing impoverishment of a major part of the population, existing evidence suggests that widening inequality fuels conflict and may itself be a cause of future recessions. This is both because of the political conflict often associated with high levels of inequality and because of short term, distortionary policies that this type of growth appears to engender.[14]

Several measures of inequality can be informative about how shared prosperity is. The most common is the Gini coefficient, which roughly measures the "excess" share of income captured by richer percentiles of the income distribution. For example, a Gini coefficient of zero would mean perfect equality, while a Gini coefficient of one would represent a situation in which only one person, or a very small fraction of people,

---

[13] For a similar analysis, see Chapter 3 in this volume by Atiyas and Bakış.

[14] See Alesina and Perotti (1996) on the link between income inequality and instability. Alesina and Rodrik (1994) and Persson and Tabellini (1994) claimed that high inequality also leads to lower growth, but the link between inequality and growth appears to be more multifaceted (e.g., Banerjee and Duflo, 2003). Nevertheless, the literature on economic populism supports the notion that high inequality fuels distortionary macroeconomic policies as well as other inefficiencies in the economy (e.g., Dornbusch and Edwards, 1991, Kauffman and Stallings, 1991, Weyland, 2001).

command all of the income or wealth in the economy.[15] Although shared prosperity can in principle be achieved by redistribution, in most instances it emerges as a result of a growth process which leads to employment growth (since unemployment is often very unequally distributed, its burden tends to be felt by less educated and poorer segments of society) and broad-based wage growth. Entry barriers, cozy government-business deals, and corruption often contribute to greater inequality by creating artificial advantages and conferring excessive economic or political power on some of the players in the economy.

What factors underpin high-quality and shared growth? Though there is no universal consensus on this question, the recent literature emphasizes institutions as major determinants of both high-quality growth and the distribution of resources. North (1982, 1991) stressed the importance of institutional factors. More recently, Acemoğlu *et al.* (2001, 2005) provide cross-country evidence, exploiting colonial origins of different types of institutions, documenting the major role of institutions and long-run growth. Hall and Jones (1999) and Caselli (2005) show that measures of productivity, such as TFP, are correlated with such institutional differences. Acemoğlu *et al.* (2003) document that countries with better economic institutions are much more stable and do not suffer as severe recessions as those with worse institutions.

Acemoğlu and Robinson (2012) further develop the theory of institutions and present several historical cases bolstering the notion that better institutions are associated with less unequal and more shared prosperity. In addition, they provide some simple definitions of the most important prerequisites of the institutional complex that undergird high-quality and shared growth. They propose the notion of "inclusive economic

---

[15] More formally, the Gini coefficient is computed from the Lorenz curve of income. The Lorenz curve plots the cumulative fraction of total income of different percentiles of the distribution of income. The Gini coefficient is defined as the area between the Lorenz curve and the 45° line (which represents perfect equality) divided by 1/2. This explains why a Gini coefficient of zero represents perfect equality, and when the cumulative fraction of total income of all percentiles except the very top is zero, this area is equal to the entire triangle below the 45° line and is thus equal to 1/2, giving a Gini coefficient of one. In addition to the Gini coefficients, we sometimes report shares of national income accruing to bottom 50% and top 1% of the population from the World Inequality Database.

institutions" to capture the most important aspect of this complex. They write (p. 74):

> "Inclusive economic institutions ... are those that allow and encourage participation by the great mass of people in economic activity that make best use of their talents and skills and that enable individuals to make the choices they wish. To be inclusive, economic institutions must feature secure private property, an unbiased system of law, and the provision of public services that provides a level playing field in which people can exchange and contract; it also must permit the entry of new businesses and allow people to choose their careers."

They further stress that inclusive economic institutions are unstable unless they are bolstered by "inclusive political institutions", which distribute political power and voice broadly in society, introduce effective checks on political and economic elites, and have the capacity to enforce laws, tax and regulate economic activity, and provide effective public services. This definition highlights that inclusive political institutions must be democratic, as non-democratic regimes will lead to the monopolization of political power in the hands of a narrow segment and will exclude the majority of the population from effective political participation. Nevertheless, elections are not sufficient for political institutions to be inclusive. Electoral democracies may still entail little effective political competition and may be propped up by clientelistic policies based on selective transfers or the mobilization of ethnic or religious groups. They may also fail to place sufficient constraints and checks on elected officials.

We will see these links between inclusive economic and political institutions and high-quality, shared growth in the Turkish context as well.

The difficulties of emerging economies to transition from their existing economic structure have also received attention in recent debates. Some economists have claimed the existence of a "middle income trap" whereby emerging economies find it difficult to break away from the middle-income status into higher levels of income.[16] This is particularly

---

[16] The concept was first introduced by Gill and Kharas in a World Bank report on East Asia in 2007; see Gill and Kharas (2007). For a retrospective by the authors a decade later, see Gill and Kharas (2015).

true because such a transition often necessitates greater investments in technology, faster productivity growth, and more efficient allocation of resources (e.g., Eichengreen *et al.*, 2014). Though there is some evidence indicating that many emerging economies find a transition to a higher-quality growth difficult, this appears to be related to their institutional structures. Economies, such as South Korea, have swiftly broken through such a "trap" because of major political and economic reforms (e.g., Acemoğlu *et al.*, 2019).

A more recent case illustrates the same point. Poland, starting from a fairly low level of income per capita in the 1990s, undertook major economic and political reforms, in part as a result of its accession to the European Union (EU). These institutional reforms came with rapid productivity growth and technological improvements. As a result, Poland has almost tripled its GDP per capita (in PPP) in two and a half decades (Piatkowski, 2018).

In the rest of the chapter, we interpret the recent Turkish macroeconomic developments through the lenses of this framework. We start by documenting how high-quality economic growth and shared prosperity have evolved over the last three decades and then explain their relationship with Turkey's economic and political institutions.

2.3. The Quality of Recent Turkish Growth

Figure 2.4 plots the evolution of GDP growth in Turkey since the 1960s. In addition to the high volatility of macroeconomic performance visible from this series, the bold line, which depicts the five-year moving average, reveals a number of important patterns. First, Turkish growth slowed down appreciably after the 1960s to an average annual pace of less than 2% in the 1970s. After a short-lived boost in the early 1980s, partly as a result of economic reforms implemented by then Prime Minister Turgut Özal, growth once again lost momentum and returned to under 2% throughout the 1990s.[17]

---

[17] For a detailed account of Turkish economic growth since 1820, see Pamuk (2018).

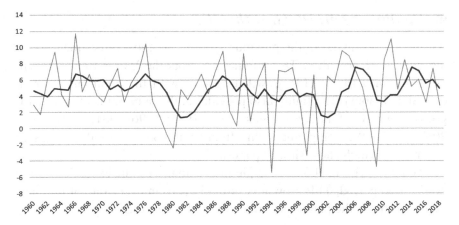

Figure 2.4. Long view: GDP growth (%) (bold line corresponds to five-year moving averages)

Note: This figure shows the annual GDP growth in the Turkish economy and its five-year moving average. GDP growth numbers from 1998 are based on new National Income Accounts data released in December 2016, while for prior years we use growth rates from the old data series.

Source: TurkStat and our calculations

This was followed by a notable increase in the growth rate in the early 2000s reaching an average of around 7.6% per annum during 2002–2006. This rapid growth window was then punctured by the effects of the global recession in 2009. Turkey subsequently returned to relatively rapid growth, even if this has fallen short of the levels of the early 2000s.

The rest of this section probes the quality and nature of this growth experience, documenting that with the exception of the 2002–2006 interlude, growth has been low-quality — with little-to-no productivity growth — and far from shared.[18]

---

[18] Several data revisions, most notably the 2016 revision of the National Income Accounts data and the 2014 revision to labor/employment data, create breaks in Turkish economic time series. We overcome these challenges by splicing historical series using growth rate estimates (based on old data) and percentages of GDP by sector. The old and revised series are similar when we go back in time, with the most dramatic differences concentrated in the post-2009 period.

a. *Quality of Turkish Growth: TFP*

As already discussed in the previous section, the most direct measure of the quality of growth is TFP. Figure 2.5 plots the World Bank's recent estimates of Turkish TFP growth (together with the contribution from capital and labor). The figure also provides at the bottom the average TFP growth rate over four sub-periods (1989–1995; 1996–2001; 2002–2006; 2007–2017). We complement this figure with our own calculations in Figure 2.6, which show similar patterns.[19]

What is striking about these pictures is that with the exception of the 2002–2006 period, TFP growth is virtually zero in every one of our sub-periods. This is the pattern summed up by the World Bank as,

"economic growth in Turkey since the 1980s has been driven largely by factor accumulation, with only periodic boost in productivity."

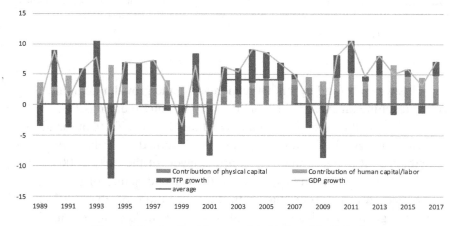

Figure 2.5.   Productivity growth in Turkey: World Bank

Note: This figure is reproduced from data provided by the World Bank; period averages are calculated as simple arithmetic averages.

Source: World Bank (2019).

---

[19] See World Bank (2019). Chapter 3 in this volume by Atiyas and Bakış yields similar results.

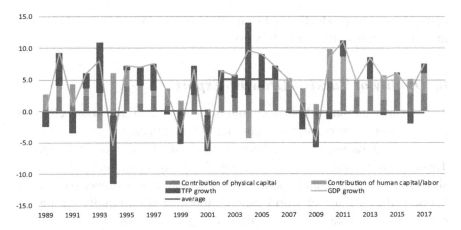

Figure 2.6. Productivity growth in Turkey: Our calculations

Note: Calculations are based on a standard growth accounting framework as in Hall and Jones (1999), with weights of 1/3 and 2/3 assigned for capital and labor shares, respectively. Capital stock series has been derived from gross fixed capital formation, applying the standard perpetual inventory method and has been adjusted for capacity utilization, while human capital stock stands for employment adjusted for education using Mincerian returns.

Source: Our calculations.

In contrast, the average TFP growth during the 2002–2006 window is 4.1% in the World Bank data and 5.2% in our own estimates. This unusually rapid TFP growth explains a large part of the growth surge during this window, approximately 54% and 68%, respectively. Put slightly differently, without TFP growth, Turkish GDP during this short five-year period would have grown only by a relatively unimpressive 2–3%.

The post-2009 era is particularly noteworthy in this respect. On the one hand, GDP growth returns to a relatively high level, averaging around 6.5% per annum. But TFP growth almost completely disappears. In the World Bank data, there is essentially zero TFP growth, while our estimates put TFP growth at slightly negative.[20] In sum, TFP estimates paint a picture of persistently low-quality growth in Turkey, punctured with an

---

[20]The post-2007 period is affected by the sharp drop and then recovery associated with the global financial crisis. If we leave these years out and focus from 2011 to 2018, average

episodic rise in productivity during 2002–2006. We will see that other indicators point in the same direction.

b. *Quality of Turkish Growth: Exports*

TFP growth measures both technological upgrading and more efficient allocation of resources in the economy. A complementary gauge for technological upgrading is the technology content of the country's exports. Turkey's merchandise exports increased rapidly in the early 2000s, as shown in Figure 2.7, and continued to rise, albeit at a slower pace, after 2008. Turkey's share of world exports, too, increased rapidly during the early 2000s, and stabilized thereafter, as Figure 2.8 indicates.

The changes in the technology content of exports reveal a more nuanced pattern, however. In Figure 2.9 we present the evolution of the composition of Turkish exports in the past three decades. We report the fraction of exports in high-tech, medium-high-tech, medium-low-tech and

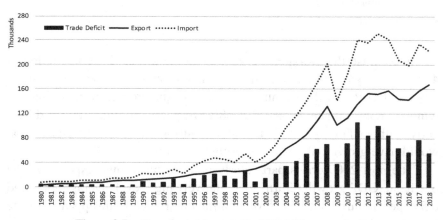

Figure 2.7.   Exports and imports (in USD billion, nominal)

Note: Figures are in current US dollars; export values are reported in f.o.b., import values in c.i.f.

Source: TurkStat.

TFP growth (our estimates) is slightly better, 0.4% per annum, which is still much lower than the average between 2002 and 2006, 5.2% per annum.

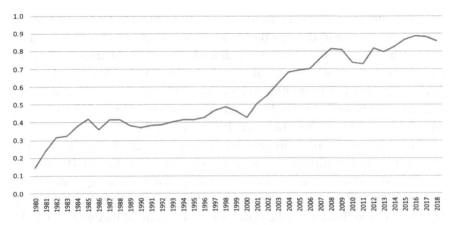

Figure 2.8. Turkish exports/World exports (%)

Note: The figure shows Turkish merchandise exports as a share of world total exports. Exports are measured f.o.b., in current US dollars.

Source: World Bank.

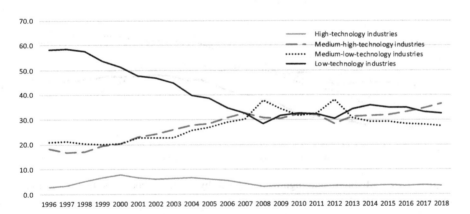

Figure 2.9. Turkey's exports by technology intensity (as % of total manufacturing exports)

Note: The figure shows Turkey's manufacturing exports according to technology intensity, based on the Organisation for Economic Co-operation and Development's (OECD) ISIC Rev. 3 classification, which provides technology content in four categories: high-tech, medium-high-tech, medium-low-tech, and low-tech.

Source: TurkStat.

low-tech categories.[21] As the figure shows, from the late 1990s until about 2007 there is a rapid drop in the share of low-tech industries and a substantial increase in the share of medium-high-tech industries in Turkish exports. For example, Turkey now exports less in textiles (its share of Turkish exports fell from 40% to less than 20% between 1999 and 2007) and more in household durables and vehicles (the share of these goods rose from around 10–30% between 1999 and 2007).

Notably, both of these improvements stop after 2008. Turkish exports show no further quality or technology upgrading over the last 10 years.

This slowdown of technology upgrading is not a consequence of the fact that Turkey has already reached a high level. Figure 2.10 shows, based on World Bank data, the evolution of the share of medium and high-tech exports in total manufactured exports for a number of countries since

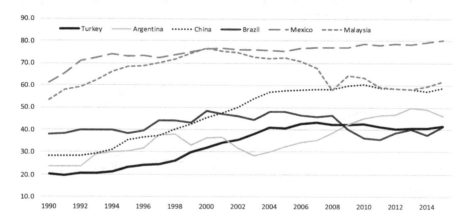

Figure 2.10. Medium and high-tech exports by selected countries (as % of total manufacturing exports)

Note: This figure shows the evolution of medium and high-tech exports as a percentage of total manufacturing exports.

Source: World Bank.

---

[21] This classification follows the OECD. High-tech includes aircraft and spacecraft, pharmaceuticals, computing machinery; medium-high-tech includes, among others, motor vehicles, trailers and semi-trailers, railroad equipment, electrical machinery and apparatus; medium-low-tech includes building and repairing of ships and boats, rubber and plastic products, basic metals; and low-tech includes textiles, tobacco, food and beverages.

1990. Turkish exports appear to be less technology intensive than those of Mexico, Malaysia, China, and comparable to those of Brazil and Argentina.[22]

In one of its recent biannual surveys on the Turkish economy (OECD, 2016), the OECD summarizes the situation as follows:

"While Turkey incorporates an increasing share of foreign value added in its own exports (backward participation), its capacity to provide intermediate inputs other countries' exports (forward participation) is still limited."

It goes on to state that there is "substantial room for progress in corporate governance and managerial skills, as well as the use of ICT tools in production and management processes."

In sum, it is remarkable how little technological upgrading and productivity improvement there has been in the Turkish economy during the last decade, despite its relatively rapid growth.

c. *The Quality of Turkish Growth: Education*

Skill shortages are one of the major reasons for lack of productivity growth and technology upgrading around the world.[23] We will see that Turkey made important progress in the 2000s, especially as educational spending increased (World Bank, 2014), but Turkey lags behind other OECD countries and many emerging economies in terms of educational

---

[22] Figure 2.10 uses World Bank data, which are available at a different level of aggregation than the OECD data used in Figure 2.9. In particular, the World Bank computes the technology content of exports from UN Comtrade data, which combine high- and medium-tech exports into a single category (following the SITC Rev. 3 classification). This has no bearing on the evolution of technology content of Turkish exports since, as shown in Figure 2.9, Turkey's high-tech and medium-high-tech shares closely follow each other, and their behavior is essentially identical to that of medium and high-tech exports in Figure 2.10.

[23] See Cappelli (2015) for a general discussion and Acemoğlu and Restrepo (2019) for the role of skill shortages in productivity and technology adoption in the context of automation.

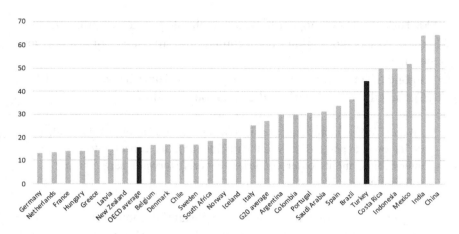

Figure 2.11.   Educational attainment of 25–34-year-olds: Below upper secondary, 2017
Source: OECD, Education at a Glance.

attainment, and the quality of education has remained low and regressed further over the last several years.

This can be seen in Figure 2.11, which plots the fraction of 25–34-year-olds with less than upper secondary education in 2017. At 44%, Turkey fares much worse than the OECD average (15%) and also underperforms other emerging economies including Argentina, Colombia, Brazil, and Saudi Arabia.[24]

The quality of education may be even more important than its quantity (e.g., Hanushek and Woessman, 2016), and here the situation for Turkey looks even grimmer. Figure 2.12 presents the evolution of the gap between the PISA scores in reading, math, science, and average skills of Turkish high school students and the OECD average for five periods, 2003, 2006, 2009, 2012, and 2015.[25] Turkey starts significantly behind the OECD

---

[24] Though educational attainment has increased in Turkey over the last two decades, this has been more or less at the same pace as the rest of the OECD, leaving Turkey's relative standing roughly unchanged.

[25] PISA is the OECD's Program for International Student Assessment. Every three years it tests 15-year-old students from all over the world in reading, mathematics, and science. The tests are designed to gauge how well the students master key subjects in order to be

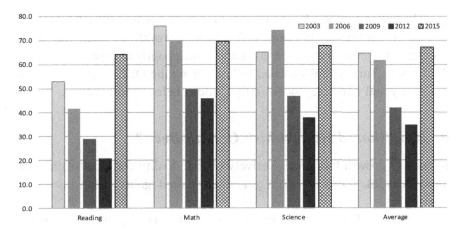

Figure 2.12. The education gap between international average (OECD) and Turkey

Note: Shows the difference between the OECD international average and Turkey's results in three key subjects (reading, mathematics, science) and their averages.

Source: OECD, Program for International Student Assessment (PISA).

average in all areas in 2003. As remarked earlier, we then see some notable improvements as this gap, especially in math and reading, narrows during the next three periods. This favorable trend reverses suddenly in 2015, however, and all of the gaps shoot back up to the same or even higher levels than in 2003.[26]

---

prepared for real-life situations in the adult world. PISA cycles are referred to by the year in which the students were tested.

[26] For an analysis of the narrowing of this gap between 2003 and 2012, see Rivera-Batiz and Durmaz (2014) and Gürsel and Durmaz (2014). To our knowledge, there is no formal analysis of the sudden widening of this gap in 2015, although government's 2012 education "reforms" are likely to have played a role. Comprehensive reforms introduced in March 2012 raised compulsory schooling from 8–12 years (primary, junior-high, and senior-high), but simultaneously changed the curriculum away from math and science, and allowed vocational tracks after four years of compulsory primary education. These vocational tracks notably included religious (*imam hatip*) schools. According to data from the Ministry of Education, the number of religious schools increased from 1,624 in 2011–2012 to 3,394 in 2018, now making up 29% of all schools.

The patterns shown by the OECD Survey of Adult Skills (PIAAC) are similar. According to this survey, the Turkish workforce lacks the skills necessary to perform complex tasks and scores poorly at problem solving. As a result, Turkey ranks second to last among the OECD countries both in literacy and numeracy skills (only Chile is below Turkey).[27]

d. *How Shared Has Turkish Growth Been?*

If Turkish growth has been relatively of low quality for most of the last three decades, has it at least generated shared gains? The answer is broadly no.

Figure 2.13 shows the Gini coefficient for Turkey from the World Bank. Two patterns are noteworthy. First, the level of inequality in Turkey

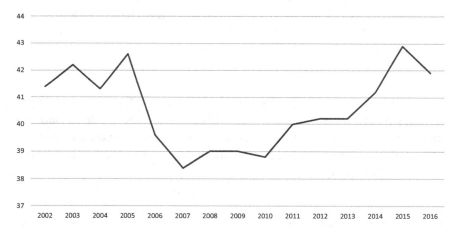

Figure 2.13. Gini coefficient

Note: The figure reports the Gini coefficient for Turkey, which is discussed in detail in Section 2.2. The World Bank data we prefer to use here (as explained in footnote 28) are available through 2016 only, but this does not change our narrative. It is nevertheless useful to add that the Gini continues to rise slightly through 2017–2018 according to TurkStat data.

Source: World Bank.

---

[27] PIAAC measures adults' proficiency in three key information-processing skills: literacy, numeracy, and problem-solving in technology-rich environments. See Kavuncu and Polat (2019) for a detailed assessment of Turkey's numbers.

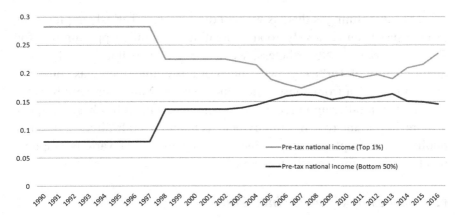

Figure 2.14. Income inequity (share of total, %)

Note: This figure reports the income shares of the top 1% and bottom 50% of income distribution.

Source: World Inequity Database (WID).

is relatively high, comparable to those in China, Argentina, and Mexico. (For comparison, the Gini coefficient is around 0.30 in Germany and Sweden.)

Second, and equally notable, is the evolution of the Gini over the last two decades or so. It declines from almost 0.43 in the beginning to the 2000s to just over 0.38 by 2006. However, from 2007 onward the Gini starts increasing, and now stands at around 0.42 again.

Comparison by income percentiles, based on the World Inequality Database, reveals broadly similar trends. The share of national income accruing to the bottom 50% first rises but then falls, while the share going to the top 1% first declines but then rises significantly approaching 25% (see Figure 2.14).[28]

---

[28] In contrast to the behavior of the Gini coefficient from World Bank data and the top income share from the World Inequality Database, Gini numbers from TurkStat do not show as clear an increase in inequality until 2014. The World Bank and TurkStat data draw on the same household surveys, but use different methodologies. Among other differences, TurkStat implements an adjustment for the age composition of households.

The silver lining is that, as we will discuss next, Turkish employment growth has been relatively robust, creating economic opportunities for Turkish workers.[29] Nevertheless, we will see that in line with the low-quality nature of Turkish growth, much of this employment has come not from industry but from construction and services. Moreover, with private-sector growth faltering in recent years, the government has begun to play a more important role in employment generation both directly through public-sector employment and indirectly by means of various employment subsidies for the private sector.[30]

e. *Sources of Growth since 2007*

The patterns we have documented so far raise an obvious question: if there is no TFP growth, little technological upgrading and only limited improvements in the skills of the workforce, how and why has the Turkish economy grown over the last decade or so? The answer to this question is important both for understanding the causes of low-quality growth in Turkey, and for assessing the nature of the difficulties the Turkish macroeconomy is currently experiencing.

The answer is that Turkish growth in this period has largely been fueled by credit and has been in part driven by a massive surge in the construction sector. Figure 2.15 shows the evolution of the credit to GDP ratio in the Turkish economy since the late 1980s. After decades of relatively stable (and low) credit availability, credit growth outstripped GDP growth starting in the mid-2000s. As a result, the credit to GDP ratio, which stood at less than 30% in 2006, rose to above 65% by late 2017.[31]

---

[29] See Chapter 6 in this volume by Uysal, Paker, and Pelek.

[30] According to TurkStat figures, the public sector has hired about 1 million more workers since early 2018, while (non-agricultural) private-sector employment has declined by about 1.5 million. While the change in the status of some 700,000 outsourced workers (from private to public sector) in early 2018 has played a major role in this. The shift does not fully account for the scale of the change in public- versus private-sector employment levels in this period.

[31] About one-fourth of this credit is to the household sector, while the rest is to (non-financial) corporations. Much of the latter category is denominated in foreign currency, and currency fluctuations account for the volatility in the last few years.

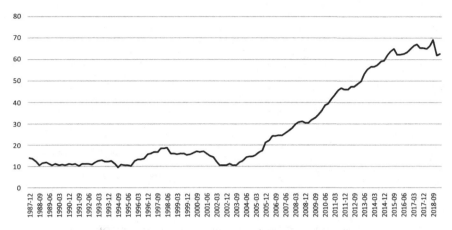

Figure 2.15.   Credit to private sector (as % of GDP)

Note: Total credit to private sector (households and non-financial corporations).

Source: The Central Bank of the Republic of Turkey.

This credit expansion and other government policies (documented in the following paragraphs) propelled a rapid construction boom.[32]

Correspondingly, Figure 2.16 shows the composition of investment (gross fixed capital formation as a percent of GDP).[33] After a rebound in the aftermath of Turkey's 2001 crisis, machinery and equipment investment declined as a percent of GDP between 2006 and 2009, and essentially stagnated thereafter. In sharp contrast, construction investment has increased from less than 10% of GDP in the early 2000s to about 18% at present.[34]

---

[32] See Figure 12 in Domaç and Işıklar (2019), which shows that the allocation of credit has been visibly tilted toward non-tradable sectors, the construction sector, in particular.

[33] The data from the Central Bank used in Figure 2.16 are constructed with a different methodology and from different sources than the BIS series used in Figure 2.3. Nevertheless, the two series are very similar.

[34] The fact that machinery and equipment investment was high between 2002 and 2006 but only construction investment surged after this date suggests that investment has not been constrained by lack of savings or credit, but has been shaped by economic and political incentives, which encouraged construction projects and made other (especially

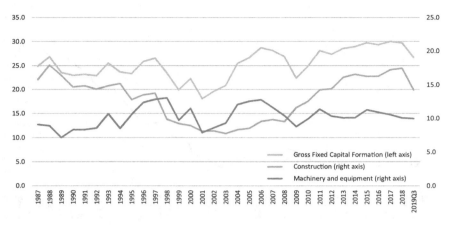

Figure 2.16.   Gross fixed capital formation (% of GDP)

Note: The figure uses December 2016 National Income Accounts data from 1998 through 2018 for total investment, and from 2009 through 2018 for machinery and equipment and construction investment sub-components, which are available since 2009 only. Prior years have been derived using the old GDP series. See Note to Figure 2.4.

Source: TurkStat.

Much of this investment was in residential and commercial property, for which there now appears to be a huge oversupply, perhaps as large as 2 million dwellings.[35] The government has played a defining role in the construction boom, both through public–private partnership projects, which supported infrastructure investments, and through TOKİ, the State Housing Agency, which has built a large number of low-income and more recently, luxury dwellings. Taking into account investments, fees, and other transfers, the contract value of the public–private partnership projects is estimated to have reached some $140 billion.[36]

---

manufacturing) investments less attractive since around the time of the global financial crisis.

[35] For an analysis of the construction sector dynamics during this period, see IMF (2016), Demiralp *et al.* (2015), as well as Chapters 3 and 5 in this volume by Atiyas and Bakış, and Günçavdı and Bayar, respectively.

[36] See Presidency of Strategy and Budget, koi.sbb.gov.tr. The liabilities created by both the public–private partnership projects and TOKİ's investments are off balance sheet and are not included in the government's spending and deficit numbers.

Figure 2.17. Loan growth: Private and public banks (FX adjusted, 13-week moving average, annualized)

Note: The coverage differs slightly before and after 2014 so that the credit series include only the deposit banks prior to 2014, but both the deposit and participation banks thereafter.

Source: BRSA and our calculations.

Government interventions have also been a major contributor to credit growth during recent years. With private banks increasingly unwilling or unable to lend in recent years (concerned about their own balance sheets as well as the balance sheets of their customers), the government has asked state banks to take over lending as the patterns documented in Figure 2.17 make it clear.[37]

Sectoral employment trends, presented in Figure 2.18, paint a similar picture. Between 2002 and 2006, there is a rapid decline in agricultural employment (by about 1.3–1.4 million), but this is counterbalanced by robust increases in both industrial (0.4 million) and service (0.9 million) jobs. Employment has continued to grow since 2010, but this growth has been growing disproportionately in services and construction: service and construction employment grew by about 55% and 60%, respectively,

---

[37] In particular, over the last five years the share of loans by state banks rose from 30% to almost 45% while the share of private banks declined from 70% to 55%.

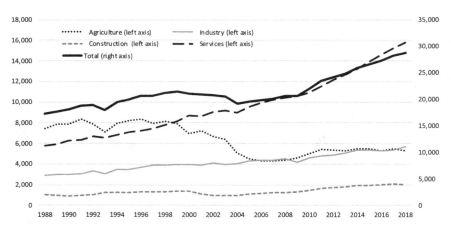

Figure 2.18.   Employment ('000 persons)

Note: Absolute number of employed by sector; total is shown on the right axis.

Source: TurkStat, Uysal and Furkan (2019) and our calculations.

between 2007 and 2018, while employment in industry and agriculture grew about 20%.[38]

One of the major aspects of low-quality growth we have already emphasized is its fragile nature. This fragility is visible in the recent Turkish experience. As Figure 2.7 illustrates, credit-fueled growth has led to much more rapid expansion of imports than exports, causing a significant current account deficit (averaging around 5% of GDP in the last 10 years),[39] and may be one of the factors contributing to high inflation (around 10% during 2010–2019 and around 12% as of early 2020).

---

[38] Revised TurkStat data are available from 2014. These data are extended back to 2005 by TurkStat, and further to 1988 by us using growth rates of old series. There is a very sharp jump in employment in 2014 in the revised TurkStat data. Following the recommendation in Uysal and Kavuncu (2019), this jump is smoothed using the geometric average with 2013. Differences in sectoral classifications between the old and new time series introduce additional measurement error in the sectoral time series. For a comprehensive assessment of labor market trends, see Chapter 6 in this volume by Uysal, Paker and Pelek.

[39] In 2019, current account deficit has disappeared, but this is largely owing to the sharp contraction in economic activity.

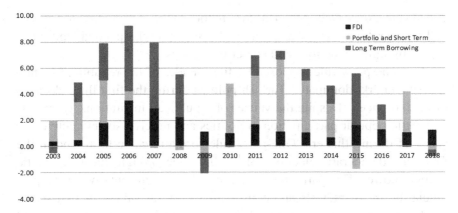

Figure 2.19.   Capital flows (as % of GDP)

Note: The figure shows (net) capital inflows in three broad categories: FDI; long-term borrowing by residents, mainly loans contacted by the private sector; and the sum of portfolio flows and short-term borrowing.

Source: CBRT, Balance of Payments Statistics.

Another indication of this fragility has been the composition of capital inflows into the Turkish economy. Figure 2.19 shows that the share of foreign direct investment (FDI) and long-term capital flows have been replaced by shorter-term, more fickle flows. FDI flows (excluding real estate), which were essentially zero in early 2000s, rose to 3% of GDP in 2006 and then stayed around that level for a few years, but then declined to 0.5% of GDP recently.

2.4. The Institutional Foundations of Low-Quality Growth

The prime cause of low-quality and unshared growth in Turkey is to be found in the nature and evolution of Turkish institutions. Though the Republic of Turkey, founded in 1923, repudiated much of the institutional heritage of the Ottoman Empire and undertook sweeping reforms, Turkish institutions never became truly inclusive. The military and bureaucratic elites were excessively powerful throughout, politics remained top-down, and democratic activity was periodically suppressed, upended, and interrupted by military actions and sometimes coups.

The one-party rule, imposed by the founder of the republic, Mustafa Kemal Atatürk, dominated Turkish politics during the first three decades of its existence.[40] Despite the veneer of republican institutions, there was very little popular participation in politics and no civil society activity to speak of during this era. One-party rule formally came to an end in the first semi-democratic elections of 1950, which brought the Democratic Party to power. This party, fashioning itself as a representative of the provincial business interests and conservative cultural values, at first spearheaded an economic and political opening of the country, but by the end of the decade had turned increasingly authoritarian and repressive. In 1960, the military moved against the Democratic Party and proceeded to hang its leader, Adnan Menderes. The military then engineered two more coups, in 1971 and 1980, and also brought down a coalition government in 1997 (in which the Islamist party was the majority partner) with the threat of a coup, subsequent to which the Constitutional Court closed the party. Even during periods of electoral democracy, the military frequently intervened in matters of state and foreign policy.

Lack of democratic and popular participation created an environment without proper political checks, and consequently, government–business relations remained opaque and were mired in irregularities and systematic favoritism. For most of this period, connections to the government created myriad advantages for certain businesses, breeding corruption and limiting the competitiveness of the Turkish economy.

This political environment did not encourage broad-based, high-quality public good provision and contributed to underinvestment in education and skills. It was also not conducive to FDI, which was for the most part discouraged by the authorities. This took away one of the most direct channels via which the technology of Turkish industry could be upgraded.

---

[40] See Zurcher (2004) and Pamuk (2018) for a summary of Turkey's 20th century political and economic histories, respectively. For a history of Turkey's economic institutions since 1980, see Chapter 1 in this volume by Pamuk.

It also made the economy more prone to current account imbalances. Much of the growth of the economy, as a consequence, has been highly volatile, with periods of growth followed by sharp recessions as our Figure 2.4 shows.

These institutional weaknesses have been a mainstay of the Turkish economy more recently too. In its regular biannual survey of the Turkish economy, the OECD concluded (2016, p. 89):

> "Turkey's participation in [global value chains] remains below potential owing to institutional features that hamper efficient allocation of capital and labor, obstacles inherent in bilateral trade agreements and entry regulations, underdeveloped human capital and insufficient investment in innovation, R&D and knowledge-based capital."

Bolstering the plausibility of our interpretation — on a causal link from institutions to low-quality growth — is the fact that Turkey's high growth episode between 2002 and 2006 overlapped with major institutional and political changes. During this brief period of five years, there was a general opening in economic institutions, raising competitiveness, reducing macroeconomic and microeconomic policy uncertainty, stemming bureaucratic and government corruption, and bringing a modicum of rule-based decision-making instead of the extreme discretion that had characterized earlier periods. These changes in economic institutions started in 2001, in the aftermath of Turkey's severe financial crisis, but they were then continued by the first AK Parti (Justice and Development Party) government that came to power in 2002.

The changes in economic institutions were tightly linked to political developments. During this period, military tutelage waned, Turkish democracy deepened, and a range of ambitious political and social reforms were initiated under the auspices of the EU-accession process.

However, this brief period of institutional reform did not last and was followed by major reversals in both economic and political institutions, as we explain in this section. Consistent with our interpretation, as institutions started deteriorating after 2006, low-quality growth set in again, and prosperity became less shared.

a. *The Evolution of Turkish Economic Institutions*

Let us start with economic institutions. The evidence suggests that the 2000s witnessed a major change from the previous decades in terms of "delegation of the decision-making power to relatively independent agencies, and the establishment of rules that constrain the discretion of the executive" (Atiyas, 2012).

A key pillar of macroeconomic policy reform was the granting of greater independence to the Central Bank starting in 2001. A new law defined the sole objective of the Central Bank as achieving and maintaining price stability in the context of first implicit and then formal inflation targeting, and prohibited direct lending to the government.

Monetary policy reforms were complemented by equally major fiscal reforms. Most notably, two new laws enacted transparent controls on ministerial spending, borrowing and off-budget expenditures. The first, the Public Finance and Debt Management (PFDM) Law of 2002, brought all central government borrowing under strict and transparent rules and imposed uniform reporting requirements on all debts. The second, the Public Financial Management and Control Law (PFMCL) of 2003, rationalized fiscal management and established "principles and merits, multi-year budgeting, budget scope, budget execution, performance management and strategic planning, internal control, accounting, monitoring and reporting." The sum total of these two laws was to significantly increase fiscal accountability of the government, and they duly introduced much greater discipline to public finances.

Equally sweeping was a new procurement law, introduced under pressure from the IMF and the World Bank in 2002. This law targeted the high levels of corruption and irregularities in public procurement, which had become commonplace under the auspices of the highly politicized and ineffective State Procurement Law of the early 1980s. The new laws increased transparency and opened the tender process to competitive bidding. There were similar changes in the regulatory front and a number of new independent autonomous agencies were founded or were further empowered.[41]

---

[41] Prominent examples include the Public Procurement Authority, the Banking Regulatory and Supervision Agency, the Energy Market Regulatory Authority, the Telecommunications

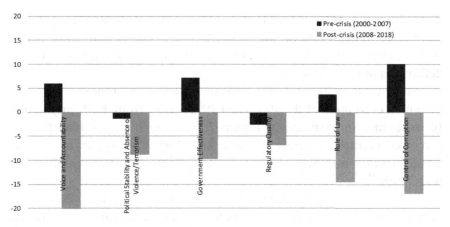

Figure 2.20. Institutional reforms

Note: This figure reports the difference in ranking in six governance indicators during the pre-crisis (2000–2007) and post-crisis (2008–2018) periods.

Source: World Bank.

In sum, there were striking steps toward best-practice laws and regulations during this short period of time, and many of these reforms started having immediate effect. Even if from the beginning some of them were not as ambitious as they first appeared and there were systematic inconsistencies, the reforms created a sea change in public finances and signaled the coming of a more accommodating environment for domestic and foreign businesses.

In part as a result of these reforms, the overall institutional environment in the Turkish economy improved significantly in the early 2000s. Figure 2.20 provides the World Bank's assessment of changes in various dimensions of Turkish economic institutions for two sub-periods,

---

Authority, the Competition Authority, and the Capital Markets Board. These agencies professionalized the bureaucracy and reduced discretionary government influence over regulation and the policy uncertainty that this entailed. The Banking Regulatory and Supervision Agency was particularly instrumental in carrying out Turkey's banking sector reform and restructuring program (Bredenkamp *et al.*, 2009).

2000–2007 and 2008–2017.[42] Indices of voice and accountability, government effectiveness, rule of law and control of corruption all show major improvements during the early 2000s (see the notes to Figure 2.20 for the definitions of these indices).

Particularly important for Turkish business environment was the mounting corruption of the 1980s and 1990s. Data from the Transparency International, summarized in Figure 2.21, show a steady reduction in perceived corruption during this era, with Turkey's position in international rankings improving from around high-70s to just above 50 in the mid-2000s.[43]

But this encouraging picture soon started to crumble from 2006/2007 onward. First came the complete stalling of the structural reform efforts. This was followed by the dismantling of some of the earlier reforms and

---

[42] These indicators come from the Worldwide Governance Indicators project of the World Bank, which constructs aggregate indicators for six broad dimensions of governance, based on the views of a large number of enterprise, citizen and expert survey respondents in industrial and developing countries. The six dimensions are: (1) Voice & Accountability (perceptions of the extent to which a country's citizens are able to participate in selecting their government, as well as freedom of expression, freedom of association, and a free media), (2) Political Stability and Lack of Violence (perceptions of the likelihood of political instability and/or politically-motivated violence, including terrorism), (3) Government Effectiveness (perceptions of the quality of public services, the quality of the civil service and the degree of its independence from political pressures, the quality of policy formulation and implementation, and the credibility of the government's commitment to such policies), (4) Regulatory Quality (perceptions of the ability of the government to formulate and implement sound policies and regulations that permit and promote private-sector development), (5) Rule of Law (perceptions of the extent to which agents have confidence in and abide by the rules of society, and in particular the quality of contract enforcement, property rights, the police, and the courts, as well as the likelihood of crime and violence); and (6) Control of Corruption (perceptions of the extent to which public power is exercised for private gain, including both petty and grand forms of corruption, as well as "capture" of the state by elites and private interests).

[43] The Corruption Perception Index ranks countries and territories based on how corrupt their public sector is perceived to be. A country or territory's score indicates the perceived level of public-sector corruption on a scale of 0–100, where 0 means that a country is perceived as highly corrupt and 100 means it is perceived as very clean. A country's rank indicates its position relative to the other countries and territories included in the data set.

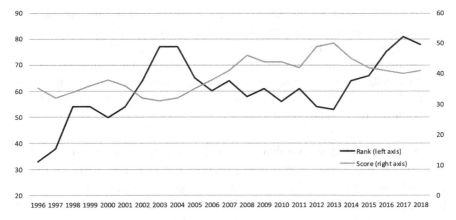

Figure 2.21. Corruption Perceptions Index

Note: This figure reports the evolution of the Corruption Perception Index (CPI) and Turkey's rank among countries in Transparency International's data set. CPI scores are between 100 (highly clean) and 0 (highly corrupt), while a higher figure corresponds to a lower rank.

Source: Transparency International.

deterioration in the overall institutional environment. The institutional slide accelerated during AK Parti's third term that began in June 2011.

The gutting of the procurement law, which was introduced with great expectations and initially had some impact, is indicative of the extent and nature of the reversal in the quality of economic institutions during this period. It also signals that AK Parti was never at ease with the new law, seeing it from the very beginning as a constraint on its infrastructure investment plans and the funneling of state resources toward its own constituencies. As the party gained confidence and control, the procurement law was gradually weakened and sidelined. There was first a significant expansion of "exceptions", which undercut the transparency and competitiveness of the procurement process. These were followed by major changes in the tender rules (from open tenders to restricted ones), the introduction of various advantages for domestic bidders, and the implementation of rather high minimum monetary limits, below which procurement of goods and services would be exempted from the law. In the words of the EU Progress Report in 2014,

"Turkey's public procurement legislation remains not in line with the acquis in a number of aspects. This includes numerous derogations and exemptions from the scope of the law. Both the classical and utilities sectors are formally subject to the same law and procedures, thus making the legislation for the utilities sector more restrictive than envisaged by the EU Utilities Directive. [...] There have been various allegations of political influence on public tenders."

As documented by Gürakar (2016), the number of contracts that were left outside the transparent public procurement practices increased substantially starting around 2005. By 2011 about 44% of all contracts were taking place outside of the confines of the new law, and the number of contracts awarded by open tender had dwindled.[44]

The procurement law was in fact not as comprehensive as it first appeared, as important budgetary items were not covered by the law. These included spending, public–private partnerships and most importantly, the State Housing Development Administration, TOKİ, which was at the time directly attached to the Prime Minister's Office.[45] As detailed in Atiyas (2012), although TOKİ's exemptions were originally limited to public housing projects, in 2011 these were extended to procurement for other public-sector construction projects (e.g., stadiums, public parks, and buildings). Because TOKİ was further exempted from the budgetary rules imposed by PFMCL, this critical part of the public procurement process was never subject to effective monitoring. The organization has also played an increasingly unaccountable role in taking over and redistributing land in many urban areas. The EU's Progress Report of May 2019 summarizes the situation as follows:

"The vast and increasing number of exemptions inserted into the framework law on public procurement has become a matter of growing

---

[44] Gürakar (2016), pp. 53–54. Also see Gürakar and Meyersson (2016) who look specifically at the construction auction projects and find that "increased discretion in public procurement not only increased costs — in terms of both the winning bid and rebate value — but also increased the likelihood of the winning firm being politically connected to the ruling AKP."
[45] After the switch to the presidential system, TOKİ has been brought under the purview of the Ministry of Environment and Urban Planning.

concern. In particular, tenders at municipal level and for public–private partnerships for large infrastructure investments remained prone to corruption."

Arguably more ominous was the aggressive attacks by the government on autonomous agencies. As explained in Özel (2015), after some *de facto* meddling in the affairs of these agencies (e.g., in the form of influencing the election of board members or the hiring and firing of staff), the government formally ended the independence of these agencies in 2011. Decree No. 649 legislated that ministers would have "the authority to inspect all transactions and activities of the related, attached and affiliated agencies" (which included the autonomous regulatory agencies), thus giving the ministers and their staff the ability to restrict the independence of these agencies. At around the same time, the idea of independent regulatory institutions has been dealt another blow, with the then-deputy prime minister Ali Babacan stating that "it was time for some independent agencies to re-delegate their authority" (Özel, 2015). This "re-delegation" has subsequently intensified, and with systematic political meddling, these agencies have duly lost all independence.

The evolution of the Central Bank independence illustrates these institutional dynamics. Starting in the second half of the 2000s the Central Bank came under heavy pressure from the then Prime Minister Erdoğan to reduce interest rates. Even though the Bank's leadership was fairly compliant to the prime minister's demands, the pressure on the institution mounted. In July 2019, its governor, already hand-picked by the government, was abruptly sacked for not being sufficiently accommodating. Thereafter, the Central Bank started reducing the interest rates, used its cash reserves to finance the government budget deficit, and initiated backdoor sales of foreign exchange reserves to state banks to bolster the value of the lira. The whole episode is damaging not just because of its implications for macroeconomic policy, but because it demonstrates the unwillingness of the administration to be restrained even by the most pliable organizations.[46]

---

[46] In fact, later during a speech in parliament in early November 2019, President Erdoğan would openly declare that they "fired the previous central bank governor because he wouldn't listen and we have decided to move on with our new friend", practically ending whatever was left of central bank independence till then.

This sharp reversal in economic reforms had immediate effects on economic institutions. Figure 2.20 based on World Bank governance indicators reveals major deterioration in all dimensions of economic institutions — including stability and regulatory quality where Turkey was already not doing very well, and voice and accountability, government effectiveness, rule of law, and control of corruption where Turkey had shown improvements in the early 2000s. Consistent with these patterns, Figure 2.21 reveals an abrupt turnaround in corruption perceptions, most likely reflecting mounting non-transparency and discretion in public procurements and intensifying government involvement in business decisions.

b. *The Evolution of Turkish Political Institutions*

We have argued that the turnaround in Turkey's economic performance is a reflection of the turnaround in economic policies and institutions, including the stalling or reversal in the process of much-needed structural reforms. But this only provides a proximate answer to the deeper question of why economic policies and institutions improved in the first phase and then went into a reversal. We argue that both the initial improvements in economic institutions and their subsequence slide have political roots.

During its first five years of rule the AK Parti became, largely unwittingly and perhaps even unwillingly, an instrument of political reform. This period witnessed the broadening of the political base as the military tutelage in Turkish politics, probably the most important factor holding back Turkish democracy and civil society, ended. A confluence of factors came together to make the early 2000s a propitious time for such a fundamental transformation in Turkish politics. But this period, and the resulting political opening, was short-lived.

The AK Parti came to power after a basic structure of economic reforms had been put in place following the 2001 financial crisis. The party at first lacked a deep bench of qualified experts to take over the relevant bureaucracies, limiting its reach and ambitions.

Equally important was that the AK Parti was elected with a limited mandate, with just 34% of the vote, and as a partial outsider to the corridors of power. It was viewed more as a representative of an increasingly disenfranchised and dissatisfied segment of Turkish society. This segment included provincial, conservative businessmen, the urban poor (who were often recent migrants), and the rural population (excluding Kurds and Alevis). These less Westernized, more religious, and more conservative social groups were never welcomed by the Republic's rulers, the so-called "Kemalist elites", named after their ideological commitment to the principles of Mustafa Kemal Atatürk, and often defined to include the military, the bureaucracy and big, urban-based conglomerates, and argued to be represented by the state's party, the Republican People's Party. The reality was more nuanced, however. Conservative ideology associated with the base of the AK Parti was not systematically excluded from power for most of the republican period and became particularly important both in school curricula and as the active rhetoric of many governments since the 1980 military coup, especially as a strategy to combat the presumed threat from the left.

This nuance did not stop many conservative Turks from feeling excluded and sidelined politically and culturally. Many started seeing a powerful culture war in Turkey, in which they felt they were disadvantaged. It is this culture war that was invoked and bombastically summarized by Prime Minister Recep Tayyip Erdoğan's famous statement:

"In this country there is a segregation of Black Turks and White Turks. Your brother Tayyip belongs to the Black Turks."[47]

The AK Parti's rise to power thus came to be seen as the political empowerment of this previously-excluded group. During their early rule, they conceived their survival to depend on democracy (which they interpreted as respecting the electoral results rather than succumbing to a military intervention against them).

Additionally, the AK Parti came on the scene when EU–Turkey relations were revitalized. The party presented itself as a staunch supporter of EU accession. The process leading up to the accession negotiations,

---

[47] While the exact timing of this statement is a matter of debate, it first rose to prominence when quoted in a *New York Times* interview with the newly-elected Erdoğan by Deborah Sontag in May 2003.

launched on October 2005, had started reasonably earnestly and had gained significant momentum by 2006, and had the strong backing of the Turkish public.[48]

The initial optimism about the EU accession process provided a powerful anchor to institutional reforms in Turkey. Many agreed with the sentiment of a widely discussed report from 2004:

> "Our starting assumption is that it is likely that accession negotiations would start during 2005, but that they would last for quite some time, with membership materialising only around 2012–15. We therefore take a long-term perspective and explore particular areas in which the EU and Turkey could cooperate during the long interim negotiating period." (The European Transformation of Turkey, Derviş *et al.*, 2004)

Consequently, the role that the IMF and the World Bank played on bolstering economic reforms in the aftermath of the 2001 financial crisis came to be complemented by the EU as a guarantor of political reforms.

Indeed, EU accession process was vital for kickstarting sweeping advances in civil and political rights, reducing the military's role in politics, initiating judicial reforms, and providing a template for best-practice legislation in a wide range of areas. The EU pressure also enabled the initiation of various difficult reforms, including improved property rights for non-Muslim religious foundations, the lifting of draconian penalties against speech construed as criticizing Turkish identity, the introduction of the ability of civilian courts to try military personnel, the banning the trials of civilians in military courts, laws protecting children, improved trade union rights (including the right for public service workers to sign collective labor agreements, removing previous bans on political and solidarity strikes), and permission for individuals to apply to the Constitutional Court in cases where their freedoms of fundamental rights are violated (Hale, 2011).

---

[48] According to surveys conducted by the German Marshall Fund, those in favor of EU rose from 40% in the late 1990s to 70% around 2004–2005, but dwindled rapidly thereafter (see in the subsequent paragraphs).

These were followed by the lifting of bans against Kurdish protests and legislation allowing state-run Turkish radio and television to broadcast in Kurdish, the ending of the emergency rule over the last two of the 13 Kurdish-majority provinces, the introduction of broad civilian supervision over defense expenditures, and the removal of National Security Council presence in the oversight of cinema, video, musical works, and radio and television as well as a shift in the government's willingness to generally respect rulings by the European Court of Human Rights. These reforms were by and large a direct result of EU–Turkey engagement (Gürsoy, 2011; Kirişçi, 2011).

The military and nationalist forces were opposed to these reforms, and in all likelihood they would have been more strenuously resisted in the absence of the shepherding role of the EU.

Equally critical was that the prospect of EU accession acted as an anchor and a carrot to the ruling party — there were major economic gains from closer ties with Europe. However, it was not just the economic benefits of EU accession that motivated the AK Parti. Since the AK leaders viewed themselves under constant threat from the military, closer ties to EU appeared as an attractive insurance strategy against a military coup. Since the majority of the population was increasingly keen on becoming part of Europe, the cards were stacked against any moves that would alienate Turkey's European partners.

The overall consequence of this battery of reforms was a clear improvement in the perceived quality of Turkish political institutions. Figures 2.22 and 2.23 present the evolution of a measure of political rights and a measure of freedom of expression from the Freedom House. They both show improvements during the early 2000s, but even sharper deteriorations thereafter, reflecting the about-face in the character of Turkish politics after the mid-2000s. This reversal reflected several trends coming together.

First, the economic institutional framework put in place after the 2001 crisis ceased to constrain AK Parti elites and mayors as they found myriad ways of circumventing the regulations and laws, as we recounted in the case of the procurement law.

Second, the 2002 election brought the beginnings of the end of the two major center-right parties, with their votes going almost in block to

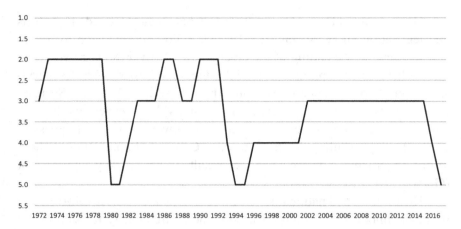

Figure 2.22.   Freedom House: Political Rights

Note: The Political Rights index measures the degree of freedom in the electoral process, political pluralism and participation, and functioning of government. Until 2003, average ratings for political rights that fell between 1.0 and 2.5 were designated Free; between 3.0 and 5.5 Partly Free; and between 5.5 and 7.0 Not Free. From 2003 onward, average ratings that fall between 3.0 and 5.0 are Partly Free, and those between 5.5 and 7.0 are Not Free.

Source: Freedom House.

the AK Parti in the 2007 elections. The AK Parti thus became a much more formidable electoral force and by 2011 commanded almost 50% of the vote.

Third and perhaps even more importantly, the balance between the AK Parti (and its base) and the Kemalist forces changed dramatically. Much of the military establishment was already unhappy about both the AK Parti's rise to power and their increasingly marginalized role in the 2000s, when the AK Parti nominated its number two, Abdullah Gül, for the presidency. The military, and their civilian allies, were alarmed by the fact that Gül's wife wore a headscarf and would represent Turkey in international forums and inhabit Atatürk's presidential palace.

This, combined with their general unease about the political direction of the country, made the military top brass move to threaten another coup with a web memorandum in April 2007. The Constitutional Court started proceedings to close the AK Parti for anti-secular activities. But the

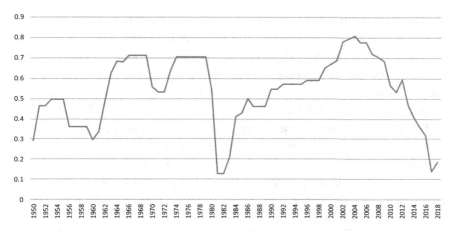

Figure 2.23. Freedom of Expression Index

Note: This figure reports the Freedom of Expression index, which measures to what extent the government respects press and media freedom, the freedom of ordinary people to discuss political matters at home and in the public sphere, as well as the freedom of academic and cultural expression. The scale is from low (0) to high (1).

Source: Freedom House, V-Dem.

situation was different in 2007 than in 1960 or 1997. The AK Parti had already organized deeper social networks within modern Turkish society, and had taken control of large parts of the bureaucracy and the increasingly heavily militarized police, while the status of the traditional military within Turkish society was at an all-time low. As noted previously, the EU accession process also provided a strong bulwark against military meddling in Turkish politics. The military's threat this time came to nothing.

This episode not only sidelined perhaps the most powerful opponent of the AK Parti, the Kemalist generals, but also further radicalized the AK leadership. According to some insider accounts, leading AK figures are reported to have packed their bags during the events of April 2007, fully expecting the military to come to power and put them in jail. Their David and Goliath reading of Turkish history — where the victimized "Black Turks" are stamped out by the conspiracy of Kemalist "White Turks" — was both confirmed and embellished. They may have concluded that they had to destroy the anti-AK military elites. They may have even come to see the dismantling of the existing institutional structures, which they saw as biased toward hostile groups, as a political necessity.

This is also the period during which the collaboration between AK Parti supporters in the bureaucracy and the members of the secretive Gülen movement, led by the reclusive Islamic preacher, self-exiled in Pennsylvania, Fethullah Gülen, may have become stronger. The Gulenists had already taken sometimes open, sometimes clandestine root in many parts of the bureaucracy, police force, and the military. They now started working more closely with the government to purge Kemalists and independents from these positions. Particularly notable were the sham Ergenekon and Sledgehammer trials, targeting former and some current mid-ranking soldiers and generals.[49]

Finally, the EU's anchor for Turkish institutional reforms and leverage over Turkish politicians came to an abrupt end at around 2010 as the accession process almost completely stalled. Several factors played a role in this rupture. The first stumbling block was Cyprus. The collapse of the UN-sponsored talks on a comprehensive settlement and Turkey's unwillingness to extend the Customs Union to Cyprus brought relations to a standstill and caused the suspension of eight ongoing chapters in 2006. During this period, the government and many nationalist elements in the population intensified their resistance to the legal and human rights reforms, which they saw as strengthening Kurds and other minorities. Furthermore, there was a backlash against Turkey in some of the key European countries, most notably in France's referendum and the rise of Nicholas Sarkozy, with an explicitly anti-Turkish accession platform. These developments started transforming attitudes toward the EU within the Turkish population. As disillusionment set in, support for EU took a tumble, falling from above 70% in 2004 to a low of 40% in 2007 (Acemoğlu and Üçer, 2015).[50]

The implications of all of these trends for the Turkish political institutions have been striking. After 2007, the government started cracking

---

[49] On the Ergenekon trials, see Jenkins (2011). On the Sledgehammer case, see Rodrik (2014).

[50] For a more thorough account of the reasons behind Turkey's disillusionment with the EU, see Chapter 7 in this volume by Aktar, on Turkey's disillusions and shortcomings.

down against various critical media outlets and independent societal organizations, many of which had started flourishing thanks to the greater freedoms of the early 2000s. In May 2013, protests erupted in Gezi Park, near İstanbul's Taksim Square. The protests were a reaction to the Turkish government's plans to demolish the park to build a replica of the Ottoman-era Taksim Military Barracks (of symbolic importance to the Islamist movement in Turkey) that would include a shopping mall, but they quickly turned into a broader movement critical of government policies and corruption, and started articulating demands for greater freedom of belief, expression, and media. Similar protests got underway in other major cities. Hopes that there would be a dialogue between the government and the protesters were soon dashed, and a heavy-handed crackdown followed.

The mid-2010s also witnessed three other developments, with major implications for Turkey's institutions. The first was a sharp reversal in the government's Kurdish policy, most notably with the complete reversal of the so-called "peace process" that Erdoğan himself had initiated. Simultaneously, Erdoğan started courting nationalist votes and took a much more hardline attitude toward Kurdish demands. The result was a significant deterioration in the security situation and the resumption of armed conflict in the southeast of the country.

The second was a falling out between Erdoğan and Gülen (and their supporters). Their power struggle culminated in a botched coup attempt in July 2016, which appears to have been masterminded by Gülen's allies in the military. The failed coup attempt was followed by a state of emergency and a systematic purge of both Gulenists and other critics of the government from the bureaucracy and security forces, that ended up with the arrest or dismissal of some 140,000 state employees (Kingsley, 2017). Though by all accounts Gulenist penetration in the bureaucracy and security services was real and highly damaging to Turkish institutions, the post-coup purges were often carried out without due process and the whole process further weakened the independence of the judiciary.

The third major development was the narrow approval of Erdoğan's proposed change in Turkey's constitution in an April 2017 referendum, transforming the country from parliamentary to a presidential system.

The new constitution concentrates on significant powers in the hands of a directly elected president, who now controls all executive authority, sets economic and foreign policy, has sweeping appointment powers, and is subject to very weak checks and balances. Though the new presidential system is still in flux, it has already massively expanded executive power, reduced political pluralism, and removed *de jure* and *de facto* constraints on political discretion (see Makovsky, 2017; Alirıza, 2018; Demirtaş, 2019; Kirişçi and Toygür, 2019).

All of these changes have been associated with a broader weakening of democratic institutions, further restrictions on the freedom of speech, less independence for media, and a further deterioration in Turkey's record on human and civil rights. The indices shown in Figures 2.22 and 2.23 above confirm these trends.

Equally telling is the number of journalists jailed in Turkey, which is plotted in Figure 2.24 together with the total number of imprisoned journalists in the world. Despite the fact that most journalists today are allied with the government, happy to faithfully toe its line, Turkey not only tops

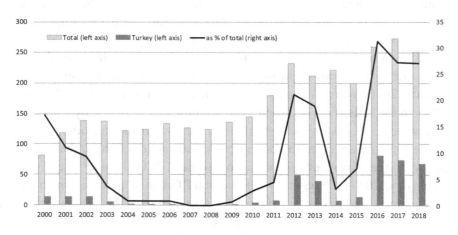

Figure 2.24. Journalists imprisoned

Note: The figure shows the total number of imprisoned journalists around the world and in Turkey, as well as the ratio of imprisoned journalist in Turkey as percent of total.

Source: Committee to Protect Journalists.

the list of countries where it is most precarious to be a journalist, but accounts for a staggering 25–30% of total number of jailed journalists in the world.

All in all, Turkish political institutions, which became more democratic and more inclusive in the first half of the 2000s for a variety of reasons, started moving in the opposite direction, and the last 10 years or so have witnessed a significant deterioration in civil rights, freedom of speech, and media freedom as well as a less constrained political environment with more curtailed participation from society and societal organizations. There is a strong overlap between the timing of the political reversal and the volte-face in economic institutions.

2.5. The Way Forward

The account of the Turkish macroeconomy we have provided has three major implications.

First, the achievements of the Turkish economy have been hampered by its institutional structure that has made its growth low-quality and often unsustainable. The economy has not generated shared prosperity either, because the same institutional characteristics have underpinned a more unequal distribution of resources in the economy.

Second, the brief interlude between 2002 and 2006 demonstrates that improvements in political institutions, bolstered by significant weakening in Turkey's democratic institutions, are feasible and can bear dividends relatively quickly in terms of productivity growth, more rapid economic change, and more equally shared prosperity.

Third, these socially costly dynamics notwithstanding, there is no reason to expect the political process to bring such high-quality growth by itself. Indeed, the 13 years since 2006 have witnessed the resurgence of low-quality growth driven by deteriorating economic and political institutions. The fallback from this episode of relatively rapid but low-quality growth has been a familiar one: the specter of protracted economic stagnation.

In the rest of this concluding section, we briefly discuss what our framework and prospective suggest as the best way forward.

Because low-quality growth has been sustained by rapid expansion of credit to households and especially to the corporate sector, we may be in the midst of a triple balance sheet slowdown. The corporate sector is heavily indebted and anecdotal evidence suggests that a significant fraction of companies are already facing serious financial difficulties. Problems on household balance sheets may further increase the strains on the system, especially as they may lead to a sharp decline in demand for housing, worsening the already precarious situation facing the construction sector.[51] Finally, the balance sheet of the banking sector looks compromised. The fraction of non-performing loans on the balance sheets of private banks has increased sharply and now (as of early October) exceeds 5% of all loans, and in the absence of efforts to systematically clean these balance sheets, this fraction is only likely to grow in the near future.[52]

These problems could spell trouble for short-term prospects of the Turkish economy. Although the more sanguine view of a "V-shaped" recovery, similar to Turkey's experience in the 2001 and 2009 recessions, is popular among some commentators, business representatives and government officials, a more prolonged period of stagnation or perhaps even a "second-dip" may be more likely in the years ahead.[53] This is partly because of the persistently low-quality nature of growth we documented previously that appears to have run out of steam, and partly because of the aforementioned balance sheet problems among banks, corporations, and households, coupled with the absence of any comprehensive restructuring framework, which raise the likelihood of a lengthy period of low investment and weak or even negative job growth.

---

[51] Indeed, home sales have shrunk at an annual rate of about 20% through the first eight months of 2019, while the construction sector shed some 700,000 jobs (about one-third of sector's total employment) in about a year and a half. See Chapter 6 in this volume by Uysal, Paker and Pelek.

[52] In all likelihood, this number is a severe underestimate because of the large size of so-called Stage II loans (i.e., loans in the watch list) and lax regulations, making banks themselves unwilling to declare non-performing loans. The government instructed banks in September 2019 to recognize a portion of these non-performing loans, amounting to TL 46 billion (around $8 billion). See also Dalgın and Sak (2019) and IMF (2019b).

[53] See also Chapter 4 in this volume by Yazgan that arrives at a similar conclusion.

The way forward, therefore, must involve not only a focus on how to improve the quality of Turkish growth in the medium term but also proactive steps to redress the balance sheets of households, firms, and banks.

The solutions to these problems are linked. The Turkish economy can avoid a sharp recession by strengthening corporate and banking balance sheets, which in turn necessitates robust capital inflows. The only way to attract capital inflows on favorable terms and maturity structure is to improve the business environment as perceived by foreign firms and investors. This means embracing the same types of economic reforms that Turkey undertook in the early 2000s, including major institutional reforms and a less discretionary and more predictable microeconomic policy framework.

The most important institutional reforms, just as in the early 2000s, include improving the legal system (both in terms of its efficiency and independence from the executive), reducing policy uncertainty (for example, by restoring the independence of the Central Bank and other regulatory agencies, and reducing politician discretion in economic decisions), increasing competitiveness, and stemming corruption. Such reforms can only be credible, however, if they are underpinned by genuine reforms strengthening Turkish democracy.

None of this is easy or even likely. As emphasized in Acemoğlu and Robinson (2012) as well as in our aforementioned account of the evolution of Turkish political institutions, political change and reform seldom happen simply because there is an urgent need for them; rather, they follow their own logic, often depending on political balances and the formation of the relevant coalitions. Unless political change takes place, deep-rooted economic reforms remain unlikely.

Perhaps the greatest danger for Turkey then is a further worsening of the political situation together with half-hearted interventions to prevent corporate and banking failures, without dealing with the root causes of Turkey's low-quality, unsustainable economic growth.

References

Acemoğlu, D. (2009). *Introduction to Modern Economic Growth*, Princeton University Press.

Acemoğlu, D., Aghion, P. and Zilibotti, F. (2006). "Distance to Frontier, Selection, and Economic Growth", *Journal of the European Economic Association*, Vol. 4, No. 1, pp. 37–74.

Acemoğlu, D., Johnson, S. and Robinson, J. A. (2001). "The Colonial Origins of Comparative Development: An Empirical Investigation", *The American Economic Review*, Vol. 91, No. 5, pp. 1369–1401.

Acemoğlu, D., Johnson, S. and Robinson, J. A. (2005). "Institutions as the Fundamental Cause of Long-Run Growth", in P. Aghion and S. Durlauf (eds.), *Handbook of Economic Growth*, Vol. 1, Elsevier, pp. 385–472.

Acemoğlu, D., Johnson, S., Robinson, J. and Thaicharoen, Y. (2003). "Institutional Causes, Macroeconomic Symptoms: Volatility, Crises and Growth", *Journal of Monetary Economics*, Vol. 50, pp. 49–123.

Acemoğlu, D., Naidu, S., Restrepo, P. and Robinson, J. A. (2019). "Democracy Does Cause Growth", *Journal of Political Economy*, Vol. 127, No. 1, pp. 47–100.

Acemoğlu, D. and Restrepo, P. (2019). "Automation and New Tasks: How Technology Displaces and Reinstates Labor", *Journal of Economic Perspectives*, Vol. 33, No. 2, pp. 3–30.

Acemoğlu, D. and Robinson, J. (2012). *Why Nations Fail*, Crown Publishing Group.

Acemoğlu, D. and Üçer, M. (2015). "The Ups and Downs of Turkish Growth, 2002–2015: Political Dynamics, the European Union and the Institutional Slide", *The Search for Europe: Contrasting Approaches*, BBVA Open Mind Press.

Alesina, A. and Perotti, R. (1996). "Income Distribution, Political Instability, and Investment", *European Economic Review*, Vol .40, pp. 1203–1228.

Alesina, A. and Rodrik, D. (1994). "Distributive Politics and Economic Growth", *Quarterly Journal of Economics*, Vol. 109, No. 2, pp. 465–490.

Alirıza, B. (2018). "Erdoğan Takes Total Control of 'New Turkey'", Center for Strategic and International Studies.

Atiyas, İ. (2012). "Economic Institutions and Institutional Change in Turkey during the Neoliberal Era", *New Perspectives on Turkey*, No. 14, pp. 45–69.

Banerjee, A. and Duflo, E. (2003). "Inequality and Growth: What Can the Data Say", *Journal of Economic Growth*, Vol. 3, pp. 267–299.

Bredenkamp, H., Josefsson, M., Lindgren, C.-J. (2009). "Turkey's Renaissance: From Banking Crisis to Economic Revival", *Successes of the International Monetary Fund*, Palgrave Macmillan.

Cappelli, P. H. (2015). "Skill Gaps, Skill Shortages, and Skill Mismatches: Evidence and Arguments for the United States", *Sage Journal*, Vol. 68, No. 2, pp. 251–290.

Caselli, F. (2005). "Accounting for Cross-Country Income Differences", *Handbook of Economic Growth* (ed. 1), Vol. 1, pp. 679–741.

Dalgın, B. and Sak, G. (2019). Re-ensuring Flow of Credit to Return to Growth: The Case for a Turkish Troubled Assets Restructuring Program.

Demiralp, S., Demiralp, S. and Gümüş, İ. (2015). "The State of Property Development in Turkey: Facts and Comparisons", Koç University-Tüsiad Economic Research Forum, Working Paper 1503.

Demirtaş, S. (2019). "The First Year of Turkey's Presidential System", *Hürriyet Daily News* (July 10).

Derviş, K., Emerson, M., Gros, D. and Ülgen, S. (2004). *The European Transformation of Modern Turkey*, Brussels: Centre for European Policy Studies, Istanbul: Economics and Foreign Policy Forum.

Dollar, D., Kleinberg, T. and Kraay, A. (2013). "Growth Still is Good for the Poor", Policy Research Working Paper No. WPS 6568. Washington, DC: World Bank.

Domaç, İ. and Işıklar, G. (2019). "Turkey Economics View: Strong Growth will Require Less Perspiration and More Inspiration", Citi Research Economics.

Dornbusch, R. and Edwards, S. (1991). *The Macroeconomics of Populism*, University of Chicago Press.

Eichengreen, B., Park, D. and Shin, K. (2014). "Growth Slowdowns Redux", *Japan and the World Economy*, Vol. 32, pp. 65–84.

Gill, I. S. and Kharas, H. (2015). "The Middle-Income Trap Turns Ten", World Bank, Policy Research Working Paper, No. 7403, Washington, DC.

Gill, I. and Kharas, H. (2007). "An East Asian Renaissance: Ideas for Economic Growth", World Bank, Washington, DC.

Gordon, R. J. (2017). *The Rise and Fall of American Growth: The U.S. Standard of Living since the Civil War*, Princeton University Press.

Gürakar, E. (2016). *Politics of Favoritism in Public Procurement in Turkey Reconfigurations of Dependency Networks in the AKP Era*, Palgrave Macmillan.

Gürakar, E. and Meyersson, E. (2016). "State Discretion, Political Connections and Public Procurement: Evidence from Turkey".

Gürsel, S. and Durmaz, M. (2014). "Large but Insufficient Increase in Quality of Education?", BETAM Research Brief.

Gürsoy, Y. (2011). "The Impact of EU Driven Reforms on the Political Autonomy of the Turkish Military", in Part I. "Turkey and the European Union: Accession and Reform", guest edited by Avcı, Gamze and Çarkoğlu Ali, South European Society and Politics.

Hale, W. (2011). "Human Rights and Turkey's EU Accession Process: Internal and External Dynamics, 2005–10", in Part I. "Turkey and the European Union: Accession and Reform", guest edited by Avcı, Gamze and Çarkoğlu Ali, South European Society and Politics.

Hall, R. E. and Jones, C. I. (1999). "Why Do Some Countries Produce So Much More Output Per Worker Than Others?", *Oxford University Press*, Vol. 114, No. 1, pp. 83–116.

Hanushek, E. and Ludger, W. (2016). "The Role of Education Quality for Economic Growth", World Bank Policy Research Working Paper No. 4122.

Hidalgo, C. A. and Hausmann, R. (2009). "The Building Blocks of Economic Complexity", *PNAS*, Vol. 106, No. 26, pp. 10570–10575.

International Monetary Fund (2016). "Understanding Turkish Residential Real Estate Dynamics", in Turkey: Selected Issues, Country Report, No. 17/33, pp. 45–64.

International Monetary Fund (2019a). Saudi Arabia: Article IV Consultation Staff Report, September.

International Monetary Fund (2019b). Turkey: Staff Concluding Statement of the Article IV Consultation Mission, September.

Jenkins, G. (2011). "Ergenekon, Sledgehammer, and the Politics of Turkish Justice: Conspiracies and Coincidences", Rubin Center.

Kauffman, R. R. and Stallings, B. (1991). *The Political Economy of Latin American Populism*, University of Chicago Press.

Kavuncu, F. and Polat, S. (2019). "A Brief Assessment of Adult Skills in Turkey: Results from Survey of Adult Skills (PIAAC)", TÜSİAD — Sabancı University Competitiveness Forum Working Paper No., 2019–1.

Kingsley, P. (2017). "Erdoğan Says He Will Extend His Sweeping Rule Over Turkey", *The New York Times*.

Kirişçi, K. (2011). "The Kurdish Issue in Turkey: Limits of European Union Reform", Southern European Society and Politics.

Kirişçi, K. and Toygür, İ. (2019). "Turkey's New Presidential System and a Changing West: Implications for Turkish Foreign Policy and Turkish-West Relations", Foreign Policy at Brookings, Turkey Project Policy Paper, No. 15, pp. 1–21.

Makovsky, A. (2017). "Erdoğan's Proposal for an Empowered Presidency", Center for American Progress.

North, D. C. (1982). *Structure and Change in Economic History*, W. W. Norton & Company.

North, D. C. (1991). "Institutions", *Journal of Economic Perspectives*, Vol. 5, No. 1, pp. 97–112.

OECD (2016). OECD Economic Surveys: Turkey.

Özel, I. (2015). "Reverting Structural Reforms in Turkey: Towards an Illiberal Economic Governance?", Global Turkey in Europe Series Policy Brief (2015, May).

Pamuk, Ş. (2018). *Uneven Centuries: Economic Development of Turkey since 1820*, Princeton University Press.

Persson, T. and Tabellini, G. (1994). "Is Inequality Harmful for Growth?", *American Economic Review*, Vol. 84, pp. 600–621.

Piatkowski, M. (2018). *Europe's Growth Champion*, Oxford University Press.

Rivera-Batiz, F. L. and Durmaz, M. (2014). "Why Did Pisa Test Scores Rise in Turkey?", BETAM Research Brief.

Rodrik, D. (2014). "The Plot Against the Generals".

Schularick, M. and Taylor, A. M. (2012). "Credit Booms Gone Bust: Monetary Policy, Leverage Cycles, and Financial Crises, 1870–2008", *American Economic Review*, Vol. 102, No. 2, pp. 1029–1061.

Uysal, G. and Kavuncu, F. (2019). "Tüik Temel İşgücü Göstergelerinin Geriye Doğru Revizyonu (1988–2018)".

World Bank (2008). Commission on Growth and Development.

World Bank (2014). Turkey's Transitions: Integration, Inclusion, Institutions, Country Economic Memorandum.

World Bank (2019). "Firm Productivity and Economic Growth in Turkey", Country Economic Memorandum.

Weyland, K. (2001). "Clarifying a Contested Concept: Populism in the Study of Latin American Politics", Comparative Politics, Ph.D. Programs in Political Science, City University of New York, Vol. 34, No. 1, pp. 1–22.

Zurcher, E. J. (2004). *Turkey A Modern History*, I.B. Tauris.

Chapter 3

Productivity, Reallocation, and Structural Change: An Assessment

Izak Atiyas and Ozan Bakış

3.1. Introduction

The basic narrative of the Turkish economy up until mid-2000s was one of successful structural change. After a decade of macroeconomic instability and highly volatile growth that characterized most of the 1990s, and following the adoption of a wide-ranging economic program in 2001, Turkey exhibited respectable economic growth in the 2000s, at least until the global financial crisis. Further, growth in that period was accompanied by rapid increase in total factor productivity (AFP) (Atiyas and Bakis, 2014) as well as successful performance in structural change, i.e., reallocation of labor from low productivity agriculture to higher productivity services and industry (Atiyas and Bakis, 2014, 2015; Rodrik, 2010). Further, this period was characterized by significant improvements in both political and economic institutions (Acemoglu and Üçer, 2015; and Chapter 2 by the same authors in this volume). By contrast, there is widespread agreement that Turkey's economic performance has deteriorated in the last few years. With the loss of the European Union (EU) anchor, and increase in authoritarian tendencies, there is also widespread concern about institutional degradation, including in areas such as independence of the judiciary, freedom of the press, and the overall quality of

91

governance (see Chapters 2, 7, and 8). The purpose of this chapter is to evaluate how the narrative of successful structural change needs to be modified to accommodate the developments of the last four decades.

The chapter makes several contributions: First, it will update the growth accounting exercise presented in Atiyas and Bakis (2014) and examine the contribution of TFP to aggregate growth. Second, the growth accounting exercise will be extended to the construction industry. The construction industry is believed to have played a significant role in recent years, and to the best of our knowledge, this chapter is the first to examine the characteristics of growth in this industry in an accounting framework. It is also worthy to note that the recent severe depression in this sector played a crucial role in the recession of 2018. Third, to assess whether structural change has continued to play a positive role, the chapter will examine the contribution of reallocation of labor to the growth of aggregate labor productivity (LP). Finally, based on the premise that structural transformation and technological upgrading eventually show up in the increase in international competitiveness, the chapter will provide evidence on slowdown in the improvement of the quality of Turkey's exports.

Throughout the chapter, we try to follow a uniform scheme of periodization of the last four decades. The period 1981–1989 covers the period of economic liberalization and reform under the Özal governments, up to the capital account liberalization that took place in 1989. The period 1990–2002 covers the "lost years" of 1990s, when Turkey struggled with macroeconomic instability, high inflation, and large budget deficits made worse by off-budget expenditures. The excesses of the 1990s culminated in a financial crisis in 2000–2001, and an economic reform program supported by the International Monetary Fund (IMF) and the World Bank was launched in 2001–2002. The year 2002 is a year of high growth, reflecting a "rebound" effect of a severe contraction experienced in 2001. We include the year 2002 in the "lost years" segment, both because the contraction and the rebound growth cancel each other out and also because the Justice and Development Party (AK Party) government was formed in November 2002 and Recep Tayyip Erdoğan became Prime Minister in March 2003.

We will refer to the years 2003–2013 as the "first AK Party period". We further subdivided this period into three phases: The years 2003–2007 correspond to a period of intensive economic and political reform as well as an orientation toward accession to the EU. These are years when, overall, institutions of economic policymaking were more rule based than traditionally has been the case in Turkey (Chapter 7). While a new business class was supported by the government, the prospect of EU accession and the adoption of EU regulations provided the traditional elite with security. The years 2008–2010 correspond to the period of global economic crisis, causing a substantial drop in GDP in 2009, followed by a rebound in 2010. Even though growth was high in 2010, it reflected a rebound from a low base. We therefore include the year 2010 in the same period as 2008–2009, and call the whole cycle "the crisis period". The period 2014–2018 corresponds to what we call the "second AK Party period" when a fundamental change in the mode of governance is clearly visible. Following the Gezi protests in 2013, successive AK Party governments turned increasingly authoritarian, a tendency that peaked following the 2016 failed coup attempt. When exactly the change occurred is a matter of controversy. Some observers underline the year 2012 as the year when the rift between AK Party and the Gülen movement became visible.[1]

An important contribution of this chapter is that we carry out the growth accounting exercise in four sectors: agriculture, industry (comprising mining, manufacturing, electricity, water, and gas), construction, and the services. We include construction as a separate industry because its role in the economy has been important and controversial, especially in the last decade and a half. There is a widespread view that economic growth in the last few years has relied too heavily on growth in the construction industry. The construction sector has been promoted both because it generates jobs, and because it is a sector where generation and allocation of rents to politically connected firms is relatively easy. Rents can be generated both through changes in regulations (e.g., changing zoning regulations can generate significant rents in construction of buildings) especially in construction and through public procurement (e.g., building of motorways or projects with private-sector participation). Moreover, many of the new business groups associated with the ruling AK Party are

---

[1] In February 2012, prosecutors allegedly associated with the Gülen movement revealed an investigation against the president of the National Intelligence Organization who was closely associated with the leadership of the AK Party.

in the construction business (Buğra and Savaşkan, 2014). Gürakar (2016) examines public procurement data and finds that "In the AK Party period, …, the majority government has used public procurement as an influential tool both to increase its electoral success and build its own, loyal elites" (p. 107). At the same time, the role of politics in the development of the construction industry is nothing new. For example, granting titles to illegal urban settlements in exchange for political support has always been an important dimension of political clientelism in Turkey. These considerations make it worthwhile to examine the characteristics of growth in this sector in some detail.

The chapter is organized as follows: The next section presents our data and methodology. The third section discusses the results of the growth accounting exercise at the aggregate level. Section 3.4 examines the role of factor accumulation and TFP growth in agriculture, industry, construction, and services. Section 3.5 investigates the role of reallocation in aggregate growth of LP. Section 3.6 provides a brief analysis of the quality of Turkey's exports. Section 3.7 concludes.

3.2. Data and Methodology

a. *Methodology*

The starting point for TFP estimation is the assumption of a production function. Almost all past studies estimating TFP start with the basic production function $Y_t = A_t K_t^\alpha L_t^{1-\alpha}$. Then, from this function TFP growth is derived as follows:

$$\ln\left(A_{t+1}/A_t\right) = \ln\left(Y_{t+1}/Y_t\right) - \alpha \ln\left(K_{t+1}/K_t\right) - \left(1-\alpha\right)\ln\left(L_{t+1}/L_t\right) \quad (1)$$

where α is the share of capital in GDP. So, TFP growth is measured as a residual, and usually it is called Solow's residual. The reason for this labeling is that Solow's (1957) was the first paper to compute TFP in this way. Once α is estimated or assumed, we need time series data on Y, K, and L to estimate TFP growth. One common problem is the lack of capital data. And a typical solution is using the following investment data and perpetual inventory equation:

$$K_{t+1} = (1-\delta)K_t + I_t \tag{2}$$

to obtain a time series of capital data. This equation requires the initial level of capital, which is not available unfortunately. Again, the common practice is to assume that the economy is in a steady state so that GDP and capital grow at the same constant rate (g) so that we have the following equation that pins down the initial capital stock:

$$K_0 = \frac{I_0}{g+\delta} \tag{3}$$

Here, I_0 is usually the first observation of investment data, g is the average growth rate for the period we want to compute the capital stock for, and finally δ is the depreciation rate for the capital stock.

For sectoral TFP growth, we use the following variant of Equation (1):

$$\ln\left(A_{t+1}^i / A_t^i\right) = \ln\left(Y_{t+1}^i / Y_t^i\right) - \alpha^i \ln\left(K_{t+1}^i / K_t^i\right) - \left(1-\alpha^i\right)\ln\left(L_{t+1}^i / L_t^i\right) \tag{4}$$

where superscript i refers to sector. In this chapter, these are agriculture, industry, construction, and services. We are allowing sectors to have different capital shares.

b. *Data*

Before presenting details of our data, we should expose our sectoral classification. For TFP analysis, we present both aggregate results and sectorial results where sectors are agriculture, industry (mining, manufacturing, and public utilities), construction, and services. The main constraint for TFP analysis, as we will see in subsequent sections, is the construction of a long capital stock series, which is only feasible for the four aforementioned sectors. Since we do not need capital stock data for LP analysis, we enlarge the number of sectors to nine: agriculture; mining; public utilities (electricity, water, and gas); manufacturing; construction; wholesale and retail trade; financial institutions, insurance and real estate; transport, storage and communications; and community, social, personal and government services.

i. *Setting parameters*

To estimate Equation (2) (which also requires estimation of Equation (3)) we need to determine parameters α and δ, along with GDP, investment, and employment series both at aggregate and sectoral levels. Following the literature, we set depreciation rate to 6% for aggregate analysis. For sectoral depreciation, we let agriculture have a lower depreciation rate, 3% in the baseline specification and the same depreciation rate for all sectors as a robustness check (6%). For capital share, our main specification uses a value of 1/3 for capital share when we analyze aggregate TFP as most of the literature, respectively. Another reason why we prefer 1/3 is that Atiyas and Bakis (2014) show that aggregate labor share adjusted for self-employment is around 2/3, which is widely used by TFP literature.

However, starting from December 2016, the Turkish Statistical Institute (TurkStat) made an important revision to national accounts. Both composition and level GDP change in important ways. One wonders whether the finding by Atiyas and Bakis (2014) on adjusted labor share still holds in the new GDP series. One disadvantage of the new series of "GDP by income approach" released by TurkStat is that it covers only the 2009–2018 period. Nevertheless, if we compute aggregate labor share adjusted for self-employment from this more recent data, it is around 2/3, actually 64.3% to be precise (see Bakis and Acar, 2020, for details). For sectoral TFP analysis there is no such consensus on factor shares. However, different sectors are expected to have different factor shares. For sectoral factor shares, we rely on Valentinyi and Herrendorf (2008), who measure sectoral income shares for the USA, we use capital share, $\alpha = 0.55$ for agriculture, $\alpha = 1/3$ for industry and services, and finally $\alpha = 0.21$ for construction. A hasty reaction to these numbers may be that the capital share for agriculture is too high. But given that land is part of the capital stock for agriculture, and for many farmers land is the principal input in production, it seems more convincing than it looks.

The concerns about a constant depreciation rate that is common to all sectors are well known; however, given the lack of convincing data, most of the literature stick with 6% of constant depreciation rate. This part of the problem is unavoidable. There is an inherent problem in calculating a unique and constant depreciation rate when capital is made, in varying proportions, of communication technology equipment, machinery as well as buildings, land, animals, and office equipment. Studies by Jorgenson (1996) and Hulten and Wykoff (1981) show that depreciation rate is lowest in agriculture, highest for construction, and in between for manufacturing and services. This is why we prefer a depreciation rate of 6% for aggregate analysis, but for sectoral analysis, we favor 4% for agriculture, 8% for construction, and 6% for both industry and services.

In addition to other data problems, we want to construct a time series that goes back as far as possible. This is necessary to have reliable TFP numbers. Since our oldest observation for aggregate investment goes back to 1948, we construct GDP and employment series going back to 1948 as well. For aggregate GDP, we easily find a series going back to 1948. For investment and employment, it is relatively more difficult but still feasible. The most difficult task was finding sectorial investment series going back to 1948. In the following sections, we provide a detailed discussion of how each variable used in the TFP analysis is constructed.

ii. *GDP*

We use real GDP as a measure of output from the TurkStat. One major difficulty in the construction of "real GDP" data for Turkey is its changes in activity classification. Looking at TurkStat data, we see that different classifications are used through time. First, we have the International Standard Industrial Classification of all Economic Activities (ISIC) Rev. 2, which covers years 1948–2006. Then, we have NACE Rev. 2, which covers years 1998–2018. Actually, in practice we had other classifications such as NACE Rev. 1, which covered the years 1998–2011.

But when TurkStat updated activity classification, it extrapolated to earlier years so that between 1948 and 2018 we have only two classifications for GDP. Meanwhile, when TurkStat switched to chain-linking technology, the activity classification, NACE Rev. 2, did not change, but the treatment of "Financial intermediation services indirectly measured" changed in the new series. Before, in the 1998-based GDP, it was a separate item that was needed to be added to sectorial total along with taxes and subsidies to get GDP at purchaser's prices. But with new chain-linked series taking 2009 as the reference year, it is distributed to individual sectors so that we need to add only taxes and subsidies to sectorial total to get GDP at purchaser's prices. To be consistent across time, we are assuming that whatever is common to all sectors (such as FISIM or taxes and subsidies) is distributed across sectors following their share of value added in sectorial total. Once the problem regarding FISIM and taxes and subsidies is solved, it is not difficult to construct sectorial employment for nine sectors. For details and the conversion table we use for different classifications, see Bakis and Acar (forthcoming).

iii. *Capital*

We use the Gross Fixed Capital Formation (GFCF) and the perpetual inventory method (PIM) to derive capital stock. Since we rely on steady-state assumption to compute initial capital stock, it is better to compute it as early as possible so that any error we commit in the initial estimate disappears in the long run. In this chapter, we calculate the aggregate capital stock in 1948 and we report TFP results for 1980 and later years. So, we have a 32-year gap between the time we calculate TFP and initial capital stock estimation. By iterating the following perpetual inventory equation:

$$K_t = K_0 \left(1 - \delta\right)^t + \sum_{i=0}^{t-1} I_i \left(1 - \delta\right)^{t-1-i}$$

we see that any error made in the estimation of initial capital stock disappears exponentially with a growth rate of $-\delta\%$. Therefore, we tried to go back as far as possible to estimate the initial capital. Since our first observation of investment is in 1948, we estimated the initial capital stock in 1948. Assuming a depreciation rate of 6%, only a small portion of the initial capital (as much as $(1 - \delta)^{32} = 13.8\%$) is rested for year t. So, 86.2% of any error we made in the estimation of initial capital disappears by 1980.

Our major difficulty in this chapter, regarding data, was the construction of sectoral capital stock for the Turkish economy. The reason is that DPT published investment series using "housing" as a sector instead of "construction". Since it is difficult to disentangle housing from other construction investments, previous literature avoided sectoral TFP beyond three sectors (agriculture, industry, and services where construction is put either in industry or services). But as we discussed in Section 3.1, construction is an important sector both for understanding the dynamics of the Turkish economy and political economy-related issues in Turkey. Consequently, we tried our best to come up with a capital stock for construction sector. Unfortunately, it is not possible to build reliable capital series for nine sectors as it is the case for GDP and employment.[2] Thus, we restrict the number of sectors to four (agriculture, industry, construction, and services). Also, publicly available data that can be used to separate housing investment from other construction is available for the 1992–2015 period, with three different economic activity classifications (ISIC, NACE Rev. 1, and NACE Rev. 2). For details and the conversion table that we use, see Bakis and Acar (forthcoming).

Once a deprecation rate is decided, we compute the initial level of capital in 1948 using Equation (3) as $K_0 = I_0 / (\overline{g} + \delta)$, where $\overline{g}$ is theoretically the growth rate of capital and output in the steady state. In practice, we use the average growth rate of GDP over 10 years following the year 1948. Equation (3) is commonly used in the literature and it assumes that economy is in a steady state in 1948. For investment, we use the GFCF, again as does the literature. Once we have an estimate for initial capital stock, we assume a 6% depreciation rate and add new investment in year t to the next year's capital stock to obtain aggregate stock of capital for the Turkish economy.

There is another problem when one builds sectoral physical capital series. Knowing the aggregate level of capital does not help in determining how much of it goes to each sector. Following Caselli (2005), we use the non-arbitrage condition between sectors. The idea is that the marginal firm (or investment) should earn the same rate of returns in each sector. Assuming a Cobb–Douglas production function where we allow capital

---

[2]The sectors are: agriculture; mining; public utilities (electricity, water and gas); manufacturing; construction; wholesale and retail trade; financial institutions, insurance and real estate; transport, storage and communications; and community, social, personal and government services.

share to be sector-dependent (in the following equation a is used for agriculture, i for industry, c for construction, and s for services):

$$Y_j = A_j K_j^{\alpha_j} L_j^{1-\alpha_j}, \ j = a,i,c,s$$

The non-arbitrage condition can be written as (where P_i denotes prices of sector i and $P_i Y_i$ is the sectoral GDP in current prices for sector i)

$$\frac{\alpha_a P_a Y_a}{K_a} = \frac{\alpha_i P_i Y_i}{K_i} = \frac{\alpha_c P_c Y_c}{K_c} = \frac{\alpha_s P_s Y_s}{K_s} \tag{5}$$

Alternatively, these equations can be written in terms of sectoral shares of GDP (v_j) and sectoral capital as well

$$K_a = K_s \frac{\alpha_a v_a}{\alpha_s v_s}; \ K_i = K_s \frac{\alpha_i v_i}{\alpha_s v_s}; \ K_c = K_s \frac{\alpha_c v_i}{\alpha_s v_s} \tag{6}$$

Instead of sectoral shares of GDP in a single year (v_{jt}), we use the average sectoral shares of over first five years ($\bar{v}_j, j = a,i,s$ over 1948–1952) to minimize the risk of measurement error, or an outlier year. Combining the aforementioned equations with the fact that the sum of the sectoral physical capital is equal to the aggregate level of capital, $K = K_a + K_i + K_c + K_s$, we can obtain initial capital levels for the year 1948 once we have the aggregate physical capital for the Turkish economy.

iv. *Employment*

There are two problems regarding generation of consistent employment data that goes back to the 1980s. The first one is the change in total employment because of an update made to the Turkish population due to the Address Based Population Registration System (ABPR hereafter, "ADNKS" in Turkish). This created a break in employment in 2004, where only 2004 and its following years are based on ABPR data. In the old series, we have an employment of 21.7 million, while in the updated ones we have only 19.6 million implying a difference of more than 2 million employees in 2004. The second problem is changes in activity classification. Even if, like GDP, many classifications (ISIC Rev. 2, NACE Rev. 1, and NACE Rev. 2) are used, it is not difficult to construct sectoral employment for the nine sectors. For both aggregate and sectoral employment, we use employment figures published by the TurkStat for the 2004–2018 period. For earlier years, we use growth rates found in the TurkStat (2007), which uses old series before ABPR update.

3.3. Trends in Overall Productivity and Basic Growth Accounting

Table 3.1 presents the basic data for growth accounting. The first panel shows the growth rates of aggregate GDP and the second panel shows the percentage contributions of capital, labor, and aggregate TFP to overall GDP growth. GDP growth is highest in the 2002–2013 period, reaching 5.7%. In fact, if one were to disregard the crisis (and rebound) years of 2008–2010, GDP growth surpassed 7% in that period. The period 1990–2002 exhibits lower average GDP growth compared to the other periods.

The first panel of the table shows that TFP growth (represented by A in the table) has been especially high in the 1980s, and in the 2003–2007 and 2011–2013 periods. The very high growth rate of TFP in the 2003–2007 period (4%) is especially noteworthy, corroborating earlier findings of Atiyas and Bakis (2014). Growth in TFP is substantially lower in the 1990–2002 period, but especially in 2014–2018. TFP growth has been negative during the period of the global economic crisis. Another important observation is that the growth rate of capital stock increased substantially in the 2000s, from below 5% in the 1980s and 1990s, to above 6% in the 2000s, reaching a high of 7.2% per annum in 2014–2018.

The second panel of Table 3.1 shows the contribution of factor accumulation and TFP growth to overall GDP growth in Turkey. As expected, the percentage contribution of TFP growth is especially high in the 1981–1989 and 2003–2007 periods. In both periods, over one half of the overall growth in GDP is accounted for by the growth of TFP. TFP growth is especially low in the 2014–2018 period. Periods with low contribution of

Table 3.1.   Basic accounting of overall GDP growth in Turkey 1981–2018 (%)

	Y	K	L	A	LP
Growth rate (%)					
1981–1989	4.7	3.8	1.1	2.7	2.3
1990–2002	3.4	4.9	1.2	1.0	1.9
2003–2013	5.7	6.3	2.6	1.9	3.2
2003–2007	7.0	6.2	1.5	4.0	5.6
2008–2010	1.4	6.4	2.9	–2.7	–1.4
2011–2013	7.8	6.5	4.1	2.9	3.8
2014–2018	4.8	7.2	2.4	0.8	2.5
Contribution (%)					
1981–1989		27.1	15.6	57.4	
1990–2002		47.0	23.6	29.4	
2003–2013		37.1	30.1	32.8	
2003–2007		29.3	14.3	56.4	
2008–2010		154.1	137.1	–191.2	
2011–2013		27.9	34.8	37.3	
2014–2018		49.6	32.9	17.5	

Note: Y: GDP, K: Capital, L: Labor, A: TFP, LP: Labor productivity. The second panel shows the percentage contribution of K, L, and A to overall growth.

TFP growth are also characterized by high contributions of accumulation of capital, moving above 47% in 1990–2002 and almost 50% in 2014–2018.

In this regard, a comparison of the 1980s and the 2014–2018 period is telling: Average annual growth in aggregate GDP in these two periods is very similar, 4.7 and 4.8, respectively. However, as indicated earlier, in the former period, which corresponds to a period of fundamental reforms, more than half of high GDP growth is accounted for by growth in productivity (57.4%). By contrast, in the 2014–2018 period, when the reform momentum was all but lost, the contribution of TFP growth is very low, about 18% on an average annual basis. As discussed in detail in Chapter 2, the period 2014–2018 also witnessed significant deterioration in both political and economic institutions.

The last column of the first panel of the table shows growth in LP. It is easy to observe that growth in LP mimics growth in GDP quite closely: periods of high GDP growth also exhibit relatively high growth in LP. A casual observation also suggests a high degree of correlation between growth in TFP and LP as well, except for the period 2014–2018. In this period, growth in LP is still relatively high (on average about 2.5 per annum), whereas growth in TFP is quite low, suggesting that relatively high LP growth is mainly due to increase in the capital–labor ratio rather than increase in TFP. This is consistent with high contribution of growth of capital (49.6%) to overall GDP growth mentioned previously.

Overall, one has to submit that economic growth in the 2014–2018 period was quite respectable, but, compared to all earlier periods investigated in this chapter, was driven more strongly by capital accumulation rather than efficiency in resource use.

3.4. Trends in Sectoral Productivity

In this section, we examine productivity trends in four sectors: agriculture, industry, construction, and services. We start with a comparison of growth in TFP in the four industries. The data are presented in Table 3.2. The first column presents the data for growth in aggregate TFP and the rest of the columns present growth in sectoral TFP.

Table 3.2. Growth in sectoral TFP

	g	g_agr	g_ind	g_con	g_ser
1981–1989	2.7	−0.9	4.5	5.2	−0.6
1990–2002	1.0	1.0	0.9	0.2	−1.6
2003–2013	1.9	1.1	3.1	4.5	−0.4
2003–2007	4.0	1.3	4.7	9.8	0.1
2008–2010	−2.7	2.3	−1.7	−6.7	−2.5
2011–2013	2.9	−0.2	5.3	7.1	0.8
2014–2018	0.8	2.2	1.6	0.5	−0.1

Note: g_X: growth in TFP sector X where X takes the following values: agr = agriculture, ind = industry, con = construction, and ser = services.

One can make several observations: First, TFP growth is much higher in industry and construction relative to both agriculture and services. TFP growth in construction is very high in high growth years, but very low in the low-growth 1990s and highly negative during the crisis years. TFP growth in construction remains quite low in the 2014–2018 period. By contrast, TFP growth in industry is less volatile. The drop in the TFP of industry during the crisis years of 2008–2010 is much smaller than the drop in the TFP of the construction sector. TFP growth in industry is also higher than that in construction in the 2014–2018 period. TFP growth in agriculture is quite low. Interestingly, it is highest in the 2014–2018 period. Finally, TFP growth in services is negative in all periods. We should note that low (or even negative) TFP growth in services is not specific to Turkey. Other studies find similar findings for the Organisation for Economic Co-operation and Development (OECD) countries and the USA (see among others Kets and Lejour, 2003; Foerster *et al.*, 2019).

It will be interesting to examine TFP growth in individual industries in some detail. Table 3.3 presents the results for agriculture. Average annual growth in the capital stock of agriculture is of the order of 2–3% throughout the period. Growth in agricultural TFP is relatively high in the 2003–2007 and 2014–2018 periods (1.3 and 2.2, respectively). In both periods, employment growth is negative (−3.4 and −2.5, respectively). As in Atiyas and Bakis (2014), we conjecture that higher TFP growth in agriculture during these periods mainly reflects the decline in hidden unemployment

Table 3.3. Factor accumulation and TFP growth in agriculture

	Y	K	L	A
1981–1989	0.8	2.9	0.4	−0.9
1990–2002	1.8	2.4	−1.1	1.0
2003–2013	2.7	2.6	0.4	1.1
2003–2007	1.2	2.6	−3.4	1.3
2008–2010	5.5	1.6	5.2	2.3
2011–2013	2.6	3.6	1.9	−0.2
2014–2018	2.6	2.7	−2.5	2.2

Note: Y: GDP, K: Capital, L: Labor, A: TFP.

Table 3.4. Factor accumulation and TFP growth in industry

	Y	K	L	A
1981–1989	6.9	2.5	2.4	4.5
1990–2002	3.5	2.6	2.5	0.9
2003–2013	6.7	6.2	2.2	3.1
2003–2007	8.6	7.5	2.1	4.7
2008–2010	0.7	4.4	1.4	−1.7
2011–2013	9.3	5.7	3.2	5.3
2014–2018	4.8	4.4	2.7	1.6

Note: Y: GDP, K: Capital, L: Labor, A: TFP.

in agriculture.[3] Given that agriculture has historically been laden with low productivity and overemployment, an increase in productivity through a reduction of hidden unemployment is a welcome development.

Table 3.4 provides the details of growth in GDP, capital, labor, and TFP in industry. One important observation is the increase in the growth rate of capital stock in the 2000s relative to the earlier two periods. While the rate of increase in the capital stock was around 2.5% in 1981–1989 and 1990–2002, it increased to 6.2% in 2002–2013 and 4.4% in 2014–2018. Increase in capital stock was high even in the crisis (and rebound) years of 2008–2010, about 4.4%. Growth in labor was between 2–3% in most of the periods. Growth in TFP industry was high in the 1981–1989 period (about 4.5% per annum) and surpassed 5% in the non-crisis years of the 2003–2013 period. It dropped to 1.6% in 2014–2018. As with the overall GDP growth, GDP growth in industry was mostly driven by increase in capital stock in the 2014–2018 period, and the contribution of TFP was low. The drop in TFP growth in the 2014–2018 period reflects a serious slowdown in technology upgrading and should

---

[3] One may note that TFP growth in agriculture during the 2003–2007 period in this chapter (2.2 per annum) is substantially lower than that for 2002–2006 as reported in Atiyas and Bakis (above 6% per annum). The difference is partly due to different periodization and partly due to differences in the calculated growth of capital stock (2.6 vs 0.7 in Atiyas and Bakis, 2014).

Table 3.5. Factor accumulation and TFP growth in construction

	Y	K	L	A
1981–1989	6.6	4.7	0.5	5.2
1990–2002	1.3	4.7	0.1	0.2
2003–2013	10.7	5.8	6.2	4.5
2003–2007	16.0	5.8	6.3	9.8
2008–2010	−1.9	4.2	5.0	−6.7
2011–2013	14.4	7.3	7.3	7.1
2014–2018	4.2	8.9	2.2	0.5

probably be interpreted as a distress signal for the future of industry in Turkey.

Table 3.5 provides similar data for construction. GDP growth in the construction industry has been high in 1981–1989 (about 6.6%), dropped to 1.3% in the 1990s, and reached a peak of 10.7% per annum in 2003–2013. In 2014–2018, it was relatively moderate, about 4.2% on average. The construction industry has attracted high levels of investment in all periods, with the rate of growth of capital stock close to 5% in the 1980s and 1990s, 5.6% in the 2000s, and reaching a peak of 8.6% in the 2014–2018 period. This relatively high rate of growth in the capital stock was accompanied by relatively high TFP growth in the 1980s and non-crisis years of the 2000s. As observed earlier, by contrast TFP growth has been highly negative during the crisis years and very low in the 2014–2018 period. The period 2014–2018 is noteworthy in this regard, when GDP growth in the construction industry is driven by very high growth rates in capital stock but very low rates in productivity growth. Another interesting aspect of the construction industry is relatively high growth rates in labor in the 2000s, especially relative to the rest of the sectors: Construction has been an important generator of employment during the 2003–2013 period (see Chapter 5).

We report similar data for services in Table 3.6. Services are also characterized by high growth rates in capital as well as labor. Growth in capital stock was lowest in the 1980s, but still high at an average of 6% per annum. It was much higher in the rest of the periods, reaching a peak annual

Table 3.6. Factor accumulation and TFP growth in services

	Y	K	L	A
1981–1989	3.9	6.0	3.7	−0.6
1990–2002	3.5	8.6	3.4	−1.6
2003–2013	5.0	9.4	3.5	−0.4
2003–2007	5.8	10.2	3.5	0.1
2008–2010	1.6	8.3	2.1	−2.5
2011–2013	7.2	9.2	5.0	0.8
2014–2018	5.2	7.4	4.2	−0.1

average of 10% in the 2002–2007 period. The rate of growth in labor, although lower than that in construction in the 2000s, has also been quite high. These high rates of factor accumulation have been associated with very low or negative growth in TFP throughout the last four decades.

It is well known that there is much heterogeneity in productivity and productivity growth among service industries. In their analysis of structural change in advanced countries, Jorgenson and Timmer (2011) draw attention to this heterogeneity and underline the need for better measurement as well as better understanding of drivers of technical change in service industries. In the case of Turkey as well, one needs a more detailed breakdown of services to understand the dynamics of low TFP growth in services. Nevertheless, persistent low TFP growth suggests that Turkey has not yet benefitted from the expansion of those service industries that are characterized by a higher intensive use of information and communication technologies and thereby enjoy higher productivity growth.

It is important to remember that the share of services in total GDP of Turkey has remained above 60%. Its share in total employment has increased from about 30% in 1980 to about 55% in 2018. It has also attracted high levels of investment throughout the period with growth rates of capital higher than those in industry. Hence, services make up a significant portion of overall economic activity in Turkey. If Turkey is stuck in a middle-income trap, part of the explanation probably lies in the fact that productivity growth has been so low in such an important part of the economy.

3.5. Trends in Structural Change

Overall productivity growth can be achieved through two main mechanisms. First, productivity growth can be achieved within individual firms through investments in better technology, employment of higher skilled labor, research and development, innovation activities, etc. Second, an increase in overall productivity can be achieved by the reallocation of factors of production from low to high productivity firms. The same is true at the level of industries: Growth in aggregate productivity can be achieved by productivity growth within industries, and by reallocation of inputs from low to high productivity industries. At the level of an industry, the former captures both productivity growth within firms and reallocation between firms. At the level of industries, the latter is often called structural change. While one would expect that structural change would make a positive contribution to productivity growth, this is not always the case. In particular, McMillan *et al.* (2014) have shown that in 1990–2005 the contribution of structural change to overall growth in LP in fact has been negative in Latin America and Africa. In other words, in these regions, labor has moved from high to low productivity industries.[4]

In this section, we concentrate on LP and decompose growth in aggregate LP into two components: a component that reflects productivity growth within industries, and second, reflecting the effects of reallocation of labor between industries. Specifically, we undertake the decomposition proposed by McMillan *et al.* (2014).

$$\Delta P_t = \sum_i \overline{s} \Delta p_{i,t} + \sum_i \overline{p} \Delta s_{i,t}$$

Here, the Δ stands for the difference between time t and $t - k$, P and p_i stand for productivity of the overall economy and of sector i, respectively, and s_i stands for the employment share of sector i.[5] Finally, the formula

---

[4] For more on the relation between sectoral productivity and changes in sectoral employment shares, see Chapter 5.

[5] As mentioned earlier, we use the following sectors for this analysis: agriculture; mining; public utilities (electricity, water, and gas); manufacturing; construction; wholesale and retail trade; financial institutions, insurance and real estate; transport, storage and communications; and community, social, personal and government services.

relies on average employment share and average productivity level of each sector where average is defined with respect to $\bar{s} = (s_{i,t-1} + s_{i,t})/2$ and $\bar{p} = (p_{i,t-1} + p_{i,t})/2$. Hence, the equation decomposes LP growth in period $t-1$ and t into two parts: the first part of the equation captures productivity growth within each sector, weighted by the beginning of period employment shares. The second part is the sum of changes in employment shares of each industry, weighted by the end of period sectoral productivity levels. The second part reflects structural change.

The results of the exercise are presented in Table 3.7. The first panel reports growth in aggregate LP (column 1), and the "within" and "between" components as reflected in the aforementioned equation (where within plus between equals growth in aggregate LP). The lower panel reports the percentage contribution of the within and between components to growth in aggregate LP (where the numbers of the two components add up to 100).

Table 3.7. Decomposing growth in LP (%)

Growth Rate (%)	LP	Within	Between
1981–1989	2.3%	1.7%	0.6%
1990–2002	1.9%	0.7%	1.2%
2003–2013	3.2%	1.6%	1.6%
2003–2007	5.6%	3.7%	1.9%
2008–2010	−1.4%	−2.8%	1.4%
2011–2013	3.8%	2.6%	1.2%
2014–2018	2.5%	1.8%	0.7%
Contribution (%)			
1981–1989		73.4	26.6
1990–2002		39.3	60.7
2003–2013		50.7	49.3
2003–2007		66.0	34.0
2008–2010		200.4	−100.4
2011–2013		68.6	31.4
2014–2018		71.0	29.0

Previous studies (Atiyas and Bakis, 2015; Rodrik, 2010) have shown that overall, the contribution of structural change to growth in aggregate LP has been positive in Turkey. Table 3.7 confirms the earlier findings. It also shows, however, the positive contribution of structural change to aggregate growth in LP has diminished in recent years. The between component of LP growth has been above 1 percentage points in all of the post 1990 periods, reaching 1.9 percentage points in the 2003–2007 period and 1.6 percentage points in the 2003–2013 period. Importantly, the between component has been positive (about 1.4 percentage points) even during the crisis years. However, it has dropped to 0.7% in the 2014–2018 period. In other words, in recent years, reallocation has played a much diminished role in promoting growth in aggregate LP.

Figure 3.1 helps explain why this has been the case. The y-axis of the figure is the log of the ratio of sectoral to aggregate LP in 2013. This ratio is equal to zero when sectoral LP is equal to aggregate LP. The x-axis shows the change in sectoral employment shares between 2013 and 2018. The size of the circles represents the share of sectoral employment in 2013. The figure shows that between 2013 and 2018, a significant amount of employment growth has happened in industries whose LP in 2013 was lower than aggregate LP, namely wholesale and retail trade (wrt) and especially community, social, personal, and government services (cpg). Moreover, these are industries with high employment shares to start with.

Figure 3.2 shows the evolution of between and within components over time. Even if the average growth is almost the same for each component, we see clearly that the within component is much more volatile. Since the within component refers to the economic efficiency and capital deepening, the sharp falls in this component in crisis and low growth years (1994, 1999, 2001, 2009, 2016) is likely to imply a decline in economic efficiency in these particular years, since there are no strong declines in physical capital stock that could justify such drops in the within component. A usual explanation for large losses in LP (and the within component) during economic crisis and strong increases in expansion period following recession is labor hoarding. Since adjusting labor input level in line with demand for products is costly for firms, they prefer to respond to these fluctuations by adjusting the utilization rate of their employment. In practice, labor hoarding may happen through a decrease in hours

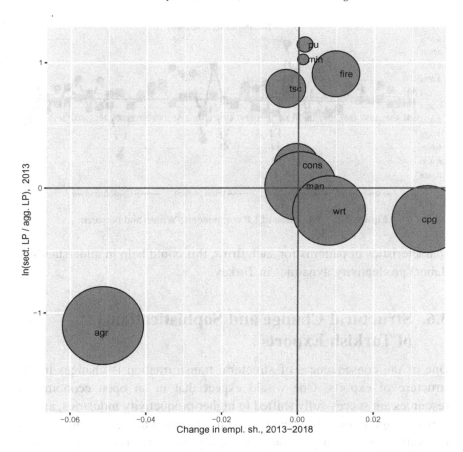

Figure 3.1. Sectoral productivity and changes in employment share: 2013–2018

Note: agr: agriculture; min: mining; pu: public utilities (electricity, water, and gas); man: manufacturing; cons: construction; wrt: wholesale and retail trade; fire: financial institutions, insurance and real estate; tsc: transport, storage and communications; cpg: community, social, personal, and government services.

worked and (partially) paid or unpaid temporary leaves during crisis. The claim is that when economic conditions are better hoarded, workers (that are supposed to be qualified and experienced) provide an extra effort to meet the hike in demand which increases labor (within) productivity. To get further insight into why the within component is so volatile in the Turkish economy, one needs to work with firm-level data and closely track firms with declining productivity. If we can find common

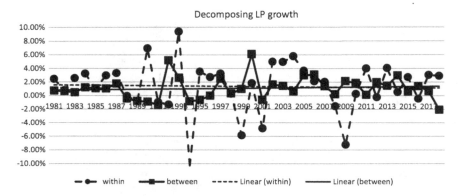

Figure 3.2.   Evolution of LP components: Within and between

characteristics or patterns for such firms, this could help in understanding (labor) productivity dynamics in Turkey.

3.6. Structural Change and Sophistication of Turkish Exports

One of the consequences of structural transformation is changes in the structure of exports. One would expect that in an open economy as resources are successfully shifted to higher productivity industries, and as firms engage in technological upgrading, research and development, and innovation, these changes would eventually enable firms to be competitive in international markets, and export more sophisticated products with higher technology content. In this section, we make a very brief assessment of changes in the structure of Turkish exports in the last two to three decades. We look at two indicators. The first is the share of goods with medium and high technology content in total manufactured exports. As shown in Figure 3.3, this share increased substantially from about 20% in mid-1990s to about 45% in 2007. This increase was mainly due to increases in the share of medium technology products, especially in the automotive industry and domestic appliances (Albaladejo, 2006). The share of medium- and high-technology products remained stagnant after 2007, vacillating between 40% and 45%. In other words, in the last decade Turkish exports did not register any improvements in terms of technology

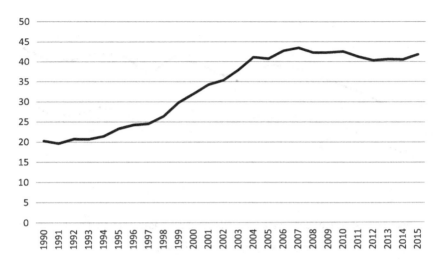

Figure 3.3. The share of medium- and high-tech exports in manufacturing exports (%)

Source: World Development Indicators.

content. One might add that the share of high-technology products in manufactured exports remained very low throughout the period, i.e., below 3%.

The second indicator reflects the "sophistication of exports", labelled as EXPY in the literature (Hausman *et al.*, 2007). Essentially, EXPY is a measure of the degree to which a country's export basket resembles those of rich countries. It is calculated in the following way: For each product (at the level of 6-digit Harmonized System), the weighted average of per capita incomes of countries that export that product is calculated. This is called PRODY. Then, EXPY of a country is calculated as the export-share-weighted sum of the PRDOYs of the products it exports. EXPY of Turkey is presented in Figure 3.4. Because the EXPY may be sensitive to the years for which PRODYs are calculated, two indicators have been calculated. For the first one, PRODYs are calculated as the average of 2002–2005 (beginning of period). For the second one, PRODYs are calculated as the average of 2010–2013. The figure shows the log of EXPY between 2002 and 2017. Even though the levels of the two indicators are different, their behavior over time is very similar. In both cases, EXPY increases relatively fast between 2002 and 2007, but slows down after

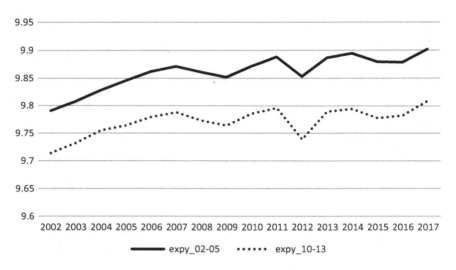

Figure 3.4. The sophistication of Turkish exports

Source: UN-Comtrade.

2007. For example, the difference in log EXPY (which approximates percentage growth) is about 7–8% between the years 2002 and 2007 but only 3–4% between 2008 and 2017.

These findings suggest a sharp contrast in the evolution of the sophistication of Turkish exports in the period 2002–2007 and 2008–2018. As emphasized earlier, and discussed in detail in Chapter 2, the period of 2002–2007 was a period of significant economic and political reforms, improvements in institutions, and high productivity growth. It seems these developments had a clear positive effect on the degree of sophistication of Turkish exports. Similarly, in the more recent period, the slowdown in economic reforms, the deterioration in both political and economic institutions, as well as the slowdown in TFP growth seems to be associated with a slowdown in the improvements of the sophistication of Turkish exports.

3.7. Conclusion

This chapter has presented the results of a growth accounting exercise both of the aggregate economy and in agriculture, industry, construction, and services. We find that while productivity growth has made a major contribution to economic growth, especially until the global recession thanks to institutional improvements, its contribution to growth has diminished substantially in the 2014–2018 period. Growth in the latter period has been driven primarily by factor accumulation, especially accumulation of capital. The slowdown in productivity gains constitutes certainly one of the main challenges that Turkish economy faces in the future.

On the other hand, this finding suggests that various programs initiated by the government to encourage the banking system to provide credit to the private sector, and the various subsidy mechanisms designed as instruments of industrial policy in order to get out of recession since 2018, have not been able, at least so far, to generate productivity increases. Our results show that these policies have most likely helped the continuation of economic growth by promoting capital investment. A corollary is that the efficiency of recent investment initiatives may be questionable.[6]

Growth accounting at the level of individual sectors reveals that TFP growth in construction has been high but also highly volatile, contracting much faster than that in industry during periods of economic slowdown and contraction. TFP growth in construction has been especially low in 2014–2018, but relative to previous periods and relative to industry. By contrast, the growth of the capital stock in construction has been much faster in construction relative to industry in this period.

Services are an important part of the Turkish economy, both in terms of share in GDP and employment. The aforementioned analysis suggests that productivity growth in services has remained poor throughout the period. This seems to present an important barrier to the growth of productivity in the future.

Our analysis of the role of reallocation of labor in aggregate LP growth suggests that the contribution of reallocation to aggregate productivity has also diminished in the 2014–2018 period. It seems that the main reason for this is that employment has increased, particularly in industries with lower-than-average productivity.

---

[6]The recent contraction in private investments and the parallel slowdown in economic growth may be signaling that this way of sustaining growth may have reached its limits. See Sönmez (2019) and Bakis and Mutluay (2019).

Overall, our analysis suggests that Turkey has missed an important opportunity to upgrade its productive capacity during the periods of high economic growth. In particular, after successfully moving from industries with relatively low technology into those with medium technology since the 1990s, transformation has not progressed any further. Interestingly, Turkey's experience especially in the earlier part of the 2000s suggests a blueprint about how to move ahead. However, the overall orientation of economic policy and performance in recent years does not provide much hope that such a blueprint will be followed.

Appendix

A3.1. *Robustness Checks for TFP Analysis*

Since there is no consensus on the method one needs to use to estimate initial capital stock, or sectoral depreciation rate, or factor shares, we want to test whether our results are sensitive to small changes in one or both of them.

Table 3.8 shows the sensitivity of aggregate and sectoral TFP growth rates to assumptions about capital share and depreciation rate. We compare our baseline specification (the first row in the table) with two others (second and third rows). It appears that capital share has more effect on results compared to depreciation rate. Since we are modifying these parameters for agriculture and construction, these two sectors are the only affected ones. When capital share goes from 0.55 to 0.33 for agriculture, the TFP growth increases considerably. For instance, in the 2014–2018 period, the average TFP growth goes from 2.2% to 3.4%. This is the highest change, but in all other periods we see positive effects. The intuition is that for a given GDP and capital growth, a lower capital elasticity makes room for a larger TFP contribution. When capital share goes from 0.21 to 0.33 for construction, the TFP growth reduces considerably. For instance, in the 2014–2018 period the average TFP growth goes from 0.5% to −0.3%. This is the highest change, but in all other periods we see a similar negative effect. Again, the intuition is that for a given GDP and capital growth, a higher capital elasticity makes room for a lower TFP contribution. The effect of the change in deprecation rate is relatively unimportant.

Table 3.8. Sensitivity of TFP growth to capital share and depreciation rate

diff alpha, diff depr

	AGR — Alpha = 0.55, Depr = 0.04				IND — Alpha = 0.33, Depr = 0.06				CON — Alpha = 0.21, Depr = 0.08				SER — Alpha = 0.33, Depr = 0.06			
	Y	K	L	A	Y	K	L	A	Y	K	L	A	Y	K	L	A
1981–1989	0.8	2.9	0.4	-0.9	6.9	2.5	2.4	4.5	6.6	4.7	0.5	5.2	3.9	6.0	3.7	-0.6
1990–2002	1.8	2.4	-1.1	1.0	3.5	2.6	2.5	0.9	1.3	4.7	0.1	0.2	3.5	8.6	3.4	-1.6
2003–2013	2.7	2.6	0.4	1.1	6.7	6.2	2.2	3.1	10.7	5.8	6.2	4.5	5.0	9.4	3.5	-0.4
2003–2007	1.2	2.6	-3.4	1.3	8.6	7.5	2.1	4.7	16.0	5.8	6.3	9.8	5.8	10.2	3.5	0.1
2008–2010	5.5	1.6	5.2	2.3	0.7	4.4	1.4	-1.7	-1.9	4.2	5.0	-6.7	1.6	8.3	2.1	-2.5
2011–2013	2.6	3.6	1.9	-0.2	9.3	5.7	3.2	5.3	14.4	7.3	7.3	7.1	7.2	9.2	5.0	0.8
2014–2018	2.6	2.7	-2.5	2.2	4.8	4.4	2.7	1.6	4.2	8.9	2.2	0.5	5.2	7.4	4.2	-0.1

same alpha, diff depr

	AGR — Alpha = 0.33, Depr = 0.04				IND — Alpha = 0.33, Depr = 0.06				CON — Alpha = 0.33, Depr = 0.08				SER — Alpha = 0.33, Depr = 0.06			
	Y	K	L	A	Y	K	L	A	Y	K	L	A	Y	K	L	A
1981–1989	0.8	3.0	0.4	-0.4	6.9	2.5	2.4	4.5	6.6	4.7	0.5	4.6	3.9	5.9	3.7	-0.6
1990–2002	1.8	2.4	-1.1	1.7	3.5	2.6	2.5	0.9	1.3	4.7	0.1	-0.4	3.5	8.5	3.4	-1.6
2003–2013	2.7	2.6	0.4	1.6	6.7	6.2	2.2	3.1	10.7	5.8	6.2	4.6	5.0	9.4	3.5	-0.4
2003–2007	1.2	2.7	-3.4	2.6	8.6	7.5	2.1	4.7	16.0	5.8	6.3	9.9	5.8	10.1	3.5	0.1
2008–2010	5.5	1.6	5.2	1.5	0.7	4.4	1.4	-1.7	-1.9	4.2	5.0	-6.6	1.6	8.3	2.1	-2.5
2011–2013	2.6	3.6	1.9	0.1	9.3	5.7	3.2	5.3	14.4	7.3	7.3	7.1	7.2	9.2	5.0	0.8
2014–2018	2.6	2.7	-2.5	3.4	4.8	4.4	2.7	1.6	4.2	8.9	2.2	-0.3	5.2	7.4	4.2	-0.1

(Continued)

Table 3.8. (*Continued*)

AGR	Alpha = 0.33		Depr = 0.06	
	Y	K	L	A
1981–1989	0.8	2.7	0.4	−0.3
1990–2002	1.8	2.2	−1.1	1.8
2003–2013	2.7	2.6	0.4	1.6
2003–2007	1.2	2.7	−3.4	2.5
2008–2010	5.5	1.3	5.2	1.6
2011–2013	2.6	3.9	1.9	0.0
2014–2018	2.6	2.8	−2.5	3.4

IND	Alpha = 0.33		Depr = 0.06	
	Y	K	L	A
1981–1989	6.9	2.5	2.4	4.5
1990–2002	3.5	2.6	2.5	0.9
2003–2013	6.7	6.2	2.2	3.1
2003–2007	8.6	7.5	2.1	4.7
2008–2010	0.7	4.4	1.4	−1.7
2011–2013	9.3	5.7	3.2	5.3
2014–2018	4.8	4.4	2.7	1.6

CON	Alpha = 0.33		Depr = 0.06	
	Y	K	L	A
1981–1989	6.6	4.8	0.5	4.6
1990–2002	1.3	4.9	0.1	−0.4
2003–2013	10.7	5.6	6.2	4.7
2003–2007	16.0	5.5	6.3	10.0
2008–2010	−1.9	4.3	5.0	−6.7
2011–2013	14.4	6.9	7.3	7.2
2014–2018	4.2	8.6	2.2	−0.2

SER	Alpha = 0.33		Depr = 0.06	
	Y	K	L	A
1981–1989	3.9	5.9	3.7	−0.6
1990–2002	3.5	8.5	3.4	−1.6
2003–2013	5.0	9.4	3.5	−0.4
2003–2007	5.8	10.1	3.5	0.1
2008–2010	1.6	8.3	2.1	−2.5
2011–2013	7.2	9.2	5.0	0.8
2014–2018	5.2	7.4	4.2	−0.1

same alpha, same depr

Table 3.9 shows different approaches for estimating capital stock and the resulting aggregate and sectoral TFP growth rates. As we see in this table, despite some minor differences, they do not change the story of productivity for Turkish economy. Our preferred approach ("aggregate ss") consists of estimating initial capital by combining the assumption of steady state and perpetual inventory equation. Then, to find how much of the K is distributed among different sectors, we follow Caselli (2005) and use non-arbitrage condition between sectors. A second alternative would be applying the steady state assumption of steady state and perpetual inventory equation at sectoral level as each sector is a separate economy. A third one is assuming $K_0 = kY_0$, where k is constant. Feenstra *et al.* (2015) compare this approach to the steady state one and claim this as the superior one: "we argue that this method actually leads to superior results, in particular in early years of the sample and in transition economies, where the data are available for a limited period of time and where the early years were particularly turbulent (p. 12 in Online Appendix)". This approach goes back to Harrod–Domar growth model where the GDP is proportional to capital stock. In economic planning literature, k is called incremental capital output ratio (ICOR), and has been frequently used in the 1960s and 1970s (see for instance Sato, 1971). Using the law of motion for capital, we can rewrite the ICOR equation as follows:

$$k = \frac{\Delta K}{\Delta Y} = \frac{I - \delta K}{\Delta Y}$$

So, the ratio of net investment to change GDP is constant, since the aforementioned function depends on capital and the knowledge of depreciation rate it is not easy to apply. Instead of using the aforementioned function, we followed a report made by the Government of India (GoI, 2012), and we computed the ratio of gross investment to GDP change ($I/\Delta Y$) for Turkish economy for the period 1949–1979, and took the median value as ICOR. Once we know k, it is easy to calculate the initial capital stock. First, we compute initial capital stock for 1948 (ICOR-1948). This is acceptable for aggregate economy. But, since data reliability has been of concern for years for sectoral investment data before 1980, we compute initial capital stock in 1980 and check whether there are significant changes

Table 3.9.　The effect of different approaches to estimate initial capital stock

Aggregate ss	g	g_agr	g_ind	g_con	g_ser
1981–1989	2.7	-0.9	4.5	5.2	-0.6
1990–2002	1.0	1.0	0.9	0.2	-1.6
2003–2013	1.9	1.1	3.1	4.5	-0.4
2003–2007	4.0	1.3	4.7	9.8	0.1
2008–2010	-2.7	2.3	-1.7	-6.7	-2.5
2011–2013	2.9	-0.2	5.3	7.1	0.8
2014–2018	0.8	2.2	1.6	0.5	-0.1

Sectoral ss	g	g_agr	g_ind	g_con	g_ser
1981–1989	2.7	-1.3	4.3	5.3	-0.5
1990–2002	1.0	0.8	1.0	0.0	-1.5
2003–2013	1.9	1.2	3.2	4.7	-0.3
2003–2007	4.0	1.5	5.1	10.2	0.2
2008–2010	-2.7	2.1	-2.1	-7.2	-2.5
2011–2013	2.9	0.0	5.3	7.5	0.9
2014–2018	0.8	2.2	1.6	0.4	-0.4

ICOR–1948	g	g_agr	g_ind	g_con	g_ser
1981–1989	2.7	-1.1	4.5	5.2	-0.5
1990–2002	1.0	0.9	0.9	0.2	-1.6
2003–2013	1.9	1.1	3.1	4.5	-0.4
2003–2007	4.0	1.2	4.7	9.8	0.1
2008–2010	-2.7	2.2	-1.7	-6.7	-2.5
2011–2013	2.9	-0.3	5.3	7.1	0.8
2014–2018	0.8	2.2	1.6	0.5	-0.1

ICOR–1980	g	g_agr	g_ind	g_con	g_ser
1981–1989	3.4	-3.7	4.7	5.1	0.7
1990–2002	1.3	0.1	1.0	0.2	-1.1
2003–2013	2.0	0.8	3.2	4.5	-0.4
2003–2007	4.1	0.8	4.8	9.8	0.2
2008–2010	-2.6	2.0	-1.7	-6.7	-2.5
2011–2013	3.0	-0.5	5.3	7.1	0.8
2014–2018	0.9	2.0	1.6	0.5	-0.1

in TFP growth (ICOR-1980). As can be seen from Table 3.9, despite some minor differences, all approaches yield similar results. The only visible differences are when we compute initial capital in 1980 using ICOR approach. While the level of capital stock generated in the three first approaches is very close to each other in 1980, the fourth approach (ICOR-1980) generates relatively a higher stock of capital, except agriculture. As a result, given investment series, the growth rate of capital stays relatively low. Accordingly, given GDP and employment growth numbers, this increases the growth rate of TFP, except agriculture. These differences tend to vanish as time passes, naturally, as the effect of initial capital weakens over time. This is why we prefer to estimate initial capital as early as possible so that any error in measurement is largely compensated by exponential decay.

References

Acemoglu, D. and Üçer, M. (2015). "The Ups and Downs of Turkish Growth, 2002–2015: Political Dynamics, the European Union and the Institutional Slide", NBER Working Paper No. 21608.

Albaladejo, M. (2006). "The Manufacturing Sector in Turkey: Challenges for Structural Change and Convergence", Prepared for Europe and Central Asia (ECA) Region Department of the World Bank's background paper to Turkey's Investment Climate Assessment (ICA).

Atiyas, I. and Bakis, O. (2014). "Aggregate and Sectoral TFP Growth in Turkey: A Growth-Accounting Exercise", *İktisat İşletme ve Finans*, Vol. 29, pp. 9–36.

Atiyas, I. and Bakis, O. (2015). "Structural Change and Industrial Policy in Turkey", *Emerging Markets Finance and Trade*, Vol. 51, No. 6, pp. 1209–1229.

Bakis, O. and Acar, U. (2020). "Türkiye Ekonomisinde Toplam Faktör Verimliliğinin Seyri: Sektörel Bakış, 1980–2018", Betam Workşng Paper Series No: 19.

Bakis, O. and Mutluay, H. (2019). "Growth Evaluation: 2019 2nd Quarter", BETAM.

Buğra, A. and Savaşkan, O. (2014). *New Capitalism in Turkey: The Relationship Between Politics, Religion and Business*, Edward Elgar.

Caselli, F. (2005). "Accounting for Cross-Country Income Differences", in P. Aghion and S. Durlauf (eds.), *Handbook of Economic Growth*, Elsevier.

Foerster, A., Hornstein, A., Sarte, P.-D. and Watson, W. (2019). "Aggregate Implications of Changing Sectoral Trends", FRB San Francisco Working Paper 2019-16.

Feenstra, R. C., Inklaar, R. and Timmer, M. P. (2015). "The Next Generation of the Penn World Table", *American Economic Review*, Vol. 105, pp. 3150–3182.

GoI (2012). "Report of the Working-Group on Estimation of Investment, Its Composition and Trend for Twelfth Five-Year Plan (2012-13 to 2016-17)", Perspective Planning Division, Government of India, New Delhi.

Gürakar, E. (2016). *Politics of Favoritism in Public Procurement in Turkey: Reconfigurations of Dependency Networks in the Ak Party Era*, Palgrave.

Hausman, R., Hwang, J. and Rodrik, D. (2007). "What You Export Matters", *Journal of Economic Growth*, Vol. 12, No. 1, pp. 1–25.

Hulten, C. R. and Wykoff, F. C. (1981): "The Measurement of Economic Depreciation" in C. R. Hulten (ed.), *Depreciation, Inflation, and Taxation of Income from Capital*, Urban Institute Press.

Jorgenson, D. W. (1996). "Empirical Studies of Depreciation", *Economic Inquiry*, Vol. 34, No. 1, pp. 24–42.

Jorgenson, D. W. and Timmer, M. P. (2011). "Structural Change in Advanced Nations: A New Set of Stylised Facts", *Scandinavian Journal of Economics*, Vol. 113, No. 1, pp. 1–29.

Kets, W. and Lejour, A. (2003). Sectoral TFP Developments in the OECD, CPB Memorandum (Dutch Centre for Economic Policy Analysis, The Hague).

McMillan, M., Rodrik, D. and Verduzco-Gallo, I. (2014). "Globalization, Structural Change, and Productivity Growth, with an Update on Africa", *World Development*, Vol. 63, pp. 11–32.

Rodrik, D. (2010). *Structural Transformation and Economic Development*, TEPAV.

Sato, K. (1971). "International Variations in the Incremental Capital-Output Ratio", *Economic Development and Cultural Change*, Vol. 19, No. 4, pp. 621–640.

Sönmez, M. (2019). "Yatırımlar Cakıldı, Krediler Sorunlu" Bülten Eylül 2019 Eki, TMMOB Makine Mühendislei Odası.

Solow, R. M. (1957). "Technical Change and the Aggregate Production Function", *Review of Economics and Statistics*, Vol. 39, pp. 312–320.

TurkStat (2007). Statistical Indicators 1923–2006 (Publication No: 3114).

Valentinyi A. and Herrendorf B. (2008) "Measuring Factor Income Shares at the Sector Level", *Review of Economic Dynamics*, Vol. 11, No. 4, pp. 820–835.

Chapter 4

Financial Cycles of the Turkish Economy: How Will It End This Time?*

M. Ege Yazgan

4.1. Introduction

The main purpose of this study is to provide predictions on the future course of the Turkish economy based on an analysis of financial cycles. This chapter focuses on financial cycles rather than business cycles. Whereas the latter are typically measured using output data, the former are measured using a number of alternatives related to credit, asset, and equity prices. A large number of research into business cycles has already been performed; however, financial cycles have recently been gaining increasing academic attention.

Financial cycles can last much longer than business cycles. Whereas business cycles, as traditionally measured, tend to last for up to eight years, financial cycles are typically found to last around 15–20 years, and appear to have grown in amplitude over the past ~40 years (Borio *et al.*, 2018). The difference in length between the two types of cycles implies

---

*I am grateful to the editors of this volume, Asaf Savaş Akat and Seyfettin Gürsel, for their useful comments and suggestions that have helped in improving the content of the chapter. The usual caveat applies.

that a financial cycle can span more than one business cycle. As a result, although financial cycle peaks tend to precede recessions, not all recessions are preceded by financial cycle peaks. It has also been found that deep financial imbalances cause recessions to be longer and deeper (Claessens *et al.*, 2011, 2012; Jorda *et al.*, 2011). Jorda *et al.* (2011) found that recessions associated with financial crises lead to deeper slumps and sharper turnarounds than normal recessions.

Financial cycles are found to be so different to business cycles that many researchers (e.g., Runstler, 2016) claim that a separate macroprudential stabilization policy from classical monetary and fiscal policy is justified. Some research has found credit growth to be the single best predictor of financial instability (Jorda *et al.*, 2011; Schularick and Taylor, 2012).

The idea that the financial system is able by itself to generate boom and bust cycles by means of endogenous credit bubbles goes back to the work of Minsky (1977).[1] The credit-based perspective on long-run economic fluctuations has gained importance in recent years, particularly following the global financial crisis of 2008, and financial crises have come to be seen as "credit booms gone wrong" (Schularick and Taylor, 2012).

The present study follows this tradition and asserts that financial cycles are important variables in assessing economic conditions and in forecasting the future course of the economy. This chapter first attempts to identify the past financial cycles of the Turkish economy, then based on an economic analysis of these cycles, past recessions, and some additional data, observations are presented and predictions for the future course of the economy are made.

The analysis presented in this chapter indicates that the Turkish economy has completed one lengthy financial cycle. However, the recession that Turkey is currently going through has not proven to be deeper than the country's past recessions. On the contrary, it has been milder than previous recessions, as the latest GDP growth data indicate, and seems very unlikely to go on longer than the normal length of past recessions. Neither has it

---

[1] See Schularick and Taylor (2012) for a historical account of the credit view argument.

led to deeper slumps or stronger turnarounds than experienced during normal recessions, as documented by Jorda *et al.* (2011). So what is happening? Is Turkey experiencing an unusual end to the financial cycle or is the country not yet at the end of the current cycle? When the recession ends, will a quick recovery follow, despite corrections in financial cycle variables (i.e., credit, debt, etc.)?

This chapter argues that a quick recovery is unlikely. The analysis presented below suggests that a long period of slow growth is awaiting. One way of minimizing the output cost of this predicted low growth period appears to be boosting net exports and increasing foreign demand to boost growth, as this has already been helpful in reducing the output cost thus far. This chapter also draws attention to the conditions that led to Turkey's successful recovery after the 2001 crisis, and compares them with current conditions in order to provide some useful recommendations for how the recovery can be assisted. Finally, we answer affirmatively the question of whether Turkish economy is at a crossroads, in the sense that Turkey will now either enter a period of slow growth until the deleveraging process is completed, or change its growth model from internal demand oriented to foreign demand oriented.

4.2. Identifying "Financial Cycles" of the Turkish Economy

Much less research has been performed into financial cycles than business cycles, and hence no consensus has been reached on the variables and patterns of their changes that characterize financial cycles. As stated by Drehmann *et al.* (2012), there is some ambiguity in which variables may be relevant. The obvious choices are credit and asset prices, but studies differ in which other variables are asserted to be pertinent. Borio *et al.* (2018) measure financial cycles using a composite index incorporating real credit, credit-to-GDP ratio, and real house prices. Drehmann *et al.* (2012) use five variables claimed to characterize financial cycles, including real equity prices and an index of aggregate asset prices, which combines residential property, commercial property, and equity prices in addition to those named earlier. In Kutuk *et al.*'s (2017) study of Turkish financial cycles, the authors use real equity prices (based on the Borsa Istanbul 100 Index) and real effective exchange rates in addition to real credit and credit to GDP ratio.

Like the aforementioned papers, the present study not only measures financial cycles using real credit and credit-to-GDP ratio but also adds a new variable: foreign debt-to-GDP ratio. Although the literature acknowledges that credit has the main role in financial crises, foreign debt is also recognized to be relevant (Reinhardt and Rogoff, 2011). Jorda *et al.* (2011) point out that external imbalances have also played a role, but more so in the pre-WWII era of low financialization than today. In the Turkish economy, external constraints are still binding and therefore constitute an important variable (Akat and Yazgan, 2012). I exclude stock prices because of the sample's small size and volatile nature. The literature also considers real property prices to be an important variable in measuring financial cycles. In the case of Turkey, real house price data are only available for recent periods; nevertheless, more than a decade of data are available and so this study's analysis also incorporates real housing prices.

This study considers foreign debt instead of total debt (the total of foreign and domestic debt) to be the most relevant debt variable. Domestic debt is captured, to some extent, by the credit variables used in the study's model. Detailed total debt variables (denominated in both foreign and domestic currencies), disaggregated into different sectors such as households, financial and non-financial corporations, and government bodies, are also available (with some limitations), and so are utilized in the analysis. On the other hand, foreign debt is believed to capture external constraints and debt represents the largest part of Turkey's total foreign liabilities. Its decomposition, between private and government debt, has important implications and will also be referred to where appropriate.

Figure 4.1 plots the quarterly debt- and credit-to-GDP ratios between 1989Q4 and 2019Q2 and year over year real GDP growth rates. Real credit (deflated by the Consumer Price Index) is not included in Figure 4.1 because it closely follows the credit-to-GDP ratio and shows identical characteristics. Gross foreign debt is used to calculate the debt-to-GDP

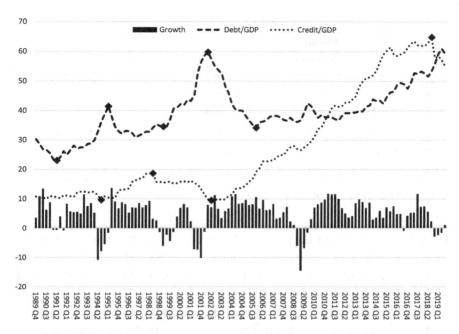

Figure 4.1. Debt- and credit-to-GDP ratios

Note: Ratios and growth rates are measured as year over year (YoY) figures.

ratio.[2] Non-financial private sector credit (households and corporations) issued by banks is used to calculate the credit-to-GDP ratio.[3]

We observe that including the recent recession, there have been five episodes of recession during the period sampled. These episodes are shown as negative blocks in the (year over year) growth rate data in

---

[2] All raw data are obtained from Turkey Data Monitor (TDM, www.tdm.com), unless stated otherwise. Where required, all further calculations are performed by the author.

[3] Other possible methods of calculation of the credit variable include credit issued to the non-financial private sector by all categories of lender (not only banks), credit issued to households from all categories of lender, and credit issued to non-financial corporations (excluding households) from all categories of lender. These data, and the credit variable data used in this study (i.e., credit to non-financial private sector from banks), are available from Bank of International Settlements (BIS) database. The credit variable data used in this study are deemed to be reliable because the BIS and local sources produce similar values; hence, this variable is preferred to others. However, the other credit variables are also utilized later in this chapter.

Table 4.1. Recessions

Period	Time since Previous Recession	Duration	Depth
1994Q2–1995Q1	—	4 Quarters	$-6.37 \times 4 = -25.5$
1998Q4–1999Q4	16Q	5 Quarters	$-3.0 \times 5 = -15$
2001Q2–2002Q1	5Q	4 Quarters	$-6.4 \times 4 = -25.7$
2008Q4–2009Q3	36Q	4 Quarters	$-7.1 \times 4 = -28.5$
2018Q4–?	37Q	3+ Quarters (ongoing)	$-2.2 \times 3 = -6.6$ (ongoing)

Note: Growth rates refer to year over year (YoY) growth rates.

Figure 4.1. The exact dates are indicated in Table 4.1. There are three recessions with a duration of four quarters and one with a duration of five quarters; the most recent recession is ongoing at the time of writing, and therefore its total duration is not known.

One of the purposes of this chapter is to form a prediction of the duration and depth of this recession. The output costs of recessions, labeled as "depth" in Table 4.1, is calculated as the (year over year) average growth rate of the recession (a negative value) multiplied by its length. The length of the gap between the 1998Q4–1999Q4 and 2001Q2–2002Q1 recessions is only five quarters. This unusually small duration between the two recessions and the relatively small cost of the first of the two leads us to take the view that the two periods constitute a single larger and bigger recession. By summing the depth and duration of these consecutive contractions we can identify a recession with a duration of nine quarters and a depth of 40.7, which is the largest ever recorded for Turkey. The two periods can therefore be treated as a single recession.

Figure 4.1 shows the peaks and troughs of credit and debt cycles identified using Harding and Pagan's (2002) algorithm. In applying this algorithm, one must specify the time duration and amplitude (or phase) boundaries to be used by the algorithm to distinguish short-term fluctuations from long-term cycles. Tables 4.2 and 4.3 provide more details about these cycles, including their phases of contraction and expansion, together with their starting and ending levels, durations, and amplitudes. Amplitudes are defined as changes from trough to peak (expansion) or peak to trough

Table 4.2. Credit cycles

Period	Nature	Duration	Starting Level (%)	Ending Level (%)	Amplitude (%)
–1994Q3	Deleveraging	—	—	10	—
1994Q3–1998Q2	Leveraging	15 Quarters	10	19	9.0
1998Q2–2002Q3	Deleveraging	17 Quarters	19	9	9.2
2002Q3–2018Q3	Leveraging	64 Quarters	9	65	55.7
2018Q3–?	Deleveraging	4+ Quarters (ongoing)	65	—	—

Table 4.3. Debt cycles

Period	Nature	Duration	Starting Level (%)	Ending Level (%)	Amplitude (%)
–1991Q2	Deleveraging	—	—	23	—
1991Q2–1995Q1	Leveraging	15 Quarters	23	41	18.4
1995Q1–1999Q1	Deleveraging	16 Quarters	41	35	6.8
1999Q1–2002Q2	Leveraging	13 Quarters	35	60	25.2
2002Q2–2005Q4	Deleveraging	14 Quarters	60	34	25.6
2005Q4–?	Leveraging	55+ Quarters (ongoing)	34	—	—

(contraction). In the following discussion, the term of cycle is used interchangeably for expansion and contraction phases, but not for the "complete" cycle, which can be measured either from peak to peak or trough from trough.

a. *Credit Cycles*

Table 4.2 describes Turkey's credit cycles. The most noticeable observation from Table 4.2 is the presence of a very long expansionary credit cycle (period of leveraging) starting shortly after the end of the 1998Q4–2002Q1 recession. This cycle ends in 2018Q3 and lasts 64 quarters (i.e., 16 years). It seems likely that this is the longest duration for any cycle (business or financial) in the economic history of Turkey. Although we do not undertake the task of identification of business cycles within our data,[4] we can easily observe the limit for an expansionary business cycle in the period of our sample is of 37 quarters (9.2 years), because this is the longest duration between the two recessions, as indicated in the second column of Table 4.1. Moreover, even a visual review of GDP figures easily confirms that such periods should be of shorter length. These findings are in line with those of other studies, which find that business cycles are considerably shorter, ranging from two to eight years, whereas financial cycles range from eight to 20 years and typically contain a number of business cycles, and hence at least one period of recession (see Drehmann, 2012; Borio, 2018). In Turkey's case, the financial cycle identified earlier (based on credit-to-GDP ratio) incorporates the 2008Q4–2009Q3 recession and appears to end in 2018Q3.

Although Harding and Pagan's algorithm indicates 2018Q3 to be the end of the previous leveraging phase, given the available data it is still possible that, as in 2009Q1 and 2016Q1, the decline in 2018Q3 may constitute only a correction and not the end of the cycle. If so, the credit-to-GDP ratio should rapidly return to its level prior to the recession. In this scenario, the recession starting in 2018Q4 would not constitute the end of this cycle; instead, credit would start to grow again and GDP growth would resume quickly and accelerate. In the alternative scenario, if 2018Q3 is the end of the cycle, the correction will take longer and even if the recession ends in its typical timeframe (four quarters),[5] the subsequent growth will remain weaker than in the first scenario. In the following section, we discuss these possibilities in further detail.

b. *Debt Cycles*

Turning attention to foreign resource constraints, Table 4.3 illustrates the properties of recent debt cycles. Unlike the single long credit cycle observed after the 1998Q4–2002Q1 recession, Harding and Pagan's

---

[4] For an analysis of synchronization of business and financial cycles in Turkey see Akar (2016).

[5] The depth of the current recession appears to be milder than previous recessions. According to the figures in Table 4.1, the average depth of a four-quarter recession can be estimated to be around 25 cumulative percentage points.

algorithm shows two distinct debt cycles taking place after 2002. The more recent and longer expansionary cycle which starts in 2005Q4, has not yet terminated. At the time of writing, the current duration of this cycle is 55 quarters (13.75 years). Although the debt-to-GDP ratio has not started to decline following the ongoing recession, it is very likely that Turkey is close to the end of this cycle because private-sector companies have already given some indications of deleveraging.[6] A sharply increasing debt-to-GDP ratio is also typical of other recessions such as 2001, especially when recessions are associated with sharp currency devaluations (or depreciations) as also seen in the most recent period. This phenomenon magnifies the contraction in GDP, as denominated in foreign-currency, caused by recessions; hence, the debt-to-GDP ratio continues to rise during recessions.[7]

The first of the two debt cycles after the 1998Q4–2002Q1 recession starts in 2002Q2 and ends in 2005Q2. This corresponds to a relatively short deleveraging period (14 quarters or 3.5 years), during which time the debt level shrank from 59.8% of GDP in 2002Q2 to 34.2% of GDP in 2005Q4. Similar to the credit cycle, the last debt cycle overlaps with the 2008Q4–2009Q3 recession, which indicates that the recession has caused a correction in both ratios and has not affected the overall cycles. The recession affects the two ratios in opposite directions, and the "cyclical" effect of the recession is more apparent in the debt cycle than the credit cycle; whereas the debt-to-GDP ratio shows sharper increases, the credit-to-GDP ratio declines gently. This more pronounced behavior of the foreign debt ratio, in general, can be attributed to the effect of depreciations in the value of the Turkish Lira that are associated with recessions. Although almost all foreign debt is denominated in foreign currency,

---

[6] Foreign Exchange Assets and Liabilities of Non-Financial Companies figures published by the Central Bank of the Republic of Turkey (CBRT) indicate that deleveraging of non-financial private corporations have already started. These figures move from −222 billion United States net foreign exchange position in January 2018 to a net position of −184 billion by July 2019. Net foreign exchange position is calculated by taking difference between total foreign exchange assets and liabilities of non-financial companies.

[7] On the other hand, if we consider instances of sharp depreciation to be the result of overvaluation of the Turkish Lira, the sharp reduction in the debt-to-GDP ratio during the period 2002Q2–2005Q4 can be partly explained by the appreciation of the Turkish Lira.

credit balances are generally denominated in local currency. Hence, unlike debt-to-GDP ratio, credit-to-GDP ratios should be expected to decrease during recessions. The discrepancy in the behavior of two ratios can be aggravated depending on the extent of depreciations.

c. *Real-Estate Cycles*

In this subsection, we focus on real-estate prices. The longest available data set on Turkish real-estate prices is the Real Estate Investment & Development Information Network (REIDIN) Residential Property Price Index (RPPI) housing price index. The index is a composite index of house prices for seven of the largest cities in Turkey. Data are available from June 2007. To obtain real house prices we deflate house price index figures using the consumer price index.[8] Figure 4.2 illustrates the real house price data.

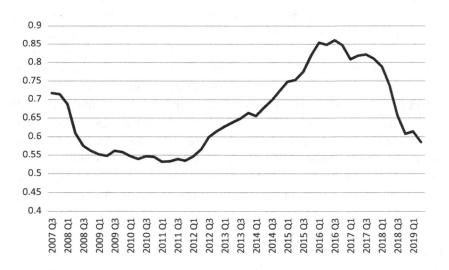

Figure 4.2.   Real house prices

---

[8] Data are available on monthly basis; for consistency with the other data in this study, these data are converted into quarterly averages. We note that a cycle analysis performed using monthly figures yields identical results.

Table 4.4. Real house price cycles

Period	Nature	Duration	Starting Level	Ending Level	Amplitude
–2011Q1	Deleveraging	—	—	0.53	—
2011Q1–2016Q3	Leveraging	22 Quarters	0.53	0.86	0.33
2016Q3– ?	Deleveraging	12+ Quarters (ongoing)	0.86	—	—

Harding and Pagan's algorithm identifies the real house prices cycles as illustrated in Table 4.4. Similar to credit and debt cycles, available data do not support the expectation that the 2008Q4–2009Q3 recession altered the course of real house price cycles. The decline in the real house price index started before the crisis in the fourth quarter of 2007. The index stagnated during and after the crisis until it began to increase in the first quarter of 2011. It could be argued that the drop in real house prices in 2007Q4 may have been corrected earlier in the absence of the crisis. Unfortunately the absence of data before 2007Q3 prevents us examining economic trends over a longer period of time in order to explore this issue further. However, it seems plausible that although the crisis may have suppressed an earlier correction in the house prices, the expansionary period in the housing cycle can be attributed to the high levels of global liquidity and associated expansion in domestic credit in the period after the crisis. The housing cycle starts later, ends earlier, and remains weaker than the credit cycle. This result is expected, because whereas our credit variable is based on credit to non-financial private corporations, property prices are affected by credit to the household sector. Data on household debt and credit are sufficient only to derive limited conclusions, but as discussed in the following sections, they indicate that household deleveraging started at the same time as the end of the real house price cycle, although credit to households started to contract earlier.

4.3. Expansionary Deleveraging, De-dollarization, and Credibility: 2002Q2–2005Q2

The previous analysis of financial cycles has revealed two distinctive behaviors in terms of debt and credit cycles in the period after the

1998Q4–2002Q1 recession; we observe a single long expansionary credit cycle, and one contractionary and one expansionary debt cycle occur in this period. The contractionary debt cycle, 12 quarters long, running from 2002Q2 to 2005Q2, corresponds to the period of the stabilization program that followed the recession. In terms of behavior of macroeconomic variables, this period is an interesting one and deserves closer focus.

In terms of debt-to-GDP ratio, the stabilization program that followed the 2001 crisis brought about a fast and sizable deleveraging, especially in the public sector. During the cycle of 2002Q2–2005Q2, while the debt-to-GDP ratio was rapidly decreasing, the proportion of total foreign debt represented by public debt reduced from 67% to 55%.[9] During this time the public debt-to-GDP ratio shrank from 39.2 to 20.1 (a relative change of 49%), and the private debt-to-GDP ratio declined more gently, from 20.6 to 16.5 (a relative change of 20%). Therefore, the private sector deleveraged less than the public sector in terms of foreign debt.

Considering the expansionary behavior of the credit-to-GDP variable (which increased from 9.9 to 15.8) during this debt cycle, we can state that the greatest share of the burden of deleveraging fell on the public sector, rather than the private sector. It should also be noted that this period was accompanied by an appreciation in the value of the Turkish Lira, and real appreciation increased by 35% from its value in January 2003, which contributed to the reduction of the foreign debt-to-GDP ratio.

Interestingly, during this cycle of debt deleveraging, annual growth averaged 7.7%, which marked one of the most rapid growth periods in Turkey's economic history. Moreover, this rapid growth was mainly driven by rapid increases in total factor productivity (Atiyas and Bakis, 2014; Atiyas and Bakış, Chapter 3 in this volume; Acemoğlu and Ucer, Chapter 2 in this volume). The period also witnessed a structural change, i.e., reallocation of labor from low productivity agriculture to higher productivity services and industry, which contributed this rapid increase in productivity (Rodrik, 2010; Atiyas and Bakis, 2014, 2015; Günçavdı and Bayar, Chapter 5 in this volume).

---

[9]The proportion attributable to public debt continuously declined until the third quarter of 2016, at which time it stabilized at around 30%, and has recently risen to 32%.

This expansionary deleveraging debt cycle also corresponds to Turkey's most successful period of disinflation; inflation fell to 7.7% in 2005 from its level of around 68% in 2001. The appreciation of the Turkish Lira in this period also played a major role in the process of disinflation (see Benlialper and Comert, 2015).[10] Despite real appreciation, this period witnessed intensification of the industrialization process, in parallel to the structural change mentioned previously. The share of total employment represented by the manufacturing sector, one of the measures of industrialization, recorded significant increases during this period (see Günçavdı and Bayar, Chapter 5 in this volume). On the other hand, real appreciation did not prevent the surge in exports neither in quantity nor in quality. Turkey's merchandise exports and its share in world exports increased rapidly in this period with significant ameliorations in their technology contents (Acemoğlu and Ucer, Chapter 2 in this volume).

What could be behind this extraordinary performance? Acemoglu and Ucer (2015; Chapter 2 in this volume) suggested it was due to the role of institutional reforms implemented during this period. In fact, this period was characterized by significant improvements in both political and economic institutions (Acemoglu and Ucer, 2015; Chapter 2 in this volume). Here, I would like to mention the role of the rapid de-dollarization as one of the key factors that made this astonishing outcome possible. Dollarization, measured by the share of total deposits represented by foreign currency deposit, reduced from 55% in 2002 to 34% in 2005.[11] De-dollarization, on the other hand, was a consequence of successful disinflation and increased

---

[10] Benlialper and Comert (2015), in their study focusing on the period between 2002 and 2008, indicated that appreciation of the Turkish Lira was tolerated during this period, whereas depreciation was responded to aggressively by Turkey's central bank. It is well known that due to Turkish production's dependence on imported inputs, exchange rate depreciation becomes inflationary via a pass-through mechanism. Moreover, because currency depreciation erodes confidence, worsening inflation expectations, and has the potential to leading to a depreciation–inflation spiral, the central bank acting in favor of appreciation of the Turkish Lira is an expected result. We comment further on this issue later in this chapter.

[11] This ratio continued to decrease until the beginning of 2013, at which time it stood at 28%. It then started to increase again, and has recently nearly attained the levels it reached at around the time of the 2001 crisis.

confidence in the Turkish Lira that disinflation created. The issue underpinning all of these was the credibility of the 2001 stabilization program. The effect of its credibility and the associated confidence in the Turkish Lira made real appreciation of the Lira possible, which in turn, contributed a favorable environment for foreign debt servicing together and strong GDP growth. This period demonstrates how a credible disinflation program backed by institutional reforms (Acemoglu and Ucer, 2015; Chapter 2 in this volume) can create rapid growth and deleveraging at the same time.

4.4. Credit Driven Growth, Recession, and the Surge of Inflation

Having analyzed a successful deleveraging period, I now examine the period after 2006. This period corresponds to the long credit and debt cycles documented earlier, and hence to periods of leveraging in both credit and debt. In this section, I provide an overview of some macroeconomic developments that have occurred during these long expansionary cycles.

As mentioned earlier, both of these cycles overlap the 2008 global financial crisis. Although the output cost of the recession following this crisis, i.e., 2008Q4–2009Q3 recession (see Table 4.1), was the largest of the recent recessions, its effect on the financial ratios considered here remained limited. In other words, the recession did not cause an interruption in the expansionary debt and credit cycles. The two ratios continued to increase after some minor corrections, especially in the case of the credit-to-GDP ratio. The recession did not affect the upward trend of the credit cycle; the trend becomes even stronger after a small drop in the ratio during the recession. Due to this increasing trend, first in credit ratio and later also in debt ratio, a quick recovery followed the recession and growth accelerated rapidly (see Figure 4.1). This quick recovery and the record high growth rates achieved during 2010 and 2011 that followed the recovery were related to the large increase in credit.

The credit expansion was, in turn, related to the surge of capital flows into emerging markets, followed by massive expansionary monetary policies in developed economies (quantitative easing, etc.). Baskaya *et al.* (2017) and Giovanni *et al.* (2017) show how capital inflows to Turkey lowered real borrowing costs and fueled credit expansion after the 2008 global financial crisis (see also Günçavdı and Bayar, Chapter 5 in this volume). In this time, the economy experienced record high current account deficits and the described surge in foreign debt.

Even though the rate of growth started to decline in the third quarter of 2012, this credit fueled growth continued until 2018Q3 (despite some fluctuations).[12] At this point it is worthwhile to mention a change in Turkey's economic policy that was designed as a response to accelerating credit growth and sharp widening of the current account deficit in the years 2010 and 2011. To react to these developments the Central Bank of Turkey and the economy administration focused on policies to neutralize the effects of the surge in capital flows, seeking to contain increases in credit and to cool down the overheated economy. The main aim was to increase the resilience of the economy to adverse external financial shocks and to prevent boom-bust cycles amplified by so called sudden stops (sudden reductions in net capital flows).

The monetary policy was gradually redesigned and a macropruden-tial policy approach became dominant concentrating on financial stabil-ity and limiting excessive credit growth (Kara, 2012, 2016a, 2016b). Because the widening current account deficit and the surge in credit were the main concerns, the macroprudential policy concentrated on simultaneously containing credit and the current account deficit. The policymakers prioritized policy tools targeting credit to households, because of its close relationship with Turkey's current account deficit. Credit to private corporations was regarded as less important, because its link to the current account deficit seemed to be weaker (Kara, 2016a, p. 131).[13] How instrumental were these macroprudential measures? While the measures were effective in terms of reducing the current account deficit (see Figure 4.5) and slowing down the economy to some extent,

---

[12] The coup attempt of 15 July 2016 caused a slight interruption in positive growth during this period. Apart from this event, the fluctuations in growth rates are mainly attributable to the global financial situation and to internal policy decisions.

[13] Aliogullari *et al.* (2015) indicate that in Turkey, whereas consumer loans are closely linked to the current account deficit, the association between commercial loans and the current account deficit seems to be weaker.

Figure 4.1 (and Figure 4.4) shows that the credit-to-GDP variable used in this study did not appear to be influenced. This issue is investigated further in the following section.

Turkish economic growth has always been, to large extent, driven by domestic demand (consumption), and external demand has never been the driver of growth.[14] As such, growth has always been constrained by the availability of domestic credit and foreign resources. In consequence, investments have been directed to the service sector (or to non-tradable sectors, i.e., those whose outputs cannot be sold in other countries) rather than to industry (or tradable sectors). During the recent period of credit-driven growth the economy became even more service-sector oriented. An increasingly large share of investment was directed to non-tradable sectors, such as big construction/infrastructure projects intended to meet the increasing domestic demand. The share of total employment attributable to the manufacturing sector,[15] as well as some other industrialization measures, have fallen steadily since 2008 (see Günçavdı and Aylin, Chapter 5 in this volume). As documented by Atiyas and Bakış (Chapter 3 in this volume), Acemoğlu and Ucer (Chapter 2 in this volume) total factor productivity ceased to derive growth and some indicators of technological upgrading such as technology content of exports have started to deteriorate.

a. *Exchange Rate Shock, the Surge in Inflation and Term Premium Jump*

In August 2018, the Turkish economy was hit with a severe exchange rate shock, triggered by a diplomatic dispute between the USA and Turkey. At the end of 31 July, TL/USD exchange rate was approximately 4.9, based on the daily average. On 13 August, however, $1 was worth 6.89 Turkish Lira (TL), indicating 40% loss in its value in less than two weeks' time. Moreover, according to intraday figures, on this day it remained at around 7.2 for some time, registering a jump of as much as 20% in a day.

---

[14] A period of a few years during the 1980s stands as an exception.
[15] This share had been on a steadily increasing trend until 2006, and particularly so between 2002 and 2006.

The Lira appreciated later but remained highly volatile for a long time. It has only recently stabilized around a level, 25–30% depreciated compared to its value at the beginning of August. This sharp devaluation of TL has induced a surge in inflation which has appeared to be somehow persistent despite weak domestic demand.[16]

The shock was triggered by a diplomatic dispute between the USA and Turkey concerning a US pastor detained by Turkey due to allegations of spying. The reaction of the financial markets indicated that they did not perceive the issue as temporary dispute between two long-allied and friendly countries, but rather regarded it as a serious issue with the potential to damage relations permanently. The fear of a structural shift in the relationship between the USA and Turkey, together with the anticipated dire consequences for financial markets, resulted in an immediate slump in consumer and investor confidence, and constituted a large negative shock for the balance sheets of the heavily indebted private sector. The economy entered recession immediately, during that very quarter.

To evaluate the importance of this adverse shock, I use the estimated term premium and risk-neutral rate (or average expected short term rate) calculated using fixed coupon government bond yields. Using the approach of Adrian *et al.* (2013), Yavuz and Yazgan (2019) provided estimates of term premiums and risk-neutral yields on government bonds for a selection of emerging market countries including Turkey. Figure 4.3 illustrates the 10-year government bond yield for Turkey and its decomposition into term premium and risk-neutral rate, using daily data.[17]

The 10-year yield is selected for analysis because it is representative of long-term expectations; however, data for two-year bonds reveal a similar pattern. For the emerging markets considered in Yavuz and Yazgan (2019), 10-year yields are generally driven by the term premium component; i.e., variations in the bond yields are mainly attributable to

---

[16] Nevertheless, it is worth noting that the depreciation of the TL had started earlier; at the beginning of 2018 the TL/USD exchange rate was around 3.77. Compared to its value of 4.90 at the beginning of August, this implies that in seven months, the depreciation of Turkish Lira had already reached almost 30% of its value at the start of the year.

[17] We have presented data starting from 1 June 2016. Earlier data are available, but show the same pattern and do not contribute meaningfully to the present discussion.

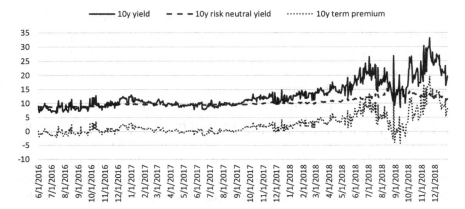

Figure 4.3.   Risk-neutral rate and term premium of 10-year government bond yields

fluctuations in term premiums. Hence, the changes in bond yields reflect the market perception regarding future uncertainty, and they seem to be unaffected by changes in average expected short rates. The risk-neutral yields, i.e., the average short-term expected rates, in general, remain relatively much less volatile than term premiums and show limited variation. Turkey is differentiated from the other countries in the study in the period from the second half of 2018 in terms of the behavior of both risk-neutral yields and the term premium component. Both components, and especially the term premium, become very volatile from June 2018. The movement in risk-neutral rate can be associated with sharp increases in expected inflation as a result of the exchange rate shock in August, whereas the movements in the term premium reflect the volatility in market perceptions of future uncertainty.

Reflecting on this behavior of the term premium, it can be argued that the financial market's concern regarding the risk of the Turkish government defaulting on its debt widely fluctuated during this period. Financial markets are notorious for erratic behavior and large amplitudes in valuations, and the present example certainly fits this description. Among the emerging markets considered by Yavuz and Yazgan (2019), a comparably high level of volatility in the term premium associated with an increase in the risk-neutral rate can only be found in Russia at the end of 2014 and the beginning of 2015, which corresponds to the period of the USA and European Union's sanctions against the Russian government. It should also be noted that the volatility in term premium and the increase in risk premium in Russia during that period remained significantly lower than those in Turkey described previously.

4.5. Has Deleveraging Started? Who is Deleveraging and Who is Not?

The recession that started in 2018Q4 heralded the end of credit cycle and probably the end of the recent regime of relatively high growth. The average growth rate over the 64 quarters-long credit cycle was greater than 5.9%, despite the presence of the severe recession of 2008Q4–2009Q3. Although the current debt cycle is already 55 quarters long and is still ongoing according to the aforementioned data, as discussed earlier, signs now indicate that it is in its final phase and will soon come to an end. Therefore, some deleveraging processes should already have started. The question is which actors are deleveraging and which are not. First, we consider the decomposition of our credit variable, then we examine the overall indebtedness of Turkey's main sectors.

Whereas the debt-to-GDP ratio calculation encompasses the foreign debt liabilities of all sectors, both private and public, the credit-to-GDP ratio calculation used in the aforementioned analysis encompasses only the non-financial private sector, which consists of households and non-financial corporations. We can further decompose credit data using the Bank of International Settlements (BIS) database. BIS provides credit-GDP ratio data for credit to households (including non-profit institutions serving households) from all sectors, including domestic banks, other domestic financial corporations, non-financial corporations, and non-residents. In contrast, the credit to non-financial private sector data used previously in this study encompasses only domestic banks. Credit-GDP ratios calculated based on credit to the non-financial sector and credit to non-financial corporations (excluding households) from all sectors are also provided by BIS. Figure 4.4 illustrates these three additional credit-to-GDP ratios. For comparative purposes, Figure 4.4 also includes the credit-to-GDP ratio used in Figure 4.1 and the earlier analysis.[18]

---

[18] To be consistent with the other measures we recalculated this variable using BIS data. The data are only available up to 2019Q1.

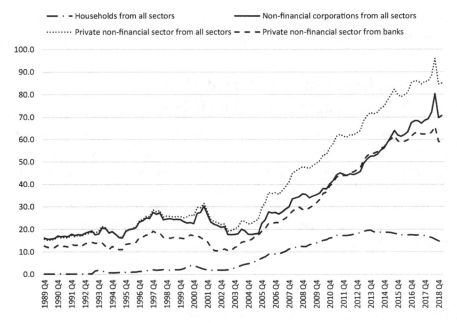

Figure 4.4. Credit-to-GDP ratios

Regarding cycle properties, all credit variables show the same characteristics except for the credit-to-GDP ratio for households. In other words, all data series follow the same cycle dates as shown in Table 4.2, except for credit to households. As is apparent from Figure 4.4, the expansionary credit cycle for households does not end in 2018Q3, as is the case for the other three credit series, but at a much earlier date, 2013Q4. Although the other three series share same cycle dates, as illustrated in Table 4.4, there are some differences between the credit-to-GDP ratio for non-financial private credit from domestic banks and the credit-to-GDP ratio for non-financial corporations' credit from all sectors.

The difference may be due to either the borrower side (households) or lender side (banks). In terms of deleveraging behavior it does not matter where the difference comes from because the conclusion remains unaltered. Non-financial corporations began deleveraging or became constrained in credit in 2018Q3, whereas households started this process earlier, in 2013Q3. So why did households start deleveraging earlier than private corporations? The answer lies in the macroprudential polices implemented in 2011 that are discussed in the previous section. As mentioned, the economic administration gave the priority to measures aimed at constraining overborrowing in consumer credits. The difference in the timing of deleveraging behavior suggests that these measures were successful in constraining household credit, as targeted, without constraining credits to non-financial firms.

To measure the extent of the ongoing deleveraging process, we now consider another data set, provided by the CBRT, featuring figures showing the level of indebtedness of specific sectors. The data set provided by CBRT is named Financial Accounts: Total Debt of Sectors. Table 4.5 illustrates the ratios of total debt (i.e., the sum of utilized loans and issued debt securities) to GDP for separate sectors.

Consistent with the credit-to-GDP data described earlier, non-financial corporations increase their leverage from the start of the sample period until 2018Q3, at which time they sharply deleveraged. Although to a lesser extent, financial corporations also experienced some deleveraging

Table 4.5. Total debt-to-GDP ratios of residents' sectors

	Non-Financial Corporations (%)	Financial Corporations (%)	Central Government (%)	Households (%)
2010Q4	41.69	14.37	47.69	16.74
2011Q4	44.28	17.84	40.08	17.12
2012Q4	52.28	21.62	33.84	19.59
2013Q4	61.82	26.23	30.51	17.80
2014Q4	67.40	26.71	30.54	17.56
2015Q4	61.82	26.23	30.51	17.80
2016Q4	67.40	26.71	30.54	17.56
2017Q4	68.25	28.39	30.20	16.98
2018Q1	69.17	28.41	29.64	16.60
2018Q2	72.20	29.61	29.33	16.30
2018Q3	79.79	33.80	32.32	15.53
2018Q4	69.13	29.24	30.04	14.70
2019Q1	70.32	29.07	31.28	14.24
2019Q2	69.09	29.81	34.12	13.90

at that time. For the non-financial private sector, the data seem to indicate that deleveraging has started and is expected to continue further to complete the contractionary credit (and debt) cycle. On the other hand, for households, the data show that deleveraging started long before the 2018Q4 recession.

4.6. What's Next? If Deleveraging, How Long and to What Extent?

Predictions on the evolution of the current recessions will be critically dependent on predictions on the behavior of the credit cycle, and will be affected by the movements of credit and debt variables. The credit-to-GDP ratio reached its maximum in 2018Q3, at a high of 65%. After three quarters of the recession it fell to 57% in 2019Q2. The 2008–2009 crisis involves a quick recovery, or a "V" type exit from recession. With the help of global ultra-loose monetary policies, the credit-to-GDP ratio recovered from 28% after a small correction in the credit. A comparison with the 2001 crisis may not be helpful because the latter was a period with much weaker private sector credit conditions; however, it also involves a "V" type quick recovery.

As we know from the available data, the economy is presently in the third quarter of a recession and the output costs of these three quarters have been much milder than costs during the 2008–2009 recession (see Table 4.1).[19] So, is achieving a "V" type quick recovery time, as was achieved in late 2002 and 2009, even easier?

Recent data on private credits signal some expansion, especially from consumer sides undertaking in the third quarter of 2019. Thanks to these recent increases it seems likely that the duration of the present recession can be restricted to three quarters, which is less than the typical four-quarter duration of recessions according to our data. This seems to be the likely outcome of the present recession because the rate of contraction has started to diminish in 2019Q2. Furthermore, GDP growth nowcasts

---

[19] However, the loss in the employment seems to be at least as costly as in previous recessions.

indicate that Turkish economy will achieve, albeit small, positive growth rate in the third quarter of, but a reasonable growth in fourth quarter of 2019 thanks, partly, to base year (quarter) effect.

Although these figures are interpreted as somehow optimistic in the sense that they may overshoot actual rates for reasons stated in the following paragraphs, some smaller but positive growth especially in the fourth quarter is very likely. These nowcasts are based on the model of Modugno *et al.* (2016) (see also Soybilgen and Yazgan, 2016, 2018) and are published by www.nowcastturkey.com (or www.simditahmin.com, in Turkish). The nowcasts published on the website are immediately updated as soon as new data on a variable, in the predictor list of the model, are released. The underlying model that generates these nowcasts was updated after the revision of Turkish GDP at the end of 2016. The updated model, as outlined by Soybilgen and Yazgan (2018), gives more emphasis on credit variables among model predictors. This update has provided more accuracy to the model compared to the initial one in Modugno *et al.* (2016), where the model was constructed using the pre-revision GDP data. The "optimistic nowcasts" generated by the model of Soybilgen and Yazgan (2018) reflect the assumption that credit channel will work this time as in previous cases. However, this time credit and link growth link cannot perform as well as in the past.

For a "V" type quick recovery to be possible and downturn to continue with accelerating growth, the credit-to-GDP ratio needs to rise quickly, up to a level of 65% again and even further. International comparisons indicate that the credit-to-GDP ratio can attain a figure even higher than 100%, based on emerging markets averages according to BIS data. Hence, an increase to 65% and higher in the credit-to-GDP ratio is technically possible for an emerging market country such as Turkey.

However, there are two main difficulties related with achieving this level of ratio. First, as stated by post-Keynesian monetary theorists, creating credit by means of the banking system has no technical boundaries (see Werner, 2016, among others), but does have some other boundaries related with business, especially investors sentiments. Even if credit is available, investors may prefer to delay making investments due to loss of confidence in the business environment. The sharp increase in the volatility of term premiums (and the risk-neutral rate), as discussed earlier, is an indicator, among others, that confidence has not yet been restored. Second, the availability of credit is to some extent is dependent on the foreign finance constraint. The foreign debt-to-GDP ratio is at its historically highest level of 60% as of 2019Q1. This ratio should be reduced, because it implies an unsustainable level for an emerging market country. Most deleveraging should come from the private sector because this sector holds a large portion of the total foreign debt, which is in contrast to the 2001 crisis. Hence, the private sector's balance sheets should undergo greater deleveraging and repayment of foreign debt. This would leave a weak private sector with low levels of appetite and capability to make new investments. Under these circumstances credit expansions relying mostly on consumers[20] may have some positive effects on growth but may remain insufficient in the absence of investment motives.

4.7. A Look at Flow Variables

So far, all analysis has been based on the behavior of stock variables. We will now take a short look at flow variables, such as current accounts and investments. As a matter of national accounting identities, a country's current account balance is identical to its savings gap, i.e., the difference between its savings and investments. In other words, the share of investments that cannot be financed by domestic resources should be financed by foreign resources. Figure 4.5 displays Turkey's current account deficit, investments (including stocks), and savings-to-GDP ratios.

The current account deficit has recently turned into a small surplus, achieved in the second quarter of 2019 after three quarters of deceleration. As can be observed from Figure 4.5, during 2008–2009 the current account deficit decelerated in six consecutive quarters, but never turned into a surplus. Hence, the economy did not pay back its foreign liabilities during the crisis; on the contrary, although the percentage reduced, it continued to accumulate new foreign liabilities. This is consistent with our earlier findings on the debt cycle, which was not disrupted by the 2008–2009 crisis. The situation was quite different in 2001; there was a current account surplus for six consecutive quarters until the beginning of

---

[20] As shown earlier consumers' balance sheets are not as constrained as private firms.

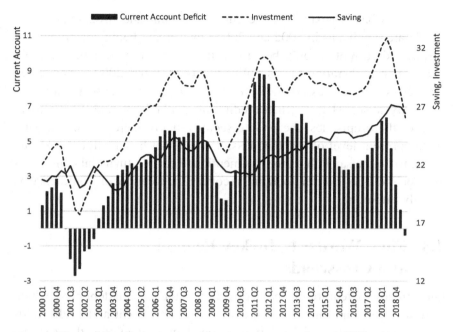

Figure 4.5. Current account, investments, and savings to GDP ratios

2003. This is also consistent with the characteristics of the debt cycle as discussed earlier. However, what is common to both 2001 and 2009 crises is that the current account deficit rapidly increased as the economy emerged from recession. Considering the fact that in the present crisis, the debt-to-GDP ratio has not yet started to decline, but will have to sooner or later, the net current account position is expected to stay in surplus for at least a few more quarters.

On the other hand, the investment ratio started to fall before the beginning of the recession, and has been declining for four consecutive quarters since 2018Q3, reducing from 33% (2018Q2) to 26% (2019Q2). In both the 2001–2002 and 2008–2009 crises, this ratio declined for five consecutive quarters, from 30% (2008Q3) to 23% (2009Q4), and from 24% (2000Q4) to 18% (2002Q1). Based on the aforementioned analysis of the credit cycle and ongoing deleveraging process of the real sector firms, we can anticipate that the decrease in the investment ratio will also continue for at least a few more quarters.

Then what is next? Will the current account and investment ratios accelerate rapidly, as in 2002 and 2009? Investment being constrained by credit, and current account being constrained by foreign debt, the rapid increase in both ratios seems unlikely. In 2002 and 2009, when quick recoveries were witnessed, the indebtedness of the private sector was significantly lower. Hence, when credit was available, as indeed it was in both of these episodes, the private sector quickly increased investment. At the present level of indebtedness, it would not be easy for the private sector to do the same this time. As mentioned earlier, financial constraints are not the only barrier to rapid recovery, restoration of confidence is equally important.

4.8. Final Words: Is Turkey Economy at a Crossroads?

Quick recovery requires a small correction in the foreign debt ratio, which in turn causes rapid increases in current account deficit and credit ratios after some corrections. The aforementioned analysis implies that such an outcome is unlikely. If Turkey is in the half way through (credit) or in the beginning of (debt) the process of deleveraging, the debt and credit contractionary cycles will continue for some time in the future. It is relevant to note that the above-mentioned literature on financial cycles documents that recessions at the end of financial cycles are deeper than those that occur in the middle of cycles. As mentioned previously, the current recession is expected to end in the third or at least in the fourth quarter of 2019,[21] but this does not seem to bring a quick recovery. The output cost of the current recession has thus far remained low (see Table 4.1). Growth will be positive but is expected to be considerably low for some time. Several studies have indicated that credit booms weaken output in the medium term (Lombardi *et al.*, 2017; Mian *et al.*, 2017) and weaken productivity growth (Borio *et al.*, 2016). There is also no reason not to expect the same outcome from Turkey's current financial cycle. Acemoğlu and

---

[21] Base year effect will also play an important role in reasonably high growth outcome in the fourth quarter.

Ucer (Chapter 2, in this volume) and Atiyas and Bakış (Chapter 3, in this volume) document low-productivity characteristics of the economic growth associated with this financial cycle of Turkey.

The length of this period of slow recovery will determine the depth of the current recession. So far in this study, the depth of recessions has been measured by the cumulative negative GDP growth rates. Although this methodology could be a fairly accurate approximation in the case of "V"-type recoveries, it underestimates the costs of recessions because it fails to account for the cost of associated low growth periods. Can the process of recovery be made relatively fast? Because fast growth driven by credit- and debt-fueled domestic demand does not seem to be possible this time, can external demand-driven growth be possible? During the present recession, one of the reasons Turkey is undergoing such a "shallow" recession is the positive contribution of net exports. Net exports, due to a large fall in imports and some increase in exports, have been able to contribute meaningfully to the growth thus far. If a continuous increase in net exports is possible, and especially if this increase comes predominantly from an increase in exports rather than a fall in imports, the output cost of the recession should remain low and some economic growth may resume.

This would require a change in the long-established credit driven growth regime of Turkey and a return to a process of industrialization that may help productivity increases. Another positive contribution may come from re-establishing damaged confidence, which is evidenced by the abrupt movements in the term premium. The need for structural and institutional reforms are emphasized by several authors in (and out of) this volume to achieve quality growth with increases in productivity.

For this purpose, a close look at the policies and reforms implemented during the expansionary deleveraging period after the 2001 crisis may be beneficial. During this period, the effect of reforms and credibility associated with successful disinflation made strong recovery possible at the same time as deleveraging in foreign debt was taking place. As discussed earlier, this period was very different to the quick recovery after the 2009 crisis, especially in terms of the nature of the growth (see Acemoğlu and Ucer, Chapter 2; Pamuk, Chapter 1, in this volume). Is Turkish economy at a crossroads? It seems that the answer is yes. If the country chooses a future direction based on a new growth regime, re-creation of business confidence for new investments, restoration of institutional framework and implementing required reforms, Turkey may achieve a path of sustainable growth. Otherwise, as explained previously, the outcome may be a long period of slow growth of the kind that Turkey has not experienced before.

References

Acemoglu, D. and Ucer, M. (2015). The Ups and Downs of Turkish Growth, 2002–2015: Political Dynamics and the European Union and the Institutional Slide, in "The Search for Europe: Contrasting Approaches", BBVA Open Mind Press.

Adrian, T., Crump, R. and Moench, E. (2013). "Pricing the Term Structure with Linear Regressions", *Journal of Financial Economics*, Vol. 110, No. 1, pp. 110–138.

Akat, A. S. and Yazgan, M. E. (2012) "Observations on Turkey's Recent Economic Performance", *Atlantic Economic Journal*, Vol. 41, No. 1, pp. 1–27.

Akar, C. (2016). "Analyzing the Synchronization between the Financial and Business Cycles in Turkey", *Journal of Reviews on Global Economics*, Vol. 5, pp. 25–35.

Aliogullari, Z., Başkaya, Y., Bulut, Y. and Kilinc, M. (2015). Turkiye'de Tuketici ve Ticari Kredilerin Cari Acikla İliskisi (in Turkish), CBT Research Notes in Economics, 15/19.

Atiyas, I. and Bakis, O. (2014). "Aggregate and Sectoral TFP Growth in Turkey: A Growth-Accounting Exercise", *Iktisat İsletme ve Finans*, Vol. 29, pp. 9–36.

Atiyas, I. and Bakis, O. (2015). "Structural Change and Industrial Policy in Turkey", *Emerging Markets Finance and Trade*, Vol. 51, No. 6, pp. 1209–1229.

Baskaya, Y., Giovanni, J., Kalemli-Ozcan, S. and Ulu, M. (2017). "Capital Flows and International Credit Channel", *Journal of International Economics*, Vol. 108, pp. 15–22.

Benlialper, A. and Comert, H. (2015). "Implicit Asymmetric Exchange Rate Peg under Inflation Targeting Regimes: The Case of Turkey", *Cambridge Journal of Economics*, Vol. 40, No. 6, pp. 1553–1580.

Borio, C., Drehmann, M. and Xia, D. (2018). "The Financial Cycle and Recession Risk", *BIS Quarterly Review*, December.

Claessens, S., Kose, M. A. and Terrones, M. E. (2011). Financial Cycles: What? How? When?, IMF Working Paper 11/76.

Claessens, S., Kose, M. A. and Terrones, M. E. (2012). "How do Business and Financial Cycles Interact?" *Journal of International Economics*, Vol. 87, No. 1, pp. 178–190.

Drehmann, M., Borio, C. and Tsatsaronis, K. (2012). Characterizing the Financial Cycle: Don't Lose Sight of the Medium Term!, BIS Working Papers, No. 380, June.

Giovanni, J., Baskaya, Y., Kalemli-Ozcan, S. and Ulu, M. (2017). International Spillovers and Local Credit Cycles. NBER WP No. 23149.

Harding, D. and Pagan, A. (2012). "Dissecting the Cycle: A Methodological Investigation", *Journal of Monetary Economics*, Vol. 49, No. 2, pp. 365–381.

Jorda, O., Schularick, M. and Taylor A. (2011). "Financial Crises, Credit Booms, and External Imbalances: 140 Years of Lessons", *IMF Economic Review*, Vol. 59, No. 2, pp. 340–378.

Kara, H. (2012). "Kuresel kriz sonrasi para politikasi (in Turksih)", *Iktisat Isletme ve Finans*, Vol. 27, No. 315, pp. 9–36.

Kara, H. (2016a). Turkey's Experience with Macroprudential Policy, BIS Papers No. 86.

Kara, H. (2016b). "A Brief Assessment of Turkey's Macroprudential Policy Approach: 2011–2015", *Central Bank Review*, Vol. 16, No. 3, pp. 85–92.

Lombardi, M., Madhusudan, M. and Shim, I. (2017). The Real Effects of Household Debt in the Short and Long Run, BIS Working Papers, No. 607.

Modugno, M., Soybilgen, B. and Yazgan, E. (2016). "Nowcasting Turkish GDP and News Decomposition", *International Journal of Forecasting*, Vol. 32, No. 4, pp. 1369–1384.

Kutuk, S., Hacihasanoglu, Y. S. and Binici, M. (2017). Are Financial Cycles Deviating from Business Cycles in Turkey? Financial Markets, Central Bank of the Republic of Turkey.

Mian, A., Sufi A. and Verner E. (2017). "Household Debt and Business Cycles Worldwide", *The Quarterly Journal of Economics*, Vol. 132, No. 4, pp. 1755–1817.

Minsky, H. P. (1977). The Financial Instability Hypothesis: An Interpretation of Keynes and Alternative to Standard Theory. Challenge (March–April), pp. 20–27.

Schularick, M. and Taylor, A. (2012). "Credit Booms Gone Bust: Monetary Policy, Leverage Cycles, and Financial Crises, 1870–2008", *American Economic Review*, Vol. 102, No. 2, pp. 1029–1061.

Soybilgen, B. and Yazgan, E. (2016). "Simditahmin.com'un Turkiye GSYH Buyume Oranları icin Tahmin Performansı (in Turkish)", *Iktisat ve Toplum*, Vol. 4, pp. 64–71.

Soybilgen, B. and Yazgan, E. (2018). "Nowcasting the New Turkish GDP", *Economics Bulletin*, Vol. 38, No. 2, pp. 1083–1089.

Reinhard, C. and Rogoff, K. (2011). "From Financial Crash to Debt Crisis", *American Economic Review*, Vol. 101, No. 5, pp. 1676–1706.

Rodrik, D. (2010). Structural Transformation and Economic Development, TEPAV.

Runstler, G. (2016). "How Distinct are Financial Cycles from Business Cycles?", *European Central Bank Research Bulletin*, No. 26.

Werner, R. A. (2016). "A Lost Century in Economics: Three Theories of Banking and the Conclusive Evidence", *International Review of Financial Analysis*, Vol. 46, pp. 361–379.

Yavuz, C. and Yazgan, M. E. (2019). What Drives Emerging Markets Term Premia?, Istanbul Bilgi University, unpublished manuscript.

Chapter 5

Structural Transformation and Income Distribution in Turkey*

Öner Günçavdı and Ayşe Aylin Bayar[†]

5.1. Introduction

The last 17 years have been an exceptional period in the history of Turkey for three reasons. First, a newly founded political party came into power after a snap election in November 2002 and has remained there as a single-party government for more than 17 years. This election also marked both a drastic change in the existing political establishment and a rise of a new one with the leadership of the AK Parti (Justice and Development Party). This political transformation has later become a reason for many to appeal for public confidence in the Turkish economy. Second, changes in the political front were accompanied by an expansionist financial policy in the world economy, and the Turkish economy was eventually exposed to a massive amount of capital inflows, which were used to expand the volume of domestic credit allowing for a consumption boom.

---

*The authors gratefully acknowledge comments on the earlier versions of the paper by Seyfettin Gürsel and Asaf Savaş Akat. Their comments and suggestion significantly improved the chapter. The authors, however, accept sole responsibility for any remaining error.

[†]Corresponding author: Öner Günçavdı; Istanbul Technical University, Faculty of Management, Süleyman Seba cd. 34367 Maçka — Beşiktaş/Istanbul, Turkey.

Third, this new political era witnessed a relatively successful economic performance, especially in the period between 2003 and 2007, by enhancing positive public perception about this new political establishment led by the AK Parti.

AK Parti had come into power in the aftermath of the worst economic crisis of the Turkish economic history. In response, distinguished economic performance in the early years in power paved the way for rising public support for the AK Parti, and this helped them consolidate the right-wing public support from the Turkish political spectrum around themselves. AK Parti has gradually become the only representative of the right-wing political discourse in the 2000s by eliminating the rivalry of other right-wing parties.[1]

The new political climate has widely been perceived as a sign of confidence in the Turkish economy by domestic and international investors. Infrastructural investment and a consumption boom, along with overvaluation of domestic currency and massive credit expansions, all served as the instruments for increasing the well-being of households, particularly of middle- and low-income families, and kept the public support high and the trust of voters on various AK Parti governments alive.

The political transformation has also been accompanied by a structural transformation in the economy. This structural transformation, beginning right after completing capital accounts' liberalization as a distinctive institutional change in the 1990s, has not been pertaining only to Turkey. A similar transformation has been observed in other developing countries, indicating that what happened in the economies of developing countries is indeed a systematic event widely occurring in response to changes in today's world economy.

This transformation process is, in fact, a continuous process, and it would not be an exaggeration to suggest that the major transformation of the Turkish economy started *far before* 2003. The origin of the transformation observed in Turkey can be traced back to those years when the Turkish economy began to become a part of the world economy in the 1980s.[2] With the help of various structural reforms undertaken during

---

[1] See Chapter 1 by Pamuk and Chapter 2 by Acemoğlu and Üçer.
[2] See Chapter 1 by Pamuk.

the 1990s, the Turkish economy was transformed from a relatively state-oriented, interventionist economic structure, into a more market-oriented one. The new institutional framework was enhanced with the economic reforms in 2001, and the economic growth policies implemented by various AK Parti governments and the financial stance prevailing in the world economy in the 2000s took place within this framework.

The structure of the Turkish economy has begun to change after 2003, *partly* due to deteriorations in relative prices between tradable and non-tradable goods and *partly* because of a change in sectoral preferences of the government in favor of non-tradable economic activities such as *construction*, *trade*, and *banking*. They have eventually become the main motive of the economic growth models during the AK Parti period. This sectoral choice can be considered an obligation of a new political establishment, which is eager to expand its public approval by providing high, as well as inclusive, economic growth to the wide layers of Turkish society. This was indeed an exceptional task, and its accomplishment was used to rely both on the availability of financial resources, and its distribution to particular economic and social groups through the most appropriate channels (such as the market) to remain in power as long as possible. De-industrialization, which can be described by an increase in the share of non-tradable economic activities in employment and total value added manufacturing, has come out *unintentionally* as an economic *outcome* of this task of the economic growth model, and it has become its distinguishing feature of this period.

The concern about de-industrialization is not new, and there have been various attempts to explain this, particularly in the process of development. The first attempt goes back to Kaldor's explanation of structural development during the development process. In his seminal contributions, Kaldor's underlying argument is the faster the rate of growth of manufacturing in the economy, the faster will be its growth of GDP (Kaldor, 1966 and 1967). Therefore, industrialization is the engine of economic growth and faster growth. It has been seen that today's advanced countries have experienced industrialization as well as de-industrialization process as in the theoretical expectation postulated by Kaldor. However, many economies of developing countries today have been de-industrialized without completing industrialization properly. This de-industrialization has been called "premature" mainly because it has started before industrialization was completed (in other words, marginal factor productivity began to fall) (Dasgupta and Singh, 2006; Rodrik, 2016).

The economic literature has put forward various causes of de-industrialization (Rowthorn and Ramaswamy, 1997), but some are worth noting in the case of Turkey. A new institutional structure (or globalization) allowing for free trade and capital flows, economic populism that is desperately required by the new political establishment to make itself be accepted largely by the Turkish society, favorable financial conditions available in international financial markets, and change in the relative prices in favor of non-tradable economic activities, can be accounted for the shift in scarce economic resources toward non-tradable sectors in Turkey.

Turkey is one of the countries in Organisation for Economic Co-operation and Development (OECD) having the worst income distribution (OECD, 2016). The purpose of this chapter is to first establish a new channel of interaction between de-industrialization and different income entities available in the economy, and then to examine the effects of de-industrialization on income distribution by using this channel of interaction. For this purpose, we reveal the presence of de-industrialization, and then examine both likely motives behind de-industrialization and its interaction with the new economic discourse politically set by AK Parti after 2003.

The chapter consists of seven sections, and its organization is as follows. The first section is to examine the political motives of the existing political establishment encouraging structural transformation moving away from the manufacturing industry. The second section exhibits some empirical observation on the state of the financial situation in the 2000s, abetting structural transformation. High economic growth rates, regarded as an indication of economic (as well as political) success in the 2000s, aim to accelerate structural transformation with the expectation of mobilizing low-income households upward, and the government was able to accomplish this aim by prioritizing some sectors in resource allocation. The third section draws attention to the high economic growth rate episodes in the last 17 years from a comparative perspective. De-industrialization in the 2000s with several well-known indicators of structural transformation is analyzed in the fourth section.

Unlike the well-known definition in the literature, de-industrialization in this chapter is defined as the share of the "non-tradable" sector in GDP and employment. In this chapter, we imagine an economy divided into three sub-sectors, namely tradable (mainly representing manufacturing), non-tradable (services and other sectors operating only domestically and having the low capability of generating income in foreign currencies), and finally agricultural (which has been the traditional sector in Turkey). The effects of international trade as a cause of de-industrialization, together with domestic demand and changes in productivity, are empirically examined in the fifth section. The relationship between structural transformation and income distribution is studied in the sixth section. Finally, the last section is devoted to some concluding remarks.

5.2. Economic Populism and Structural Transformation

This section examines the political motives behind the structural transformation, and the populist economic discourse as the ground for economic practices undertaken by various AK Parti governments is put forward as the cause of de-industrialization. The reason why we emphasize the link between economic populism and de-industrialization is that the importance of non-tradable expenditure as the most distinctive instrument of populist economic discourse has largely been missed from attention in the literature. However, the recent rise in political debate on populism in both advanced and developing countries has required establishing a likely link between populism and de-industrialization. In practice, economic populism has gained its importance in today's political debates as long as the populist political practices improved the well-being of people in need. People, extremely exhausted by the results of neoliberalism in economics, have unfortunately been left without any option other than following up on the populist discourse of today.

Economic populism has recently been the mainstream discourse in economic policy debates in Turkey and the world. This can be seen as a reaction of policymakers in the developing and even in the advanced countries to neoliberal economic policies and their economic consequences. Populism has different dimensions, and economic policies are one of the concerns of the populist discourse (Eatwell and Goodwin, 2018; Muller, 2016). Remaining within the boundary of national economies, economic populism can be considered as the implementation of economic policies that put emphasis overwhelmingly on economic growth and income distribution without considering the risk of inflation and internal and external financial constraints (Dornbusch and Edwards, 1990). Economic growth, particularly high growth, becomes the "ambition of policymakers" at any expense.

Populism in an economic sense goes back to economic policy practices of Latin American countries and even of Turkey in the 1960s and the 1970s. This version of economic populism targeted mostly the well-being of poor and low-income households. Industrialization and import substitution, practiced in a rather different institutional framework from today, was widely regarded as the engine of economic growth irrespective of its inclusiveness. The transformation of national economies from agriculture to manufacturing had mobilized the population from rural to urban areas and had constituted the cause of inequality and poverty. Populism rose in response to these defects of industrialization at the early stage of development and targeted mainly at generating benefits for the poor without taking into account the constraints of any economic practice. The populist discourse in the 1960s and the 1970s was in favor of a solution to the inequality and poverty issues by going further into industrialization and creating employment in manufacturing. The new populist practice today washowever practiced in an open environment with a relatively developed institutional structure under the pressure of international competition, and inevitably was ended up with de-industrialization. Therefore, economic populist practices in two different institutional frameworks have generated two different results in the structural transformation of the Turkish economy.

Despite the aims of economic populism, the results were not as expected and economic populism usually ended up with high inflation — in some cases hyperinflation, high debt stock as in the Latin American countries, and low economic growth in the 1970s, and left these countries to deal with various economic imbalances. Most importantly, these results constituted an excuse for worldwide acceptance of the adaptation of the neoliberal economic policies to cope with these imbalances.

After over 30 years of experience, neoliberal policies globalized the world economy at an unprecedented level and helped many developing countries to deal with economic imbalances in the short run and catch sustainable growth rates for a while. Nevertheless, the achievement of the economic growth sphere has not been sustainable and sufficiently inclusive, and inequalities in developing countries like Turkey and countries in Latin America remained as important as before.[3] Most importantly, improvements in income distribution and poverty have become extremely dependent on high economic growth; the higher the economic growth, the better the income distribution (Bayar and Günçavdı, 2020). Economic populism today emphasizes the policies that encourage economic activities generating high economic growth without being under the pressure of international competition. This partly is the reason why new populism paves the way for non-tradable economic activities. The rise of non-tradable economic activities in manufacturing value-added and employment together with an increase in non-tradable income entities become an instrument of populist economic practices.

5.3. Financial Environment and a Fall in the Cost of Economic Growth

Turkey in the 2000s was exposed to large capital inflows, and it experienced almost all symptoms of a Dutch Disease problem, such as overvaluation of the domestic currency, a consumption boom, and deterioration of relative prices between tradable and non-tradable goods due to an unavoidable increase in non-tradable prices. This is, though, not a typical Dutch Disease phenomenon as it happens in a natural resource-abundant developing country as being exposed to large foreign exchange earnings in the event of a commodity boom (Corden and Neary, 1982). Even though countries like Turkey are not resource rich, they attracted a large

---

[3] See Chapter 2 by Acemoğlu and Üçer; Acemoğlu and Robinson (2012).

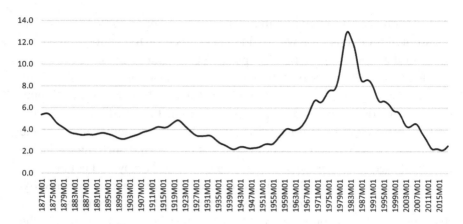

Figure 5.1.   The US monthly 10-year treasury bond rates — Trend values

Source: The raw data were obtained from the *Federal Reserve Economic Data* (FRED), https://fred. stlouisfed.org/series/T10Y2Y#0.

amount of capital after 2002 due to changes in the institutional structure allowing for capital inflows and the availability of easy borrowing opportunities at low costs in the world financial market (see Palma, 2014).

Exceptionally low-interest rates in the world financial market was another determinant of the dynamics of this situation. Figure 5.1 illustrates a secular decline in the trend value of the 10 years T-bill of the US Treasury. The trend values of monthly interest rates of the US treasury bills were calculated by the Hodrick–Prescott Filtering method. It is evident from Figure 5.1 that today's trend value of the US 10-year Treasury bond seems to have reached the level that is observed after WWII.

Turkey benefited from the financial bonanza with the institutional framework allowing her easily to access international finance. Figure 5.2 shows the extent of the capital flows between 2003 and 2019 as a difference in capital account deficits from the amounts in the finance account. The monthly data were taken from the Central Bank data distribution system and the data that correspond to the value each month are 12-month moving cumulative amounts. Positive values in Figure 5.2 indicate the excess amount of finance over current account deficits, whereas negative ones imply the lack of finance. It is clear from Figure 5.2 that despite the presence of a short period during the sub-prime crisis and many months

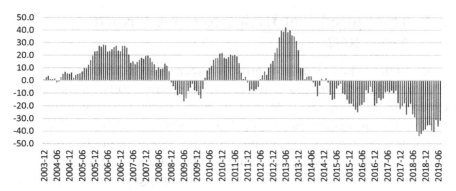

Figure 5.2. Difference between current account deficits and finance account (billion $)

Source: TCMB (Central Bank of Turkey), https://evds2.tcmb.gov.tr/index.php?/evds/serieMarket.

in the 2011–2012 period, Turkey achieves to attract more capital than the amount that the economy requires to finance capital account deficits. However, this turned in the opposite direction after 2013, and Turkey began to lack a sufficient amount of capital inflows to finance capital account deficits.

Financial liberalization and intense efforts for globalization after the 1980s gradually increased the availability of finance and led to a decrease in the cost of borrowing. An expansionist monetary policy after the sub-prime mortgage crisis also contributed to a rise in international liquidity and provided an appropriate financial environment for economic growth for developing countries.

For many developing countries like Turkey, this low-interest rate era has also been the high economic growth period. It was easier than before to find a resource to finance expenditure requiring generating high economic growth. However, the presence of severe international competition on foreign trade has been the main obstacle for some countries in this highly globalized world, and it became difficult to have high economic growth rates through tradable economic activities. Instead, non-tradable economic activities have become the new engine of economic growth due to the absence of international competition on non-tradable activities. This has been one of the reasons for some countries de-industrializing in this low-interest rate era.

5.4. The Episodes of High Economic Growth After 2002

Since attaining high economic growth is seen as an indication of macro-economic success, the government has put extra efforts into pursuing exceptionally high rates. Moreover, high economic growth is also regarded as an instrument of populist economic practices, and a relatively new political establishment, requiring extensive public approval, seeks a way of generating economic benefits for those who support this establishment. This can be done only through high economic growth, particularly without disturbing the already existing benefits in society. However, today's public policymakers are restricted to accomplish this high economic growth target. Highly liberalized trade regimes and increased pressure of international competition, unfortunately, leave little room for maneuvering for policymakers. They seem, to some extent, to have lost their control on the one side of the entire economy (namely tradable one) due to globalization, and become dependent on the non-tradable economic activities to generate economic growth that is in their control.

Economic populism emerges as the government loses its appetite for structural reforms and desperately needs economic growth to sustain high public approval, while at the same time it remains dependent increasingly on non-tradable economic activities without taking care of any cost of this dependency. However, this type of economic growth inevitably appears in the short term, and it is difficult to sustain in the long term unless the availability of finance continues.

This is particularly crucial for a country like Turkey, which has historically been suffering from the shortage of domestic savings. Turkish economic growth rates historically show high variations dependent on the availability of resources that are required to finance economic growth. This is also true for the economic growth episodes after 2002. In this regard, the economic growth performance of the Turkish economy shows mixed narrative after 2002. The early years of the 2000s emerged as a reform period, as the first AK Parti government was acting as a reformist government by accomplishing various political and economic reforms.

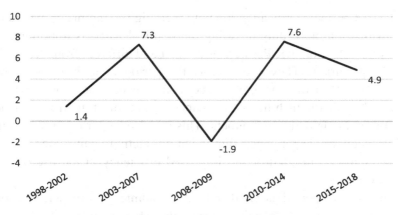

Figure 5.3.   Average growth rates (%)

Source: TurkStat, http://www.tuik.gov.tr/UstMenu.do?metod=istgosterge.

Sound macroeconomic management was astonishingly successful and inflation, interest rates, and foreign exchange rates were low enough as a sign of this good macroeconomic management. As a result, economic growth was exceptionally high; most importantly this growth was inclusive and paved the way for an improvement in income distribution (Bayar and Günçavdı, 2020).

The average growth rate of the Turkish economy after 2001 can be seen in Figure 5.3. There are five different economic growth eras in Figure 5.3. The 1998–2002 period is the pre-AK Parti period describing the condition that brought the AK Parti into power. The striking feature of this period is the institutional framework, which had been started to bring about change after 1990. Among others, capital account liberalization and easy access to international capital can be considered as two of these institutional changes. Rapid institutional changes, particularly after the 1990s, and the inability of the Turkish policymakers to adapt themselves to the requirements of this new institutional framework can be attributed for this low growth performance in this period.

The entire period between 2003 and 2018 can broadly be divided into four distinct periods in terms of the sources of economic growth (see Figure 5.3). Among them, two of them (namely the 2003–2007 and the

2010–2014 periods) draw attention with their high economic growth rates. This distinction, according to ruling the political party, is important, for those who define the AK Parti era as distinct and different from the earlier periods of Turkey. They even define the period after 2003 as "New" Turkey, based on the so-called "exceptional" economic growth performance. They distinguish this performance as a proof of good governance of a strong-single party government. This is indeed a period, in which the Turkish economy experienced significant productivity gains due to accelerated capital accumulation and improved efficiency in the use of economic resources.[4]

The second period is another high economic growth period corresponding to two crucial elections during the AK Parti ruling. In the local election in 2009, AK Parti had performed rather badly and its public support had declined to 38% due to over a 4% contraction in the economy. The government ended its reform program, and indulged in seeking a possible easy, less costly (at least in the short run) and quick way of generating economic growth. Realizing the importance of high economic growth for drawing high public support in forthcoming elections in 2010 and 2011, the government of the time increased public expenditure and encouraged expansion in the volume of domestic credit. Changes in relative prices, rather in favor of non-tradable goods (including domestic trade and construction) helped the economy generate non-tradable demand-driven economic growth in this period. Construction, trade, banking, and other services came forward as leading economic activities driving economic growth in this period. Large capital inflows were available for the use of the government of the time, allowing for a consumption boom in the economy. Capital account deficits in the tradable goods side of the economy appeared as a result of this consumption boom, whereas increases in non-tradable prices caused rigidities in the overall prices level to not fall to the level targeted by the Central Bank. Therefore, high economic growth rates in this period were obtained at the expense of high current account deficits and sustained a high price level in non-tradable goods.

Respectively, AK Parti government's coming into power after the 2003–2007 period changed its priorities in the macroeconomy, and

---

[4] See Chapter 2 by Acemoğlu and Üçer; Chapter 3 by Atiyas and Bakış.

became inclined to "mega" infrastructural projects — such as the *Third Bosporus Bridge*, the *Third Istanbul Airport*, and *The Bridge* connecting the two sides of Marmara Sea at Yalova and the Bridge over the Dardanelles Strait — in order to appeal for the public's electoral support.[5] It is important to note that all these "mega" projects are non-tradable, and they can be considered as an indication of the sectoral sources of economic growth on which the Turkish government has recently relied.

The demand components of economic growth provide important information on the common features of high economic growth episodes in the AK Parti period. Figure 5.4 was drawn to see the relative importance of each demand component in economic growth. Leaving two exceptional years 2001 and 2002 aside, the first episodes between 2003 and 2007 seem to have witnessed relatively high growth rates of investment and imports. This observation is also true for the second growth episode. Hence, these common features of high economic growth episodes imply that fixed capital accumulation and

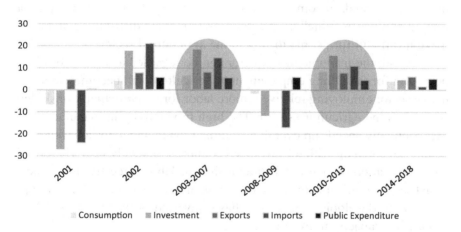

Figure 5.4.   Growth rates of expenditure components

Source: TCMB, https://evds2.tcmb.gov.tr/index.php?/evds/serieMarket.

---

[5]The government was proposing to build a water-crossing channel from the Black Sea to the Marmara Sea as an alternative passage to Bosporus. Although the project attracted huge public attention, it has been postponed now due to its huge financial cost and change in the financial stance of the Turkish economy in the international markets.

importations have been an essential condition for the high economic growth in Turkey.[6]

5.5. Structural Transformation

The route of development is theoretically expected to take place as a shift from agriculture to manufacturing. This expectation is mainly based on Kaldor's empirical observations from several advanced countries, and, according to him, the manufacturing sector is the engine of economic growth at the early stage of this route (Kaldor, 1966). However, the recent trend that we observe from developing countries challenges Kaldor's view. Among others, this Kaldorian view becomes important for a country like Turkey for two reasons. First, agricultural economic activities have been dominating the entire economy, and the agriculture sector has consequently been facing various difficulties to absorb the excess population growth due to a fall in employment. Eventually, declines in mean income in agriculture and, in some cases, a concentration of land ownership by a limited number of "elite" people deteriorate income distribution and even make it difficult for people to stay in the agricultural sector.

Second, the manufacturing sector can be regarded as the sector compensating for the falling employment in agriculture and becomes an alternative sector employing relatively more labor force (particularly unskilled ones) than the agriculture sector. The high productivity in manufacturing hypothetically speeds up overall economic growth and helps a developing country to catch up with the advanced countries relatively fast. Therefore, industrialization, which is taken as a shift of labor force from the traditional sector to manufacturing, has been seen as the condition for development, and developing countries have invested a lot to establish a production capacity in manufacturing.

---

[6]Günçavdı and Ülengin (2018), using a *CES* form for aggregate investment, empirically examined the reason behind high investment demand in these growth periods. According to their empirical finding, the rate of substitution between tradable and non-tradable components of investment was very low, and this means that its non-tradable component was required for its promised capital gains accruing as a consequence of high economic growth and domestic demand for non-tradable goods.

However, a recent trend among developing countries has become different from this in a way that labor force in traditional sectors like agriculture shift more to services (or non-tradable) instead of manufacturing as expected by Kaldor. Several interesting observations appear from the recent experiences of transforming developing countries, and this raises our concern about the nature of today's development pattern of least developed countries. Among others, some are noted as follows:

- A secular fall in the shares of manufacturing value added and employment in total. More importantly, these declines occurred at a relatively lower level of per capita income that has been for today's advanced countries in the past.
- The expected sectoral shift from agriculture takes place in some developing countries to service sectors, not to manufacturing.
- Sectoral shifts in some developing countries associated with deteriorations in income inequality. Especially in the case of shifting from an industry with having better income distribution toward a sector with high within-group inequality, the structural transformation might have changed to deteriorate overall income distribution.

It is an empirical question to examine to what extent this postulated outcome of structural transformation appears in a particular case. As countries develop, the importance of manufacturing reduces, and the workforce eventually moves from manufacturing to services. This route of development is called "de-industrialization" and it has been the route that today's advanced countries followed in the past. Basing on detailed cross-country empirical observations, Castillo and Neto (2016) postulate that today's advanced countries started this transformation when they reached US$15,000–20,000 per capita income. This structural shift from manufacturing to services has been considered as a sign of development for many years.

However, today's developing countries appear to have entered this route of development a little bit earlier than the advanced countries did in the past (Castillo and Neto, 2016; Rowthorn and Ramaswamy, 1997). Empirical observation pointed out that developing countries started to move out of manufacturing to services before the per capita income level reach

US$15,000–20,000 without completing the industrialization in manufacturing. Moreover, the workforce in agriculture today usually skips over the manufacturing sector but instead move directly to services. In some developing countries, this transformation has taken place when the per capita income was somewhere between US$3,000 and US$4,000. Since manufacturing is not sufficiently matured, this structural transformation is called premature de-industrialization (see Dasgupta and Singh, 2006; Rodrik, 2016).

Table 5.1 reports the differences between overall economic growth and growth rates of manufacturing value added for different areas of the world. The primary reason for this international comparison is to examine the impacts of different industrialization practices. For example, East Asian countries in Table 5.1 include newly industrialized countries, and some are success stories of the past in industrialization, such as South Korea, Thailand, and China. Latin American countries in the same table are also well known for their unsuccessful industrialization practices and economic crises that they have occasionally confronted in search of ambitiously high economic growth rates. Sub-Saharan countries, such as Nigeria, South Africa, and Kenya, are underdeveloped but all are in an attempt of industrialization today.

The period of Table 5.1 is sufficiently long to assess the consequences of such structural transformation, which takes time to occur. The first period, spanning from 1970 to 1980, is the period of import substitution under the controlled foreign trade regime. This is also the period when industrialization and capital accumulation in manufacturing speeded up. The second period in Table 5.1 witnessed various liberalization efforts in foreign trade regimes and financial markets. The import-substitution-industrialization strategy abounded, and re-organization of the existing capital stock according to the competitive power of the country in international markets, instead of creating new capital stock, was gained priority in this period. In the 1990s, capital controlled on external accounts was removed in many developing countries and access to international finance through external borrowing become easier than before. A fall in the cost of borrowing and increases in the availability of external finance in the world market enables many developing countries (which were named as emerging market economies afterward) to grow their economies at higher rates than before. However, all these favorable conditions inevitably

Table 5.1.   De-industrialization in some selected developing countries

	Differences between the Entire Economic Growth Rate and Manufacturing Growth Rate (%)			
	1970–1980	1980–1993	1993–2003	2004–2017
ASIA				
China	5.3	1.5	1.9	—
India	1.2	1.1	0.8	0.8
Indonesia	6.8	6.0	1.7	−0.9
South Korea	7.6	3.2	1.7	1.6
Malaysia	3.8	4.1	1.4	−0.6
Pakistan	0.5	1.3	0.9	1.1
Philippine	0.1	−0.6	−0.3	−0.1
Sri Lanka	−2.2	2.7	1.1	−0.2
Thailand	3.4	2.6	2.1	−0.4
LATIN AMERICA				
Argentina	−1.2	−0.4	−1.2	−0.6
Bolivia	1.5	—	−0.1	−0.1
Brazil	0.9	−1.9	−0.3	−1.9
Chile	−2.6	−0.7	−1.6	−1.9
Colombia	0.4	−0.2	−4.3	−1.7
Equator	1.0	−2.1	−0.6	−1.0
Mexico	0.7	0.5	0.1	−0.5
Peru	—	—	−0.6	−1.4
Venezuela	2.2	−0.8	−1.1	−2.5*
SUB-SAHARA AFRICA				
Nigeria		−3.5	−6.5	−1.4
South Africa	1.8	−0.5	−0.4	−1.0
Kenya	3.7	0.9	−1.1	−1.6
TURKEY	1.3	1.5	0.8	−1.2

*The data for Venezuela are available only for 11 years between 2004 and 2014 in World Bank's World Development Indicators. Unlike other countries, the differences in growth rates are calculated for the 2004–2014 period, not the 2004–2017 period.

Source: The data for Asia and Latin American countries between 1970 and 2003 are borrowed from Dasgupta and Singh (2006); the remaining data for 2004–2017 are compiled from *World Bank World Development Indicators* by the author. The data for Sub-Sahara Africa were also obtained from *World Bank World Development Indicators*. The data for Turkey, on the other hand, are from *Economic and Social Indicators* 2017.

hindered industrialization in some of these countries. And, the last period is the financialization of the world economy. Low-interest rates and an abundant amount of international borrowing capacity become an engine for economic growth in many developing countries.

Table 5.1 illustrates the differences between the rate of output growth in manufacturing and the entire economic growth rate. A negative net growth rate in the table indicates that manufacturing grows slower than the overall economy, and *vice versa*. In the first column of Table 5.1 net economic growth rates come up with positive signs, implying that the manufacturing sector was the engine of economic growth with higher growth rates than other sectors in the economy. This expected result was due to import substitution strategy and capital accumulation in manufacturing at any expense in the 1970–1980 period. However, in the second period between 1980 and 1990, developing countries began to differ in terms of net economic growth rates. The majority of South Asian countries exhibit positive net economic growth rates whereas almost all Latin American countries appear to have had negative growth rates. This is indeed a clear indication that South Asian countries continued industrialization in the 1980–1990 period, as the countries in Latin America, except Mexico, left it. Turkey in this period seems to continue to industrialize with the positive average net economic growth rate. In the last period, however, de-industrialization has become an event that was seen even in some South Asian countries along with Latin American countries. Turkey in this period also had a negative average net growth rate, indicating a strong sign of de-industrialization.

Further evidence on the presence of de-industrialization in Turkey can be examined in detail by employing different measures calculated for recent years. One is the calculation of the net economic growth rates as seen in Table 5.1.

As we have already pointed out, international trade is one of the reasons of de-industrialization. Turkey experienced noticeably large foreign trade deficits after 2002, and these trade deficits could be at least some extent of de-industrialization. In Figure 5.5, the share of manufacturing in GDP fell by 2.3% between 2003 and 2017, while manufacturing trade balance, during the same period, deteriorated by 41.2%. This means that domestic expenditure shifts from domestically manufactured goods to

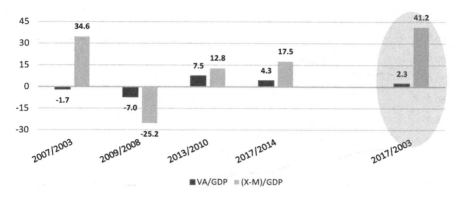

Figure 5.5.   Changes in the shares of manufacturing value added and trade balance in GDP (%)

Source: TCMB and TurkStat.

foreign ones in this period. There would be various factors causing this shift, but a number of them seem to be significant to explain the decline in the importance of domestic manufacturing. One of them is a significant fall in the price of foreign manufactured goods, which would have caused primarily by the overvaluation of Turkish Lira (TL) and increased productivity in the world-manufacturing sector due to new technological innovations. Since the domestic manufacturing sector might have come behind to adopt these technological innovations, Turkey might have lost a certain competitive power in manufacturing.

Following a similar discussion in the literature, several macroeconomic indicators can be used to show the extent of the nature of structural transformation in Turkey. Among others, a mismatch between consumption and domestic production stands out in the Turkish case. This can be seen as another reason for a fall in the share of domestic manufacturing in GDP, which would be due to changes in consumer preferences, causing a mismatch between consumer preferences and domestic production structure. As the per capita income increases, consumer preferences expectedly changes, and the already existing composition of domestic production becomes inferior for households. If changes in the composition of domestic production are slow or do not exist at all, the imports become essential to meet the need for new preferences of households. Lastly, as the

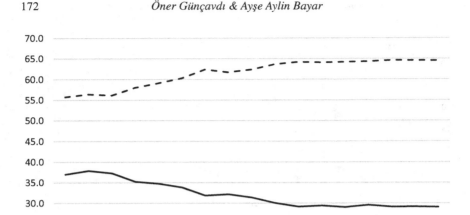

Figure 5.6.   Distribution of consumption by commodity groups

Source: TurkStat.

distribution of income worsens, the structure of demand shifts away from manufacturing toward services (see Figure 5.6). This also leads to a decline in the share of manufacturing in GDP. Households consequently demand more non-tradable from inside and more tradable from outside.

a. *The Sectoral Shares of Employment*

Figure 5.7 shows the diagram for the shares of sectoral employment for the manufacturing and services sectors (including construction). The data are readily available from *TurkStat* for the 1985–2018 period. The employment share of manufacturing is distinguished by the straight line, whereas the service sector share is given by the dash line. There are several observations worth mentioning in this respect. First, the share of manufacturing employment seems to have increased until 2008, and it began to decline afterward by rendering a *concave* functional shape for the trend function. The employment capacity of the manufacturing sector shows a decline, which started after 2009. Second, the service sector employment is an important source of employment, and it seems to have

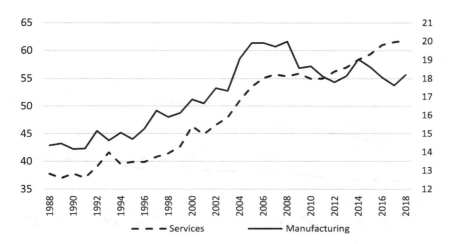

Figure 5.7. Sectoral shares of employment (%)

reached over 60% of total employment after 2016. The best-fitted trend function becomes an increasing trend line as seen in Figure 5.7. Lastly, it will not be an exaggeration if it is considered that employment in the Turkish economy is, to a great extent, *service-led employment.*

In Figure 5.8, the numbers of employment in three distinctive sectors, namely manufacturing, services, and agriculture, are depicted. It is even more evident from the earlier figure that services (including construction) seem to have become the dominant sector creating employment after 2001. In particular, relatively two sharp increases appear in the service sector employment, the first in 2004, the second in 2009. Employment in manufacturing steadily increased without any distinctive trend. The agricultural employment, on the other hand, shows a sharp decline in 2004 and seems to have remained stable afterward.

According to Figure 5.8, employment levels in the extended-service (including services and construction) and manufacturing services show a rising trend from 1988 to 2018 (see TurkStat, 2018). Among them, manufacturing employment shows a secular trend at a relatively slow pace. The extended-service sector, on the other hand, seems to have increased relatively faster than manufacturing, but it departed away from its trend with a small jump in 2010. Basing on this observation, the extended-service

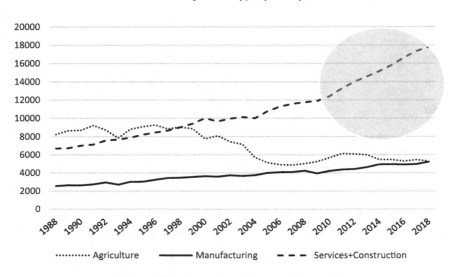

Figure 5.8. Sectoral employment (thousand)

sector has become the most important sector creating employment, particularly after 2010.[7] It is also obvious from Figure 5.8 that the agricultural sector is the only one losing employment. It appears that the employment capacity of the agricultural sector especially declined between 1999 and 2007, and then seems to have reached stability.

Unlike these conventional measures of de-industrialization, additional indicators can also be proposed here by generating them from microeconomic data sources available in Turkey. The longest data available for this purpose are *Households Budget Surveys*, covering the period between 2002 and 2017. Two indicators, namely sectoral mean income and the population shares of each income entity, are calculated and the results are discussed in what follows.

b. *Differences in Sectoral Mean Income*

In this study, the total income of households is decomposed into three components according to the sectors through which income is generated;

[7]G. Uysal and F. Kavuncu (2019). "Disables' Care and Labour Statistics". *BETAM Research Note* 19/244.

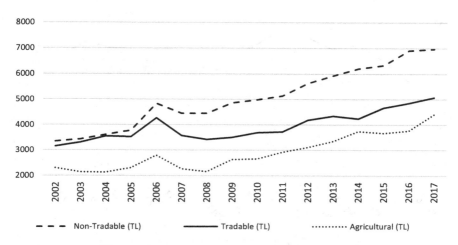

Figure 5.9.   Mean income of each income type (TL)

they are namely non-tradable, tradable, and agricultural income. The mean income level of each component can be seen in Figure 5.7. Since these figures are calculated from *Households Budget Surveys*, they are only available for the period between 2002 and 2017. In Figure 5.9, the mean non-tradable income is higher than the mean income of other income sources. Mean non-tradable income seems to have steadily increased after 2002, but this increase particularly became distinctive after 2008.

The ratios of the mean levels of non-tradable income to other income components can be seen in Figure 5.9. In 2004, tradable and non-tradable mean income levels appear to be almost equal. Then, this ratio of non-tradeable mean income became almost 1.4 times higher than the tradable mean income in 2007 and remained more or less at this level afterward. This finding implies that the mean income in non-tradable economic activities increased relatively more than tradeable mean income, particularly in the 2004–2008 period.

c. *Change in Population Shares*

"Population" in our exercise here refers to the number of income entities, and it is decomposed by income groups. Any "change" in this context

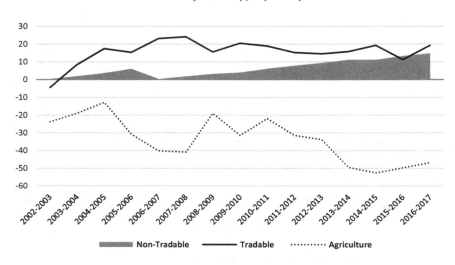

Figure 5.10.   Change in population share — Cumulative

implies a change in the number of relevant income entities. For example, any increase (or decrease) in the population share of non-tradable income is considered an increase (or decrease) in the number of income entities in the form of non-tradable activities. Figure 5.10 shows this change in each income component. Three distinctive results emerge from Figure 5.10. First, the population share of agricultural income declines after 2009. Second, tradable income items seem to surge around zero indicating no major change in the population share of tradable income. Third, non-tradable income entities, together with their population share, apparently increased after 2009.

d. *Changes in Relative Prices*

It is most likely that most developing countries are price takers in manufacturing goods and their relative prices are fully determined globally. Technological development in advanced countries experiences rapid productivity growth, which leads to a substantial amount of decline in relative prices of manufacturing through the standard supply–demand condition in the world market. This expectedly puts the pressure of low manufacturing prices on developing countries with slow technological progress in technology. These countries without strong comparative advantage in manufacturing inevitably become net importers of manufacturing goods, and begin to rely more on non-tradable sectors (such as construction, services, trade, and finance) rather than tradable economic activities (namely manufacturing) to revive economic growth. Those that are not able to avoid international competition, have to become increasingly dependent on economic activities which are controlled by domestic supply–demand conditions without being exposed to international competition originating from advanced countries. This is one reason for squeezing the manufacturing sector in employment and production. Non-tradable sector unavoidably becomes the most trusted economic activity to policymakers in developing countries to create employment and economic growth.

Figure 5.11 shows that the Turkish experience also complies with the theoretical expectation. Figure 5.11(a) illustrates a decline in the relative price of manufacturing until 2008.[8] Turkey was exposed to foreign competition mainly due to the Customs Union agreement with the EU after 1995, and manufacturing goods in any kind and competitive prices became highly accessible for Turkish customers. Overvaluation of the domestic currency, caused by large capital inflows, was a great help for

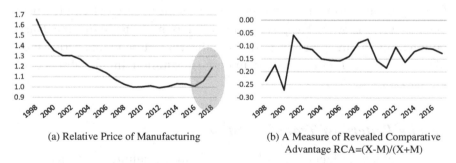

(a) Relative Price of Manufacturing

(b) A Measure of Revealed Comparative Advantage RCA=(X-M)/(X+M)

Figure 5.11. Relative prices of manufacturing and its international competition power

[8]The relative prices are derived as a ratio of the price of manufacturing to the price of service and construction. Both price series must be taken as tentative price indices, and both are obtained by dividing current values of sectoral data to those chain-linked volume values. This is not a conventional way of deriving these price indices, but a recent change in measuring national account data left no other option, other than this.

Turkey to import easily. Figure 5.11(b) also illustrates the loss of the competitive power of Turkish manufacturing. Revealed comparative advantage (RCA) was calculated as a ratio of net exports (X – M) to the volume of foreign trade (X + M). RCA values appear to be negative for all years between 1998 and 2017, indicating losses of competitive power in manufacturing.

This explanation is based on the differential technological progress in manufacturing among advanced and developing countries. This is also the reason for the rising economic populism in developing countries. The countries that have difficulties to overcome undesired effects of globalization and backwardness in technological progress seek alternative ways for generating employment, economic growth, and better income distribution. They find the recent structural shift from manufacturing to non-tradable economic activities a relief, without worrying about the binding constraint of international competition. Yet, a requirement of adopting domestic economy, most importantly political establishment, to new conditions puts a squeeze on politicians everywhere to rely on non-tradable economic activities to please the public searching for a better job and higher income. Today's populism in practice is different from the earlier one in the 1960s–1970s. The manufacturing sector and structural transformation from agriculture to manufacturing used to be the sources of employment and economic growth. The government used to intervene in income distribution through direct income policies. Industrialization in this period took place, *to a great extent*, under import substitution in the absence of globalization.

e. *The Pattern of Transformation*

The movement of labor forces has been from agriculture to services, not to manufacturing as expected. However, the shift from agriculture to manufacturing has been very limited and it seems to have stopped after 2005. This is mainly because both sectors, agriculture and manufacturing, have lost employment against services. A similar pattern of transformation in the workforce has also been observed for services, with the only exception that this shift continued to a limited extent after 2005.

The second feature of this transformation is that the shift from agriculture to services has been accompanied by declines in the relative productivities of the service and manufacturing sectors compared with agriculture until 2005. Importantly, the fall in productivity in the service sector was larger than in manufacturing. This suggests that the sectoral transformation from agriculture to manufacturing and services until 2005 was not economic growth enhancing.

Another feature of transformation is that manufacturing has been losing employment against services as seen in Figure 5.12. The fall in employment has been accompanied by a rise in the relative productivity of manufacturing compared with services. In comparison with the rising relative average labor productivity of manufacturing, the sectoral shift of labor forces to the service sector from manufacturing has little chance to exhibit a positive impact on overall economic growth.

As we have already pointed out, international trade is one of the reasons of de-industrialization. Turkey experienced noticeably large foreign trade deficits after 2002, and these trade deficits could be at least to some extent due to de-industrialization. In Figure 5.7, the share of manufacturing in GDP fell by 2.3% between 2003 and 2017, while manufacturing trade balance, during the same period, deteriorated by 41.2%. This means that domestic expenditure shifted from domestically manufactured goods to foreign ones in this period. There would be various factors causing this shift, but a few of them seem to be significant to explain the decline in the importance of domestic manufacturing. One of them is a significant fall in the price of foreign manufactured goods, which would have been caused primarily by the overvaluation of the Turkish Lira and increased productivity in the world-manufacturing sector due to new technological innovations. Since the domestic manufacturing sector might have fallen behind to adopt these technological innovations, Turkey might have lost a certain competitive advantage in manufacturing. Another reason for a fall in the share of domestic manufacturing in GDP would be changes in consumer preferences, and a mismatch with domestic production structure. As the per capita income increases, consumer preferences expectedly change, and the already existing composition of domestic production becomes inferior for households. If changes in the composition of domestic production are slow or do not exist at all, the imports

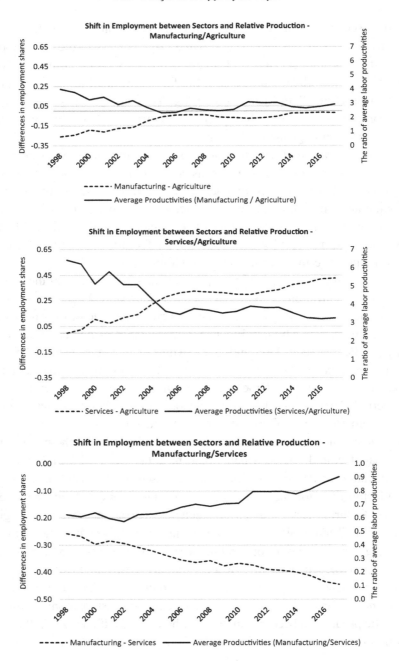

Figure 5.12.   Sectoral comparison between productivity and employment shares

become essential to meet the need for new preferences of households. Lastly, as the distribution of income worsens, the structure of demand shifts away from manufacturing toward services (see Figure 5.6). This also leads to a decline in the share of manufacturing in GDP. Households consequently demand more non-tradable goods than tradable ones from the domestic economy by relying on the importation of tradable goods from the world.

5.6. International Trade as a Cause of De-industrialization

International trade is one of the several reasons for the de-industrialization process in Turkey. The trade–employment relationship has widely been studied in the literature, but mostly for developed market economies (Acemoğlu *et al.*, 2016; Greenaway *et al.*, 1999; Krugman and Lawrence, 1993). However, the same issue has begun to drawn attention for developing market economies, especially after the (premature) de-industrialization process has also become observable for these countries. The de-industrialization, as a result of being exposed excessively to import penetration, can give rise to deteriorations in income distribution through its revealed undesirable effects on employment.

The same development has been seen in the economy of Turkey for some time, and de-industrialization has lately become visible as an apparent drop in the shares of manufacturing value-added and employment. Besides, the search for high economic growth as a result of populist economic practices and an increased reliance on non-tradable economic activities for growth ended up with high dependence on importation.

As much as the appropriate environmental factors prevailed, Turkey has been able to have *current account deficits*. In Figure 5.13, a sudden rise in current account deficits can be observed in the 2000s. However, the extent of these deficits had not been seen in the history of the Turkish economy. Moreover, as long as the economy grows above its potential level, which is historically 4.5–5% per annum, current account deficits also rise to unsustainable levels mainly because of the high dependency of the Turkish production and consumption on imports. Various AK Parti governments in the 2000s have had to rely largely on non-tradable economic activities and have easily produced high economic growth and

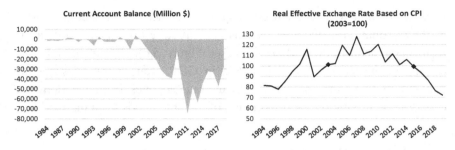

Figure 5.13.   Current account balances and real effective exchange rates

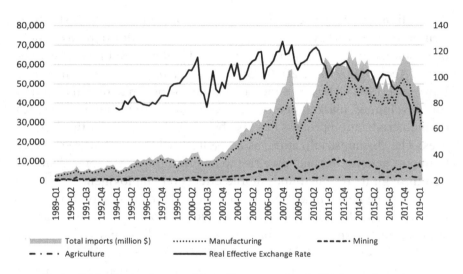

Figure 5.14.   Sectoral composition of imports and real effective exchange rate

gains in jobs by avoiding international competition to which tradable economic activities have intensively been exposed.

The sectoral breakdown of imports in Figure 5.14 also shows a drastic jump in manufacturing imports after 2002. This implies that the great extent of current account deficits was also made up of manufacturing imports. In particular, manufacturing imports, along with total imports, illustrate a firm rise up to the 2008–2009 period in which the sub-prime mortgage crisis prevailed in the world economy. It is also striking from

Figure 5.14 that this jump in import took place while Turkish Lira was appreciating. After a limited amount of a decline in the 2008–2009 period, imports revived with high economic growth and continued to remain as high as before. The imports of mining and agriculture, on the other hand, stayed relatively low.

This empirical finding implies that foreign trade in manufacturing would be one of the causes of declining share in manufacturing value added and employment. We now propose a simple method of measuring the employment effect of rising imports in the 2000s by basing on the calculation of net import penetration (NIP). The net effects of the simultaneous growth of exports and imports need to be estimated to assess the impacts of trade on de-industrialization like losses in employment. NIP offers a simple method that takes account of this net foreign trade effect simultaneously. The method we propose, as noted, is simple and well known in the literature (see Luttrell, 1978). NIP for each year t is calculated as the ratio of net imports ($M - X$) to apparent consumption ($C = Q + M - X$, where C and Q are apparent consumption and domestic production, respectively).

The data and calculated NIP for the 1998–2017 period are reported in the table in Appendix A. It is interesting that all calculated values of NIP are positive and increase over time, indicating that the manufacturing sector has lost competitive power in international trade due to the overvaluation of the domestic currency. This finding is indeed compatible with the findings of earlier research emphasizing the high import dependence of the Turkish economy on imports (Günçavdı and Kayam, 2017; Günçavdı and Orbay, 2002; Günçavdı and Ülengin, 2018). Figure 5.15, drawn by using calculated NIP values in Table 5.2, illustrates an increase in NIP while the share of the use of domestic production in total consumption declines due to losses of comparative advantage of domestic production.

Of course, high NIP could be responsible for a certain extent of losses in employment in manufacturing, and these losses can be calculated by taking into account changes in NIP values between t and $t + 1$. We first estimate a hypothetical level of employment, which is compatible with the actual change in NIP from t to $t + 1$. This estimated employment is noted by L_{t+1}^{*}, and it is calculated by $L_{t+1}^{*} = \alpha L_{t+1}$, where $\alpha = (1 - \text{NIP}_t)/(1 - \text{NIP}_{t+1})$. Thus,

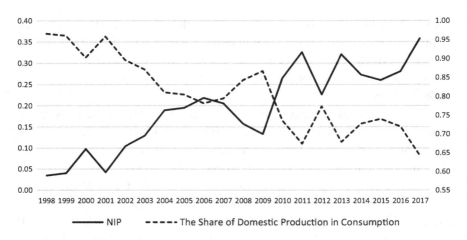

Figure 5.15.   Net import penetration and the share of domestic production in consumption

L_{t+1}^{*} is calculated as a fraction of actual employment and it is interpreted as the estimated employment level if actual employment from t to $t + 1$ was changed by the amount of change in NIP. It is evident from this that $\alpha = 1$ if there is no change in *NIP* (i.e., $\text{NIP}_{t} = \text{NIP}_{t+1}$). If $\text{NIP}_{t+1} > \text{NIP}_{t}$, then $\alpha > 1$, so that the calculated level of employment will be greater than the actual level of employment; $L_{t+1}^{*} > L_{t+1}$. Finally, the difference between the estimated and actual levels of employment will be a measure of the change in employment at time $t + 1$ (ΔL_{m}) due only to import penetration between period t and $t + 1$; $\Delta L_{m} = L_{t+1}^{*} - L_{t+1}$. The positive values of ΔL_{m} are interpreted as losses in employment, whereas the negative ones show gains in employment. These estimated values of losses (or gains) are reported in Table A1 in the appendix, and both their levels and cumulative values are illustrated in Figure 5.16. Cumulative values in Figure 5.16 show total losses in employment until the selected end year from the initial year 1998. According to the figure, import penetration has been responsible for job losses, and these losses appear to have speeded up after 2009.

In sum, Turkey was able to increase economic growth and domestic consumption after 2002, which paved the way for high current account deficits, but, at the same time, suffered from job losses due to increase in import penetration. This empirical finding shows that international trade

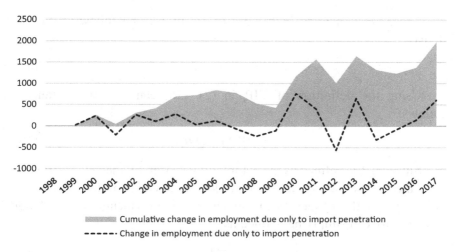

Cumulative change in employment due only to import penetration
- - - - - Change in employment due only to import penetration

Figure 5.16. Estimated job losses due to import penetration

and excessive increase in manufacturing imports accounted for a certain extent of de-industrialization, and this effect seems to have increased apparently in the period after 2009.

a. *Relative Impact of Demand, Productivity, and Import on Manufacturing Employment*

It would be useful to carry out an additional empirical examination to see the relative effects of demand, labor productivity, and imports by employing a simple accounting approach. Our method is simple and based on the decomposition of the definition of the apparent consumption variable as follows:

$$C_t = Q_t + M_t - X_t \qquad (1)$$

where C_t: consumption; Q_t: domestic production; M_t: imports; X_t: exports. Recalling the definition of net import penetration (NIP_t) as the ratio of net foreign trade balance ($M_t - X_t$) to domestic consumption (C_t), (2) can be written as follows:

$$NIP_t = (M_t - X_t)/C_t \qquad (2)$$

Then, upon dividing both sides of (1) by C_t, the following can be derived:

$$1 = (Q_t + M_t - X_t)/C_t \tag{1a}$$

Using the definition of NIP$_t$ in (2), (1a) can also be written as follows:

$$(1 - \text{NIP}_t) = Q_t/C_t \tag{1b}$$

Since NIP$_t$ is defined as the net import penetration, then $(1 - \text{NIP}_t)$ can be named as the ratio of domestic production to consumption. To make a connection with changes in manufacturing employment, average labor productivity can simply be defined as

$$A_t = Q_t/L_t \tag{3}$$

or

$$Q_t = A_t L_t \tag{3a}$$

Upon substituting Q_t from (3a) into (1b),

$$(1 - \text{NIP}_t) = A_t L_t/C_t \tag{1c}$$

Assume that S_t is the ratio of domestic production to consumption and it is substituted for $(1 - \text{NIP}_t)$. Respectively, (1c) can be written for L_t as

$$L_t = S_t(C_t/A_t) \tag{4}$$

Equation (4) describes the labor employed in domestic production in terms of consumption, domestic production, and average productivity. Respectively, proportional changes in labor can also be derived in the growth form by logarithmically differentiating Equation (4):

$$\dot{L} = \dot{C} + \dot{S} - \dot{A} \tag{5}$$

where "." over the variables above represents the growth rates of the relevant variable; i.e., $\dot{X} = \frac{(dX/dt)}{X}$. Identity (5) is an accounting identity and defines that growth rates of manufacturing employments are related *positively* to both the growth rate of total consumption ($\dot{C}$) and the growth rate of the share of domestic production in consumption ($\dot{S}$) and *negatively* to

Table 5.2. The sources of changes in employment

	Growth Rates			
	Actual Change in Employment	**Consumption**	**Domestic Production**	**Average Productivity**	**Estimated Change in Employment**
1999	2.7	−5.0	−0.6	−8.0	2.4
2000	2.3	13.9	−6.0	4.6	3.3
2001	−1.5	−14.2	6.2	−7.5	−0.5
2002	4.2	11.2	−6.5	−0.1	4.9
2003	−1.8	13.0	−2.8	11.8	−1.6
2004	2.1	21.6	−6.9	10.9	3.8
2005	6.7	10.4	−0.7	2.7	7.0
2006	1.8	13.1	−2.9	7.9	2.3
2007	0.5	5.0	1.7	6.2	0.5
2008	3.6	−5.3	6.1	−3.0	3.8
2009	−6.8	−11.4	2.8	−2.3	−6.3
2010	6.8	29.2	−15.2	2.7	11.4
2011	3.6	30.9	−8.3	15.9	6.7
2012	1.2	−10.9	14.7	1.0	2.8
2013	4.8	24.5	−12.2	4.3	8.0
2014	6.6	−0.9	7.1	−0.4	6.6
2015	0.4	4.1	1.8	5.5	0.4
2016	−0.8	6.8	−2.8	4.7	−0.7
2017	1.1	22.3	−10.8	7.9	3.6

Source: Author's calculation based on data from TUİK.

changing rate of average productivity $(\dot{A})$.[9] The statistical data are available to calculate each component in (5) from *TurkStat* for the 1998–2017 period.

The empirical results are reported in Table 5.2 and they must be taken as tentative just to examine the relative importance of three factors defined

---

[9]There are two important defects in this decomposition method. First, the accounting identity (1) is defined rather arbitrarily, and a different identity expectedly yields different results. Second, this definition ignores the effects of cross-terms and other variables that are not included here (Martin and Evens, 1981).

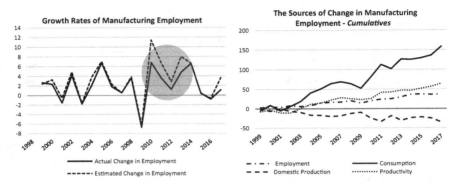

Figure 5.17.   The impacts of import penetration on employment

in Equation (5). Figure 5.17 presents a simple comparison between actual
and estimated growth rates of manufacturing employment, and the performance of the calculated growth rates looks fine. Respectively, the estimated figures show great similarity with the actual ones until 2011 and
then drift away from the actual figure until 2013. After getting closer to
each other again in the period between 2014 and 2016, the estimated
employment growth rate differs significantly from actual value in 2017.
Despite these differences, estimated results can be considered as sufficiently successful.

The results are also very informative regarding the factors that determine the change in employment in manufacturing. Two findings become
obvious in this empirical analysis. First, general consumption (or demand)
positively contributes to employment. Second, the reduction in domestic
production (due to higher import penetration) expectedly causes losses in
employment in the manufacturing sector. Third, the positive trend of the
average productivity of labor implies a decline in the average productivity
of labor.

These results indicate that domestic demand is necessary for generating economic growth and gaining employment in manufacturing, but it is
not sufficient. A certain extent of import substitution would have been
needed as a sufficiency condition to revive industrialization and create
extra employment. Unless external borrowing to finance non-tradable-
derived domestic demand and economic growth is sufficiently available,

industrialization and the tradable sector's production will be the only option for the new economic growth model.

5.7. Structural Transformation and Income Inequality

In his seminal paper, Kuznets has been the first one drawing our attention to the relationship between structural transformation and income inequality (Kuznets, 1955). Based on his empirical observations on a limited amount of countries, he argued that as low-income economies industrialize, inequality would initially increase. This is because as labor force moves from relatively low-productive industries, such as agriculture, to relatively high-productive ones, such as manufacturing, a difference would occur between the wage levels of workers already employed and endowed with appropriate skills in manufacturing and the wage level of fresh labor force previously working in agriculture with no skill for manufacturing. This postulate has later become a well-known **Kuznets hypothesis**.

This hypothesis has, however, been challenged by the experiences of today's developing countries. Kuznets's hypothesis is an empirical observation and not a deterministic relationship. The relationship between structural transformation and income inequalities is to some extent determined by the specific characteristics of the path of transformation that the country follows. In this regard, Kuznets distinguished three essential characteristics of the sectoral transformation that determine the effect on income inequality of the transformation. They are namely (i) the mean income level of the sectors that the transformation involves; (ii) within-group inequality of the sectors between which the population moves; (iii) the population share in each sector (which constitutes a population shift effect). If the labor force moves more from both low-mean income and high within-group inequality sector to high-income and low within-group inequality sector, then income inequality improves and the Kuznets hypothesis does not hold.

If we turn our attention to the Turkish experience, it can be seen that the shift of labor force takes place from agriculture to service sectors rather than manufacturing. The distributional effects of this shift are determined by the mean income levels and within-group inequality of each sector (Baymul and Sen, 2019). In this regard, what we have observed was the agriculture sector being a low-mean income (see Figure 5.9) and high within-group inequality sector (see Figure 5.20), and the service and non-tradable sectors, in general, possess the highest mean income level. Although within-group inequality in non-tradable also is high, this particular transformation from agriculture to services might have an improving effect on the overall inequality, but this can rather be concluded by examining further empirical results. However, we expect that the shift of labor from tradable to non-tradable would have deteriorating effects on entire income distribution in the economy. In this regard, Figure 5.21 in the following section clearly shows that the ratio of the mean income of both sectors remained stable after 2008. It implies that there has been no apparent deterioration in the relative mean income level of both income groups after 2008. Given the fact that within-group inequality of tradable is lower than other sectors, a shift from manufacturing, or tradable in general, would deteriorate income distribution, or at least hold it stable.

To see whether the structural transformation in Turkey has taken place by the Kuznets hypothesis, the Gini coefficients of the entire Turkish economy are depicted with the shares of three sectors, namely agriculture, manufacturing, and services, in Figure 5.18. The Gini coefficient is shown on the vertical axe, whereas the share of each sector is depicted on the horizontal axis. In the first panel in Figure 5.5(a), it seems that income inequality increases as the share of agriculture rises over time, and *vice versa*. The figure in panel (b) shows a decline in income inequality with

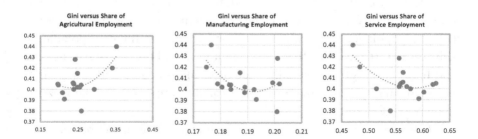

Figure 5.18.   Income distribution and sectoral shares

Sources: The raw data in the figure are obtained from TurkStat.

an increase in the share of manufacturing. They are all expected results as the Kuznets hypothesis postulates. The panel (c) in Figure 5.18 implies falls in inequality as the share of services increases.

a. *Income Distribution*

Income inequality has been one of the crucial economic issues in the Turkish economy, and this allows the Turkish policymakers to easily adopt populist approaches to combating inequality. Different estimates of income inequality are available for the period before 2002 and can be compiled from the website of the Presidential Office of Strategy and Budget of Turkey.[10] Estimated Gini[11] coefficients for the 1963–1994 are based on various empirical research previously made by the State Planning Organization and State Institute of Statistics, which had previously been responsible for economic planning and monitoring economic and social development in Turkey. A comprehensive and continued survey-based research on this issue was first started by *TurkStat* in 2002 and onward.

Undulated economic growth rates in the 1970s were surprisingly accompanied by improvements in income distribution (Figure 5.19). These improvements seem to have continued after 1980.[12] There is another interesting observation on the economic growth–income distribution relationship. It becomes evident from Figure 5.16 that as the economy

---

[10]This is a newly established governmental body working under the new Presidential Office. The same data had previously been compiled and announced as Economic and Social Indicators to the public by the Minister of Economics, but they had also been available in the publications of various governmental bodies. For the data, see http://www. sbb.gov.tr/ekonomik-ve-sosyal-gostergeler/.

[11]For the definition of the Gini coefficient and its importance in measuring income inequality, see Chapter 2 by Acemoğlu and Üçer.

[12]The data for income distribution for the period before and after 2002 are compiled from different sources. Income distribution figures for the period earlier than 2002 usually come from different studies of State Planning Office, as forecasted parameters, without relying on any organized household survey. As seen in Figure 5.6, there is also discontinuity in income distribution data before 2002 for this reason. Therefore, precaution is needed when income distribution data for the period before 2002 are used for any comparison with those calculated for the period after 2002.

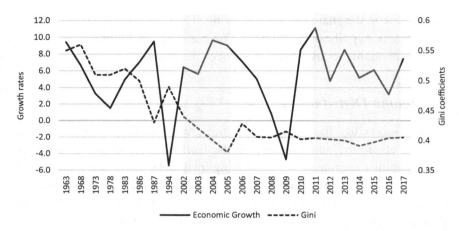

Figure 5.19. Relationship between economic growth and income distribution

encounters any economic crisis and a sharp slowdown in economic growth, income distribution immediately deteriorates. For example, in the 1994 economic crisis, once economic growth declined to −5%, the Gini coefficient, as a well-known income distribution measure, seems to have reached 0.49 in 1994 from 0.43 in 1987. Similarly, this negative relationship was also seen in the sub-prime mortgage crisis in 2008–2009, where economic growth slowed down at the rate exceeding 4% by deteriorating income distribution.

Regarding the performance in income distribution under various AK Parti governments, the entire period between 2002 and 2017 does not show a unique pattern. An evident improvement in the early 2000s (namely in the 2002–2005 period) seems to have disappeared afterward. Although a limited amount of decline in income inequality continued between 2006 and 2013, income distribution began to deteriorate after 2014. This mixed result is worth explaining.

Changes in the intuitional framework and macroeconomic priorities can account for this mixed result. In the early years of the 2000s, reforms measures and good macroeconomic governance (featured by low-interest rate and inflation and stable foreign exchange rate) took place and eradicated income gaps in the economy.[13] In an empirical work based on the

---

[13] See Chapter 2 by Acemoğlu and Üçer.

Household Budget Survey of *TurkStat*, Bayar and Günçavdı (2020) postulate that good macroeconomic governance is the crucial factor for the improvement in income equality in the early years of the 2000s. In particular, despite their small shares in total income, financial earnings have been the most important determinant of income inequality, and a drastic decline in interest rates during the reform period, together with lowering inflation, helped income inequality decrease (Bayar and Günçavdı, 2020). Additionally, labor and entrepreneurial income were other influential income items that were also affected by sound macroeconomic management in the reform period. Despite the presence of small ups and downs, improvements continued until 2014 and then began steadily to increase once again.

In another paper, Bayar and Günçavdı (2018) decompose the total income of households concerning their sources and define three different income groups whose income is earned from three distinctive economic activities. They are namely (i) Non-tradable income, which is earned only from non-tradable economic activities, such as services, construction, and trade; (ii) Tradable income, which is earned from tradable economic activities such as manufacturing; finally (iii) Agricultural income, which is earned from agricultural activities.[14] Accordingly, some households in the survey would have only one or a combination of these income items as total household income. We divide these incomes by their sources and cumulate them as three separate income items regardless of households themselves. Therefore, instead of using a household as a unit of observation, we use only these income entities and examine how they interact with changing macroeconomic conditions. When one looks at Figure 5.20, the share of non-tradable income is seen to be far higher than other income entities in selected years.

In Figure 5.21, inequality levels, measured by Gini coefficients, of three income groups are shown. Within-group inequality seems to be lower in tradable income than others. Non-tradable income has the highest

---

[14] Agricultural goods are also tradable goods, but the agricultural sector has great importance in the Turkish economy and constitutes a large share in the entire economy, we consider agricultural income separately from tradable goods. Besides, macroeconomic policies targeting particularly at agricultural activities are sector-specific policies and differ in nature from those for tradable.

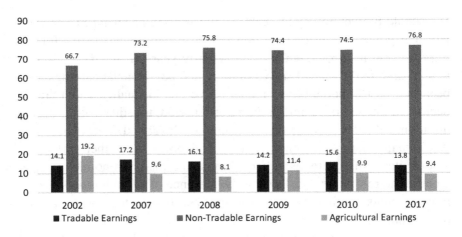

Figure 5.20. Shares of each source of income in total (%)

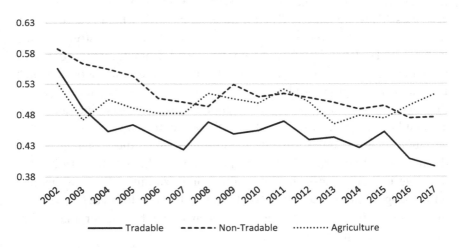

Figure 5.21. Within-group inequalities — Gini coefficients

within-group inequality due to having more variability in size and their nature among income items than those of other income types. The same is true for agricultural income, which is earned according to the size of land owned by households. These differences in inequality offer two candidates that possess a detrimental impact on the entire inequality. Any measure aiming at improving income distribution must then target these two distinctive income types by improving their within-group inequalities. In particular, a non-tradable income group has great potential in an improvement in the entire distribution of income in the economy.

This type of decomposition is particularly important in examining structural transformation. Each income group is not a perfect substitute for others, and they would be affected *differently* by changes in macroeconomic policies, relative prices, and incentives. Most importantly, the markets, which constitute the sources of income entities, would show different responses to shocks due to their structural differences. For example, tradable income and tradable goods markets are highly globalized and are exposed to severe international competition and external shocks. Accordingly, macroeconomic policies regarding the tradable goods market and tradable income are assumed to be determined in coordination with the need for international markets. On the other hand, non-tradable goods market and non-tradable income are easily taken under control by policymakers without worrying about the restrictiveness of international competition. The policies regarding non-tradable income might become independent from external shocks.

Non-tradable sectors are relatively closed to international competition, and to a great extent, present freedom for policymakers and politicians to implement independent economic policies according to the needs of society and the economy. In particular, after globalization took away the control of policymakers over a certain part of the economy, non-tradable activities and non-tradable sectors have gained importance to intervene directly in the economy to generate economic growth, and even to exercise populist policies. In the case of having difficulties in creating economic growth, non-tradable activities and income become easy for policymakers to encourage. This feature of non-tradable activities also allows policymakers to establish a novel "rent-transfer-via-markets" mechanisms to "selected" or "privileged" groups of people in the economy.

As we discussed earlier, Figure 5.7 illustrates the mean income of each income type between 2002 and 2017 based on our calculation from the household survey data. The great extent of income entities in the household budget surveys is non-tradable income. And, the real mean

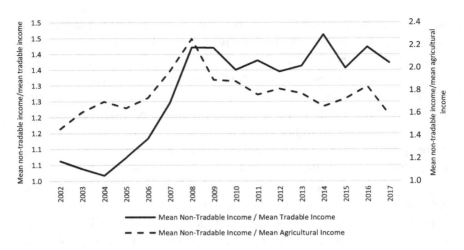

Figure 5.22. Mean non-tradable incomes to tradable and agricultural incomes

level of this income seems to be the highest among others. It is clear that the difference of mean non-tradable income, particularly from tradable one, drifted away after 2008. Although real mean tradable income also shows a secular increase after 2008, its pace seems to have been slower and its level has been lower than mean non-tradable income. These empirical findings, altogether, imply that non-tradable income is the most crucial income entity that would most likely affect unprivileged households' income.

Figure 5.22, on the other hand, shows the ratios of mean non-tradable income to mean tradable and agricultural income. It is also clear from the figure that the ratio of the real mean non-tradable income to tradable one increased sharply between 2002 and 2008. However, this relative income ratio somewhat remained constant after 2008. The same trend can be observed for the ratio of non-tradable mean income to mean agricultural income, except its decline after 2008. It is obvious from Figure 5.22 that non-tradable income shows a secular increase in the early reform period.

Based upon the presumption that different measures of macroeconomic policies might affect the different components of income differently, the total household income can be decomposed into its components according to its sources, and the relationship between these income components and macroeconomic measures can be established. In a recent paper, Bayar and Günçavdı (2018) decompose total household income into their components by their functions. They use the Household Budget Survey, which allows for six different functional forms of income. They are namely labor earnings, which are the most dominant income type and nearly consist of 55–60% of total income, of which agricultural entrepreneurial earnings are 7–8%, entrepreneurial earnings are something around 20%, financial earnings are less than 1%, retirement earnings are 10–11%, and finally transfer earnings are only 4–5% of total household income. The last two income sources in Turkey are received by households, not in return of any productive contribution to creating value added, they could be treated as transfer payments to households to maintain social justice. Then, they calculate the relative contribution of each income type into overall income inequality by employing Shorrocks (1982) and Jenkins decomposition methods.[15] The empirical results obtained from Jenkins's decomposition method is borrowed from Bayar and Günçavdı (2018) and are illustrated in Figure 5.23.

As seen in Figure 5.23, each income source contributes to overall income inequality differently. Entrepreneurial and financial earnings stand

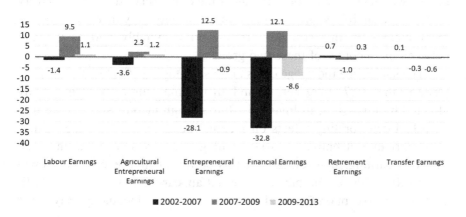

Figure 5.23.   Contribution of different income sources in overall income inequality

---

[15] For a detailed explanation of both decomposition methods and adaptation of them to the Turkish household data, see Bayar and Günçavdı (2018).

out as the most influential income in the 2002–2007 reform period. This implies that entrepreneurial and financial earnings accounted for the improvement in income inequality in the early 2000s. In addition, both income sources were influenced by low inflation, interest rate, stable exchange rate, and high economic growth, which were all products of good macroeconomic governance. Another interesting finding is that social nets practices, as an integral part of the recent World Bank–IMF backed reform program, were widely adopted by the central government and local municipalities in the early reform period, with new public institutions introduced for this purpose.

There is, of course, a widely expected presumption that these transfer payments would contribute to the improvement in inequality, which could have deteriorated after the economic crisis. However, in the Turkish case in the 2002–2007 period, the contributions of transfer earning were negligible. Retirement earnings, on the other hand, appear to have deteriorating effects on income inequality. This paradoxical result is rather related to the fact of widespread informal employment without any social security protection. This group of people is deprived of any retirement payment when they get retired. Retirement income becomes a privilege for some people who had worked formally under the umbrella of the social security system and can be a source of inequality in society. Any increase in retirement income in this structural framework inevitably widens the gap between the incomes of these two groups.[16]

The sub-prime mortgage crisis and its contagion effect in Turkey took place in the 2007–2009 period, and all income sources were inevitably affected by this crisis. In Figure 5.20, four main income sources seem to have had deteriorating effects on income inequality, namely labor earnings, agricultural entrepreneurial earning, entrepreneurial earning, and financial earning. Interestingly, in this period of high economic growth (2010–2013), the economic crisis period appears to have had no significant effects, except on financial earnings, or income inequality. Bayar and

---

[16] Gürsel *et al.* (2000) also note a similar result regarding the impact of overall transfer payments (rather than retirement payment) on income distribution. In the comparison of household income between 1987 and 1994, they find that transfer payment exhibits a deteriorating effect on income distribution.

Günçavdı (2018) postulate that the improving effect on income inequality of financial earnings is not surprising. A consumption boom, derived by credit expansion, and low-interest-rate earnings took place to revive economic growth after the crisis, and most likely, households, particularly low-income ones, were discouraged to hold savings in the financial system. High-income households, on the other hand, remained in the banking system due to their relatively high *propensity-to-save*, and interest rate earners became a more homogeneous group after the fall in interest rate than before. Additionally, the weight of interest rate earnings in total income drastically declined after the reform, and their impacts on entire income distribution inevitably decreased.

Sectoral decomposition of household income would also be informative to draw an inference about the effects of de-industrialization, defined as a rise in the share of non-tradable economic activities, on income distribution. Following the same methodology of decomposing income by their functions in production, non-tradable, and agricultural income groups, this time, are used as a unit of account (instead of equivalent disposable income of individuals[17]). Then, the impacts of tradable, non-tradable, and agricultural income on inequality are calculated by using the Shorrocks decomposition method, and the results are depicted in Figure 5.24. According to the results, the contributions of non-tradable income into income inequality have been the highest in all selected years. This implies that any economic growth strategy relying on expansion in non-tradable economic activities, rather than tradables, and income would likely account for having a detrimental effect on income inequality.

In this regard, the contributions of three income sources, namely agricultural, non-tradable, and tradable income, are estimated by using the Jenkins decomposition method, and the results are reported in Figure 5.25. This decomposition aims to understand whether different sources of

---

[17] In the literature, studies mainly employ equivalent disposable income of individuals for examination. The fact is that in a particular household, there may be some individuals who do not have any income may benefit from the incomes of the other individuals in these households. Therefore, this reality has to be taken into account when estimating the income inequality measures. In this respect, an equivalent scale is used as a tool to assess individual equivalent disposable income measure.

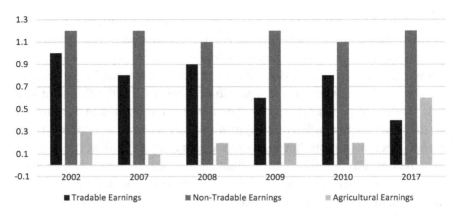

Figure 5.24. Relative contribution of income sources to inequality — Shorrocks decomposition

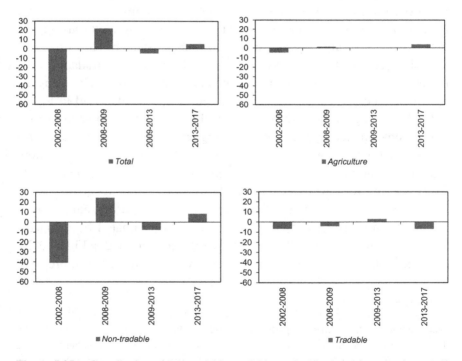

Figure 5.25. Contribution of non-tradable, tradable, and agricultural incomes in overall income inequality

income matter in combating inequality. Unlike the Shorrocks decomposition method, Jenkins (1995) suggests another method allowing for a dynamic comparison over time regarding the contributions of different income sources into overall inequality. It is clear from the figure on the top left of Figure 5.25 that the great extent of improvement in inequality taken place in the AK Parti period occurred in the first period between 2002 and 2008. It also appears that the sub-prime mortgage crisis caused a deterioration in income distribution in the 2008–2009 period. However, the limited amount of improvement took place in the high economic growth period between 2009 and 2013. The moderate levels of economic growth in the last period seem to have accompanied a deterioration in income distribution again. Interestingly, this finding indicates that maintaining high economic growth rates, as happened in the 2010–2013 period, is not the only requirement to have a significant improvement in inequality. The type of economic activity on which economic growth relies is also a crucial factor to determine income distribution.

The impacts of agricultural income seem to have remained very small but have been in the directions of changes in overall inequality in all periods. Among three distinctive income sources in our examination, non-tradable income stands out by exhibiting a distinctively high contribution to changes in overall inequality. In particular, the contribution of non-tradable incomes to a change in inequality was highest in the 2002–2008 period, and non-tradable income can be accounted for overall improvement in this period. Besides, non-tradable income seems also to have been responsible for the great extent of the deterioration in inequality in the period corresponding to the sub-prime crisis. This is also the period when non-tradable income increased relatively more than other income groups. The ratio of the mean non-tradable income to the mean income from tradable activities appears steadily to have increased until 2008, and it remained stable for the rest of the period (see Figure 5.20).

Tradable income, as a product of manufacturing, is a crucial income source, taking up almost 20% of GDP after non-tradable activities. Except for the 2009–2013 high-economic-growth period, tradable income in Figure 5.25 seems to have generated negative impacts on changes in inequality, and became the second income group improving income distribution. Figure 5.25 also shows that tradable income in the first period enhanced the improving impact of non-tradable income on inequality. However, this harmony between both income groups ruptured in the third period, in which non-tradable activities increased relatively more than tradable ones and paved the way for exceptionally high non-tradable-driven economic growth. While non-tradable incomes continued to improve income distribution, tradable incomes' contribution moved, albeit in a small way, in the direction of deterioration in 2009–2013. The same disharmony between the two income groups continues in the last period when non-tradable income caused an increase in inequality whereas trad-able ones decreased it. This is partly because financial resources began to run out, and foreign borrowing became difficult to find easily as in the beginning of the 2000s. This is also due to the high reliance of non-trad-able-driven economic growth on finance. Turkey in the third period has been experiencing economic growth at moderate rates. This finding implies that the *more the economic growth relies on non-tradable eco-nomic activities, the better the overall income distribution will be.*

The high economic growth in 2009–2013 continued to be a non-tradable-driven one, and the increasing reliance on non-tradable activities in this period caused even more de-industrialization than before. In addi-tion to economic growth rates, it is also clear from Figure 5.25 that an increase in non-tradable economic activities and income this time resulted in a deterioration in income distribution (see their positive contributions in the fourth period in Figure 5.25). This rather puzzling result postulates that increases in non-tradable economic activities are *necessary*, but are not *sufficient* to have an improving effect on income distribution. Unlike our expectation, the reason for why non-tradable-driven economic growth in the fourth period caused a deterioration in income distribution must be sought in the developments in the relative prices. Unlike in other periods, the long-term stability in the foreign exchange rate halted in the fourth period, and the nominal exchange rate became volatile.[18] The substantial

---

[18] As an example, the $/TL foreign exchange rate increased by almost 23% from 2009 to 2013. However, the same exchange rate increased by 92% between 2003 and 2007. In the early years of AKP ruling in power between 2003 and 2008, the same exchange rate seems evident to have declined by almost 14% (TCMB, https://evds2.tcmb.gov.tr/index. php?/evds/serieMarket).

increase in expenditure on non-tradable economic activities began to cause an increase in the foreign exchange rate. This is, in fact, a new development in the Turkish economy that we had not experienced before. Therefore, this brings us to the conclusion that *non-tradable-driven economic growth is likely to result in an improvement in income distribution as long as the relative prices of non-tradable to tradable activities are stable.*

5.8. Conclusion

Turkey has gone through political and economic transformations in the 2000s, but the origin of this transformation goes back to the 1980s when economic liberalization and integration to the world economy started. Her distinguished macroeconomic performance after the economic crisis in 2001 particularly drew attention in the beginning. However, Turkey was not alone in having this macroeconomic success, as other emerging market economies had experienced high economic growth in the same period.

This high performance with growth was accompanied by a distinctive transformation in their economic structure and bought about a fall in the importance of tradable economic activities in creating manufacturing value-added and employment. These economies, including Turkey, eventually became dependent on non-tradable economic activities to generate high economic growth and additional employment. This process was then called de-industrialization. Although de-industrialization in the normal course of development, as noted by Kaldor (1966), is expected to take place after the marginal factor productivity of manufacturing begins to fall, it occurred early in many developing countries including Turkey.

In this chapter, the experience of Turkey with de-industrialization is examined, and several factors are put forward to explain this early occurrence of de-industrialization, as follows:

- economic populism as an extension of the political power struggle in Turkey, and an increase in non-tradable economic activities as an effective instrument of populist economic practices;
- the high availability of financial resources in the international markets and their low cost during the 2000s, allowing financial resource

deficient developing countries to finance expenditure on non-tradable economic activities easily;

- the institutional structure of emerging market economies, which become more and more similar to those in advanced countries; on the international trade side, this similarity made developing market economics be more exposed to international competition; on the financial side, a globally similar financial structure paved the way for easy access to international finance;
- the mismatch of domestic consumption preferences with domestic production, the importation of tradable goods, mainly manufacturing goods, as a result, are all examined as causes of de-industrialization in Turkey.

This chapter also puts a particular emphasis on the observation from the Turkish economy that economic populism is exercised by an extension of non-tradable expenditure and economic activities such as construction, services, trade, banking and insurances, and public services. While economic populism requires high job creation as a result of high economic growth, non-tradable activities come forward to accomplish these tasks. Since any tradable-driven economic growth, the policy is under the constraint of international competition, policymakers, especially those who feel the pressure of severe political struggles, become dependent on non-tradable economic activities without feeling any pressure coming from international competition. However, this change in preferences between economic activities distorts the quality of economic growth, which increasingly becomes non-tradable-driven, creating less employment and value added than expected. However, this type of growth model has little ability to create foreign currency income, and requires finance, particularly from international capital markets. Moreover, this makes the economy vulnerable to external shocks. Any change in the prevailing favorable conditions in international capital markets easily creates instability and uncertainty about the prospects of economic growth.

The empirical investigation shows that a structural shift toward non-tradable activities from both tradable and agricultural has taken place in the case of Turkey. Based on micro Household Budget Survey data, we observe that the mean income level of non-tradable activities appears to have increased substantially. More importantly, the number of non-tradable income entities in total income has also increased along with an expansion in non-tradable economic activities. This feature of the Turkish transformation is expected to generate a positive impact on income distribution. It is indeed true for the first years of the AK Parti government in the period between 2003 and 2008. We observed that income distribution in this period drastically improved until 2008, but then remain almost stable afterward. Our research also indicates that rises in non-tradable income in the early years of the 2000s must account for the improvement in income distribution. Besides, financial earnings stand out as the income source that generates the highest improving effect on income distribution in the 2002–2007 period. Importantly, our findings postulate that non-tradable-driven economic growth is likely to result in an improvement in income distribution as long as the relative prices of non-tradable to tradable activities are stable.

References

Acemoğlu, D., Autor, D., Dorn, D., Hanson, G. H. and Source, B. P. (2016). "Import Competition and the Great US Employment Sag of the 2000s", *Journal of Labour Economics*, Vol. 34, No. S1, pp. S141–S198.

Acemoğlu D. and Robinson, J. (2012). "Why Nations Fail: The Origins of Power, Prosperity and Poverty", 1st ed, Crown.

Bayar, A. A. and Günçavdı, Ö. (2018). "De-industrialization and Poverty in Turkey", *Efil Journal*, Vol. 1, No. 4, pp. 36–71. (in Turkish)

Bayar, A. A. and Günçavdı, Ö. (2020). "Economic Reforms and Income Distribution in Turkey". Forthcoming in *Economic Systems*.

Baymul, Ç. and Sen, K. (2019). "Kuznets Revisited: What Do We Know About the Relationship between Structural Transformation and Inequality?" *Asian Development Review*, Vol. 36, No. 1, pp. 136–167.

Castillo, M. and Neto, A. M. (2016). "Premature Deindustrialization in Latin America". *United Nations ECLAC*, Production Development Series 205. Santiago, Chile: United Nation Publication.

Corden, M. W. and Neary, P. J. (1982). "Booming Sector and De-industrialisation in a Small Open Economy", *Economic Journal*, Vol. 92, No. 368, pp. 825–848.

Dasgupta, S. and Singh, A. (2006). "Manufacturing, Services and Premature Deindustrialization in Developing Countries". *United Nation University-WIDER* Research Paper No. 2006/49.

Dornbusch, R. and Edwards, S. (1990). "Macroeconomic Populism", *Journal of Development Economics,* Vol. 32, pp. 247–277.

Eatwell, R. and Goodwin, M. (2018). *National Populism: The Revolt against Liberal Democracy,* Penguin Books.

Greenaway, D., Hine, R. C. and Wright, P. (1999). "An Empirical Assessment of the Impact of Trade on Employment in the United Kingdom", *European Journal of Political Economy,* Vol. 15, No. 3, pp. 485–500.

Günçavdı, Ö. and Kayam, S. S. (2017). "Unravelling the Structure of Turkish Exports: Impediments and Policy", *Journal of Policy Modeling,* Vol. 39, pp. 307–323.

Günçavdı, Ö. and Orbay, B. Z. (2002). "Exchange Rates, Domestic Market Structure, and Price-Cost Margins: Evidence from a Developing Country", *Applied Economics,* Vol. 34, No. 6, pp. 783–789.

Günçavdı, Ö. and Ülengin, B. (2017). "Tradables and Non-Tradable Expenditure and Aggregate Demand for Imports in an Emerging Market Economy", *Economic Systems,* Vol. 41, No. 3, pp. 445–455.

Günçavdı, Ö. and Ülengin, B. (2018). "Credit Boom and Investment Puzzle in Turkey", *Unpublished Paper,* İTÜ Economic and Social Research Centre.

Gürsel, S., Levent, H., Selim, R. ve Sarica, Ö. (2000). *Individual Income Distribution and Poverty in Turkey: Comparison with European Union.* TÜSİAD Report, No: TÜSİAD-T/2000-12/295. İstanbul: TÜSİAD. (in Turkish)

Jenkins, S. P. (1995). "Accounting for Inequality Trends: Decomposition Analyses for the UK", 1971–86, *Economica,* Vol. 62, pp. 29–63.

Kaldor, N. (1966). "Marginal Productivity and the Macro-Economic Theories of Distribution: Comment on Samuelson and Modigliani", *Review of Economic Studies,* Vol. 33, No. 4, pp. 309–319.

Kaldor, N. (1967). *Strategic Factors in Economic Development,* New York State School of Industrial and Labour Relations, Cornell University.

Krugman, P. and Lawrence, R. (1993). "Trade, Jobs, and Wages", *NBER Working Papers,* No. 4478, National Bureau of Economic Research, Inc.

Kuznets, S. (1995). "Economic Growth and Income Inequality", *The American Economic Review,* Vol. 45, No. 1, pp. 1–28.

Luttrell, C. B. (1978). "Imports and Jobs: The Observe and Unobserved". *Federal Reserve Bank of St. Louis Review,* pp. 2–10.

Martin, J. P. and Evans, J. M. (1981). "Notes on Measuring the Employment Displacement Effects of Trade by Accounting Procedure", *Oxford Economic Papers*, Vol. 33, pp. 154–164.

Müller, J.-W. (2016). *What is Populism?*, University of Pennsylvania Press.

OECD, (2016). *Society at a Glance 2016*, OECD Books.

Palma, J. G. (2014). "De-industrialisation, 'Premature' De-industrialisation and the Dutch-Disease", *Revista NECAT* — Ano 3, No. 5. Jan–June de 2014.

Rodrik, D. (2016). "Premature De-industrialization", *Journal of Economic Growth*, Vol. 21, pp. 1–33.

Rowthorn, R. and Ramaswamy, R. (1997). "Deindustrialization: Cause and Implications", *IMF Working Paper* WP/97/42, IMF.

Shorrocks, A. F. (1982). "Inequality Decomposition by Factor Components", *Econometrica,* Vol. 50, pp. 193–212.

TurkStat. (2018). "The Turkish Labour Statistics", access from: http://tuik.gov.tr/PreTablo.do?alt_id=1007.

Uysal, G. and Kavuncu, F. (2019). "Disables' Care and Labour Statistics", *BETAM Research Note* 19/244.

Appendix A

Table A1. The impacts of NIP on employment

	Domestic Output Q	Exports X	Imports M	Domestic Consumption $C = Q + M - X$	Net Import Penetration $NIP = (M - X)/C$	$\alpha = (1 - NIP_t)/(1 - NIP_{t+1})$	Actual Employment L	Estimated Employment if No Increase in Import Penetration $L^* = \alpha L$	Change in Employment due only to Import Penetration $\Delta L_m = (L^* - L)$	Cumulative Change in Employment due only to Import Penetration $\Sigma(L^* - L)$
1998	107 988 631	6.274.512	10.130.374	111.844.493	0.03	—	3463	—	—	—
1999	102 002 782	10.115.334	14.357.507	106.244.955	0.04	1.01	3555	3575	20	20
2000	109 201 105	15.930.255	27.768.846	121.039.695	0.10	1.06	3638	3871	233	254
2001	99 491 693	35.624.083	39.985.146	103.852.755	0.04	0.94	3582	3373	-209	45
2002	103 484 915	51.048.050	63.079.511	115.516.377	0.10	1.07	3731	3990	259	304
2003	113 629 475	66.081.574	82.963.498	130.511.399	0.13	1.03	3664	3770	106	410
2004	128 676 609	85.195.572	115.237.975	158.719.011	0.19	1.07	3742	4019	277	686
2005	141 064 789	92.753.202	126.975.817	175.287.404	0.20	1.01	3994	4024	30	716
2006	154 926 320	115.717.473	159.031.341	198.240.188	0.22	1.03	4066	4187	121	837
2007	165 378 668	131.317.815	174.080.748	208.141.600	0.21	0.98	4088	4021	-67	770
2008	166 204 969	161.539.002	192.535.574	197.201.541	0.16	0.94	4235	3992	-243	527
2009	151 436 401	148.169.489	171.446.739	174.713.651	0.13	0.97	3949	3840	-109	418
2010	165 969 976	158.697.259	218.462.335	225.735.051	0.26	1.18	4216	4970	754	1172
2011	199 202 715	211.900.033	308.175.727	295.478.409	0.33	1.09	4367	4763	396	1568

2012	203 704 562	257.866.643	317.532.864	263.370.784	0.23	0.87	4420	3853	-567	1001
2013	222 669 208	269.787.785	374.998.394	327.879.817	0.32	1.14	4632	5275	643	1644
2014	236 241 645	322.121.426	410.757.462	324.877.681	0.27	0.93	4936	4610	-326	1318
2015	250 183 050	365.709.840	453.643.595	338.116.805	0.26	0.98	4956	4871	-85	1232
2016	259 788 258	404.353.635	505.607.742	361.042.364	0.28	1.03	4915	5054	139	1372
2017	283 498 084	537.708.285	695.937.381	441.727.180	0.36	1.12	4969	5571	602	1974

Source: Author's calculation based on data from TUIK.

Chapter 6

Labor Market Challenges in Turkey*

Gökçe Uysal, Hande Paker, and Selin Pelek

6.1. Introduction

The labor market in Turkey is characterized by persistent unemployment rates (UR) that follow the volatile growth performance of the Turkish economy. Tackling unemployment has proven particularly challenging in the years following the Great Recession. Annual rates indicate that in the past decade, the lowest level was 7.8% in 2012, and the highest 13% in 2009.

Turkey has a relatively high unemployment rate of approximately 11%. The data in Table 6.1 indicate that Latin American countries are similar to Turkey in this regard. Asian economies such as the Republic of Korea and Indonesia have lower unemployment rates presumably depending on their development strategies. Hungary and Poland, two central European countries whose GDP per capita levels are comparable to that of Turkey, have lower unemployment rates. Of course, they are European Union (EU) members and thus benefit from a labor market that extends into Europe. Yet, being an EU member is not sufficient for attaining low unemployment rates. Spain and Greece, both seem to have a severe

---

* The authors would like to thank the editors Asaf Savaş Akat and Seyfettin Gürsel for their insightful comments, as well as Furkan Kavuncu and Cem Sahin for excellent research assistance. This chapter has benefited extensively from the findings of TUBITAK Project No. 113K365 and TUBITAK Project No. 117K200.

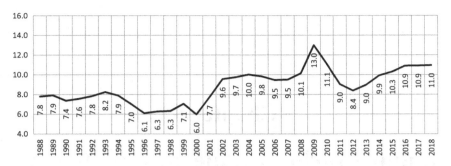

Figure 6.1. Annual unemployment rates (%)

Source: HLFS, own calculations.

Table 6.1. GDP per capita *and* unemployment and labor force participation, 2018

Country	Unemployment Rate (%)	GDP per Capita (Current US$)
Mexico	3.3	9,698
Poland	3.7	15,424
Hungary	3.7	15,939
Korea, Rep.	3.8	31,363
Indonesia	4.3	3,894
Chile	7.2	15,923
Colombia	9.1	6,651
Argentina	9.5	11,652
Italy	10.2	34,318
Turkey	**10.9**	**9,311**
Brazil	12.5	8,920
Spain	15.5	30,524
Greece	19.2	20,324
South Africa	27.0	6,340

Source: World Bank.

unemployment problem. Brazil, South Africa, and Turkey are marked by relatively lower GDP per capita and higher unemployment rates.

The unemployment rate since 1988 is displayed in Figure 6.1. Note that following the 2001 economic crisis, the unemployment rate increased from 6% to around 10%, where it stayed until the Global Recession hit in 2008–2009 and the unemployment rate soared to 13%.

Following an economic boom, as summarized in Chapters 1 and 2, the unemployment rate decreased fast to 8.4%, falling to a level lower than the pre-crisis one. However, this recovery was merely transitory given the increasing vulnerabilities of the economy. By 2018, the annual unemployment rate had hit 11% as the economy was hit by a recession. Monthly data indicate that this trend will continue into 2019. As the latest data show, unemployment soared to 14.3% in July 2019.

This chapter will focus in depth on the discussion of the cyclical and structural reasons behind this persistent unemployment. In doing so, certain characteristics of the labor market will also be briefly analyzed. The global recession, political instability following the *coup d'état* attempt in July 2016, and high inflation period beginning by the end of 2017 are the main cyclical factors that feed into higher unemployment rates.

Yet, even during some periods when the growth performance of the economy is remarkably high, its job creation capacity remains insufficient in significantly reducing the unemployment rate. A fast-growing labor force, the mismatch between the skill set of the workers and that demanded by firms, the limited opportunities for employees to build new skills, stark regional unemployment differences, as well as competitive pressures due to globalization are the main structural features of the severe unemployment problem faced by Turkey.

Furthermore, weakening growth rates are beginning to take a toll on the labor market as non-farm unemployment rates reached 16.7% in July 2019. The outlook is bleak given that the growth performance is not expected to recover soon, particularly when coupled with the existing structural problems of the labor market.

The primary dataset used in this chapter is the Household Labor Force Survey (HLFS), conducted by the Turkish Statistical Institute (TurkStat). Macrolevel data from the HLFS is released monthly, and microlevel data are released yearly. We use both macro and microlevel for the analysis herein, and supplement it with other datasets when needed. We focus on the 2005–2018 period given that monthly data are only available after 2005. Note that seasonally adjusted series by TurkStat are also based on the same data. Furthermore, there was a major revision in the HLFS data in 2014, entailing population projection updates, a new definition of unemployment which was aligned with that of EuroStat, International Labour Organization (ILO), and other institutions as well as some other minor changes.[1] Clearly, such a revision creates a break in the time series. Using a methodology developed previously to correct the series for the probable jumps, we create new series for key labor market statistics, and use them whenever possible.

The rest of the chapter starts with an overview of the cyclical patterns in unemployment and unearths the dynamics that govern unemployment in the short run. The structural problems that tarnish the labor market in the medium to long run are presented next. One particularly important structural predicament is the low labor force participation rates (LFPRs) of women, which is discussed in detail in the following section. The chapter concludes by raising questions for the upcoming decade in terms of tackling high unemployment and other structural issues that need to be addressed.

6.2. Economic Growth and Unemployment Cycles in the Period of 2005–2019

As elucidated by Pamuk in Chapter 1 as well as Acemoğlu and Üçer in Chapter 2, the GDP growth performance of the Turkish economy is far from pursuing a stable path, but rather suffers from sizable booms and busts. Since the magnitude of the changes in the GDP directly effects those in employment, as well as the unemployment dynamics, it evolves in substantial cycles as shown in Figure 6.2. Nevertheless, the ups and downs in employment levels are not the unique factors that affect the unemployment rate. Labor force has its own dynamics. First of all, it should be noted that the working-age population is still increasing, although at a slower pace. As for the labor force dynamics, they are affected by fewer hires during recessions as they discourage entries into the labor market thereby mitigating labor force increases on the one hand, and on the other, they are affected by the acceleration in the female labor force participation, witnessed during the recent years in particular. Last but not least, a structural shift in the job creation capacity of economic

---

[1]The previous definition of unemployment entailed "searching for a job in the previous 3 months". The new definition shortened this period to the "reference month", in line with ILO's definition.

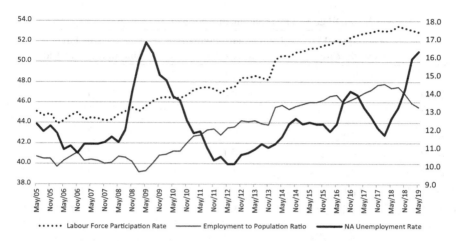

Figure 6.2. Labor force participation, employment, and non-agricultural unemployment rates

Source: HLFS, own calculations from seasonally adjusted data.

growth occurred after the recession of 2008–2009, grading up the employment-growth elasticity sizably.

Before going through the unemployment cycles of the 2005–2019 period, which has been shaped by these complex dynamics, note that the unemployment rates that rule over Turkey are high. Indeed, even in the years following periods of high economic growth, the general employment rate remained above 8.4% and the non-agricultural rate above 10.3% (Table 6.2). The causes of this resilient unemployment must be sought in the various structural impediments that exist. They will be discussed in the next section.

Figure 6.2 represents the quarterly non-agricultural labor force participation and employment rates as well as the non-agricultural unemployment rates, all taken from the seasonally adjusted series.[2] Since 2005, Turkish labor market went through five different phases or cycles.

---

[2] Unless otherwise stated, the rest of this section uses non-farm unemployment rates to discuss labor market dynamics in Turkey. Agricultural production is dominated by small family farms, productivity is very low, and agricultural unemployment is almost zero in Turkey.

Table 6.2. GDP growth rates and main labor market indicators, 2005–2018

	Annual GDP Growth Rate	Total Unemployment Rate (%)	Non-Farm Unemployment Rate (%)
2005	9.0	9.5	12.0
2006	7.1	9.0	11.1
2007	5.0	9.2	11.2
2008	0.8	10.0	12.3
2009	−4.7	13.1	16.0
2010	8.5	11.1	13.7
2011	11.1	9.1	11.3
2012	4.8	8.4	10.3
2013	8.5	9.0	10.9
2014	5.2	9.9	12.0
2015	6.1	10.3	12.4
2016	3.2	10.9	13.0
2017	7.4	10.9	13.0
2018	2.8	11.0	12.9

Source: TUIK and HLFS, own calculations.

The first phase, 2005–2007, can be characterized by three basic facts: high GDP growth of 7% on average, yet modest job creation that implies a resilient unemployment rate over 11%. As highlighted in Chapter 2 by Acemoğlu and Üçer as well as in Chapter 3 by Atiyas and Bakış, this period is characterized by productivity led growth, and a rather low employment-growth elasticity of 0.5 is shown in Table 6.3. Then came the shock of the Great Recession (2008–2009) that caused a jump in unemployment shaking up the usual dynamics of the labor force and employment. GDP growth decreased dramatically to 0.8% in 2008 and contracted violently by 4.7% in 2009. As expected, employment was effected adversely as employment rate decreased from 41% to 39% (Figure 6.2). The unemployment rate soared as the increase in the labor force did not diminish. At this stage, the "added worker effect" also kicked in, forcing inactive women to enter the labor market in the form of self-employment, mainly via precarious jobs (Ayhan, 2018).

Table 6.3.   GDP, employment growth and employment-growth elasticities over time

	GDP Growth	Total Employment Growth	Employment-Growth Elasticity	Non-Farm GDP Growth	Non-Farm Employment Growth	Non-Farm Employment-Growth Elasticity
2005–2007	12.5	2.93	0.23	14.1	7.14	0.51
2008–2009	−4.7	0.05	−0.01	−5.0	−0.75	0.15
2010–2012	16.4	9.51	0.58	18.2	11.10	0.61
2013–2015	11.6	8.21	0.71	11.7	8.97	0.77
2016–2018	10.9	5.89	0.54	12.0	7.51	0.63

Source: TUIK and HLFS, own calculations.

Non-agricultural unemployment, which attained its zenith at 16.9% in April 2009, came down in the following two years, as rapidly as it had jumped, thanks to a strong economic revival beating world GDP growth records at, respectively, 8.5% and 11.1%.[3] A subsidy package introduced in May 2008 also helped as the entrepreneur's contribution of social security taxes was lowered by 5 percentage points, subsidies were introduced for youth and female employment, and other subsidies were provided to mitigate the effects of the economic crisis on the labor market. These subsidies had differential effects at the gender divide, and will be discussed in the following sections.

Indeed, at the beginning of 2012, unemployment was just over 10%, significantly below the level before the Great Recession had stricken Turkish economy as can be seen in Figure 6.2 and Table 6.2. Another factor that explains this success, although to a lesser degree, is a structural shift in the job creation capacity of economic growth as the employment-growth elasticity increased from 0.5 to 0.6 in the period 2010–2012, and then jumped to 0.8 in the following period (Table 6.3).[4]

In the period of 2012–2015, albeit being volatile, average GDP growth was quite high, achieving a cumulative rate of 6%. Yearly average

[3] For the factors behind this economic boom, please see Chapters 1 and 2.
[4] Even though the increase in the employment creation capacity of growth helped bring unemployment rates down, it also decreased the contribution of the total factor productivity to GDP growth.

increase in non-agricultural employment reached 820,000 (Table 6.2), partly thanks to the improvement in job creation capacity. Yet, there was a slow but persistent increase in non-agricultural unemployment, finally reaching 12.4% in 2015.

So, why did unemployment increase instead of decreasing? The straightforward answer is, because the labor force began to impressively increase. Indeed, an acceleration in the female labor force participation was observed, and the average yearly increase of the whole labor force attained 1 million 20 thousand. During this period, more and more women in Turkey entered the labor market. More surprisingly, this willingness to work increased more among women with lower education levels. The driving forces remain to be explored. All in all, this period provides evidence that neither relatively high economic growth nor a high job creation capacity of the growth may suffice to bring down unemployment in Turkey.

The last four years constitute one of the most unstable periods in the economy. As detailed in other chapters of this book, GDP growth rates became extremely volatile, macroeconomic imbalances erupted, and strong unemployment cycles abounded. While economic growth was already showing signs of a slowdown in the second quarter of 2016, the failed coup attempt in July caused a contraction in the third quarter, and the GDP growth declined to 3.2% in 2016. Relatively low GDP growth implies an insufficient job creation performance that fails to compensate for an increase in the labor force. As a result, non-farm unemployment started a rapid rise from the second quarter onward, which continued until the second quarter of 2017.

The macroeconomic outlook changed drastically in 2017. To fight low growth and its corollary, high unemployment, different types of subsidies (e.g., tax breaks, campaigns for increasing employment, including but not limited to subsidies, an impressive amount of credit distribution to small and medium-sized enterprises guaranteed by The Treasury, etc.) were activated to stimulate domestic demand.[5] The GDP growth jumped to 7.4%.

---

[5]The political environment that gave rise to such generous government spending is explained by Yeşilada in Chapter 8.

The economic boom in 2017, as might be expected, paved the way for a sharp decrease in unemployment. However, such high levels of growth are not sustainable. The economy overheated, the current account deficit expanded, and inflation exceeded 20% by 2018. Turkish economy dove into recession from the second quarter of 2018 onward. The GDP growth rate of 2018 was quite low at 2.8% and the growth forecasts of 2019 were around 0%.[6] Thus, a new rise in unemployment that started in February 2018, mainly caused by the extreme crisis raging in the construction sector, is not a surprise. Employment in this sector fell by more than 700,000 from February 2018 to July 2019. Furthermore, employment losses in industry and services occurred along with the recession in the second half of 2018, causing the employment rate to decrease significantly while the decrease in the LFPR was rather modest (Figure 6.2). To date, the non-agricultural unemployment rate reached 16.7% as of July 2019, almost as high as its peak of April 2009.

Given the macroeconomic imbalances hampering a sustainable growth path, as well as the structural problems of the labor market summarized in the next section, high unemployment rates will constitute a major challenge in the foreseeable future.

6.3. The Structural Issues of the Labor Market

a. *Strong Increases in the Labor Force*

The labor force in Turkey is characterized by sustained growth over the long term. As presented in Figure 6.3, the labor force grew from 21.7 million in 2005 to 32.3 million in 2018, growing by over 10 million, i.e., by almost one half, over the course of 13 years.

There are several structural factors that contribute to this long-term trend. In addition to a young population that feeds the demographic dividend, Turkey also benefits from an increase in the female LFPR. Moreover, as the early retirement schemes that were made available in the 1990s are phasing out, more and more people stay in the labor market longer. More recently, and unexpectedly, the Syria crisis has also had

---

[6]The targeted growth rate for 2019 in the official New Economic Program is 0.5%.

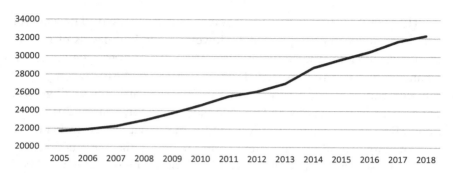

Figure 6.3.   Labor force between 2005 and 2018

Source: HLFS, own calculations.

repercussions on the labor market in Turkey. As Syrians started entering Turkey in 2011, they also started to enter the labor market to sustain their livelihoods. Note that even though this latter group is not reported in the official statistics on the labor market, they are currently in the labor market nonetheless, and will have an impact on the dynamics as well. Each of these factors is briefly discussed in the subsequent paragraphs.

Figure 6.4 presents the age composition of the labor force in Turkey. Even though the labor force is gradually getting older over time, close to one-third of the labor force is still between the ages of 15 and 29. Furthermore, inactivity rates are disappointingly high among the youth. Around 68.1% of young men and 37.3% of young women are in the labor market. In other words, inactivity, in large part, remains a gender-related structural problem as many young women become homemakers, staying out of the labor market. To sum up, simple demographics imply that the labor force will keep growing in the medium run.

Following a sustained increase in the female labor force during the past decade, female LFPR increased from 21.8% in 2005 to 34.2% in 2018, as shown in Figure 6.5. The first reason that comes to mind is the increasing education level of the population over this time period. Furthermore, this effect is more pronounced in Turkey as the female labor force participatation rate (FLFPR) varies drastically by education. The LFPR among women without a high school degree is around 30%, while it is almost 75% among those with a tertiary education. As more and more

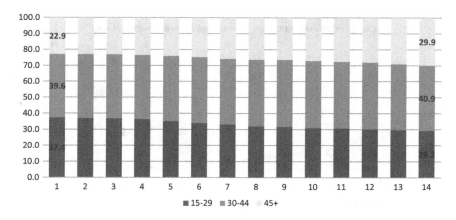

Figure 6.4. Age composition of the labor force (%)

Source: HLFS, own calculations.

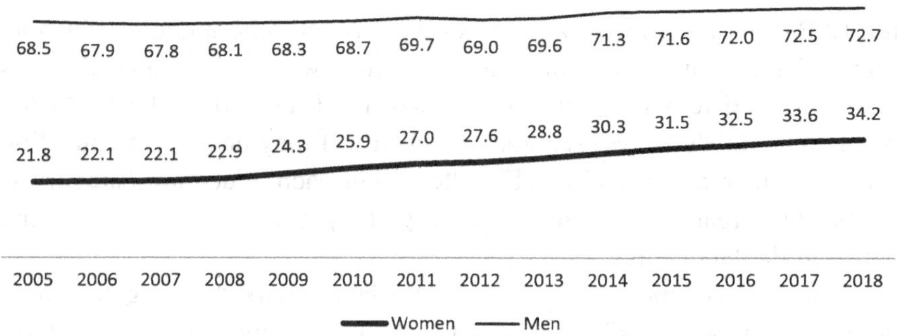

Figure 6.5. Labor force participation rates by gender (%)

Source: HLFS, own calculations.

women get tertiary education degrees, the FLFPR increases. Yet, this composition effect is merely a part of the total picture.

A simple decomposition exercise reveals that out of the 11.5 percentage point increase over this time period, 5 percentage point increase is due to the rising education levels, and 6.5 percentage points come from an increase in FLFPR within education levels (Figure 6.6). More specifically, 6.4 percentage points comes from the fact that there are more women with a tertiary education degree, and 5.4 percentage points is due to an increase

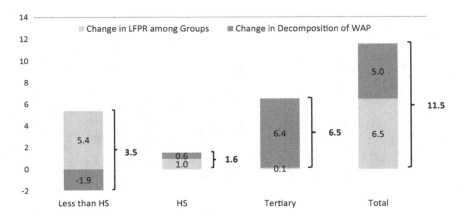

Figure 6.6. Decomposition of change in female labor force participation between 2005 and 2018

Source: HLFS, own calculations.

in FLFPR among women who do not have a high school degree. Such an impressive rise in participation among women with the lowest skill set is intriguing and remains a puzzle that will be discussed in the following paragraphs. In short, two separate effects are at play here: both education levels are increasing, and the FLFPR within each education category is increasing, creating a strong surge in participation among women, and hence in the labor force.

Not only do more people enter the labor market during this time period, but fewer people exit as retirement is postponed. In the 1990s, facing high unemployment rates, the government introduced several laws that made early retirement possible for people as young as 35–40 years old. Given the current social security system in Turkey, it is almost impossible to have an estimate of the average age of retirement in Turkey. However, income data from the Survey of Income and Living Conditions show that, in 2010, there were still about 800,000 people between the ages of 35 and 49 who were receiving pension payments (Gürsel *et al.*, 2013).[7] On the one

---

[7] Survey of Income and Living Conditions contains detailed data on different sources of income. Individuals who receive pension payments were identified using this dataset. As a reminder, note that an individual has to fulfill three requirements to be able to receive pension payments: a minimum age, a minimum number of working days, and a minimum

hand, the option of early retirement is another reason why LFPRs are low. On the other hand, given that retiring at such an early age is clearly not sustainable from an actuarial perspective, early retirement regulations were reversed in early 2000s. Data show that as early retirement is phased out, more and more workers stay in the labor force. HLFS data show that the participation rates of men over the age of 45 increased from 50.3% to 58.5%, that of women in the same age group from 13.3% to 22.4%.

Last but not least, 3.6 million Syrians that were displaced following the Syrian civil war are currently under temporary protection in Turkey, according to data released by the Directorate General of Migration Management.[8] Indeed, a mass migration of this scale is bound to have sizeable impact on the Turkish labor market. ILO reports that 2.1 million Syrians in Turkey are of working age. Given that Syrians left under dire circumstances, emergency help was mobilized by Turkey and by the EU. However, given the sheer number of Syrians in Turkey, cash transfers are, by and large, insufficient to sustain their livelihoods, and thus many Syrians are active in the labor market. Even though official data on the number of Syrians in the labor market are unavailable, estimates suggest that about 1 million Syrians are currently informally employed (Del Caprio *et al.*, 2018). In short, Syrians currently active in the labor market, as well as children who are completing their education in Turkey and are expected to enter the labor market, should also be taken into account when considering the labor force and employment trends over the medium to long run.

b. *Structural Transformation of Employment*

Being an upper middle-income country, Turkey is still in the process of structural transformation. As production shifts out of agriculture into non-agricultural sectors, so does employment. Even though the share of

---

number of days for which they pay social security premiums. Therefore, there are also individuals who meet one or two of these requirements, but not all three, and therefore, who do not qualify for pension payments. These individuals are not included in the numbers cited here.

[8] The statistics of Ministry of Family, Labor, and Social Services are available at https://www.ailevecalisma.gov.tr/media/3372/yabanciizin2017.pdf.

agriculture in GDP stood at around 8% in 2005, about one in every four workers were employed in agriculture. The share of agriculture in GDP has declined to about 6%, and the share in employment to about 18.4%. Taken together, this data imply that agriculture suffers from drastically low productivity levels, as production is dominated by family farms.

On the other hand, the share of services in total employment has increased from 47.3% in 2005 to 54.9% in 2018. As workers move out of agriculture, they flood into other sectors, and more specifically into the service sector where skill requirements may be relatively lower.

During this time period, the changes in manufacturing and construction seem more limited. Yet, the share of manufacturing has declined from 21.6% to 19.7% (Figure 6.7). As detailed by Günçavdı and Bayar in Chapter 5, for an economy that yearns for a more industrial structure, this fall shatters hope. Again, during this time period, employment in construction first jumps from 5.6% in 2005 to 7.2% in 2011. Observe that it remains at this level until 2017 as the construction sector enjoys a boom. However, following a major downfall in this sector, its share declines to 6.9%. Monthly data show that employment in this sector had been on an almost continuous and unprecedented decline from February 2018 to July 2019, shedding more than 600,000 workers.

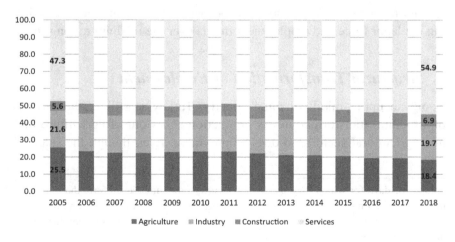

Figure 6.7.   Sectoral composition of employment (%)

Source: HLFS, own calculations.

To sum up, labor productivity in agriculture remains low, implying that agriculture will continue to release labor into other sectors. Construction is not expected to recover soon, either. Perhaps not surprisingly, labor that moves out of agriculture and construction feeds another vulnerable group in the labor market, low-skilled labor supply in manufacturing and services.

c. *High Informality*

Informal employment, i.e., holding a job that is not declared to the Social Security Institution, has been one of the most prominent characteristics of the Turkish labor market. Even though the share of unregistered employment is high, it hides an important dichotomy: Informality among the wage earners and informality among the self-employed and the unpaid family workers are two different phenomena. For the wage earners, the responsibility to register the employee and to pay the payroll taxes fall upon the employer, whereas the self-employed and the unpaid family workers decide for themselves and their households.

The vast majority, that is 87.3%, of the unpaid family workers are employed informally. The self-employed follow suit at 65.5%. This high and persistent incidence of informal employment among unpaid family workers and self-employed is related to the structure of Turkish agriculture which is based on smallholder farmers. It should be emphasized that the social security system in Turkey covers the whole family. Therefore, the registration of the family head allows all other family members to benefit from health and retirement benefits.

As seen from Figure 6.8, the share of informal workers has been on a uniformly decreasing trend, falling from 48.2% in 2005 to 33.4% in 2018. The main reason lies in the aforementioned feature of informal employment. Even though the share of informality among self-employed workers and unpaid family workers remains almost stable during the period considered, that among the wage earners decreased sizably from 32% to 18%.

Formalization of employment among the wage earners may be attributed to a number of factors: (i) Education levels are increasing, and previous research on informal employment in Turkey highlights the negative correlation between educational attainment and the probability of holding

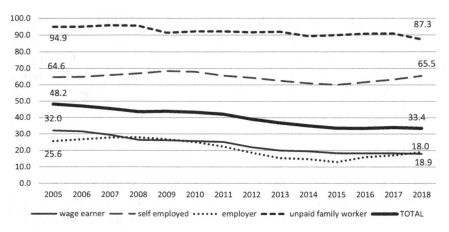

Figure 6.8. Share of informal workers by working status (%)

Source: HLFS, own calculations.

an informal job (Başlevent and Acar, 2015; Kan and Tansel, 2014; Salem *et al.*, 2011). (ii) New firms that enter manufacturing and services are more likely to create formal employment opportunities to benefit from various investment susbsidies. (iii) Public policies such as "the Action Plan to Fight against the Informal Economy" (KADİM) Project.

Note that most of the decrease in informal employment among the wage earners was recorded by 2015, and the share of informal employment has been almost stagnant since then. The reasons remain unclear. One potential explanation might be the massive migration of Syrians and their access to the informal labor market. If and when informality monitoring is increased, labor market access of Syrians is restricted. Therefore, the State may have eased monitoring as a policy to allow access to livelihoods. Data confirm this conjecture. Even though there are more than 3.6 million Syrians currently under temporary protection in Turkey, recent data provided by Directorate General of International Labor of the Ministry of Family, Labor, and Social Services,[9] indicate that the total number of working permits issued is approximately 21,000. Therefore,

---

[9]The statistics of Ministry of Family, Labor, and Social Services are available at https://www.ailevecalisma.gov.tr/media/3372/yabanciizin2017.pdf.

almost all Syrian refugees in the labor market in Turkey are engaged in informal work.

This is confirmed by the recent academic studies assessing the impact of mass migration on Turkish labor market as well. Aksu *et al.* (2018) find that men in the host community were able to switch from informal jobs to formal jobs, but that women in the host community suffered a decline in total employment and in labor force participation. Ceritoğlu *et al.* (2017) and Del Carpio and Wagner (2015) find that the migrant flow has dramatically displaced the young, the less educated and the women in the informal labor market. Even though Syrians are not a part of the HLFS, the expansion of informal employment would affect the host community's job prospects as well.

Another potential reason as to why the decline in informality has stalled may be the substantial increase in the minimum wage in January 2016. In the presence of a dualistic labor market structure, such as the one in Turkey, a rise in the minimum wage will result in a fall in employment in the formal covered sector. As the displaced workers flood into the uncovered sector, employment in the informal sector will rise. Pelek (2015) confirmed that these predictions hold in the labor market in Turkey as well, following a major increase in the minimum wage in 2004. More recent research indicates that this may indeed be the case after 2016 as well (Gürsel *et al.*, 2018a).

d. *Wages and Hours*

The structural problems of the labor market are also closely linked to wages and hours worked. As discussed in the following paragraphs, part time work is rare in Turkey, particularly among the wage earners, and thus wage bargaining is mostly done over monthly wages. Furthermore, as the firms pay both their own and worker contributions of the labor taxes, workers receive and report net wages. To minimize measurement error, we report monthly net wages. Table 6.4 summarizes the main wage indicators from 2005 to 2018. It should be noted that the real wages have followed an upward trend. The recent devaluation of the mean real wage stems from an increasing inflation rate.

Table 6.4. Main wage indicators between 2005 and 2018

	p10	Median Wage	p90	Mean Wage	Minimum Wage	Kaitz Index
2005	250	500	1,000	599	350	0.58
2006	300	500	1,200	680	380	0.56
2007	350	600	1,340	761	411	0.54
2008	400	700	1,500	873	492	0.56
2009	400	750	1,700	987	537	0.54
2010	450	800	1,900	1,038	588	0.57
2011	500	850	2,000	1,147	644	0.56
2012	600	1,000	2,360	1,289	720	0.56
2013	650	1,000	2,500	1,416	788	0.56
2014	750	1,200	2,800	1,552	869	0.56
2015	830	1,300	3,000	1,695	975	0.58
2016	1,000	1,500	3,500	1,982	1,301	0.66
2017	1,100	1,700	3,800	2,182	1,404	0.64
2018	1,200	2,000	4,200	2,474	1,603	0.65

Source: HLFS, own calculations.

Unequivocally, the minimum wage is not binding in the informal labor market, as informality is widespread. The minimum wage lies above the 10th percentile. Furthermore, it clearly does not support a conjecture that the firm and the employer may be sharing the payroll taxes that were evaded among themselves.

One relative measure regarding the minimum wage and how it relates to the rest of the labor market is the Kaitz index, the ratio of the minimum wage to the average wage. In Table 6.4, the Kaitz index is reported for the entire employment, and not only those who are covered by the minimum wage law, i.e., the formal labor market. Recent research has shown that even though the minimum wage may not be binding in the informal labor market, it has a lighthouse effect (Belman and Wolfson, 2016; Calavrezo and Pelek, 2011).

The Kaitz index confirms that the minimum wage is relatively high in Turkey, above 50% of the average wage in the labor market. Furthermore, the minimum wage spike in 2016 has triggered an upward jump from

0.58 to 0.66. It is also possible to look at the ratio of the minimum wage to the median wage, a better measure of the central tendency of the wage distribution. By 2018, this ratio had increased to 80% (1603/2000).

On the one hand, the purpose of the minimum wage is to protect workers against unduly low pay and to provide a minimum pay to those who are employed. In this regard, the minimum wage may be considered as high compared to the average wage. However, minimum wage plays a significant role in the wage bargaining process, particularly in Turkey where trade unions have little jurisdiction as membership is merely around 10%. Two recent studies, by Pelek (2018) as well as Bakış and Polat (2015), examine the wage distribution trends in Turkey and show that the minimum wage increase in 2004 compresses the entire wage distribution, decreasing wage inequality by increasing low wages substantially.

Figure 6.9 illustrates commonly used statistics of wage inequality, the upper-tail (90/50), lower-tail (50/10), and overall (90/10) measures. The latter is the most prevalent indicator and enables an international comparison. Beginning from 2009, a decreasing trend in overall wage inequality is observed while the lower-tail inequality remains unchanged. Global Wage Report 2016/17 published by ILO highlights that the overall wage inequality has a decreasing trend in several developing countries including Argentina, Brazil, Chile, Hungary, Greece, Israel, Portugal, and the

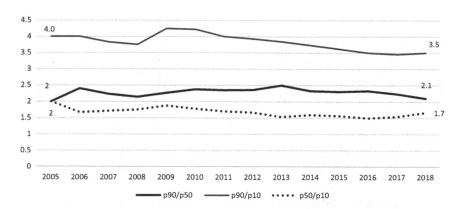

Figure 6.9. Wage inequality indicators between 2005 and 2018 (*buradayım*)

Source: HLFS, own calculations.

Russian Federation (ILO, 2016). In these countries, the 90/10 ratio ranges between 3 and 5, which is comparable to Turkey. The upper-tail wage inequality fluctuates around 2.5. Raw data imply that the significant minimum wage increase which occurred in 2016 does not seem to have had a strong impact on the wage inequality. This unexpected result in comparison with the compressing impact of the previous increase in 2004 should be examined in future research.

Another important dimension of informality in Turkey is the widespread underreporting of wages by firms. Underreporting practices are a hybrid form of informal employment within an otherwise formal labor contract. When the firms choose to underreport, employees receive their wages in two parts, an officially declared wage and an undeclared cash-in-hand wage. Pelek and Uysal (2016) estimate that at least 65.7% of the individuals who are reported to earn minimum wages actually earn more. According to their results, this underreporting causes tax losses of US$12 per worker and US$600,000 in total per month.

Lastly, hours worked in Turkey are considerably long parallel to the quasi-fixed labor costs. According to the Organisation for Economic Co-operation and Development (OECD) statistics presented in Figure 6.10, Turkey has an unusually long work week, averaging 47 hours a week, placing itself in second place among other OECD countries, following closely behind Colombia with an average 47.7 as of 2018.

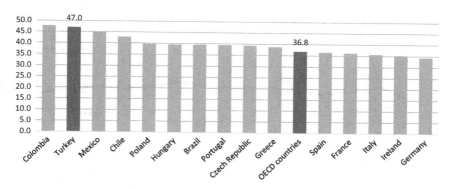

Figure 6.10. Average usual weekly hours worked on the main job, 2018

Source: OECD, https://stats.oecd.org/Index.aspx?DataSetCode=AVE_HRS#.

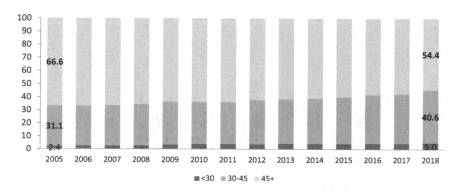

Figure 6.11. Regular working hours shares of wage earners (%)

Source: HLFS, own calculations.

HLFS data confirm this finding. Figure 6.11 presents the distribution of hours worked for wage employment, regardless of formality status. About 54.4% of wage earners work over the legal limit of 45 hours per week as of 2018.[10] Note that only 5% of all wage earners are in part-time employment, i.e., they work less than 30 hours a week.

e. *Is the Labor Market Flexible?*

The flexibility in the labor market in Turkey, or lack thereof, is a topic of discussion among academics and policymakers alike. The dualistic nature of the labor market implies that the formal labor market is highly regulated, whereas the informal labor market is completely off the books, and no regulations are binding.

Surrounding the discussions on increasing flexibility in the labor market are the voices of firms and the trade unions. Yet, the representation power of the unions is doubtful. According to trade union statistics released by OECD for the year of 2015 (latest available data), only 8% of

---

[10] Data confirm that the self-employed and the family workers adjust their working hours more easily. The share of people working more than 45 hours per week among all workers is down to 51%.

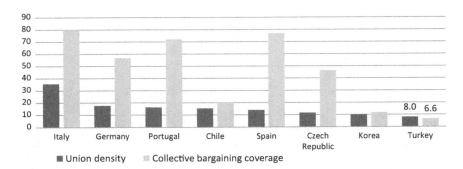

Figure 6.12.   Union density and collective bargaining coverage in OECD countries
Source: OECD, https://stats.oecd.org/Index.aspx?DataSetCode=TUD.

wage earners have a union membership in Turkey. It has also the lowest collective bargaining coverage among OECD countries, which is about 6.6%, 25% less than the OECD average as shown in Figure 6.12. Although trade unions are strictly opposed to the labor market reforms allowing more flexible forms of employment and the transformation of severance pay system, the employers consider the labor market to be rigid and claim that some of the regulations constitute an obstacle to a better-functioning labor market.

According to a commonly used measure of labor market flexibility provided by the OECD, the strictness of employment protection provided in Figure 6.13, the labor market in Turkey is not an outlier compared to similar countries. Two dimensions are included in this measure: strictness of regulation on dismissals and the use of temporary contracts. It is a synthetic indicator, calculated for each country by taking into account the related labor market regulations in force, such as notification procedures in the case of individual dismissals, severance pay, length of trial periods, compensation following unfair dismissal. The latest data reported by the OECD that provide information on comparable countries are from 2012. According to this index, Turkey is ranked 14th out of 43 countries.

Once again, the low share of part-time employment, which is 9.9% among all employed and solely 5% among wage earners, pinpoint to relatively rigid working conditions. Needless to say, limited opportunities of part-time employment are considered to be obstacles to work–life

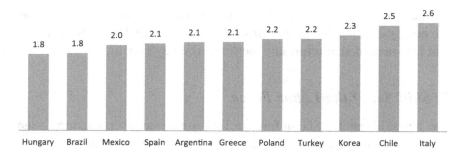

Figure 6.13. Strictness of employment protection in 2012 for selected countries
Source: OECD, https://stats.oecd.org/viewhtml.aspx?datasetcode=EPL_R&lang=en#.

reconciliation. Given the wide-spread traditional division of labor in households in Turkey, the unavailability of part-time work constitutes an additional barrier for female job seekers, given their role in home production.

Among the measures included in the index, one that has been an issue of public discussion for an extended period of time is the severance pay regime. The severance pay is not only paid in case of retirement but also in involuntary job loss. In both of these cases, one monthly gross salary for each year of work is to be paid by the employer. Even though there is a slack cap on the last month's salary in the calculation of the severance pay, there is no limit on the number of years for which the worker is eligible. In other words, if the worker had been working for 20 years in the firm prior to dismissal, they are entitled to 20 times the last month's pay as severance pay. This regulation has been implemented in 1970s, when the unemployment insurance was not in force and was not changed though the latter was introduced in 2003.

Such a generous severance pay system has unintended consequences on the labor market. First and foremost, given that severance pay increases with tenure, young workers are more likely to be laid off, further increasing youth unemployment rates. Secondly, anecdotal evidence suggests that firms bully the workers into resigning or fire and hire workers at the end of 11 months, right before the workers can start claiming their severance pay (Gürsel and İmamoğlu, 2012).

A reform proposal is perpetually on the policy agenda. Yet, trade unions harshly oppose the change by threatening with a general strike.

Furthermore, some of the employers that can avoid paying also resist it as the new system will increase their labor costs. As of 2019, the government had not succeeded at reforming the severance pay system.

f. *Skill Set of the Labor Force*

The low skill set of the labor force in Turkey is yet another structural issue that needs to be addressed. The educational distribution of the labor force is provided in Figure 6.14. In 2005, close to two-thirds of the labor force still did not have a high school degree. Just about 20% had high school degrees and a little over 10% had tertiary education. The education levels increased over time, partly due to the recent education reform of 2012, commonly known as the 4+4+4 system. Under this reform, compulsory education was increased to 12 years, the first four in elementary, the second four in lower secondary, and the last four in upper secondary education.

However, the new system does not require attendance in all types of schools, allowing some students to stay marginally attached to the education system. Hence, the graduation rates have not improved drastically. Many young people, particularly young men, enter the labor market at age

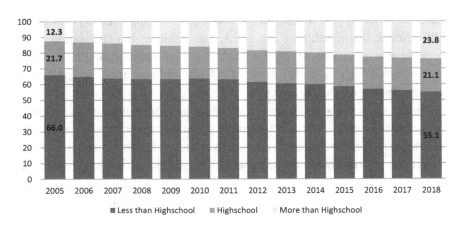

Figure 6.14. Years of education distribution of the labor force

Source: HLFS, own calculations.

15. Data also show that work and school are difficult to reconcile (Uysal and Acar, 2019). Nevertheless, from 2012 to 2018, the share of the labor force without a high school degree dropped to 55.1% and the share of the labor force with more than high school degree increased to 23.8%.

There is a stark distinction across the gender divide, both in the cross-sectional data and over time. First, note that both men and women have higher education levels in 2018 compared to 2005 (Table 6.5). Over this time period, the improvement in women's education is stronger. Among men, the share of high school graduates remained stagnant, that of lower education levels decreased, and as a result, the share of men with a tertiary education degree increased from 10.8% to 20.7%. As for women, both the share of those without a high school degree and those with a high school degree declined. As a result, the share of women with a tertiary education degree rose from 16.5% to 30.3%.

The second observation pertains to the gender differences in education levels in the labor force. Interestingly, women in the labor force are better educated than men. Unlike in other countries, this is not a reflection of higher levels of education among women than men in the working-age population. It stems from the fact that the LFPRs of women differ considerably across education levels. Women with a tertiary education have much higher rates than those without a high school degree, as detailed in the following sections. Given that better educated women are more likely to participate; the labor force is more likely to contain women with higher education levels.

Table 6.5.   Educational distribution by gender in 2005 and 2018

	Less than High School	High School	More than High School	Total
MALE				
2005	66.4	22.8	10.8	100.0
2018	56.5	22.9	20.7	100.0
FEMALE				
2005	64.9	18.6	16.5	100.0
2018	52.3	17.5	30.3	100.0

Source: HLFS, own calculations.

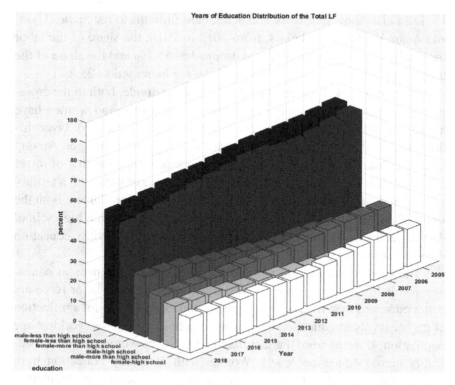

Figure 6.15.   Education level by gender from 2005 to 2018

Source: HLFS, own calculations.

Figure 6.15 provides a visual representation of how the education distribution of men and women evolved from 2005 to 2018 separately. Note that the columns that represent the shares of women's education and the columns that represent that of men should add up to 100% separately. Over time, the share of high school graduates remains stagnant, both for men and women. As the share of the labor force with only a primary education degree declines, that with a tertiary education increases, again for both men and women.

Although the education distribution provides a good summary of the skill set of the working-age population, it says little about the quality of education, and thus the actual human capital. It is notoriously difficult to measure human capital that allows international comparisons. A relatively

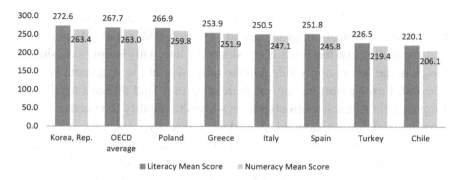

Figure 6.16. PIAAC scores by country

Source: OECD, https://www.oecd.org/skills/piaac/about/#d.en.481111 (accessed on 11 September 2019).

recent effort by the OECD, called Programme for the International Assessment of Adult Competencies (PIAAC), aims to provide information on the information-processing skills, such as literacy, numeracy, and problem-solving, comparable across a wide range of countries. Reported in Figure 6.16 are the results of the latest PIAAC test.

The OECD average is 267.7 for literacy scores and 263 for numeracy scores. Turkey's scores are 226.5 and 219.4, respectively. The implications for the human capital stock in Turkey are clear. The working-age population's literacy and numeracy skills are below average. Furthermore, gender gaps in both numeracy and literacy are among the highest among participating countries. In most countries, men and women have statistically similar scores in literacy skills, but men outscore women in numeracy skills. In Turkey, men score 11 points higher than women in literacy, and there are only a handful of countries (e.g., Chile, Singapore, and Indonesia[11]) where this gap is greater than 7. In numeracy, men score 27 points higher than women, resulting in the largest gender gap in numeracy among the participating countries. It is important to note that the gender gap does not stem from the men doing better (e.g., 37 points worse than OECD average in numeracy), but from women doing worse (51 points worse than OECD average in numeracy) (Kankaraš *et al.*, 2016).

---

[11] Only Jakarta participated in PIAAC in Indonesia.

Both the level of education, as measured by educational degrees, and the quality of education, as measured by the PIAAC scores, demonstrate that the skill set of the force is considerably low. This is only one side of the coin, the labor supply side. On the other side of the same coin is labor demand. Firms report having vacancies that they find difficult to fill. The Employment Agency routinely surveys firms to identify the needs of labor demand, and publish annual Labor Market Assessment reports. According to their data, 20.9% of firms report having a hard time filling their vacancies (Karagöl *et al.*, 2018). Almost three out of four of these firms state that they cannot find workers with the necessary qualifications.

Even though there is ample anectodal evidence on skill mismatch, hard data are more difficult to come by. According to McGowan and Andrews (2017), there is considerable overskilling and underskilling in Turkey. Using a skills-mismatch measure that combines self-assessment with proficiency scores provided in PIAAC, they document that, using literacy scores, 13% of the workers in Turkey are overskilled (versus 11% on average in the OECD) and 4% are underskilled (versus 2.5% on average in the OECD). Another measure provided by the OECD indicates that the qualification mismatch is 43% in Turkey whereas the OECD average is 35.7%.[12]

Bartlett (2013) uses yet a different measure of mismatch: the ratio of unemployed to employed workers in a given education level. Contrary to other countries where mismatch is considerably lower for tertiary education graduates, they draw attention to the fact that women with tertiary education levels also suffer from a high level of mismatch, and mention that it may be due to labor market discrimination. Their findings are in line with the significantly high unemployment rates among women with tertiary education levels, as discussed in the subsequent section.

g. *Youth Unemployment and Inactivity: Not in Employment, Education, or Training (NEET)*

In most labor markets, youth unemployment rates are higher than the overall unemployment rate. Reasons identified in the literature are

---

[12]The qualification mismatch statistics of OECD are available at https://stats.oecd.org/Index.aspx?DataSetCode=MISMATCH#.

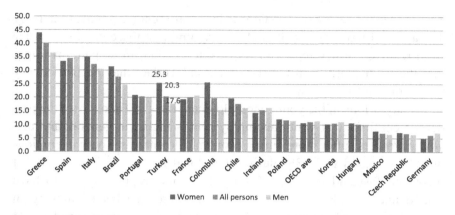

Figure 6.17. Youth unemployment rates by gender in 2018

Source: OECD, https://data.oecd.org/unemp/youth-unemployment-rate.htm (accessed on 25 September 2019).

manifold (Choudhry *et al.*, 2012; Marelli *et al.*, 2013). First, young people have lower tenure, and are thus less likely to build firm-specific human capital. Second, workers with lower tenure are less likely to qualify for severance pay, and when they do, they have relatively lower firing costs.[13] Third, school-to-work transitions prove challenging for young workers in the labor market.

Cross-country data confirm these findings. As shown in Figure 6.17, OECD data indicate that youth unemployment rates are relatively high. In Turkey, youth unemployment stands at 20.3% in 2018, whereas the OECD average is 11.1%. Note that the highest youth unemployment prevails in Greece, Spain, and Italy, where the rates are well above 30%. As is well known, the economies and hence the labor markets in these countries suffered greatly following the Great Recession and the economic downturn in the EU.

Another interesting pattern emerges in the gender gap in youth unemployment rates. In the OECD countries on average, the female unemployment rates are lower than male rates, 10.7% versus 11.4%. Nevertheless, this pattern is reversed for countries that have high youth unemployment.

---

[13] Remember that the severance pay system in Turkey dictates that the worker receives one month's pay for each year they have worked in that particular firm.

The gender gap favors men in Greece by 7.5 percentage points, in Italy by 4.4, and in Turkey by 7.7. It is also intriguing that these countries suffer from relatively low female LFPRs. Taken together, these patterns imply that the labor markets in Greece, Italy, and Turkey may be particularly unwelcoming for women.

A closer look at the youth unemployment rates in Turkey over the past decade confirms that youth unemployment is higher in general, and that young workers suffer more during economic downturns. Youth unemployment rate soared to 25.3% during the global recession. Even though it recovered fast and fell to 17.5% by 2012, its progress seems to have stalled since. Youth unemployment rate in Turkey has been following an upward trend, and the number of unemployed young people aged 15–24 has increased continuously (Table 6.6). Annual data show that youth unemployment increased to 20.3% in 2018. Unfortunately, the current outlook is even grimmer. Following the recent increasing trend, youth unemployment soared to 27.3% by July 2019.

Table 6.6. Youth unemployment by gender between 2005 and 2018

	Unemployment Rate	UR Men (%)	UR Women (%)	Gender Gap in UR
2005	19.9	19.5	20.5	0.4
2006	19.1	18.3	20.6	0.8
2007	20.0	19.5	20.8	0.5
2008	20.5	20.1	21.2	0.4
2009	25.3	25.4	25.0	−0.1
2010	21.7	21.0	23.0	0.7
2011	18.4	17.1	20.7	1.3
2012	17.5	16.3	19.9	1.2
2013	18.7	17.0	21.9	1.7
2014	17.9	16.6	20.4	1.3
2015	18.5	16.5	22.2	2.0
2016	19.6	17.3	23.7	2.3
2017	20.8	17.8	26.1	3.0
2018	20.3	17.6	25.3	2.7

Source: HLFS, own calculations.

Consistent with the findings of the OECD, the gender gap in unemployment rates favor men, except for 2009, the year in which the labor market was hit hard by the Great Recession. There may be a couple of reasons behind the disappearing gender gap in 2009. The tax subsidies to female and youth employment facilitated adult women's access to jobs (Uysal, 2013). The effects were similar among the youth, young women were more likely to benefit from the subsidy. Furthermore, the manufacturing sector was affected more adversely during this time period, and thus men were more likely to suffer job losses. Lastly, the added worker effect implied that women entered the labor market during the economic crisis as self-employed individuals. Unfortunately, as the labor market recovered and the unemployment rates fell, the gender gap in unemployment rates has been on an upward trend, and has widened considerably since then. This is partially due to the fact that coverage of the tax subsidy was expanded to include men who participate in vocational training programs, thereby shrinking the gender differential cost of labor that promoted women's employment.

Table 6.7 provides a brief overview of the evolution of the gender gap over time by education levels. First, note that the gender gap favors women in the lower education groups. The culprit is the size of the agricultural sector in this case. Women with low education levels are primarily employed in agriculture, mainly as unpaid family workers. In 2005, the gender gap was larger among high school and vocational high school graduates, and relatively lower among the tertiary education graduates. By 2018, the gender gap among tertiary education graduates widened to 11.2%, as the unemployment among women in this category skyrocketed to 35.5%.

Table 6.7. Unemployment rates by gender and education in 2005 and 2018

	2005			2018		
	Female	**Male**	**Gender Gap**	**Female**	**Male**	**Gender Gap**
Less than HS	11.1	17.4	−6.3	15.6	15.8	−0.2
High School	32.1	21.6	10.5	26.7	21.6	5.1
Vocational High School	32.4	22.4	10.0	29.2	16.8	12.4
University or higher	32.0	28.7	3.3	35.5	24.3	11.2

Source: HLFS, own calculations.

Another interesting observation pertains to high school graduates, both from vocational and general tracks. From 2005 to 2018, the unemployment rate among young women with a general high school degree declined, whereas that among men with similar education levels stagnated. On the other hand, the unemployment rates among vocational high school graduates fell among both men and women, albeit faster for men. Taken together, these findings indicate that the gender gap among high school graduates fell, yet that among vocational high school graduates actually widened. In other words, vocational training does not seem to improve the school-to-work transition rates, and it seems to be even less effective for young women. Such a differential effect needs further elaboration, yet there are no existing studies on it.

Youth employment and inactivity as measured by the not in employment, education or training (NEET) rate reflect the typical gender divide that characterizes the labor market in Turkey, i.e., the LFPRs are low among young women, and the unemployment rates are higher, pulling employment rates down (35%) and pushing the NEET rates high (24.5%). Even though there is a large decline from 2005 to 2018, the NEET youth rate still remains the highest level in OECD, indicating that Turkey is failing at using its labor efficiently.

h. *Persistent Regional Differences in Unemployment*

The last structural problem in Turkish labor market that will be discussed is the existence of huge inequalities in the regional unemployment. Figure 6.18 shows non-agricultural unemployment rates in 26 regions (NUTS2) published by Turkstat for 2018.[14] Data show that there are large

---

[14] Annual data from the HLFS entailing the main regional labor market indicators are published by TurkStat in the month of March. 2018 is the last available data. Note that the overall unemployment rates may particularly be misguiding when analyzing regional differences in unemployment rates, as agricultural employment also differs significantly across regions. In other words, regions with higher shares of agricultural employment have systematically lower unemployment rates since unemployment is close to zero in agriculture. Therefore, non-agricultural rates are reported here. For example, in Ağrı region the non-agricultural unemployment rate is the double of the overall rate, the former being 10.7% and the latter 5.3%. Gürsel *et al.* (2018b) provide a systematic overview of the

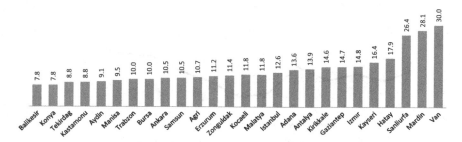

Figure 6.18. Non-farm unemployment rate by regions in 2018

Source: HLFS, own calculations.

disparities in non-agricultural unemployment rates across regions: the highest rate (30%) in Van in the southeast is almost four times higher than the lowest rate (7.7%) in Balıkesir in the northwest. Furthermore, the three regions with the highest unemployment rates by a clear margin are all situated in the east and the southeast of Turkey. The labor markets in these regions are characterized by lower LFPRs as well as lower employment rates, which are among the lowest in particular for women.

Labor theory predicts that, as long as there is a single labor market with rather flexible national rules and intraregional mobility of the labor force is not restricted, regional inequalities in unemployment rates decrease even if the country may start with a relatively large inequality across regional labor markets or inequality prevails following an external shock that affects regional economies differently.[15] Obviously, this is not the case in Turkey. Indeed, the standard deviation (SD) among 26 regions, as a measure of unemployment inequality, followed an almost uniformly increasing trend after 2012 and reached 6.0 in 2018 (Figure 6.19) while unemployment at the country level was moving up and down according to the dynamics of the labor force and employment as discussed in detail in other sections.

This rise is certainly a clear indicator that there is no convergence of regional unemployment rates to the country rate, signaling the presence of

---

overall rate. That said, standard deviations in overall and in non-agricultural unemployment rates across regions do not differ sizeably.

[15] For a comprehensive review of applied research, see Elhorst (2003).

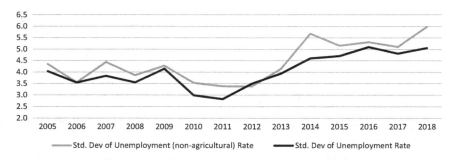

Figure 6.19. Standard deviations of regional unemployment rates between 2005 and 2018

Source: HLFS, own calculations.

serious obstacles to intraregional mobility of the labor force. Moreover, previous research has documented that unemployment changes in a given region may be independent of the movements in overall unemployment, even in opposite directions in some cases (Gürsel *et al.*, 2018b). This asymmetrical functioning at the regional level implies the existence of independent regional labor markets to some extent, a fact that might constitute a relatively high floor for unemployment even during periods of high GDP growth.

At this point, it is useful to compare the regional inequalities in unemployment in Turkey to countries of a similar size in the EU. Clearly, some countries are similar, and others are not. Among the EU countries, with labor markets of comparable sizes, Spain and Italy have both high unemployment rates at the country level, and large regional inequalities that do not display any convergence. More specifically, the standard deviation in Spain has been estimated at 6.0 and 5.5 in Italy in 2018. On the other hand, in Germany, regional unemployment rates converged toward a very low rate at the country level. Indeed, the standard deviation in Germany was slightly over 3 points in 2007 and has decreased to 1 point in 2018 (Genç *et al.*, 2019).

To sum up, large and persistent regional unemployment inequalities exist in Turkey as regional labor markets do not move in tandem, constituting a serious threat to the fight against unemployment in Turkey.

i. *Female Labor Force Participation*

Low female LFPRs are arguably the most important structural problem in the labor market in Turkey, and thus deserve a thorough discussion. The following paragraph is a detailed account of the female LFPR in Turkey, both how it compares to other countries and how it has fared over time. It is clear that education is the main driving factor of labor force participation among women. Yet, data show that its explanatory power remains limited in Turkey where the FLFPR lies considerably lower than what the famous U-shaped relationship between GDP per capita and FLFPR predicts. After documenting these findings, the analysis focuses on the institutional, social, and political factors that also play a role in shaping female labor supply, and will be complemented by findings on how labor demand approaches women's employment.

a. *Female LFPR from a comparative perspective (cross-sectional)*

Despite a clear upward trend in the past years, the FLFPRs in Turkey remain relatively low. The FLFPR of a group of comparable countries is provided in Figure 6.20. Not only does Turkey rank lower compared to Eastern European countries such as Poland and Hungary, it also falls behind Latin American countries such as Argentina, Brazil, and Colombia.

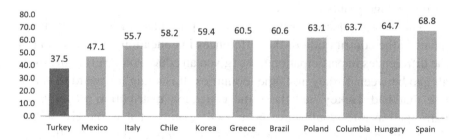

Figure 6.20. Female LFPRs in selected countries (%)

Source: World Bank, https://data.worldbank.org/indicator/SL.TLF.ACTI.FE.ZS?end=2018&name_ desc=false&start=2018&view=map (accessed on 2 September 2019).

The burning question is whether Turkey will ever be able to reach the rates of Southern European countries, like Italy and Greece, which have the lowest LFPR in Europe, even if the upward trend continues.

b. *Not everything can be explained by education*

The differences in education levels may be the culprit. Given that Turkey still aspires to become a member of the EU, a closer look at the difference between Turkey and these countries is pertinent. The education distributions are drastically different across countries. The share of women who do not have a high school degree stands at 66.4% in Turkey, whereas the same share in Italy is 38.2%, and in Greece, 27.9%. This finding is reflected in lower shares of more educated women in the working-age population in Turkey. However, note that the differences in education levels fail to explain the entire gap in participation rates between Italy and Turkey (16.5 percentage points), and between Greece and Turkey (20.8 percentage points).

Generally speaking, the female labor force education levels in Table 6.8 display the expected pattern, and participation rates increase with education within each country.[16] First, note that the participation rates are lower for women in Turkey across all education levels, including those with tertiary education degrees. Second, and perhaps more surprisingly, the gap between Turkey and other countries considered here is widest for women who hold secondary education degrees, and it increases to 23 percentage points for Italy.

This simple decomposition exercise, presented in Table 6.9, helps quantify the contribution of the differences in education levels and that of the differences in participation rates (given an education level) to the overall gap between Turkey and other countries. It is straightforward to calculate that had Turkey had the same education distribution as Italy, the participation rate would have been 42.4%, and yet it is merely 38.5%. These numbers imply that 3.8 percentage points of the total difference

---

[16] It is not always possible to find data using the same source. Here, we use Eurostat since it also provides information on the education level of the working age population, a crucial statistic for the decomposition exercise conducted here. Yet, for international comparisons, we use wider datasets as Eurostat focuses on the Euro area by nature.

Table 6.8. Shares in working age population and labor participation rates of women by educational attainment in Greece, Italy, and Turkey (%)

	Less than High School	High School	Tertiary Education	Total
Share in WAP				
Greece	27.9	43.0	29.2	100.0
Italy	38.2	42.1	19.7	100.0
Turkey	66.4	17.4	16.2	100.0
LFPR				
Greece	36.9	57.6	83.2	59.3
Italy	33.5	62.1	82.0	55.1
Turkey	29.9	39.1	73.4	38.5

Source: Eurostat, https://ec.europa.eu/eurostat/web/products-datasets/product?code= lfst_r_lfp2actrc (accessed on 15 October 2019).

Table 6.9. Differences in LFPR and education (%)

	Less than HS	HS	Tertiary	Total
Difference in LFPR				
Greece	7.0	18.5	9.8	20.8
Italy	3.6	23.0	8.6	16.5
Difference in education				
Greece	−38.5	25.5	13.0	
Italy	−28.2	24.6	3.5	
Had Turkey had their education levels	Actual rate in Turkey	Difference	Remainder	
Greece	46.5	38.5	8.0	12.8
Italy	42.4	38.5	3.8	12.7

between Italy and Turkey (16.5 percentage points) stems from factors that cannot be explained by education, whereas 12.7 percentage points of the total difference is caused by differences in education.

The data pertaining to Greece paint a similar picture. The total difference in participation rates is wider at 20.8 percentage points. Had Turkey had Greece's education levels, the participation rate would have been 46.5%. Out of the 20.8 percentage point difference, 8 points stem from differences in participation rates within education levels, and again 12.3 points stem from differences in education levels across the two populations. This finding insinuates that even if Turkey reaches the education levels of Italy and Greece in the future, it might still lag behind in FLFPR if other obstacles are not removed. This issue will be discussed in the following section.

c. *U-shaped female labor force participation*

The famous U-shaped female labor force participation curve as coined by Goldin (1995) posits that as economies develop, FLFPR first declines, and then rises. As output and employment shift from agriculture to industry, and then from industry to services. Clearly, the structural transformation of the economy is paralleled by the increase in education levels, which, in turn, affect women's participation as well. Other factors that feed into increasing participation rates include, but are not limited to, the diffusion of household appliances as stated by Greenwood *et al.* (2005), the contraceptive technologies as discussed by Bailey (2006), and the World War II as presented by Goldin and Olivetti (2013).

Comparative studies show that Turkey is still an outlier in terms of female labor force participation. A simple regression of FLFPRs and log of GDP per capita was performed to document the U-shape.[17] The results are provided in Figure 6.21. The regression results indicate that Turkey lies beneath the predicted curve. In other words, given its current GDP per capita, the predicted female participation rate for Turkey is 47.1%, clearly much higher than the current rate at 33.5%.[18]

The time trend of FLFPR paints a more hopeful picture as also confirmed by Tansel (2001). According to data in Figure 6.22, the FLFPR decreased from 34.3% in 1989 to 22.3% in 2004–2005. The secular increase started in 2006, and the FLFPR has reached 34.2% in 2018. A rise of almost 12 percentage points over the course of 12 years is

---

[17] The regression results are available upon request from the authors. Data are from the World Bank.

[18] Again, note that data from different sources may be slightly different. Some of the difference stems from the particular age groups, e.g., 15 or older versus 15–64.

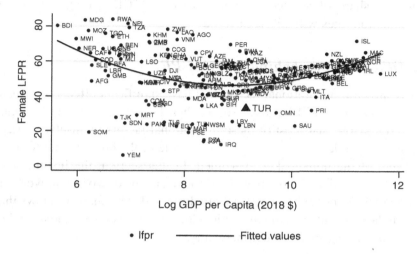

Figure 6.21.   GDP per capita and female labor force participation

Source: World Bank, own calculations.

Figure 6.22.   FLFPRs over time

Source: HLFS, own calculations.

impressive, yet, insufficient to catch countries of similar economic development levels.

Ileri and Sengul (2017) show that the share of services is still relatively low in Turkey compared to the rest of the OECD countries, yet argue that this is not the root of the problem. They show that even when Turkey's share of services increases to the OECD average, women's participation rates will still lag behind.

d. *Other reasons behind low FLFPR*

There are other institutional factors that have significant effects on female labor supply that will be discussed further. However, it should be highlighted up front that most of these institutional factors themselves reflect traditional gender roles, which assign the role of the breadwinner to men, and that of the homemaker to women. In this section, the institutional, social, and political factors that shape the decisions of women to work, or alternatively become homemakers, are discussed. The analysis shows that the fundamental underlying dynamic which crosscuts institutional, social, and political factors is gender inequality.

i. Institutional factors

First, an important factor that has an impact on women's LFPR is the lack of publicly provided, widely available, and adequate institutional dependent care in Turkey. Existing studies show that the lack of high-quality care services impacts adversely the labor force participation decision of women (Balaban and Sarıoğlu, 2008; Beşpınar, 2010; Dedeoğlu, 2010; İlkkaracan, 2012; Paker and Uysal, 2019). This is especially true for childcare services, considering the fact that women are seen as the primary caregivers for children, by both women and men. The gendered division of labor that assigns childcare to women as their main responsibility has a direct impact on the capability of women to work in a context where institutional childcare is scarce.

Additionally, gendered notions also shape how institutional childcare is perceived. Women see childcare institutions more as places of socialization and education than as an appropriate substitution for care at home (Paker and Uysal, 2019). This perception has negative implications for women's labor force participation in general and for women's labor force participation with children between the ages of 0 and 3 years in particular, which is the group with the lowest LPPR. Even higher educated women, who can earn higher incomes compared to lower educated women and can afford private childcare, attribute educational purposes to childcare institutions.

The availability of flexible working conditions such as part-time work is especially important for women who have opted out of the labor market. As noted previosuly, the share of part-time employment among the wage earners is a mere 5%. Previous research shows that there is a group of inactive women who are willing to work provided that they can find flexible forms of work such as part-time work (Paker and Uysal, 2019). While increasing opportunities for flexible work may increase LFPR in the short-run, the policy implications of flexible working conditions are mixed in terms of establishing gender equality in the labor market in the long term, which will be discussed further.

Reflecting the society's approach to gender roles, the legal framework is predicated on the gendered assumption that childcare is solely the responsibility of women. The current legal provisions offer 16 weeks of paid maternity leave to women and only three days to men. This framework, far from facilitating work–family life reconciliation, actively discourages men from taking an equal part in parenting. Moreover, it reproduces the gendered notion that it is the woman who can and should give primary care to children. In a similar vein, the law also provides women who get married a severance package within a year if they decide to leave the workforce upon getting married. In this way, the legal framework reproduces the gendered notion that the fundamental role of women is defined by the private sphere.

An additional factor that has a negative effect on female LFPR is discrimination and harassment women face in the work place. Discrimination is manifested in glass ceilings, occupational segregation, and wage discrimination. Women point to glass ceilings and mention that they are discriminated against because they are seen as less committed workers because of their roles in the private sphere as mothers and homemakers, which are seen as primary. As a result, they are overlooked when opportunities for promotion come up (Paker and Uysal, 2019). They also receive less mentoring because higher positions are taken mostly by men. Another dimension of discrimination is occupational segregation, through which women are sorted into certain occupations or certain aspects of occupations. For instance, women work in customer relations where they are expected to use their sexuality and physical appearance or are directed to administrative work in male-dominated jobs such as engineering or architecture (Paker and Uysal, 2019). Occupational segregation leads to loss of work experience for women, disadvantaging them in career development.

Even though the overall labor market does not seem to display a significant gender wage gap (only 4.5%), the picture changes when the differences in education levels are controlled (Uysal and Genç, 2019). As shown earlier, an average woman is more educated than an average man in the labor market. Once the differences in the education distributions are taken into account, the gender gap widens: 12.8% among the tertiary education graduates, 15.1% among high school graduates, and 21.6% among primary education graduates. The gap widens further along different parts of the wage distribution. At its worst, women earn half as much as men at the lower skill sets and at the lower part of the wage distribution.

To complete the picture, harassment emerges as a reality for a significant portion of the female labor force. A representative survey with 3,600 women in Turkey has found that 9% of women have experienced sexual harassment in the workplace, which must be taken as a minimum baseline considering the problem of underreporting (Paker and Uysal, 2015). Women are harassed by their bosses, co-workers, and customers. All of these conditions negatively impact the working life of women and weaken their labor force attachment, possibly leading to high exit rates.

ii. Social factors

Social roles and norms and the fact that they are shaped by gender inequality are crucial in understanding the low FLFPR in Turkey. This traditional division of labor gives rise to a number of mechanisms which shape the labor force participation decisions of women as summarized further.

First, gender roles determine the division of labor in relation to home production, which falls heavily, if not exclusively, on women. Time-use studies around the world show that women still do more housework than men, even though the gap is closing in some regions (Milkie *et al.*, 2009; Sayer, 2005). Women in Turkey undertake most of the home production (Paker and Uysal, 2019). This means that if and when they participate in the labor market, they must do a "double shift" (Hochschild, 1990), working longer hours compared to men, combined at work and in the home.

Second, traditional gender roles dictate that women are the parents who are the most capable of providing childcare by virtue of their motherhood. This conceptualization is so strong that it is seen as inherent and natural rather than socially constructed. Women, to a large extent, have internalized norms attached to motherhood in Turkey (Paker and Uysal, 2019). The internalization of motherhood as irreplaceable in parenting leads to an inner conflict which creates a dilemma for women between working (and by implication, neglecting their "main" role of mothering) and staying at home (and by implication, fulfilling their "natural" responsibility of childcare). The inner conflict, which does not exist for men, constitutes one of the most serious obstacles to female labor force participation.

Finally, the labor force participation decisions of women are formed by the competition between the values women attach to working and being homemakers. The value of work consists of financial independence, socializing at work, feeling productive, prestige, and self-confidence. It is important to note that the various aspects of empowerment are very well recognized and recounted by women who are in the labor force. Inactive women also find financial independence crucial and define its absence as a loss (Paker and Uysal, 2019). Hence, the importance of policies that will increase FLFPR should be emphasized since a long-lasting transformation of gender inequality in the labor force will be easier because more women will recognize the non-pecuniary value of being in the labor market as they increasingly participate in the labor market.

iii. Political factors

In terms of political factors, political discourse used by the President, members of the government, bureaucracy, and most of the opposition parties is a major hurdle that affects the policymaking processes, legal change and its implementation, representation of the issue in the media, and general public attitudes. The discriminatory approach in this political discourse that reproduces gender inequality is represented at the top of the state in the following words of President Recep Tayyip Erdoğan:

"A woman who avoids motherhood because she is working is a woman who denies her womanhood. This is my genuine opinion. A woman who denies motherhood, gives up taking care of her home is in danger of

losing her authenticity. She is deficient, only half a woman. No matter
how successful she is in the business world."

AK Parti (AKP) governments have followed conflicting strategies
regarding female labor force participation since they came to power. On the
one hand, they advocate and endorse a discourse which assigns women
traditional gender roles, and emphasizes that women neglect their home and
children when and if they work. This discourse is so strong that women who
work are represented as "deficient", as the aforementioned quote shows. On
the other hand, AKP is the first government to introduce tax subsidies to
female employment. Similarly, they passed legislation to allow the use of
headscarves in public workplaces, as of 2013, removing a potential obstacle
to entry. It is easy to envisage that the number of university graduate women
with a headscarf increased when the headscarf ban was lifted in universities.
Even though quantitative analysis on this issue is scarce (Leckcivilize
and Straub, 2018), qualitative studies show that wearing the headscarf may
hinder finding gainful employment (Weichselbaumer, 2016).

Thus, there is a paradoxical situation created by policies that facilitate
female labor force participation on the one hand, and a conservative political discourse that strictly defines women's role in the family, on the other.
It is beyond the scope of this chapter to analyze the reasons for this para-
dox but further research is absolutely necessary to understand its impact.
For instance, there is no research on the counterfactual exercise that tack-
les the question of what the FLFPR would have been, had these regulations not been passed. Increasing FLFPR is one of the foremost challenges
in relation to the Turkish economy and further research that analyzes the
impact of the paradoxical approach of the government can shed light on
how Turkey moves on from the current crossroads.

e. *Labor demand side: How do firms approach female workers?*

As noted previously, the legal framework that regulates labor in Turkey is
based on a traditional division of labor, where the man is the breadwinner
and the woman is the homemaker. (a) A newly married woman can qualify

for severance pay within a year of getting married if she declares that her husband does not want her to work. From the firm's perspective, any single woman is a risky asset as she may collect severance pay if she gets married. (b) The firms are required to provide or pay for child care if they have more than 100 female employees.[19] This regulation dissuades firms from hiring women who are at childbearing age. (c) Similarly, women can benefit from a 16-month paid maternity leave following child birth, whereas paternity leave is merely 3 days for men. Unfortunately, a more equal distribution under parental leave is not covered. (d) Women who have children can retire earlier.[20] (e) Women whose deceased husbands or fathers were entitled to retirement benefits can claim a certain percent of these benefits if they are single and not working. In trying to protect women whose primary role is defined to be that of the caregiver, the regulations usually increase the cost of labor disproportionately for firms who employ women. As a result, the regulatory framework dissuades firms from employing women who become costlier workers.

In addition to the costs outlined earlier, firm-level qualitative analysis also demonstrates the existence of other types of costs in male-dominant workplaces. Buğra (2010) argues that some workplaces accommodate a completely male worker group. Therefore, even building toilets and bathrooms for women are perceived to be an extra cost by the firm. She also highlights that some firms in more conservative provinces complain that providing gender-mixed environments are costly. In sum, firms' approach to female employment may be shaped by perceived costs, where the perceptions depend heavily on the traditional gender roles whereby women are homemakers, and not breadwinners.

As a result, there exists a substantial gap in unemployment rates in Turkey. Furthermore, as presented in Figure 6.23, the gender gap in unemployment rates have been increasing over time. It was also discussed

---

[19] Most firms prefer to pay the penalty as the penalty is lower than the cost of child care.

[20] To retire, workers need to meet three different requirements. To fulfill a certain number of days of work, to pay social security premiums for a given number of days, and to reach a certain age. Women who had children can decrease the number of days for which they have to pay social security premiums for up to two years for each child.

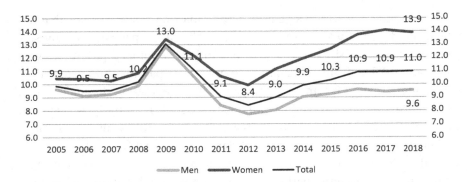

Figure 6.23. Unemployment rates by gender

Source: HLFS, own calculations.

previously that the FLFPR is on the rise during the period under study, particularly for women with lower skill sets. Due to a combination of this surprising rise and the increasing education levels, the number of women in the labor market soared. Therefore, one could potentially argue that not all the newcomers were able to find jobs. However, the unemployment rates by education level reveal another unexpected finding. During the period under study, the gender gap in unemployment rates among the lower education groups, i.e., those without a high school degree and those with only a high school degree, remained stagnant. It is among the women with tertiary education degrees that unemployment skyrocketed. In 2017, the UR was 8.9% among men and 18.6% among women (Gürsel *et al.*, 2019).

A deeper look into different age groups uncovers that the unemployment rates among women with tertiary education degrees are particularly high for young women. The unemployment rate among 20–29-year-old educated women is a whopping 29.6% in 2017 whereas the same rate is 17.5% among men (Gürsel *et al.*, 2019). Clearly, younger and more educated women are having a rough time making their transition from education to the labor market. Some potential issues are raised above.

6.4. Main Challenges Ahead

Note that unemployment had hit 14.3% and non-farm unemployment 16.7% in July 2019. The short-term movements in unemployment are driven by the growth dynamics of the economy. Recent developments have revealed that without changing the structure of the labor market, a relatively stable path of 5% growth is required to bring down the unemployment rates, and even then, the unemployment rate may stay relatively high. Yet, putting Turkey on a sustainable growth path is still the main challenge today. Whether Turkey will be able to rise to the challenge is discussed in various other chapters in this book.

Meanwhile, as unemployment rates stay at high levels, Turkey should focus on protecting the workers. Given that most households in Turkey are characterized by a single breadwinner model, it is inevitable that they are going to suffer financially in the short run. Unemployment insurance can provide a useful tool, yet, the eligibility conditions are tight, and very few unemployed workers can actually qualify. Data released by the Turkish Employment Agency reveal that in any given month, around 200,000 unemployed individuals apply to benefit from unemployment insurance, and only about 100,000 qualify.[21] Over the course of 2018, there were approximately 1.3 million applicants, and around 840,000 received some payments. In a setting where the number of unemployed has exceeded 4 million, the coverage of the unemployment insurance is inapt. Relaxing the eligibility requirements will open up a solid route to protect workers and their families against unemployment and poverty.

Another possible route to bring down the tenacious unemployment rates is to increase the employment generation capacity of growth. Providing incentives for more flexible forms of work may help in this regard, particularly given the low incidence of part-time work. Similarly, severance pay reform is frequently brought up in public discussions. However, such policies should be supplemented by those that protect workers who may find themselves in precarious jobs or in unemployment more frequently. Furthermore, in the medium run, increasing the employment generation capacity of growth is bound to hurt labor productivity, thereby leaving Turkey struggling within the bounds of the middle-income trap.

In this context, the only sustainable way of tackling persistently high unemployment lies in addressing the structural issues of the labor market in Turkey. These issues include, but are not limited to, high informality rates, long hours for full-time work, but low incidence of part-time work,

---

[21] Data are available at https://www.iskur.gov.tr/kurumsal-bilgi/istatistikler/ (accessed at 17 October 2019).

high rates of inactivity among the youth and women, stark regional differences. Note that there are cross-cutting solutions that can address multiple issues that restrain the labor market.

One such solution is reskilling the labor force. Building strategies to reskill the labor force will help (1) decrease inactivity rates among youth and women, (2) facilitate the labor market integration of Syrians, (3) increase the employability of individuals who are postponing retirement and (4) enhance labor productivity and thus may help decrease informality rates. Furthermore, reskilling the labor force is essential in keeping up with the demands of technological change. Nevertheless, reskilling is not an easy task, particularly given that the current vocational training programs in Turkey are not efficient. Investing in the quality of education, whether it be for general or vocational education, with the ultimate goal of creating a pliable work force that can adapt to technological change, is key in this regard.

Another solution is lowering quasi-fixed labor costs as they hinder both formal job creation and limit part-time work opportunities. Decreasing labor costs will help bring down high informality rates, and it may help increase more flexible forms of work, which are particularly important for the youth and women, who may be more likely to take up such work arrangements. In the short run, flexibility will help with the school-to-work transition paths of the youth, and the work–life reconciliation mechanisms generally. Yet, part-time work is also likely to create pits in the medium run, as it pays less, has fewer opportunities for promotion, and usually implies lower job security. Therefore, this strategy should be complemented with regulations that protect workers in face of insecurity and address the disadvantages that are usually paired with part-time work.

Addressing the labor market integration of Syrians will also help with various problems of the labor market. First, and foremost, providing cash transfers to 3.6 million people is an impossible policy tool. Sooner or later, policy will have to shift toward labor market integration. Even though the government has made efforts to facilitate access to formal employment opportunities, the number of working permits issued to Syrians under temporary protection is well below 100,000. Therefore, facilitating access to formal job opportunities will surely help fight high informality rates. Moreover, Syrians are likely to replace women and the youth in informal jobs in the labor market, thereby increasing unemployment and inactivity among these subgroups. Opening up a place in the table for Syrians will help more vulnerable groups in the labor market.

Given that the Syrians were subject to forced displacement, labor market integration will remain a challenge as most lack the necessary language skills, many cannot prove the labor market skills that they have, e.g., educational degrees, labor market experience. Meanwhile, those who do find jobs face unfavorable working conditions, working in jobs that nobody else wants to work in, for wages that are well below those of Turkish workers, for longer hours than Turkish workers, and they complain about discrimination by employers and by co-workers (Uysal *et al.*, 2018). In short, Syrians' integration and adaptation to the labor market remains a challenge as it is bound to create social problems if not addressed at the earliest.

Increasing women's labor force participation is the other main challenge that Turkey faces today. Given that low FLFPR in Turkey is a complex issue with multiple dimensions, policymakers and civil society actors who work on the issue need to adopt a comprehensive approach that integrates all the factors discussed earlier in order to initiate a long-term transformation. In this regard, it is absolutely crucial that policymakers take into account the fact that gender roles cross-cut almost all other obstacles to labor market participation.

A commonly suggested policy is the provision of affordable, high quality childcare, compatible with work hours. This is a basic requirement to facilitate the labor market participation of women, who are responsible for most dependent care, if not all, as discussed previously. However, it should also be recognized that the increase in the availability of affordable and high quality institutional care will not automatically increase FLFPR. Research shows that the decision to send children to daycare is affected by deeply embedded gendered notions around women and mothering. Thus, perceptions of the purpose of childcare institutions, currently defined in Turkey in terms of socialization and education of children rather than care, need to change as well.

Work–life reconciliation mechanisms should be established and strengthened where they exist, with particular attention to whether they are effectively implemented. Research shows that the lack of flexible forms of work creates an obstacle to labor market participation of women and providing such forms of work can be a policy option. The availability of flexible forms of work, however, will not change who is responsible for the private sphere in the long term, locking women into part-time work and reproducing the gender gap in wages and promotion.

The regulatory framework that increases the cost of female workers relative to that of men should be revised to achieve a gender-neutral stance. The severance pay that married women qualify for should be abolished. All childcare responsibilities should either be defined by the number of workers, rather than the number of female workers, or should be assumed by the state. All social transfers that women receive should be supplemented with labor market activation policies. Legal framework needs to be strengthened through provisions that aim to change discriminatory laws. An immediate example is parental leave which is currently designed as maternity leave only. The existing laws prohibiting discrimination are not widely known. Raising awareness on anti-discrimination clauses and practices provide another important policy tool.

Finally, a longer-term transformation is possible only by changing gendered notions and practices, which is easier said than done. Despite the enormity of the challenge that lies ahead, there are a number of actions that can be taken. Civil society actors can play a crucial role here by raising awareness through campaigns and other means, but also by pushing the government toward gender mainstreaming, making the required legal and policy changes, and weeding out discriminatory approaches from their discourses.

To sum up, if growth performance is weak and the structural problems are not addressed, Turkey will keep struggling with high unemployment rates, which will have its toll on social stability and gender inequality. Turkey will not be able to transform itself into a high-income country without ameliorating its labor market.

References

Aksu, E., Erzan, R. and Kirdar, M. G. (2018). "The Impact of Mass Migration of Syrians on the Turkish Labor Market", IZA Discussion Papers, No. 12050.

Ayhan, S. H. (2018). "Married Women's Added Worker Effect during the 2008 Economic Crisis — The Case of Turkey", *Review of Economics of the Household*, Vol. 16, pp. 767–790. https://doi.org/10.1007/s11150-016-9358-5.

Bailey, M. J. (2006). "More Power to the Pill: The Impact of Contraceptive Freedom on Women's Life Cycle Labor Supply", *The Quarterly Journal of Economics*, Vol. 121, No. 1, pp. 289–320.

Bakış, O. and Polat, S. (2015). "Wage Inequality in Turkey, 2002–10", *Economics of Transition*, Vol. 23, No. 1, pp. 169–212.

Balaban, U. and Sarıoğlu, E. (2008). "Home-based Work in Istanbul: Varieties of Organization and Patriarchy", Bogaziçi University Social Policy Forum Working Paper.

Bartlett, W. (2013). "Skill Mismatch, Education Systems, and Labor Markets in EU Neighbourhood Policy Countries", Search Working Papers WP5/20. http://www.lse.ac.uk/europeanInstitute/research/LSEE/PDFs/Latest%20 Research/WP05.20-WORKING-Paper.pdf] (Accessed on 10 September 2019).

Başlevent, C. and Acar, A. (2015). "Recent Trends in Informal Employment in Turkey", *Yildiz Social Science Review*, Vol. 1, No. 1, pp. 77–88.

Belman, D. and Wolfson, P. (2016). "What Does the Minimum Wage Do in Developing Countries?: A Review of Studies and Methodologies", International Labor Organization. Inclusive Labour Markets, Labour Relations and Working Conditions Branch Conditions of Work and Employment Series No. 62.

Beşpınar, F. U. (2010). "Questioning Agency and Empowerment: Women's Work-related Strategies and Social Class in Urban Turkey", *Women's Studies International Forum,* Vol. 3, No. 6, pp. 523–532.

Buğra, A. (2010). *Toplumsal Cinsiyet, İşgücü Piyasaları ve Refah Rejimleri: Türkiye'de Kadın İstihdamı*, TÜBİTAK. https://spf.boun.edu.tr/sites/spf. boun.edu.tr/files/1439799128_aysebugra_kadinistihdami_tubitak_0.pdf (Accessed on 30 September, 2019).

Calavrezo, O. and Pelek, S. (2011). «Les Emplois Du Bas De L'echelle Salariale En Turquie: Une Description Des Salaires Des Secteurs Formels Et Informels, Hors Agriculture», *Travail et Emploi*, No. 126, pp. 45–60.

Ceritoglu, E., Yunculer, H. B. G., Torun, H. and Tumen, S. (2017). "The Impact of Syrian Refugees on Natives' Labor Market Outcomes in Turkey: Evidence from a Quasi-Experimental Design", *IZA Journal of Labor Policy*, Vol. 6, No. 1, p. 5.

Choudhry, M. T., Marelli, E. and Signorelli, M. (2012). "Youth Unemployment Rate and Impact of Financial Crises", *International Journal of Manpower*, Vol. 33, No. 1, pp. 76–95.

Dedeoğlu, S. (2010). "Visible Hands-invisible Women: Garment Production in Turkey", *Feminist Economics*, Vol. 16, No. 4, pp. 1–32.

Del Carpio, X. V., Seker, S. D. and Yener, A. L. (2018). "Integrating Refugees into the Turkish Labor Market", *Forced Migration Review*, Vol. 58, pp. 10–13.

https://www.worldbank.org/en/news/opinion/2018/06/26/integrating-refugees-into-the-turkish-labor-market (Accessed on 10 September 2019).

Del Carpio, X. V. and Wagner, M. (2015). The Impact of Syrians Refugees on the Turkish Labor Market. https://doi.org/10.1596/1813-9450-7402 (Accessed on 10 September 2019).

Elhorst, J. P. (2003). "The Mystery of Regional Unemployment Differentials: Theoretical and Empirical Explanations", *Journal of Economic Surveys*, Vol. 17, No. 5, pp. 709–748.

Genç, Y., Gürsel S. and Polat, S. (2019). "Regional Unemploment Inequality in Turkey", WP presented in TEK Congress.

Goldin, C. and Olivetti, C. (2013). "Shocking Labor Supply: A Reassessment of the Role of World War II on Women's Labor Supply", *American Economic Review*, Vol. 103, No. 3, pp. 257–262.

Goldin, C. (1995). "The U-Shaped Female Labor Force Function in Economic Development and Economic History", in T. P. Schultz (ed.), *Investment in Women's Human Capital and Economic Development*, University of Chicago Press, pp. 61–90.

Greenwood, J., Seshadri, A. and Yorukoglu, M. (2005). "Engines of Liberation", *The Review of Economic Studies*, Vol. 72, No. 1, pp. 109–133.

Gürsel, S., Bakış, O. and Genç, Y. (2018a). "Asgari Ücret Artışı Kayıtlı İstihdamı Olumsuz Etkiledi", *BETAM Research Brief*, Vol. 18, p. 220. https://betam.bahcesehir.edu.tr/wp-content/uploads/2018/01/ArastirmaNotu220-2.pdf (Accessed on 15 October 2019).

Gürsel, S., Bakış, O. and Genç, Y. (2018b). "The Worsts and the Bests in Regional Unemployment", *BETAM Research Brief*, Vol. 18, p. 227. https://betam.bahcesehir.edu.tr/wp-content/uploads/2018/05/ResearchBrief227.pdf (Accessed on 15 October 2019).

Gürsel, S. and İmamoğlu, Z. (2012). "Kıdem Tazminatı Reformu Sorunlar ve Çözümler", BETAM Research Report Series, No. 05.

Gürsel, S., Uysal, G. and Acar, A. (2013). "Artık Daha Geç Emekli Oluyoruz", *BETAM Research Brief*, Vol. 13, p. 151. https://betam.bahcesehir.edu.tr/wp-content/uploads/2013/09/ArastirmaNotu155.pdf (Accessed on 13 September 2019).

Gürsel, S., Uysal, G. and Şahin, M. C. (2019). "Labor Market Outlook: September 2019: Stop in Increase of Non-agricultural Unemployment", https://betam.bahcesehir.edu.tr/wp-content/uploads/2019/09/LaborMarketOutlook2019M09.pdf (Accessed on 29 September 2019).

Hochschild, A. R. (1990). *The Second Shift: Inside the Two-Job Marriage*, Penguin Books.

International Labor Office. (2016). *Global Wage Report 2016/17: Wage Inequality in the Workplace*, ILO.

Ileri, S. G. and Sengul, G. (2017). *Rise of Services and Female Employment: Strength of the Relationship.* Central Bank of the Republic of Turkey Research and Monetary Policy Department Working Papers, No. 17/02.

İlkkaracan, İ. (2012). "Why So Few Women in the Labor Market in Turkey?" *Feminist Economics*, Vol. 18, No. 1, pp. 1–37.

Kan, E. O. and Tansel, A. (2014). "Defining and Measuring Informality in the Turkish Labor Market", MPRA Paper, No. 57739.

Kankaraš, M., Montt, G., Paccagnella, M., Quintini, G. and Thorn, W. (2016). *Skills Matter: Further Results from the Survey of Adult Skills. OECD Skills Studies*, OECD Publishing. [https://www.oecd.org/turkey/Skills-Matter-Turkey.pdf] (Accessed on 11 September 2019).

Karagöl, A., Atan, M., Karadeniz, O. and Ergene, T. (2018). *2018 İşgücü Piyasası Araştırması Türkiye Raporu.* T.C. Aile Çalışma ve Sosyal Hizmetler Bakanlığı & İŞKUR, Ankara, https://media.iskur.gov.tr/22554/2018-yili-turkiye-geneli-ipa-raporu.pdf (Accessed on 11 September 2019).

Leckcivilize, A. and Straub, A. (2018). "Headscarf and Job Recruitment — Lifting the Veil of Labor Market Discrimination", *IZA Journal of Labor Economics*, Vol. 7, No. 1, p. 11.

Marelli, E., Choudhry, M. T. and Signorelli, M. (2013). "Youth and Total Unemployment Rate: The Impact of Policies and Institutions", *Rivista Internazionale di Scienze Sociali*, Vol. 121, No. 1, pp. 63–86.

McGowan, M. A. and Andrews, D. (2017). "Skills Mismatch, Productivity and Policies", OECD Economics Department Working Papers, No. 1403. http://dx.doi.org/10.1787/65dab7c6-en (Accessed on 11 September 2019).

Milkie, M. A., Raley, S. B. and Bianchi, S. M. (2009). "Taking on the Second Shift: Time Allocations and Time Pressures of US Parents with Preschoolers", *Social Forces*, Vol. 88, No. 2, pp. 487–517.

Paker, H. and Uysal, G. (2015). "İşgücü Piyasasında Ayrımcılık ve Taciz", *BETAM Research Brief*, Vol. 15, p. 187. https://betam.bahcesehir.edu.tr/wp-content/uploads/2015/09/ArastirmaNotu187.pdf (Accessed on 15 October 2019).

Paker, H. and Uysal, G. (2020). "Factors that Shape the Labor Force Participation Decision of Educated Women in Turkey: Gendered Preferences and Practices", in E. Nuroğlu and Ç. Çaytak (eds), *The Role of Women in Turkish Economy*, Peter Lang GmbH, pp. 19–38.

Pelek, S. (2015). "The Employment Effect of the Minimum Wage: An Empirical Analysis from Turkey", *Ekonomi-tek-International Economics Journal*, Vol. 4, No. 1, pp. 49–68.

Pelek, S. (2018). "The Impact of the Minimum Wage on Wage Distribution: The Evidence from Turkey", *Ekonomi-tek-International Economics Journal*, Vol. 7, No. 1, pp. 17–59.

Pelek, S. and Uysal, G. (2016). Envelope Wages, Underreporting and Tax Evasion: The Case of Turkey. *unpublished paper.*

Salem, M. B., Bensidoun, I. and Pelek, S. (2011). "Informal Employment in Turkey: An Overview", *Région et Développement*, Vol. 34, pp. 57–84.

Sayer, L. C. (2005). "Gender, Time and Inequality: Trends in Women's and Men's Paid Work, Unpaid Work and Free Time", *Social Forces*, Vol. 84, No. 1, pp. 285–303.

Tansel, A. (2001). *Economic Development and Female Labor Force Participation in Turkey: Time-Series Evidence and Cross-Province Estimates*, ERF.

Uysal, G. (2013). "Incentives Increase Formal Female Employment", *BETAM Research Brief*, Vol. 13, p. 151. https://betam.bahcesehir.edu.tr/en/2013/07/incentives-increase-formal-female-employment/ (Accessed on 16 September 2019).

Uysal, G. and Acar, U. (2019). "15–19 Yaş Aralığındaki 1,3 Milyon Genç Ne Eğitimde Ne İstihdamda", *BETAM Research Brief*, No. 19, p. 242. https://betam.bahcesehir.edu.tr/wp-content/uploads/2019/05/ArastirmaNotu242.pdf (Accessed on 15 October 2019).

Uysal, G. and Genç, Y. (2019). "Kadınlar Erkeklerden Daha Az Kazanıyor", *BETAM Research Brief*, Vol. 19, p. 237. https://betam.bahcesehir.edu.tr/2019/03/kadin-lar-erkeklerden-daha-az-kazaniyor/ (Accessed on 15 October 2019).

Uysal, G., Uncu, B. A. and Akgül, M. (2018). "Suriyeli Çalışanlar ve İşgücü Piyasasında Ayrımcılık", *BETAM Research Brief*, Vol. 18, p. 232. https://betam.bahcesehir.edu.tr/wp-content/uploads/2018/09/ArastirmaNotu232-1.pdf (Accessed on 16 October 2019).

Weichselbaumer, D. (2016). "Discrimination against Female Migrants Wearing Headscarves", *IZA Discussion Papers*, No. 10217.

Wolfson, P. J. and Belman, D. (2016). "15 Years of Research on US Employment and the Minimum Wage", *Tuck School of Business Working Paper*, No. 2705499.

Chapter 7

European Union and Turkey: Why It Failed? What is Next?

Cengiz Aktar

7.1. Introduction

It is safe to say that in the history of the European Union's (EU) enlargement, starting on 1973 with the accession of Denmark, Ireland, and the UK, the first spectacular failure is the candidacy of the Republic of Turkey. It is also safe to say that this missed opportunity is the making of a coalition of unwilling between the parties concerned. Finally, the consequences of the failure, although a tad early to conclude, could be likened to a lose–lose situation which goes well beyond the parties' interests *per se,* to encompass Islam's synergy and coexistence with the rest of the world. As for Turkey, implications of the post-candidacy go beyond the simple consequences of a failed EU candidacy. By diverging from the EU path, the country consolidates and seals its de-Westernization drive to start sailing toward uncharted waters.

7.2. Short Reminder of Early Stages of Turkey's 60-Year-Old EU Venture

Turkish candidacy to the then European Economic Community (EEC) has been concretized with a number of milestones: Following a formal application for association with the EEC on July 31, 1959 and the start of negotiations on September 27, 1959 parties have signed the Association Agreement (Ankara Agreement) on September 12, 1963 which entered into force on December 1, 1964. This founding treaty, still into force, has been completed by an Additional Protocol signed on November 11, 1970 entering into force on January 1, 1973, reiterating the initial commitment for membership[1] and detailing its stages.

While the European party was initiating the membership of continent's two south-eastern neighbors, Greece and Turkey, the latter (and the former alike), was struggling with military takeovers. Indeed, Greece had been ruled by colonels between 1967 and 1974. And Turkey has gone through three *coup d'états*, in 1960, 1971, and 1980 since the beginning of its EU venture.

It goes without saying that such undemocratic practices were not conducive to concrete advancement toward the membership goal.

Following the *coup d'état* of 1980, when the parliamentary system was reinstated, the newly elected government of late Turgut Özal has, kick-started as a matter of priority the frozen relationship by lodging a formal membership application on April 14, 1987. Nevertheless, the European Commission (Commission) in its opinion has rejected Turkey's application on December 18, 1989. The opinion was adopted by the European Council on February 3, 1990. In its opinion the Commission pointed[2] that Turkey was ready for membership negotiations neither economically nor politically.[3] Instead it encouraged Turkey to concentrate its

---

[1] Article 28 of Association Agreement: "As soon as the operation of this Agreement has advanced far enough to justify envisaging full acceptance by Turkey of the obligations arising out of the Treaty establishing the Community, the Contracting Parties shall examine the possibility of the accession of Turkey to the Community". http://trade.ec.europa.eu/doclib/docs/2003/december/tradoc_115266.pdf.

[2] http://europa.eu/rapid/press-release_MEMO-96-52_en.htm?locale=EN.

[3] "In the particular case of Turkey, moreover, it emerged clearly from an in-depth analysis of economic and social conditions by an interdepartmental working party established by the Commission that despite the substantial progress made since 1980 in restructuring the Turkish economy and opening it up to the outside world, there was still a considerable lag when compared to levels of development in the EU. In addition, although Turkey had returned to parliamentary democracy, there were still problems in the form of restrictions on political pluralism, constant Human rights violations and lasting disputes with one particular Member State, plus, of course, the issue of Cyprus."

efforts to comply with the deadline announced in the Additional Protocol whereby the completion of a customs' union is foreseen by 1995. Turkish government, disheartened but still keen, focused on the requirements of the Customs Union and successfully reached the deadline. On December 22, 1995 the decision 95/1[4] on a Customs Union between EEC and Turkey was approved by the European Council following its approval at the European Parliament (EP) few days before, on December 13.

Having survived many crises so far, the Customs Union remains a critical bond between the parties since its entry into force on January 1, 1996. In 2019, the amount of trade[5] between Turkey and the EU has stood €138,065 billion, ranking Turkey at the sixth position with 3.4% of EU's total trade. Turkey ranks sixth among EU's import and export partners.

And finally, the landmark decision was made in 1999 in Helsinki when the European Council placed Turkey on the same footing as the newly independent states of Central and Eastern Europe to join the EU. The Helsinki decision, the Ankara Agreement alike were historical turning points, posing a two-fold challenge, for Turkey and for the EU itself.

Through the Ankara Agreement, the EU countries as Turkey's neighbors have initiated a new era of relations with their south-eastern neighbor. Turkey's reception in Brussels during these coldest years of the Cold War should be seen within the framework of East–West relations, also called "free world" versus "un-free" world of communism. Right after the end of the WWII, Turkey, together with Greece was invited to join this free world throughout the membership of European and Atlantic institutions, i.e., the Council of Europe, North Atlantic Treaty Organization (NATO), Organisation for Economic Co-operation and Development (OECD), Western European Union, and obviously the EEC.

As for the post-Cold War Helsinki decision it constituted the climax of Turkey's strategic partnership with the West and the strongest tie that is established between Turkey and the rest of the continent since 1918, when the Ottoman Empire had been excluded from it.

The Union's founding philosophy and objectives encompass aspects contained in all post-war institutions. In addition, the size and the scope of transfer of sovereignty by member states to supranational bodies, by

---

[4] http://trade.ec.europa.eu/doclib/docs/2003/december/tradoc_115267.pdf.

[5] https://trade.ec.europa.eu/doclib/docs/2006/september/tradoc_122530.pdf.

far, make out of the Union a unique integration process. Turkey, who has been a mere spectator of the European integration since its inception following WWII, has become a full partner and a potential actor following the 1999 Helsinki Summit.

7.3. Helsinki Summit and Its Rationale

"Enlargement is one of the European Union's most powerful policy tools. The pull of the European Union has helped transform Central and Eastern Europe from communist regimes to modern, well-functioning democracies. More recently, it has inspired tremendous reforms in Turkey, Croatia and the Western Balkans. All European citizens benefit from having neighbors that are stable democracies and prosperous market economies. It is vitally important for the European Union to ensure a carefully managed enlargement process that extends peace, stability, prosperity, democracy, human rights and the rule of law across Europe."

These are the opening words of a key strategy paper[6] published by the Commission on November 9, 2005 right after the start of membership negotiations with Turkey.

The document spells out the geopolitical approach underlying the hope of continuing to admit new members into the then 25-nation EU. It describes the official paradigm behind the decision to open accession negotiations with Turkey in October, less than 18 months after the admission of 10 new members, mainly from Central and Eastern Europe, the biggest ever expansion. And it makes clear that Turkey should be admitted for the same vital reason as new members: To expand the zone of peace, prosperity, and stability in the continent that the EU has succeeded to build over the past half century since the end of WWII.

Indeed, very rapidly after the end of the Cold War, the West realized that the former communist countries of Central and Eastern Europe would have to be fully integrated into the EU, as well as into the NATO, if the continent was to enjoy sustainable stability. Left to themselves, the former Soviet satellites would probably have ended up in chaos, since their internal dynamics would not be sufficient to reform and renovate their societies and institutions.

---

[6] https://eur-lex.europa.eu/LexUriServ/LexUriServ.do?uri=COM:2005:0561:FIN:EN:PDF.

It is a fact that, in order to prepare for EU membership, the Central and Eastern European countries underwent an unprecedented political, economic, and social transformation. Today 11 former communist countries are EU members. The remaining six candidates for membership (Western Balkans 6 or WB-6) are on their way to become open societies and modern democracies. At least, the challenge is there.

Turkey's candidacy has been reviewed in 1999 in line with these new rules of the enlargement policy deriving from the sudden end of the Cold War and the urgency to cope with the *fait accompli*. Although the oldest candidate, Turkey has been asked to comply with the new criteria designed for the former communist countries of Central and Eastern Europe. Accordingly, it has been considered as part of the new Europe that was taking shape in the post-Soviet era.

The politico-philosophical approach to include Turkey in EU's latest enlargement cycle originated from the so-called "Laeken spirit", the climax of the political project based on solidarity and partnership in the post-Cold War European continent and beyond. The Laeken spirit was meant to be the adequate response to the emerging situation in the continent after the end of the Cold War, in 1989. The Europeans crowned this project — which signaled a reborn continent — by launching works on a "European Constitution" in Laeken, Belgium in December 2001.

Thus, the decision to include Turkey in the latest enlargement wave and to invite it to join the European family was not an act of charity. It was a genuine political act taking mutual interests into full consideration. Through the integration process, the EU aimed at laying the foundations for a sustainable economic, political, and social stability in Turkey. In turn, normalization and stability in Turkey and in the former candidate countries of Central and Eastern Europe likewise, was considered as the best guarantee for the freedom, peace, security and stability of the continent as a whole.

Concretely, the integration process would avert centrifugal temptations that might emerge if Turkey were kept out of the European integration. Similarly, issues high on the common agenda such as the divided island of Cyprus, the disputes with Greece over the continental plateau in the Aegean Sea and the respective ethnic minorities in both countries, relations with northern Iraq, asylum seekers, unauthorized migration, drug and human trafficking could have been better tackled if Turkey was included in the joint consultative mechanisms of the EU.

The potential advantages of a young and dynamic population, the economic attractiveness of an unsaturated market of then 70 million consumers, the economies of scale that could be generated with the southern and eastern neighbors as well as the Central Asian States that are ethnically kin to Turkey and the geographic position of the landmass *vis-à-vis* the energy routes were surely taken into consideration as well.

Integrating a secular but predominantly Islamic country in an ensemble where Christian values shape the common references for the majority of citizens, however much they live in a secular environment, was (and still is) a huge challenge in itself.

In Helsinki, political leaders of the EU have taken a politically courageous decision to show and prove that *"Grande Europe"* as a future world power will be able to integrate different countries on the basis of shared common values despite their diverse cultural roots. In this sense, Turkey appeared as a significant test case since it personifies a number of values that are allegedly in contradiction with European values. Furthermore, the success of such undertaking would no doubt serve as an example for the Islamic countries around the Mediterranean basin, by demonstrating that modernity is within the reach of a secular Muslim society.

Turkey would have had a lot to gain from the process of integration to the EU as well. It would have had the opportunity to benefit from the experience and the techniques of its partners to brilliantly achieve the 200-year-old Western-inspired modernization process; a process in which Turkey has always been half way toward attaining a genuinely stable and prosperous democracy. It would also learn to live without having to detect enemies all around, be able to reconcile first with itself, and with its arch-enemies. It would have the opportunity to rediscover its past, confront its memory and history, and recover certain customs it had to sacrifice in its attempt to acquire a "modern European appearance". All these would be realized in an environment of mutual confidence which would enable Turkey to feel at home in Europe. And the bet was a winning one, at least partially, for the period 1999–2005. Today this fairy tale is over! The responsibility lies on both parties.

7.4. Belittling Laeken Spirit and Refuting Helsinki Act

The new European project defined in Laeken on December 14–15, 2001 was based on federalist principles and a constitutional citizenship. But the future political entity has faded away as quickly as it had developed. As a result of petty national calculations, outdated hostilities, politicians with no foresight but yet underestimating successful EU policies casting shadow over their poor performances, the wind quickly turned to the opposite direction.

And Turkey was immediately perceived as a burden, a hunch on Europe's back that has lost the Laeken spirit for good. Or perhaps, Turkey's membership bid triggered the vanishing of the Laeken spirit; we will probably never know for sure.

The slowly dying Laeken spirit affected the integration process as well. With the rejection of the Constitutional Treaty by France and the Netherlands, the dream of federal Europe was postponed to some vague future. Incidentally, Turkey, participant in the preparatory work as well as the signing ceremony of the since rejected Constitutional Treaty in October 2004 in Rome, was not invited to the signing ceremony of its avatar, the "Lisbon Treaty" in December 2007.

As Turkey embarked on a long and challenging path to membership, two *modus operandi vis-à-vis* the newcomers emerged. Firstly, while few disputed the European credentials of new members and new candidates, opponents of Turkish accession have raised somber questions as to whether Turkey is a European country — in terms of geography, culture, politics, economics, and religion. Secondly and consequently, the prospect of Turkish accession has generated far more controversy and debate than preceded the entry of the Central and Eastern European countries — with a flurry of illogical arguments against this potential newcomer.[7]

Opposition to Turkish membership has originated from all sides. The Commission itself has been reluctant to include Turkey in the post-Cold War enlargement wave. For instance, the Council Regulation to establish Pologne Hongrie Aide à la Reconstruction Economique (PHARE), the

---

[7] It was, for instance, argued that Turkey would negatively impact on the EP as it would have the biggest national group thanks to the size of its population, as tough Europarliamentarians vote according to their nationality. For a detailed account cf. Aktar (2003, 2004).

first comprehensive financial support package for countries that were liberated from the communist rule, was adopted on December 18, 1989. Fatefully, the opinion of the Commission mentioned earlier, that rejected Turkey's membership application was also issued on December 18, 1989.

Indeed, in a landmark communication "Agenda 2000: For a stronger and wider Union"[8] presented on July 16, 1997 the Commission set out the parameters of the enlargement to Central and Eastern European countries. The blueprint needs to be compared to Commission's opinion on Turkey in which the arguments to reject Turkey were valid for all new candidates but were not taken into account in the assessment for membership.

It would be inadequate to base Commission's stance on purely objective reasons, as explained in the Commission's opinion on Turkey. Nor on a sort of historical indebtedness of the western part of the continent to its eastern part. Nor on the urgency of a strong political answer from the EU to the fluid situation in the east of the continent following the collapse of the Soviet system.

EU's perception of Turkey and its membership perspective in spite of tremendous changes after 1999 has always been on negative territory. Its size and its relative feebleness have been a systematic cause for concern. Deep down, its religious and historical features have puzzled constantly the minds.

European political spectrum, ranging from the extreme right to the extreme left has developed countless arguments and dubious theories against the membership. Some of the subtlest opponents of a Turkish entry argued that Turkey would be a Trojan horse, covertly importing Islam, and would put an end to Europe's dreams of becoming a world power. If Turkey, with its different culture, was to be integrated into the European Union the argument ran, the identity edge between Europe and non-Europe would disappear, as would the possibility of Europe becoming an influential and respectable actor in the international stage. Instead, in order to build Europe as a world power, the EU should put an end to enlargement and consolidate itself inside its identity frontiers.

---

[8] https://eur-lex.europa.eu/legal-content/EN/TXT/PDF/?uri=CELEX:51997DC2000& from=EN.

The debate raised a number of fundamental questions. Is cultural identity, for example, an adequate political basis on which to build Europe as a world power in the 21st century? If so, what are the peculiar cultural characteristics common to Europe if they are not those of a community of religion, and yet by overseeing the arch-old schisms within Christianity?

Was it consistent to conceive of the European project as creating of a new breed of "Euronationals", when the project had a proper meaning and a respectable future if it superseded national, regional, and religious identities and gave birth to the first post-national political entity? It was precisely and still is the post-national, post-religious values of the European project that interested the rest of the world. These are the basis of the new "political identity" that was widely thought to be giving European ideals universal recognition.

Likewise, was it possible for Europe to become a world power by remaining at home and preaching from a distance, without giving itself the means to act? Could Europe be maintained like an aging and fragile puppet's house when it is besieged from all sides by the pressures of a rapidly changing world?

During the last enlargement, the EU owed the stability in Central and Eastern Europe to the conditionality principle. Candidates were asked to follow the so-called Copenhagen Criteria,[9] meet membership obligations in order to be EU members. And at the end they joined the Union. Thanks to enlargement, the EU protected itself and the former communist countries — with the exception of Yugoslavia — from devastating wars similar to the ones that took place in Yugoslavia. It brought stability to these countries and to the continent.

Let us for instance imagine what kind of adventure Hungary would have been dragged into, if as a country exclusively bordered with Hungarian minorities since the Trianon Treaty in 1920, did not have an EU perspective. That, being able to curb similar potential revisionist conflicts and bring along lasting stability in Eastern Europe have been achieved through the conditionality principle of the enlargement policy, a vital tool of proactive engagement or EU's soft power.

---

[9] https://ec.europa.eu/neighbourhood-enlargement/policy/glossary/terms/accession-criteria_en.

Unfortunately, in the Turkish case, such political and strategic concerns had little impact on the stereotypes and Turkey's religious difference disqualified it in the eyes of those who confound politics and religion.

7.5. European Resistance Gets Organized

Europeans started gradually to handle the Turkey file as a crisis management case. Although the candidate was ready to start the membership negotiations by the end of 2002, fulfilling the minimum requirements as applied to other candidates, the pivotal Franco-German couple (at the time President Jacques Chirac and Chancellor Gerhard Schröder) did not dare to decide on the start and postponed it until the end of 2004.

Disillusioned but still resolute, the newly elected Justice and Development Party (AK Parti, ruling Turkey since November 2002) government continued the reform process inherited from the previous coalition government and accelerated the reforms through several "harmonization packages".[10] Qualified by Turkey watchers as revolutionary, the reforms had tremendous impact on every single aspect of state and society's life. By mid-2004 it looked almost certain that the EU would respond positively as much work had been completed.[11] That was what happened in Brussels on December 16–17, 2004. It was followed by the actual beginning of negotiations on October 3–4, 2005 due to additional requirements which were fulfilled in the meantime.[12]

Turkey was subjected to the rules applying to all negotiating countries enshrined in the Negotiating Frameworks which were decked out with numerous provisions referring to open-ended processes as well as numerous reservations and derogations. Nevertheless, such uncertainty was less a problem for Central and Eastern European countries than with Turkey which has always been the odd man out.

---

[10] https://www.ab.gov.tr/files/pub/prt.pdf/.

[11] "In view of the overall progress of reforms, and provided that Turkey brings into force the outstanding legislation mentioned above, the Commission considers that Turkey sufficiently fulfills the political criteria and recommends that accession negotiations be opened". https://eur-lex.europa.eu/LexUriServ/LexUriServ.do?uri=CELEX:52004DC0656:EN:HTML.

[12] https://www.bumko.gov.tr/Eklenti/2989,ms3enpdf.pdf?0.

Likewise, the double standard operated for the budget allocations. Despite its size, Turkey received substantially less pre-accession assistance than other candidates, almost five times less. But as importantly, the Commission, i.e., the executive secretariat of the enlargement, lacked imagination to prepare and handle such a large country as Turkey. For Brussels Eurocrats, Turkey and for instance Estonia were at the same footing. The Commission pretended to cover more than 780,000 sq. km country from its capital when obviously sub-offices were necessary to familiarize the citizen with the EU and *vice versa*.

On the bilateral political front mainly Christian Democrats in Austria, Belgium, Denmark, France, Germany, Luxembourg, and the Netherlands have been vocal in their opposition through endless negative statements. But the champion was the French, through the future President Nicolas Sarkozy who dared to disregard a key international principle, *pacta sunt servanda*, whereby the ratification by France of legal documents pertaining to Turkey's membership prospects was simply ignored.

"Turkey has no vocation to integrate Europe. It will be associated as a privileged partner. This position that we had endorsed at our National Council of May 9, 2004 under the chairmanship of Alain Juppé, I ask you to confirm it," he uttered to President Chirac.[13]

European policymakers never dared to take any pedagogical initiative toward their public opinion massively uninformed about the enlargement of the Union and for Turkey, massively packed of clichés.[14] Instead, they surfed on these negative opinions.

At the end, Turkey's open-ended accession talks and staunch French hostility toward its membership achieved to empty the content of the conditionality principle. Conversely, a sort of negative conditionality took over, whereby member states having difficult relationship with Turkey

---

[13] "La Turquie n'a pas vocation à intégrer l'Europe. Elle y sera associée comme partenaire privilégié. Cette position que nous avions entérinée lors de notre Conseil national du 9 mai 2004 sous la présidence d'Alain Juppé, je vous demande de la confirmer».

[14] EU's opinion poll taker body Eurobarometer's polls on enlargement have clearly shown public's unawareness and a constant stiff opposition to the membership of Turkey. Even the most positive opinion, that of Spaniards was below 50%.

like Cyprus and France gladly abused the negotiation process by putting, through a number of Brussels techniques (opening benchmarks, silent procedures) unrealistic requests to Turkey. At the end, several negotiation chapters were blocked because of the negative conditionality.[15]

Such course was dangerous and indeed fatal; but with some distance it looks as though it was intentional. Some member states, instead of inviting Turkey to the right track, were satisfied to see Turkey lagging behind in EU works. The more the preparations for membership would fail, the more the relations would cool and Turkey would stay away from the Union.

As a matter of fact, while reforms in Turkey were slowing down, the EU was taking things easy, appeasing constantly. A Union that had no solid perspective to offer to Turkey handled the relationship through annual Progress Reports and frail statements heard once in a while, used excuses of elections to speak even less loudly, and had nothing straight to say to the Turkish government and to Turkish public for the matter.

7.6. Turkish Disillusions and Shortcomings

In face of EU's disheartening strategy and tactics, Turkish governments' reactions were different in content and objective according to periods. Whereas in the beginning one can spot some sort of disappointment, after 2007–2008 the government took an increasingly divergent path when it comes to pre-accession works to finally discard the EU project after 2013.

---

[15] Eight chapters were frozen on December 2006 by the European Council for non-compliance with the requirements of the Additional Protocol to the Customs Union agreement, namely the inclusion by Turkey of the Republic of Cyprus within the Customs Union framework as a new member state. These chapters are: (1) Free Movement of Goods, (3) Freedom to Provide Services, (9) Financial Services, (11) Agriculture, (13) Fisheries, (14) Transport Policy, (29) Customs Union, (30) External Relations. The Republic of Cyprus has unilaterally frozen six more chapters on December 2009.

Four additional chapters together with the Agriculture chapter already frozen by the European Council were frozen in June 2007 due to the position of France who refused to let those chapters directly pertaining to full membership to be opened for negotiations, in line with Sarkozy government's policy to block full membership of Turkey: (17) Economic and Monetary Policy, (22) Regional Policy, (33) Budget, (34) Institutions. France under the presidency of François Hollande has reversed its decision.

In the beginning, six factors seem to have been determinant in the loss of interest by Turkey in the process: The wish of some EU countries to keep Turkey at bay right from the launch of the pre-accession process and to refrain from giving clear perspectives regarding accession[16] was in sharp contrast with simultaneous and constant demands to fulfill the membership requirements.

Eventually, the EU appeared to take the form of a "stick without the accompanying carrot", in other words, engineering the failure of the conditionality principle right from the beginning. The lack of clear membership perspective has acted as a powerful domestic disincentive as well and was extensively used by Turkish anti-EU opposition against the government. But not only by those ones…

A Turkey which was not capable of seeing its future in the EU would have had difficulties to absorb the political and economic rights resulting from the EU-inspired reforms, and would fail to get rid of its old habits and fears, to conduct business. Even an ordinary civil servant who stands no chance of becoming an EU citizen would not be fond of the EU-related reorganization of his/her unit. In this case, the civil servant and Turkey along would easily fall back to their own familiar patterns. Thus, the failure of the negotiations is not only *inter alia* due to the attitude and/or resistance of some member states but also to the reluctance of Turkish authorities to engage in economic and political sacrifices without having an assurance for membership.

Secondly, the ruling AK Parti's grassroots felt ostracized when on June 29, 2004 a landmark decision of the European Court of Human Rights (ECtHR), although not an EU institution, failed to consider the headscarf ban at the academia as an attempt to the European Convention on Human Rights, a ban inherited from old secularist elites. While female students are free to dress as they want in European universities they, according to that ruling, are barred from entering classes with a headscarf in Turkey. The decision of the ECtHR had a devastating effect on the ruling party's constituency.[17]

---

[16] Indeed, the EU has never considered a reasonable yet very symbolic accession date for Turkey, like for instance 2023 the centenary of the Turkish Republic, see Aktar (2007).

[17] Lawyer Hüsnü Tuna who was following several cases in the ECtHR, said for instance: "The ECtHR has made different decisions in cases related to the problems of the majority of Muslims in the case of Southeast, Alevis and other sections. It has reinforced this anxiety.

Thirdly, the disappointment was felt at EU's failure to adopt a well-adjusted Cyprus policy for the divided island, to honor its moral obligations *vis-à-vis* the north of the island where a UN sponsored plan for a settlement (Annan Plan) was largely accepted in a referendum and consequently to shield the Republic of Cyprus abusing the stalemate to hamper Turkey's membership negotiations.[18]

Indeed one year after the opening of the membership negotiations on December 2006 the European Council, as previously mentioned, has frozen eight chapters for non-compliance with the inclusion by Turkey of the Republic of Cyprus within the Customs Union framework as a new member.[19] Three years later, six more chapters were added unilaterally to

---

Many of them are about the headscarf and after Leyla Şahin's case, they call at least 10 clients and they see if they want to withdraw their applications on the grounds that political decisions are given instead of objective decisions. These people are moving away from the idea that the EU process will be positive for them in the same way"

İbrahim Solmaz, former President of the İmam-Hatip (Imams and Preachers' Schools) Graduates Association (ÖNDER), said that with the Leyla Şahin case, the confidence of the ECtHR has diminished. Solmaz stated that the attitude emerging in the EU Progress Reports on the issue is not very different from that of ECtHR, saying: "The EU has not made any attempt to deal with the majority. The pious people who give great support to the EU process will definitely be considering their positive opinions." Yeni Şafak newspaper issue of November 19, 2005, in Turkish. https://www.yenisafak.com/gundem/aihmin-karari-abye-olan-guveni-sarsiyor-2717900.

[18] On April 24, 2004, a week before the accession of the then candidates including the Republic of Cyprus, a simultaneous referendum took place in Greek and Turkish parts of the divided island regarding a settlement plan bearing the name of the then Secretary-General of the United Nations Kofi Annan. Greek Cypriots voted against the Plan being assured of the accession which was already ratified in Athens months before (Athens Treaty) whereas Turkish Cypriots voted in favor. The European Council at a meeting on April 29, 2004 decided to not to penalize the Turkish Cypriots any longer but failed to deliver its promises like for instance the Free Trade Regulation benefiting the northern part of the island.

[19] The Ankara Agreement shall be applicable to Turkey and to all member states of the European Union as enlarged through the Treaty concerning the accession of the Czech Republic, the Republic of Estonia, the Republic of Cyprus, the Republic of Latvia, the Republic of Lithuania, the Republic of Hungary, the Republic of Malta, the Republic of Poland, the Republic of Slovenia and the Slovak Republic to the European Union (Treaty of Accession) which was signed in Athens on April 16, 2003 and entered into force on May 1, 2004; https://www.mfa.gr/images/docs/kypriako/ankara_agreement_protocole.pdf.

the first eight by Nicosia.[20] Today, after some distance in time, one can speculate that if the reunification of Cyprus would have succeeded then, Turkey's EU venture might have been in a quite different path.

Fourthly, it concerns the Kurdish issue. Turkish governments in line with the EU requirements have introduced groundbreaking political reforms in the direction of citizens of Kurdish extract, particularly the partial lifting of the ban on education in Kurdish language and the abolition of the death penalty which benefited automatically the jailed Kurdish leader Abdullah Öcalan. Concomitantly, the Kurdish side (PKK) has declared a unilateral ceasefire right after the capture of Öcalan, which never received any adequate response from the old establishment still holding strategic positions in the State apparatus and which was eager to use them against the AK Parti government (Balta, 2005).[21] Indeed, no one in Ankara has embraced the ceasefire; instead PKK camps were continuously bombed and occasional land operations were carried out. Finally, after five years the PKK ended the unilateral ceasefire on June 1, 2004 arguing the continued attacks and provocations of the Turkish Armed Forces. The violent turn in Turkey's critical Kurdish question was not only interpreted and publicized by the opposition, the circles close to old establishment but also some governmental figures, as a direct consequence of EU-inspired reforms which, they argued, were the main culprits of Kurds' endless demands, endangering thereby the unity of the nation.

---

[20] It is worth noting that the accession of a divided island looks now as a mistake in the sense that it rendered the reunification impossible, quite to the contrary of what was expected from the accession of the sole southern part.

[21] "But rather than ease the government's task, the ceasefire may have complicated it, because the neo-Islamists are under equally strong pressure from the military-civilian elite not even to appear to negotiate with Kurdish nationalism, and especially not the PKK, as everyone still calls the group. Echoing (the Chief of General Staff) Hilmi Özkök, the National Security Council urged the government in Ankara to brush off the Kurdish party's overture in order to preserve 'the independence of the nation and the indivisibility of the country.' An unnamed 'senior foreign ministry official' hastened to tell Agence France Presse: 'Those people (the PKK) are terrorists and it is not possible for us to qualify their actions either as positive or negative.' At Ankara's behest, Belgium blocked a PKK press conference. The ceasefire has underlined how Turkey is caught between the demands of a rocky EU accession process and the vested interests of domestic groups." https://www.merip.org/mero/mero083105.

Fifthly, it was disclosed at the hearings of Ergenekon[22] trial that in early 2004, military top brass with the exception of the Chief of General Staff Hilmi Özkök, has requested the Prime Minister Recep Tayyip Erdoğan to slow down the EU reform process.[23]

Sixthly, the negative statements by the governments of some member states, in particular that of France as mentioned earlier, have had a shattering effect on both the government and the public regarding the likelihood of the country to become one day a member of the EU.[24]

As a consequence, Turkish hesitations start to display during 2004–2005. A significant mishap was the avoidance of nominating a chief negotiator for the accession talks as it is the practice, for a long period of time. At the end, the appointed official, the Minister of Economic Affairs Ali Babacan lacked time and insight. Following the actual opening of accession talks on October 4, 2005 the government gave the impression that it was satisfied with the outcome so far and some pause if not backpedalling was now needed. It also wanted to transform the historic success of reaching the ultimate negotiation phase before membership into votes in the next general elections, without pushing further the reform process.

In 2005–2006 the reforms were eroding and, in some cases (Anti-Terror Law, Law on Police Duties and Powers), they were reversed to take an illiberal turn.

The second period of the Turkish retreat started in 2007–2008. Galvanized by the big win at the first general elections of 2007 after their

---

[22] On July 1, 2008 a firearm cache has been discovered in a suburb of Istanbul. That discovery revealed a huge conspiracy of civilian and military activists aiming at overthrowing the government by organizing ostentatious crimes of all nature to provoke the public opinion and create unrest. The trial has been unexpectedly terminated by the very same AK Parti government with all defendants acquitted.

[23] Balyoz Indictments; Balyoz I, pp. 115, 116, 130, 144 and Balyoz II, p. 130, in Turkish.

[24] Countless public opinion polls conducted over years in Turkey on country's membership prospects have systematically shown the wish to see Turkey becoming member. This being said, the public opinion has as systematically expressed the view that Europeans would never admit Turkey in. A recent poll taken by the Center for American Progress reconfirms this trend. https://www.americanprogress.org/issues/security/reports/2018/09/27/458537/snapshot-turkish-public-opinion-toward-european-union/ (Figures 1 and 2). Such suspicion has also been double-checked by European opinion polls in member states, systematically rejecting the prospect of Turkish membership.

arrival to government in 2002[25] and running from success to success, the rulers of "world's rising star" and "the model country" have quickly fallen into overconfidence. In those days, Turkish rulers were quick to belittle the West caught in the consequences of sub-prime crisis and to pretend that they do not, after all, need anyone but the "Great Turkey", heir of the "Great Ottoman Empire".

Impact of an imperial past on the difficulties of Turkey to integrate with an entity in which national sovereignty is superseded by post-national institutions and policies, need to be considered and studied as another likely basis for the Turkish contempt.

Later on, the second period of Turkish retreat was marked with the so-called Arab Spring and the "model country" label that was laid on the achievements of the Turkish Political Islam. Applauses and greetings were for those who managed to spell Islam and democracy in the same sentence. Their stewardship for other Muslim countries was globally assumed. Combined with already overblown self-confidence, Turkey's rulers felt increasingly as the bearers of a new Islamic leadership which was overtaking the humiliating EU venture. Unfortunately, they were incapable to sense that the new role was largely due to EU-related achievements.

During the same period Turkey became more and more visible regionally and internationally, not only in the vicinity as well as in the Turkic republics of Central Asia but also in Africa and even South America. Trade agreements, military cooperation agreements, new embassies, peace initiatives with neighbors, cultural centers, visa waivers, scholarships, university chairs, new flight destinations of the flag carrier, non-permanent membership of the Security Council, presidency of the Council of Europe's Parliamentary Assembly, secretariat-general of the Organization of Islamic Conference and many more countless diplomatic and political initiatives were there to rubberstamp Turkey's rise. Along the same lines, the country's economic performance was noteworthy, as explained in other chapters of this book. All in all, these developments have fed and strengthened the illusion that Turkey can make it by itself.

---

[25] For the sake of comparison, the ruling AK Parti received 34.42% in 2002, it got 45.68% in 2007.

The last period of the retreat from EU has taken the shape of an over-all retreat from the West and anything Western. In 2013, the social peace was first devastated in June by the harsh repression of a peaceful civilian protest in Istanbul's Gezi Park (Gole, 2013). Later in the year, on 17 and 25 December a massive fraud and embezzlement accusations against the ruling elite exacerbated the uproar.[26] Thus, in 2013 a noticeable retreat from EU's norms, standards, principles have started and has since been in full swing. Today, Turkish rulers take every opportunity to disregard EU's fundamentals in order to claim Turkey's singularity if not superiority.

In fact, the EU paradigm and its content have become liabilities in front of an increasingly authoritarian regime in which the arbitrary of the one-man rule has become the rule. This trend has accelerated since the so-called *coup d'état* of July 15, 2016 when the regime blessedly (sic) took the opportunity to suppress any meaningful dissent. Centuries old anti-Westernism of Turkish politics now rides the waves and Europe/West-bashing has become the favorite topic of Turkish political life.

7.7. Deepening Authoritarianism

Actually, Turkey now under the rule of Political Islam, is exposed to an iron will to inverse the 200-year-old Westernization, let alone the EU membership. The reversal of modernity and de-Westernization are visible in many domains: The status of women — actually her recommended place at home despite the fact that women were becoming more active in public life paradoxically thanks to the "decriminalization" of the head-scarf; the education system which is increasingly religion inspired and anti-evolutionist, an anti-Western stance in foreign relations. Let us pick on the last one.

Turkey's foreign relations closely followed its Western path for the past two centuries and the pattern has taken a strategic turn after the end of WWII when Turkey joined the "free world" and its post-war institutions. Among those, the EEC and NATO represented a cluster of those norms, standards, principles, and especially values which are now system-atically challenged by Political Islam. And the critical example of this

---

[26] For an analysis of the impact on the economy, particularly FDI, Simet *et al.* (2015).

turn of events is the *de facto* termination of unsuccessful membership negotiations with the EU, whose requirements have become liabilities for regime's unchecked way of rule, as mentioned earlier. As for NATO, Turkey's uncluttered relationships with Russia and *jihadist* organizations classified as terrorist, constitute an anti-Western stance fitting within the overall de-Westernization. The purchase of Russian S-400 air defense systems and the US retaliation terminating Turkish participation in the development of the new military aircraft, F-35, look like the paroxysm of the state-of-the-art regarding de-Westernization in foreign relations.

Last not least, Turkish disillusionment and search for alternatives to the EU and the West in general, unveil a deeper socio-political unease directly stemming from Turkish polity's characteristics maturing since the mid-19th century.

The ill-reputed Ottoman sultan Abdulhamid II's absolutist regime,[27] the ill-reputed Young Turks' Jacobinist regime (Aktar, 2014a), and the authoritarian pro-Western republicanism are certainly the niches of the prevailing political culture in Turkey. Regardless the ideology underneath, Turkish *homo politicus* is against power sharing, decentralization, and pluralism; is keen of justice only if that justice serves the followers of the "tribe" (*asabiyya*); is eager to preserve the master–obedient servant relation, worships a radical Turkish nationalism that is anti-Western and is predisposed to violence; is in total opposition to European norms,

---

[27] The title of Edhem Eldem's talk on February 2018 "The authoritarian shift in Turkey: Break with the past or continuity?" is self-explanatory regarding the permanence of the political culture. Here is how the talk is presented by the Institut d'Etudes Avancées of Nantes: "In recent years, Turkey has been dominated by a very clear trend towards the political and ideological hardening of the governing party, the Justice and Development Party (AKP), under the authority of its founder and leader, president Erdoğan. For many, this represents an authoritarian shift which is fueled by nationalism and Islamism, coupled with populism and majoritarianism. For historians, the challenge is not so much to describe and analyze a system that is still in its infancy, but rather to examine the existence (or lack) of permanency that could explain the emergence of this regime. Does Erdoğan represent a break with a political tradition which seemed to be moving towards a greater liberalization, or is he merely a kind of epiphenomenon, driven by an age-old movement which links him to Kemalist or Young Turk traditions, or even older movements, going as far back as the reign of Abdulhamid II?"

standards, principles, and values. In one word, *homo politicus alla turca* cruelly lacks democratic culture.

Turkish Political Islam, under which the EU membership venture has thrived, was not exempted from those characteristics and actually was completely subjugated by them. The only novelty Political Islam has brought to Turkish *homo politicus* was to complete prevailing anti-Westernism with a pro-Islamic thus anti-Christian onus.

Thus, expecting a groundbreaking change to embrace the antithetic European paradigm amounted obviously to "mission impossible" in addition to many odds on the EU side to discourage any Turkish goodwill to push forward. After all, former communist states of Central Eastern Europe were democratically no better equipped democratically, to familiarize and adopt the European paradigm but they were not as discouraged as Turkey.

7.8. State of Play

Turkish public does not feel since some time the benefits of the so-called pre-accession phase during which a candidate country thoroughly prepares for membership. Harmonization of the national legislation with the *acquis communautaire* (the corpus of adopted common laws and principles) bring already during that phase a sort of foretaste of future adhesion. Felt between 1999 and 2005 the EU dynamics started to fade away slowly.

The government, after 2005 doing very little as EU works, ended up by doing almost nothing. The citizens, unable to benefit from the EU process alienated themselves from the EU affairs. There is an obvious "homecoming" in terms of European political and economic criteria as spectacularly summarized in the political push for the reinstitution of the death penalty, otherwise abolished in 2002.

Starting in 2005 the erosion of anything relating to the EU has been slow but steady. Year after year, Progress Report after Progress Report, the EU prospects and perspectives gradually disappeared from Turkey's radar. As of mid-2020, it is not an exaggeration to note that the EU is no more in Turkey's agenda. Ankara, through its actions and declarations rejects the membership even when it pays lip service to it in front of the European and international money lenders. As for the public, according to another relatively recent report,[28] 73% and 67% of Turks, respectively, have unfavorable views of the EU and the NATO.

Technically speaking, in addition to the abolition of the ministry in charge of the EU affairs in July 2018, ministerial sub-committees in charge of EU preparations in public administration have been dismantled. The pre-accession funds (€4,453 billion for the EU budgetary period for 2014–2020) are severely underutilized (10% only) due to lack of adequate projects.

As of mid-2020, accession negotiations were at standstill with no less than 14 chapters out of 35 blocked in connection with Cyprus dispute; there was no progress on the 15 chapters under negotiation; only one chapter's negotiation was done and the Turkish party looked uninterested in opening three chapters without any hindrance, as they relate to domestically delicate issues such as social policy, competition policy, and public procurement.

Relations with the EU institutions are becoming increasingly difficult. The Commission is busy pushing papers and the outgoing Commissioner in charge of the enlargement, Johannes Hahn has paid a very limited number of visits to Turkey during his tenure compared to WB-6 countries. The negotiations are at standstill because of the unyielding opposition of Austria, France, and the Netherlands who block any official meeting pertaining to negotiations with Turkey in Brussels, in addition to the aforementioned old blockages by Cyprus. The Commission's yearly Progress Reports on Turkey's advancement toward membership which look more and more like "Regress Reports" are ostensibly thrown in the paper basket by the Turkish officials.

Relations with the EP are at the lowest level; recommendations of the Parliament to freeze and later to suspend the negotiations with Ankara have been patently ignored by Ankara.[29] The EP's outgoing Rapporteur for Turkey was an undeclared *persona non grata* in Turkey. Europarliamentarians are, with very few exceptions, against Turkey's

---

[28] https://www.americanprogress.org/issues/security/reports/2018/02/11/445620/turkey-experiencing-new-nationalism/.

[29] cf. the latest recommendation of the EP dated February 8, 2018, which summarizes the past resolutions on the issue. http://www.europarl.europa.eu/sides/getDoc.do?pubRef=-//EP//NONSGML+TA+P8-TA-2018-0040+0+DOC+PDF+V0//EN.

membership, especially since the April 16, 2017 referendum which triggered a regime change by instituting a strong presidential executive void of checks and balances.

Bilateral relations with the EU member states' politicians and public opinions are at the lowest as well, where any non-complacent declaration or action by Europeans is countered with accusations of "Nazis" and "Fascists" by the Ankara regime. Some governments have introduced in their governmental action plan the rebuttal of Turkey's membership, like Austria and Germany. Others like France have openly told their Turkish counterparts about the same outcome. Every single European decision maker knows that in Brussels' terminology, Turkey does not comply anymore with the Copenhagen Criteria, the compulsory benchmark for every candidate country. In Europe, there is neither one government nor public opinion in favor of Turkey's EU membership left.

This state of affairs has been translated into a Council decision which took note of the standstill and declared on June 26, 2018: "The Council notes that Turkey has been moving further away from the European Union. Turkey's accession negotiations have therefore effectively come to a standstill and no further chapters can be considered for opening or closing and no further work towards the modernisation of the EU-Turkey Customs Union is foreseen".[30] The declaration is short of formal end of membership negotiations as it looks difficult to reach the unanimity as some member states would refrain from publicly antagonizing Turkey for the sake of their vested interests. Nevertheless, Turkey's exclusion is indirectly mentioned in several official documents.[31] Finally, there is no more political dialogue on issues of common concern except *ad hoc* deals such as policing refugee movements

---

[30] https://www.consilium.europa.eu/media/35863/st10555-en18.pdf.

[31] Neither the Commission nor the European Council mentions explicitly Turkey in their key official documents relating to enlargement. The Commission in its landmark communication of February 2018 on enlargement foresees even a tentative accession year, 2025 for some candidates. https://ec.europa.eu/commission/sites/beta-political/files/communication-credible-enlargement-perspective-western-balkans_en.pdf. Similarly, the Council in its latest 18-month program covering the presidencies of Germany, Portugal and Slovenia from July 1, 2020 to December 31, 2021 does not mention Turkey together with the WB-6 enlargement countries. https://data.consilium.europa.eu/doc/document/ST-8086-2020-REV-1/en/pdf.

by Ankara and monitoring the Islamic State of Iraq and Syria (ISIS) terrorists who recently escaped from jail by taking advantage of the latest Turkish military assault in Syria that started in early October 2019.

Membership negotiations now put aside by a tacit understanding of parties, there remain two key issues on which the Ankara regime seems stubborn: The revision of the Customs Union and the Schengen visa waiver for Turkish citizens.

Into effect since January 1, 1996 the Customs Union decision needs indeed to be reviewed and readapted. Advantages Turkey has acquired since the making of the deal have now being eroded over years. Globalization, EU's 2004 and 2007 eastward enlargements, exclusion of services and unprocessed agricultural goods from its coverage, visa requirements for Turkish business people whereas their EU counterparts travel visa-free to Turkey, and most importantly the lack of progress in the membership bid are the most important reasons to cite.

One should recall that the Customs Union was always considered as a step before full membership. And without the membership it would always remain half-done. Although its revision is long overdue, the EU party has been slow to react whereas the Turkish party has been more vocal. Now with the deep-freezing of formal relations and unyielding opposition by some member states and the EP, it looks very difficult to go ahead with that revision.[32] Those who still hope to tie the revision of Customs Union to conditions of economic and political good governance are having illusions with the present regime as its codes are structurally anti-European. Likewise, those member states which are against the continuation of negotiations are also against the revision of the Customs Union. Not to mention the recommendation of the EP in late October 2019 by huge majority, to suspend completely Customs Union as a retaliatory measure following the Turkish assault on Syrian territory. Within these bleak perspectives, remains the Free Trade Agreement option, like with any third country, maybe an enhanced one as Turkey is an old partner.

---

[32] In March 2014, the World Bank, asked by the Commission has published a comprehensive report on the needs and requirements to revise the Customs Union which became obsolete over years as full membership did not occur as expected. cf. www.worldbank.org/content/dam/Worldbank/document/eca/turkey/tr-eu-customs-union-eng.pdf.

The exemption from Schengen visa for Turkish citizen has been wrongly negotiated since 2013 (Aktar, 2016). At this stage, one should note that although visa-free travel is, legally speaking the right of Turkish citizens, the ultimate obstacle remains political. The presence of Turkish nationals among the *jihadists* of the ISIS ranks, a growing Islamophobia and Turcophobia in Europe, huge numbers of unemployed as well as potential Turkish asylum seekers whose number is increasing due to the political situation, are taken into account by the EU policymakers, thus preventing any positive outcome.

Therefore, for Europeans, prospects of Turkey's EU membership and the feasibility of binding agreements (revision of the Customs Union, visa exemption) have become remote. This is why they seem more willing to deal with the current regime and on transactional basis like in the case of refugee policing. As from now on, Turkey is just another third country for the EU, independent from the way it is being ruled. The only difference between Turkey and other Third World countries is that the former is geographically right next to Europe.

Indeed, the EU has still two headaches remaining, both based on geography. Ankara could destabilize the continent's security equilibrium by getting closer to Russia, and could become a long-lasting destabilizing factor in the region due to its coercive actions toward Cyprus, Greece, and Syria. The risk of open hostilities with these two EU member states and a serious emigration potential of Syrians and Turks through and from Turkey as consequences of war and internal instability, need to be taken into account. A third issue is the EU companies' investments in Turkey.

Let us have a closer look to those new deals that are emerging from the failed relationship.

7.9. The Post-Candidacy Era

Every party benefited from the short EU–Turkey synergy. Europeans certainly, despite a deep disregard *vis-à-vis* the achievements which paved the way for the first time in recent history for a common future with a country otherwise considered as Europe's nemesis, its perennial "Other". The decision of 1999 was, as extensively discussed earlier, not an act of charity but a well-thought strategic vision. But now a Turkey without the EU perspective is visited by constant nightmares. Consequences of the ongoing authoritarian restoration and Turkish permanent warfare in the Middle East and in the Mediterranean are perilous to all, to the extent that it could sweep away the continental stability, relatively settled in after the latest enlargements toward the east.

Indeed, things seem quite complicated as witnessed in the chaotic responses to the lifeless candidacy. Technically speaking Turkey is a unique case in the history of enlargement since 1973 of a failed candidacy. Europe does not have any institutional memory on how to deal with, somewhat like for United Kingdom and Brexit.

Similarly, EU's spineless behavior *vis-à-vis* the regime's authoritarian drive illustrate how directionless is the EU in the post-candidacy era. The biggest lesson of the Turkish failure is that the EU cannot benignly close *ad hoc* deals pertaining to its interests and security with Turkey, which does not feel bound by any membership and/or partnership obligation. It would be difficult to bet on the EU (and NATO) ties to, for instance, ease tensions with neighbors, or to call upon Ankara to be in conformity with the *acquis communautaire* in terms of environmental protection and disaster prevention.

This is probably the biggest loss directly stemming from the failure of the conditionality principle. The failure is even more dramatic as, unlike Russia that the EU does not know better how to deal with, Turkey could have become that partner throughout its membership course, which never was an option for Russia.

Let us examine the post-candidacy "battlefield". As for the economy, European-vested interests are cause for greatest concern. As mentioned previously, Customs Union has been beneficial to parties but with the clear lead of the EU side. The trade volume between Turkey and the EU has reached €138,065 billion. The stock of FDI originating from the EU countries was standing at 73.8% of the total of $201.3 billion since 2002 until end 2018. There are thousands of EU companies[33] producing and trading in Turkey and they are often European companies at both ends. Yet

---

[33] Latest available statistics by the Ministry of Industry show 23,248 EU companies out of a total of 65,957, led by 7,333 German, 3,137 British, 2,880 Dutch and 1,453 Italian companies. https://tuys.sanayi.gov.tr/Handlers/DokumanGetHandler.ashx?dokumanId=c2b1d5fa-c5b3-4a29-a5ed-68dc65434498 in Turkish.

there is the overcautious approach to any radical move or word against the regime. Lately, safeguarding EU's industrial, commercial, and financial interests in Turkey through supporting the Turkish economy in crisis was the main headache for Europeans.

To begin with, the regime has accumulated economic mistakes over years, refrained from in-depth structural reforms, and ended up by becoming dependent on high interest rates to continue to attract speculative capital in order to keep the economy afloat and fill the deficits. Lack of proper investment security, very high unemployment, limited growth based solely on infrastructure–energy–domestic consumption spending, weak research and development (R&D), a pathetic education system, lack of natural resources, low savings rate, an outdated fiscal system, fast drying foreign direct investment (FDI), a severe brain drain, all these structural problems make for an explosive cocktail. Turkish economy that has lost its European anchorage will be fundamentally unsustainable.

Strategically speaking, Europe and the West in general are adamant to keep Turkey out of the Russian sphere of influence and within NATO, as long as it goes and despite the ever-growing anti-NATO attitude of both the regime and the public. Although a Russo-Turkish strategic partnership is, historically speaking, an oxymoron, one should never underestimate the weight of anti-NATO moods of the regime in the Turkish society and even in the army. Temptations to challenge old strategic bonds, courting Russia or to go by itself, although overblown and technically unworkable, will remain high as long as Ankara will feel freed of its EU obligations. It will incriminate Washington and the West for being friendlier to Kurdish claims in Syria while Ankara itself is friendlier to the Muslim Brotherhood, to hardline Salafists, and their countless offshoots in the region. A tragic case of West's and in particular EU's powerlessness *vis-à-vis* Ankara's violent *fait accompli* is the recent assault on Syrian territory, with bogus arguments and much warfare, potentially destabilizing and dangerous for the security *inter alia*, of Turkey's European NATO partners.

Moreover, the failure of Turkey's EU membership bid cancels and supersedes the achievements of last 20 years in terms of good bilateral relations with EU member states, particularly Greece. The bellicose rhetoric and actions of the last years against a number of EU countries, EU politicians, and citizens are also strong signals of the Turkish centrifugal drive.

Turkey's contractual obligations toward its neighbors deriving from EU membership prospects were not limited to diplomatic relations. Today two mammoth infrastructure projects that have a direct bearing on EU countries and which require due environmental as well as strategic impact assessment (Environmental Impact Assessment and Strategic Impact Assessment) are going ahead without any independent assessment. These are the Akkuyu nuclear power plant project built not surprisingly by Russia's Rosatom, across Cyprus and situated in a zone prone to earthquakes. The second one is the so-called Crazy Project, a second and artificial Bosporus, considered by experts as potentially fatal for the entire Black Sea region including the rivers feeding it, the Marmara Sea, and beyond (Aktar, 2014b).

Tactically speaking, as for patrolling EU's south-eastern borders and the fate of the so-called refugee agreement of March 18, 2016, one should note that even if the out-of-control displacements of summer 2015 have now been checked, the movement of refugees and migrants continues at a growing pace toward Greece. Not to mention the migratory potential the recent Syria assault by Turkey creates in the region and beyond.

Within this framework, although Ankara's regular threats to "unleash the hordes" of refugees toward Europe is a legitimate cause for concern, there is not much one could afford to reverse the migratory potential for all those stranded in Turkey without any future, including Turkish citizens. Yet the pressure will continue until genuine return and repatriation prospects come forward for Syrians. All things considered; the refugee/migration factor is a major negative assumption if not a non-starter when the EU engages with Ankara. Even more so when one duly recognizes the very role of Ankara in keeping alive the refugee-like situations in Syria by fueling the civil war instead of supporting the searches for a lasting ceasefire and peace-making.

Within the same framework, the prosecution of captured *jihadists* which was sub-contracted to authorities in the region, including Turkey, is a non-starter as well. The likelihood that European *jihadists* will be duly convicted is close to zero in Turkey, which was their undeclared sponsor.

Ethically speaking, after the collapse of the candidacy, EU has preferred to turn a blind eye to skyrocketing human rights violations in Turkey while paying lip service to the universal importance of those rights. The bluntest example is, when asked about the seizure of a media group (Zaman) on March 2016 right at the time of the infamous refugee agreement of March 18, 2016 with Ankara. The then German Interior Minister, Thomas de Maizières directly said, "We are not a referee regarding human rights." Similar cynicism was been showed by the outgoing President of the Commission Jean-Claude Juncker on October 28, 2015 in a famous speech before the EP: "We can say that EU and the European institutions have outstanding issues with Turkey on human rights, press freedoms and so on. We can harp on about that but where is that going to take us in our discussions with Turkey? We know there are shortcomings, but we need to involve Turkey in our initiatives." At the time he was in deep parleys with Ankara on the ways to cap the mass influx of Syrians to EU members Bulgaria and Greece.

Not much margin for action is left to Europeans out of such an unpromising context. Not many options are at hand on what is still feasible regarding the future of EU–Turkey relations and on how to contain a regime that has become the *de facto* leader of Muslim Brotherhood in the region at large.

As for the containment, in the lack of any concrete leverage there are no quick fixes. The sole leverage lies with a possible European/Western economic embargo if illegal use, invasion, or annexation of an EU territory (land but also sea) in the Aegean or Eastern Mediterranean becomes a fact. Strings could be attached to credits loaned at very advantageous conditions to Ankara by European and international financial institutions thanks to its "negotiating candidate country". Indeed, European Investment Bank loans exceeds €30 billion, those of the European Bank for Reconstruction and Development hover around €11 billion. The World Bank, as well as the Council of Europe's Development Bank, is fully involved in extending cheap credit to Turkey. National lending institutions have also loaned billions to Turkey, like France's AfD and Germany's KfW.

Never considered, this conditionality could be functional in an otherwise weak relationship.

Let us now turn to the other looser, Turkey. The country has benefited considerably from the enlargement dynamics despite all odds, paving the way to transform itself in a relatively short period of time.

With its EU candidate status confirmed, Turkey has undergone remarkable changes since 1999. The incentive of a future membership was backed by a weighty part of Turkish society and its growing aspirations to transform and democratize itself. It has led to a period of unprecedented political and economic stability. That happened despite the weight of Turkish polity's structural shortcomings described previously, as well as EU circles' constant discouragements and their reluctance to endorse the final objective of membership.

With the EU membership perspective gone, Turkey has entered uncharted waters. The EU dynamic needed to transform and to reform was fading away to leave the ground to old behaviors. The political class, the government, and the opposition alike have abandoned the EU perspective, leaving not much room to the civil society to continue to be the supporter of the process. We know the rest. Turkey has not only resigned from being a candidate for membership but took the opposite direction to approve a new regime which has blatant authoritarian traits and supported by at least half of the population.

It goes without saying that such turn of events cannot be charged to the failure of the EU membership of Turkey, yet the very failure has most probably triggered the metamorphosis. The first years of the process between 1999 and 2005 have been so successful in terms of economic, social, and political achievements that Turkey became suddenly an affluent country. The overconfidence resulting from it has had a critical effect on the illusion of being capable to go alone in world affairs. The regime coined even a bizarre motto for the country: "the precious loneliness" to describe its awkwardness. Over years, the so-called precious loneliness has become a challenge to the world personified in the one-man rule of President Recep Tayyip Erdoğan.

Finally, the peripheral looser: The wider region and the Arab and Muslim worlds...

It is a fact that three Caucasus nations, Armenia, Azerbaijan, and Georgia, Turkey's eastern neighbors were hoping to get closer to the EU thanks to Turkey's membership. This perspective now has vanished; these countries are to stay in the backyard of Russia despite some frail European bonds.

As for the Arab and Muslim worlds, a future EU member Turkey was representing something historic. A country which has similar pedigree as them was making to the world of those patronizing them since long time. It is no coincidence that Arab nations have closely followed all major decisions concerning EU–Turkey relations. The inhabitants of the region were eager to see whether Europe will choose to associate with a "different" country and thus sending a message of international solidarity. The EU decision of December 17, 2004 to start membership negotiations with Turkey, adding brand new "southern dimension" to Union's policies, has thus received exceptionally dense media coverage in Arab countries. The EU's decision was promising a global impact going well beyond Turkey's membership and the future of Europe.

To recapitulate: It looks as though the fairy tale is over, the historic rendezvous missed.

References

Aktar, C. (2003). "Turkey Membership Bid Cannot Be Judged on the Basis of Misguided Clichés". politico.eu.

Aktar, C. (ed.) (2004). *Lettres aux Turco-sceptiques*, Actes Sud.

Aktar, C. (2007). "Why Turkey Should Join in 2023". politico.eu.

Aktar, C. (2014a). "Hard Times for the Champion of Political Islam". https://www.aljazeera.com/indepth/opinion/2014/01/hard-times-champion-political-i-201412782733717428.html.

Aktar, C. (2014b). "Erdoğan's Megalomaniac Projects". https://www.aljazeera.com/indepth/opinion/2014/03/erdogan-megalomaniac-projects-201432012171661127.html.

Aktar, C. (2016). "Turkey's Visa Ordeal and Europe's Refugee Deal". https://www.aljazeera.com/indepth/opinion/2016/05/turkey-visa-ordeal-europe-refugee-deal-160509130041018.html.

Balta, E. (2005). "The Ceasefire This Time" *Middle East Report Online*, 31 August.

Gole, N. (2013). "The Gezi Occupation: For a Democracy of Public Spaces". opendemocracy.net, 11 June.

Simet, G. F., Lungu, T. and Karassavoglou, A. (2015). "The Impact of Turkey's Current Corruption Crisis on ITS", *Economy, Procedia Economics and Finance*, Vol. 19, pp. 91–100.

Chapter 8

Turkey's Development Conundrum: Three Scenarios for the Next 10 Years

Atilla Yeşilada

8.1. Introduction

The final chapter of "Turkish Economy at the Crossroads" attempts to answer the question of how Turkey will evolve in the next 10 years from the perspective of development. It proposes a simple hypothesis: Turkey's development has lost momentum, and in certain key areas regression took place in the second decade of the 21st century because of a steady decline in democracy and institutions under the rule of Justice and Development Party (AK Parti for the rest of the chapter). The country shall either grow or develop below its true potential as long as the main culprit of this decline, the current regime and its founding principles, remain in power.

This chapter shall develop a fuller definition of democracy and its institutional underpinnings as it relates to economic progress and development later in this section, but to drive home the scope and depth of Turkey's recent decline, a few startling setbacks are mentioned at the onset to motivate the discussion.

- In the United Nations Development Programme (UNDP) 2018 Inequality-adjusted Human Development Index, Turkey ranked 64th, slipping four places from the previous year.

- According to World Wildlife Federation, Turkey exhausts its renewable resources 32 days earlier annually than the world average.
- According to World Bank Changing Wealth of Nations 2018 report, between 1995 and 2014, global wealth grew by two-thirds (66%), but population grew by 27%, so that the net increase in per capita wealth was only 31% (Figures 2.1 and 2.7). Per capita wealth grew fastest in middle-income countries, raising their share of global wealth, but the largest growth in absolute terms occurred in upper-middle-income countries (at nearly 120%), in part because of China. In this period, (see map in the text), Turkey's wealth declined by 5% (World Bank, 2018).
- Turkey's ranking peaked at 42 in 2016 in the Global Innovation Index (2018), only to drop to 50 in the 2018 assessment.
- In 2017 World Economic Forum (WEF) Human Capital Index, Turkey ranked 75th, compared to the 60th rank in the 2013 report.
- Turkey has ranked 109th in the World Justice Project (WJP) Rule of Law Index 2019, marking a drop of eight places compared to 2018.
- Turkey is ranked 157th out of 180 countries ranked by Reporters Without Borders' (RSF) on its 2019 World Press Freedom Index, unchanged from 2018.

As a wise person once remarked "predictions are hard, in particular if they concern the future." Long-term forecasts involve many independent variables; and in the Quantum universe we live in, there is a lot of happenstance. Thus, instead of predicting the future by a mechanical extrapolation of current trends to a singular path, this essay examines three scenarios focusing on two "switching variables". The first variable emanates from the logical question of whether the current regime will reign over the forecast period (the first and second scenarios). The second case (third scenario) is an external shock or tail-risk, made particularly relevant after Turkey's military campaign in North East Syria, dubbed as "Operation Peace Spring", and cannot necessarily be classified as "good" or "bad". Only in fullness of time shall we discover what this fateful act meant for Turkey's development.

Before we start our exploration into the future path for Turkey, the concepts of development and democracy as used in the context of this essay need to be defined carefully, because at least in Turkey "development" came to be synonymous with Recep Tayyip Erdoğan's grandiose public works such as airports, tunnels, bridges, and mosques called "mega-projects", while "democracy" was reduced to a free and fair ballot, much ridiculed by developmental economists and developing world intellectuals as an anachronism used for neoliberals to justify the existence of the capitalist world order. Neither are true.

a. *Defining Development*

Gross domestic product (GDP) per capita and its more commonly used twin purchasing power parity (PPP)-adjusted GDP per capita are useful tools in measuring a nation's success over time and across peers, but fail to provide a comprehensive narrative of how a society marches through history by adding to or subtracting from the well-being of individuals. There are many nations which manage to increase per capita GDP over time, but stagnate in all or most indicators of what constitutes human well-being.

Israel (2018) defines the "development" concept used as follows:

"Development is a process that creates growth, progress, positive change or the addition of physical, economic, environmental, social and demographic components. The purpose of development is a rise in the level and quality of life of the population, and the creation or expansion of local regional income and employment opportunities, without damaging the resources of the environment. Development is visible and useful, not necessarily immediately, and includes an aspect of quality change and the creation of conditions for a continuation of that change."

Through the years, professionals and various researchers developed a number of definitions and emphases for the term "development". Amartya Sen, for example, developed the "capability approach", which defined development as a tool enabling people to reach the highest level of their ability, through granting freedom of action, i.e., freedom of economic, social, and family actions, etc. This approach became a basis for the measurement of development by the HDI (Human Development Index), which was developed by the UN Development Programme (UNDP) in 1990.

Previous chapters have largely focused on macroeconomic growth and its components,[1] while this final one enlarges the scope, attempting to see the future through the lens of the broader concept of societal well-being.

b. *What Does Democracy Mean in the Context of Economy, Development, and Free Markets?*

Democracy, simply speaking, is a set of rules, conventions, and institutions by which a society consents to be ruled. It is intimately related to the functioning of the economic system and how development proceeds. This chapter builds on the work of Acemoğlu and Üçer (Chapter 2) to explain the comprehensive meaning of democracy used in deriving scenarios for Turkey and what its failure would mean.

Though there are no universal recipes for achieving high-quality and/or shared growth, recent research has emphasized the role of institutional factors. Of primary importance is the complex of economic institutions that Acemoğlu and Robinson (2012) refer to as "inclusive economic institutions". These are based on secure property rights, lack of coercion, and systematic discrimination in the labor market, a functioning legal system, public services, health and education investments, and a basic social safety net creating a level-playing field. These institutions, undergirded by political institutions that distribute political voice and power broadly in society and introduce basic checks on the exercise of political authority, appear to predict long-run, shared economic prosperity.

Recent research also suggests that changes in economic and political institutions can have a major impact on the extent and nature of economic growth even in relatively short periods of time. Acemoğlu *et al.* (2019) study the economic implications of a transition from a non-democratic to a democratic regime and find that democratization increases economic

---

[1] With the exception of Chapter 7 by Cengiz Aktar, which examines the troubled relationship between Turkey and the European Union (EU).

growth substantially for the next 20 years (causing approximately a 20% rise in GDP per capita). Moreover, this growth boost tends to be of high quality and shared: it is accompanied by higher taxes, more spending and better outcomes in education and health, and greater investments. Consistent with the institutional emphasis in Acemoğlu and Robinson (2012), this political change goes hand in hand with improvements in economic institutions, such as economic reforms in product, labor, and financial markets.

"Another important argument in this literature is worth mentioning. Even though inclusive economic institutions, founded on inclusive political institutions, are conducive to faster growth, there should be no presumption that they emerge swiftly. Institutions are shaped by distributional conflicts and the relative powers of competing groups and individuals in society. Institutional reform follows either the collapse of existing political balances or results from new political coalitions in favor of reform coming together. Neither of these two paths works smoothly or rapidly, if at all."

"Our basic premise in this chapter, building on our prior work, Acemoğlu and Üçer (2015), is that the recent Turkish macroeconomic experience confirms the role of institutions in shaping the extent and nature of economic growth. While Turkey has achieved considerable economic modernization and growth over the last three decades, much of this has been of low quality and the gains have been distributed rather unequally. These problems are rooted in the institutional structure of the Turkish economy. In fact, the short five years between 2002 and 2006, during which growth took a higher-quality form, accompanied with productivity improvements, and technological upgrading, took place in the context of major improvements in economic and political institutions. When these improvements were reversed in the subsequent years, the quality of growth declined and inequality rose", comment Acemoğlu and Üçer.

Thus, the question of which development path Turkey will pursue is largely reduced to whether Erdoğan will stay in power in the next 10 years. If he does, he shall further undermine democracy and institutions, thwarting development.

c. *A Very Brief History: Turkey's Rise and Fall under the AK Parti–Erdoğan Administrations*

Turkey's journey in the 21st century constitutes another conundrum for development theory. During the earlier years of the AK Parti administration, it developed very rapidly (see Table 8.1), breaking almost all

Table 8.1. Turkey's rise and fall in the 21st century[2]

Years	Economy and Development Indicators	Event Ending the Episode	
2003–2008	Rapid growth driven by total factor productivity (TFP) boom, disinflation, significant progress in development indicators and democracy, which brought Turkey to the door of EU	Constitutional Court case to shut down AK Parti, Ergenekon and Sledgehammer trials[3]	Era of rapid progress
2008–2013	Rapid but more erratic growth, driven by foreign borrowing, rising Current Account Deficit and inequality Development indicators begin to stall, EU accession stops completely	Gezi protests (Amnesty International, 2013), taper tantrum	The interregnum, slow-down in development
2013–2016	Growth slowdown, but more importantly currency instability and rising inflation Stagnation in development indicators, widespread persecution of dissidents and media crackdown	Gulenist putsch[4]	The decline
2016–now	Visible deceleration in growth, high and erratic inflation and exchange rate depreciation, erosion of fiscal discipline Turkey begins to slip in all development indicators, State of Emergency[5] effectively relegates Turkey into a semi-democratic state status Dismantlement of institutions and efforts to consolidate all levers of state power in the office of Erdoğan		Turkey at Crossroads

[2] Coauthors of other chapters use different dates for purposes of benchmarking. This table focuses on political events which altered the AK Parti's conduct.

[3] For explanation and analysis of Sledgehammer and Ergenekon trials, see Rodrik, no date of publication.

[4] For Fethullah Gulen, the Gulenist Movement, and 2016 coup attempt, see Schwerin (2018).

[5] State of Emergency, declared after the July 2016 aborted coup and lifted emergency in July 2018. However, its essential components have been transferred to subsequent legislation.

"accepted wisdom" or practical rules about what hinders a nation's progress.[6]

Between 2008 and 2013, AK Parti's proclivity to shortchange democracy in favor of social engineering to build an Islamist-conservative society began to manifest. Roughly since the 2013 Gezi Protests — though scholars would argue about the exact date — Turkey first lost its development momentum, then began regressing in almost all internationally recognized indices measuring one or the other aspect of "development", such as freedom of expression, educational achievement, technological innovation, and judicial performance. Finally, after the aborted coup attempt of 2016, all institutions, including those underpinning the free market were hallowed out by the regime's desire to have absolute control over state and society.

Parenthetically, it should be noted that Turkey's startling decline in the second decade of the 21st century could not be entirely blamed on the government. In Chapter 7, Cengiz Aktar recounts the story of how mutual mistakes and timidity caused Turkey the loss of European Union (EU) membership anchor, with some memorable comments: "(t)he consequences of the failure, although a tad early to conclude, could be likened to a lose–lose situation which goes well beyond the parties' interests *per se*, to encompass Islam's synergy and co-existence with the rest of the world. As for Turkey, implications of the post-candidacy go beyond the simple consequences of a failed EU candidacy. By diverging from the EU path, the country consolidates and seals its de-Westernization drive to start sailing toward uncharted waters."

Turkey's rapid rise-to-eclipse development cycle[7] is a very rare phenomenon in the 20th and 21st centuries,[8] for a country which is

---

[6] For instance, the notion that Moslem nations cannot cohabit with democracy, or cannot indigenously engineer development was disproven.

[7] For a brief summary of the cycle, see Serchuk (2018).

[8] Frequently, China, Argentina, and Africa at large are used to negate the argument that democracy is a precondition for development. It is worth noting that a single variable such as "democratization" cannot account for the totality of human experience. China is a unique case where the institution of state guiding people has existed in one way or another for over 2 millennia. There is no evidence that it can be replicated elsewhere. In case of Argentina, periodic institutional breakdowns may have inhibited growth, rather than democracy. In case of Africa, there are very few relevant examples of democracy with

governed by a stable government that has not experienced war, famine, or a major and permanent "external shock". Most scholars opine that it is the steady absorption of power into the office of presidency, currently occupied by President Erdoğan and AK Parti's penchant for majoritarianism superseding checks and balances, which lies at the bottom of this decline.

In other words, it is the hallowing out of the democracy, and the attendant institutions and customs which reinforce it and connect it to a free-market economy orchestrated by the regime which has thwarted development.

d. *Explaining the Choice and Probability Ranking of the Three Scenarios*

This chapter takes "Turkey's failed democracy" as an obstacle to development as its departure point in projecting the next 10 years for Turkey, but questions the pitfalls in the argument, too, introducing an alternative. Recent developments strongly suggest that President Erdoğan and the AK Parti may abandon their current policy proclivities, or even be forced to abandon power. These constitute the first two scenarios.

The last scenario simulates Turkey being subjected to external shocks of a geo-political origin juxtaposed upon the eternal trinity of its social fault lines: Islamist versus secular, Sunni versus Alevi, and Turk versus Kurd. The external shock scenario was chosen when Turkey cemented its presence in Syria by capturing several border cantons, which — as shall be explained in the last section — has the potential for causing unrest, an open-ended entanglement in the affairs of a troubled neighbor and substantial expenditure of "blood and treasure" at the expense of funds which can be devoted to economy and welfare, or

---

all its institutions reigning in any country. Turkey remains a curiosity, because under the AK Parti and Erdoğan, it had all the prerequisites for growth and development, and had managed to erect strong democratic institutions until 2008. It is the later regression of democracy, leading to slower development, rather than a take-off stage which is being examined in this chapter.

— much less likely — to end the century-long struggle between ethnic Turks and Kurds.

It is customary to assess the likelihoods of each scenario, but no probabilistic or even logical method exists to accomplish this goal. The chapter assigns probabilities to each scenario, by using the author's extensive Google search of articles examining or referring to the cases for each scenario and making a frequency comparison.[9] For instance "Turkey will regress further under the current regime" theme is more than twice as likely as external shocks one, based on the author's search. However, the former commands only 45% odds, meaning the chances of it materializing is less than a coin flip. The positive scenario commands 35% probability, which only goes to emphasize that AK Parti relinquishing power and restoration of Turkey's developmental momentum commands much higher odds compared to the majority view.

8.2. The Base Case: Turkey Will Regress Further under the Current Regime

The departure point of this scenario is the observation that as Turkey moved away from democracy, undermining "inclusive institutions", its development and eventually growth stalled. Thus, it needs to be explained how Turkey's evermore centralized and de-institutionalized governance retards development.

a. *How the Presidency's Accumulation of Power Retards Development*

Unconventional economic views held by Erdoğan, but more broadly by the conservative-Islamic tradition of the AK Parti which refutes the traditional economic practice, leads the causes: Erdoğan's aversion to "high interest rates" on account of these presumably causing higher inflation has the status of a religious dogma, but runs afoul of established practice of effective monetary policy. A striking example of Erdoğan's monetary

---

[9]To a large extent, the three scenarios, too, are selected using the same approach.

views triggering a monetary shock is his interview with Bloomberg TV on May 14, 2018, where: "Turkish President Recep Tayyip Erdoğan said he intends to tighten his grip on the economy and take more responsibility for monetary policy if he wins an election next month." On May 24, Central Bank of Turkey was forced to hike rates by 300 basis points, as Erdoğan's comments triggered a panic among investors.

However, there are many other poorly-thought economic theories the AK Parti strategists advocate. One of these is the denial of aggregate supply constraints. The government continually heaps subsidies and incentives on companies in "strategic industries" to expand the supply curve of the economy, paying scant attention to other determinants, such as regulatory visibility, property rights, economies of scale,[10] or the labor supply mismatch.[11]

Secondly, while the presidential system pays homage to democracy, it has effectively destroyed many of its pillars, claiming those are Western impositions or are not suitable to Turkey's unique conditions — a view of civilizationism, widely emulated in most strong-man regimes. For instance, a free press is not an indispensable part of democracy, neither are checks and balances among the three branches of state, i.e., the executive, the legislature, and the judiciary.

Rule of law[12] and due process have been effectively suspended in Turkey since the 2016 coup, which has had a deleterious impact on the business environment, steadily reducing non-structures capex to GDP ratio, as well as helping the government and security agencies to settle

---

[10] The AK Parti asserts that it can "onshore" manufacturing industries in intermediate goods within a year by providing the right incentives. However, one of the main reasons why Turkish final-goods producers buy from foreign suppliers is the fact that the latter had long ago reached economies of scale by establishing global markets. New-comer domestic firms can never hope to match this advantage.

[11] A recent strategy document by Industry and Technology Ministry aims to raise 500,000 new software coders, 10 Turkish unicorns with markets caps of US$1 billion each, and 23 brand-new Turkish inventions. Turkey currently graduates 8,000 software engineers per annum, has only a couple of dozen banks and conglomerates with market caps over US$1 billion, and to the best of this author's knowledge, there are no Turkish inventions with brand name recognition in the world!

[12] "Turkey Ranks Worse in Rule of Law Index", BIA News Desk (2019).

long-standing accounts with rivals or dissidents. Such indiscriminate revenge, encouraged by lower courts is causing brain drain[13] as well as disenfranchising large numbers of productive citizens.

Thirdly, Turkey witnessed wholesale destruction of institutions deemed important to the effective functioning of the free market in AK Parti's quest to achieve high growth. Led by the Central Bank, all independent regulatory agencies are firmly attached to ministries and operate under Erdoğan's orders, distorting the efficiency of free markets.

While Turkey is presumably in a free-float exchange rate regime, state banks frequently intervene in the currency market, as the government essentially dictates prices of key staples, Turkish Lira (TL) deposit and loan rates.

Finally, the education system is used as a tool to indoctrinate the youth as pious Sunni Muslims, which is anathema to essential skill building and to participation of Kurds and Alevites in socioeconomic processes. President Erdoğan's famous phrase, which has become a social media meme, "Our goal is to raise a pious and revengeful generation", still rings in the ears of Turkey's secularist minority as a call to war.

b. *What Will Happen to Turkey if Erdoğan Were to Stay in Power for the Next 10 Years?*

Before discussing economic growth, an important caveat needs to be established. The most recent revisions made to the GDP series by TurkStat

---

[13] A recent article in *The New York Times*, citing the Turkish Statistical Institute, said more than a quarter-million Turks emigrated in 2017, an increase of 42% over 2016, when nearly 178,000 citizens left the country. The number of Turks applying for asylum worldwide jumped by 10,000 in 2017 to more than 33,000.

"The flight of people, talent and capital is being driven by a powerful combination of factors that have come to define life under Mr. Erdoğan and that his opponents increasingly despair is here to stay," according to *The New York Times*. "They include fear of political persecution, terrorism, a deepening distrust of the judiciary and the arbitrariness of the rule of law, and a deteriorating business climate, accelerated by worries that Mr. Erdoğan is unsoundly manipulating management of the economy to benefit himself and his inner circle" (see Bekdil, 2019).

in 2016 had been met with suspicion by many scholars,[14] including the author of this chapter. If one uses the old series (See Pamuk, Chapter 1), the economy had begun decelerating as early as the post-Gezi era, which would have provided a very strong argument that the regime's efforts to dilute the democracy and its concomitant institutions are harmful to economic growth.

This being said, under the current regime trend economic growth is very likely to decelerate under 3% (median 2020 forecast at end of November 2019), or even toward zero, from the current historical average 5.7%, with frequent Balance of Payments shocks caused by Erdoğan's penchant for low interest rates (leading to currency shocks) and falling credibility of Turkey (triggering "sudden risk reversal" episodes in financial markets). Given the high and rapid pass through between currency depreciation and inflation, the chances of consumer price index (CPI) inflation decelerating to single digits during the reign of the current regime is estimated as very low. In the subsequent paragraphs, explanations are provided why inflation, growth rate, and trend growth would decline under the current policy set.

Foreign direct investment (FDI) and domestic capex are to remain very low, retarding absorption of Industry 4.0, AI, and Internet of Objects into Turkish economy,[15] as indispensable conditions for the accumulation of such invisible assets, namely rule of law, due process, and an effective and forward-looking regulatory environment, will simply not be created. This will slow capital accumulation, and absorption of new technology, already retarded by a visible reluctance for private-sector fixed investment, further reducing the enlargement of aggregate supply. As growth

---

[14] For a comprehensive discussion of the methodological shortcomings of the new national income series, see Aydoğuş (2017).

[15] 2018 OECD study finds that Turkey already receives less FDI than its GDP would warrant: Relative to GDP, the inward FDI stock has fluctuated in Turkey since 2008 and was equivalent to 17% of GDP in 2015. Outward FDI was much smaller and equivalent to 4% in 2015 (Figure 3). In 2015, Turkey's share of the OECD total inward FDI stock (0.9%) was about half its share of GDP (1.6%), and its share in outward stock was 0.2% of the OECD total, a fraction of its share of GDP (Figure 4). See OECD Turkey, Trade and Investment Statistical Note (2017).

stimulating policies continue, a positive output gap and currency shocks ought to steadily push inflation upward.

Misallocation of the budget toward salaries, cronies, and mega-projects is very likely to retard advancement of human capital. The new technologies mentioned earlier require highly skilled, motivated, and adaptable workforce, which many studies, including those by the Program for International Student Assessment (PISA) and Turkish Ministry of Education, have revealed are not being produced by the current education system. To make things worse, secondary schooling rates began to drop by 2017.

Further to the budget, so far, none of the mega-projects created enough revenue for the operating consortia to generate the promised return on capital, meaning *as per* the PPP contract the difference is being paid from the budget, a burden estimated to rise exponentially in the coming years, further limiting funds for social development and welfare spending.

The Ministry of Health had to adopt draconian measures to cap health spending, with a strong possibility of future governments reneging on the promise of free and universal healthcare. At this juncture, many experts claim the Social Security System, which also provides universal healthcare to a majority of citizens, is actuarially insolvent. As growth declines, so does the tax revenue growth, which will fall short of covering health needs of retirees, already numbering in excess of 12 million versus a workforce of 28.5 million as of August 2019, and poor families receiving welfare assistance, leading to a decline in life expectancy and productivity through less-healthy labor supply.

If the regime remains on the current course of foreign policy, drastic Western responses can be triggered at some point in the future, with Turkey possibly being expelled from the Council of Europe and North Atlantic Treaty Organization (NATO).[16] In such an eventuality, Turkey will lose its external drivers for progress, further weakening internal drivers of development. The country stands the risk of being shut out of valuable foreign capital and technological know-how transfers through lower FDI and cultural estrangement.

---

[16] The US threats to impose Countering America's Adversaries Through Sanctions Act (CAATSA) sanctions because of S-400 anti-missile system purchases and the resolution by the EU Parliament to end the accession process hint that decoupling may have already started.

Turkey will remain a symbolic democracy, with free elections, but the opposition will be whittled away by Putinesque methods to prevent a real challenge to his reign. As has been established at the introduction, the diminution of democracy to a free ballot is a cause for slow development.

Secular Turks and the educated youth are expected to leave the country or "switch off" at every opportunity, draining the already shallow talent pool.

The ranking of individuals according to their religious preferences or observed devotion to the AK Parti, rather than merit or know-how, will also waste talent, causing sub-optimal development. At the end, Turkey could evolve into an informal caste society, where individual rights and obligations are variegated and determined according to religious and party affiliation, ethnicity, and even gender.

8.3. The Good Case Scenario: The Demand Side of the Democracy Equation

The first scenario treated the failure of democracy as a supply problem, i.e., democracy was provided or withheld by the regime. This is a very strange view considering how nations like Britain and United States reached an advanced democratic equilibrium: by civil war, civil rights movements, and constant class struggle. Even though it failed in many of its hosts, Arab Spring, too, demonstrated in unpleasant ways that people in the developing countries are unhappy with the way they are governed and are well capable of taking matters in hand to demand change.[17] Thus, it is fair to explore a counternarrative to the "Erdoğan president for life" view which has so much currency at home and abroad among political scholars at the time of the publishing of this book.

In fact, Turkey's March and June 2019 municipal elections, where Erdoğan and the AK Parti–MHP alliance suffered a startling defeat despite some ballot tampering, and surveys taken afterward provide strong

---

[17] Arab Spring may not yet be over. The departure of Sudan's Omar al-Bashir, as well as large demonstrations in Iraq and Lebanon, hint at a new momentum for the desire for change. See Malik (2019).

evidence that there is a growing yearning for more democracy, as approval ratings for Erdoğan and the AK Parti have declined steadily since then.

In the spring 2019 municipal elections, the main opposition party, Republican People's Party (CHP) and its allies[18] captured the mayor's offices in major cities of Turkey, such as Istanbul, Ankara, Izmir, Adana, and Mersin. More than 50% of the population is now governed locally by opposition mayors. The elections signified that the AK Parti is losing votes not only to CHP but also to its nationalist ally MHP.

Erdoğan and the AK Parti's decline in approval ratings continued after local elections. In the 11 polls publicly available since the second Istanbul elections, nine reveal substantial loss of support for the AK Parti and to a lesser extent for MHP.

Polls take a static picture, wherein discerning reasons and trends are difficult to read. Ongoing processes suggest that Erdoğan's popularity will drop further, which significantly increases the odds of opposition alliance victory in the next elections. Next, the chapter reviews these processes.

a. *Are There Any Signs of Regime Change?*

First, Erdoğan's charisma and popularity have two separate pillars. First, he appeals to the hearts of the conservatives by speaking their language and responding to their aspirations. These true fans are probably around 27% of the population, according to some polling agencies which had investigated the question, like KONDA.[19] But, the rest of the AK Parti votes are mostly attracted by its ability to supply prosperity. Erdoğan presided over Turkey for a record 16 years without a major financial crisis or recession, one of the two leaders who had done so in the post-1950s' multiparty era. His ability to put more bread on the table of a majority of the families year after year slowly created a clientele relationship with voters. World Bank complimented Turkey as one of the few developing nations which tripled per capita GDP in the short span of a decade,

---

[18] Named "the National Alliance" collectively, though in strategic districts pro-Kurdish Rights HDP and the alliance backed each other, and smaller parties which stood a chance of besting the AKP or MHP rival.

[19] See Yeni Çağ Gazetesi (2019).

a magic which had faded in 2018. As this chapter is written, Turkey is either in recession, or producing an anemic growth rate of 1–2%, while Central Bank of Republic of Turkey (CBRT) September Tendency Survey forecasts only 2.2% growth in 2020. In most of the available forecasts, it is not expected to return to its former average GDP growth rates through 2022, the rate which had kept Erdoğan in power.

The increasing number of economically disadvantaged can no longer find remedies from the AK Parti's vast formal and informal social welfare apparatus, either. Room for patronage has shrunk drastically, as large municipalities switched to opposition parties and budget deficits exceeded 3% of GDP, restricting the room to spend further severely as of October 2019.

Additionally, the AK Parti's traditional allies of Sunni sects and their vast charitable networks are no longer fully at the disposal of Erdoğan, with some moving away from the party.

The growing number of economically frustrated voters appear to be hoping to find solutions for their problems in the parties currently in the process of being established by former economy minister Ali Babacan[20] and PM Ahmet Davutoğlu.[21] Polls investigating the voter potential for the Babacan and Davutoğlu movements vary, but a rough average is 11% of national vote (collectively for both pretenders to the AK Parti votes), mostly from the AK Parti. The most recent poll this chapter has access to, by reliable Metropoll Survey (2019) finds the AK Parti–MHP leading the opposition alliance by 41–39%, with 17% undecided, and Babacan–Davutoğlu swing vote determining the winner, whichever alliance they choose to join.

The infighting in AK Parti is a very rare phenomenon in the long march of Turkey's Islamist movement, known for its cohesion and devotion to the leader. The last time such a challenge occurred, Recep Tayyip Erdoğan, Abdullah Gul, Abdullatif Sener, and Bulent Arinc formed the AK Parti, splitting from the main trunk of Felicity Party. It is possible that the Babacan and Davutoğlu movements juxtaposed over economic misery precipitating a similar split.

---

[20] For an explanation of Ali Babacan's movement, see Müjgan (2019) cited in Halis (2019).

[21] For Ahmet Davutoğlu's movement, see Pitel (2019).

Nevertheless, this chapter makes no claim that either of the two new-comers will defeat Erdoğan, or will help the opposition alliance help defeat him. There is a much more nuanced policy option available to Erdoğan. He may either emulate their policy planks, or attempt to coopt them to keep his flock together. In other words, the mantra "As long as Erdoğan is president, Turkey will not develop" will end, to be replaced by Erdoğan of AK Parti's first term. If he fails to do so, new parties could claw modest to moderate amounts of supporters from the AK Parti, jeopardizing Erdoğan's chances of re-election, and potentially causing the Grand Assembly to have an opposition majority.

AK Parti's other difficulty is its alliance with nationalist MHP, which has substantially narrowed its social and diplomatic maneuvering room. Erdoğan needs MHP leader Devlet Bahçeli's support to win the next presidential election. In return for his support, Bahçeli has increasingly converted Erdoğan into a hardline nationalist and anti-Westernist, triggering an exodus of conservative Kurdish votes and urban moderates from the party. Herein, Erdoğan faces a major dilemma. For him to start a rapprochement with the West and Kurds, he needs to ditch MHP. However, in this case he needs to find a replacement among opposition parties, all of which demand a return to the parliamentary system.

Thirdly, AK Parti has lost touch with the youth (Ayata, 2017). The Internet generation in Turkey is much more tolerant to other lifestyles than AKP's elders, recognizes that a poor and heavily politicized education system is robbing them off their future, and detest AK Parti's forced Islamization policies. Recent data show significant increases in Atheism and Deism in Turkey, contrary to what many scholars claim to be deepening Islamization of the country.

Finally, an urban conservative bourgeois is emerging, which is more pragmatic in terms of religious observance, capitalist and pro-Western at least in its consumption behavior, and which instinctively understands that constant tension at home and strife with the West abroad is bad for the future. They also recognize that Erdoğan's discretionary governance system replacing the rule of law and due process in his office is bad for their property rights, for which they had painstakingly labored for over 20 years. Arbitrary confiscation risk is now a perception shared by urban secular and conservative classes.

It is possible that the AK Parti will split into two or three different parties, or at some point the youth and urban conservative vote will seek an address outside its umbrella to change the 17-year static equilibrium.

While some observers would not deny this scenario, the most frequent response is that if Erdoğan is cornered by democratic means, he will simply dispense with it and continue to rule by deployment of coercive measures.

While the absolute devotion of lower ranks of judiciary, the police, and military appears to strengthen this argument in the sense that democracy is a luxury for the current regime which it can easily do without, a closer analysis reveals major pitfalls.

First, Erdoğan has studied the case of Maduro closely, recognizing that a legitimate democratic mandate by the people is his best defense against his biggest fear: coups or interventions inspired or organized by Western foes. The convoluted story of repeated Istanbul elections is an evidence of Erdoğan's need for legitimacy (Aydıntaşbaş, 2019). CHP candidate Ekrem İmamoğlu won the first ballot by a very narrow margin, after which under intense pressure from Erdoğan and Bahçeli, the High Election Council ruled a repeat election. İmamoğlu defeated the AK Parti candidate by a landslide, at which point Erdoğan conceded defeat.

Furthermore, there is no concrete evidence that if Erdoğan were to lose a democratic majority, the coercive organs of the state will cooperate with him. Despite years of carefully selecting conservatives and nationalists to judiciary,[22] police, and even to the military,[23] these institutions have a proven habit of siding with the winner.

The reluctance to use coercion implies that adverse shocks would moderate Erdoğan's behavior and AK Parti's return to its "factory" settings, i.e., becoming more democratic within and tolerant to dissent. If the party fails to do so, it may lose its current parliamentary majority and migrations of members of parliament (MPs) to Babacan–Davutoğlu factions. Early elections will see the end of Erdoğan and the AK Parti era.

The alternative may not be a stable single-party government or a new president with a stature equal to Erdoğan, but these matter little.

---

[22] For the changing pro-AKP stance of the high judiciary, see Yetkin (2019).
[23] For the non-AKP make-up of post-coup military, see Gürcan (2017).

The opposition is slowly developing the skills of cooperation and agreeing on common denominators, which are also required for a successful coalition government. A CHP president would immediately begin devolving powers to a stronger Cabinet and the Grand Assembly.

b. *What Would Be the Implications of This Scenario for Development?*

While coalition governments of the past had a mediocre economic record, a change in administration should accelerate economic growth almost immediately, because some of the weakness is caused by falling confidence in the government, nepotism, absence of rule of law, and the extremely discretionary management principle established under the presidential system.

It is argued that a lack of experience by the opposition could cause road accidents, which is not a big problem. The opposition possesses a slew of ex-bureaucrats and qualified economists who adhere to the conventional economic theory and practice, meaning that macropolicy settings will be more pragmatic.

In fact, it is possible that realizing the gravity of the bad loan problem in the banking industry, the new administration will call in the International Monetary Fund (IMF). An IMF stand-by program would first help resolve the growing "impaired asset" or loans in arrears problem in banks, which is estimated at 12% of the total loan portfolio, which is clogging the credit channel. This problem requires external funds and close coordination between the administration, bank shareholders, debtors, and potential buyers of dud assets, an expertise only IMF possesses. IMF's arrival on the scene could further underpin confidence, accelerating the decline in inflation and bond yields via rapid inflow of financial capital.

Inflation can be expected to decelerate gradually toward the legally mandated target of Central Bank, established at 5%, because the opposition advocates an independent monetary policy.

Prior to implementation of non-orthodox policies by the AK Parti, estimates for Turkey's sustainable growth rate ranged from 4.5–5%, which could be achieved within a few years, assuming domestic capex and FDI recover to pre-2010 years.

Improving Turkey's human rights standards and rule of law shortcomings are also fairly easy, in the sense that most of the transgressions today are not committed using the loopholes in legislation, but by an overzealous judiciary and constabulary which probably has no incentive to persecute dissidents unless prodded by the new government.

The inefficiency losses by cronyism and nepotism are difficult to estimate, but one would assume that a large portion of this will be eliminated in the first term of the new administration, reinvigorating growth by improving human capital in the bureaucracy and increasing motivation to work.

Improving Turkey's educational system is a huge challenge, because of several reasons. First, the trainers must be completely re-trained in imparting relevant knowledge and analytical skills to their students. Low pay and motivation is an immense barrier to recruiting qualified staff into the teaching industry. However, some improvement is possible, as forced conversion of lay (secular) schools into clerical ones (*imam hatips*) is reversed and Sunni indoctrination courses are replaced by science and arts. The contribution of an improved labor force to TFP would be very small over the first few years of the new administration, but should reach measurable levels within a school cohort that is roughly 10–12 years.

A government which abides by the letter and spirit of the law and wows allegiance to European Court of Human Rights (ECHR) and other supra-national court verdicts ought to improve FDI flow somewhat, but how Turkey's arcane licensing and permits system and bureaucratic sleuth can be eliminated is a big question. Nevertheless, even a modest improvement in FDI could help improve Turkey's export value added, as well as ease supply constraints, increasing employment.

A less oppressive and liberal (in the sense of tolerant) government ought to help foster a more innovation-friendly ecosystem, though Turkey's backwardness in terms of producing its own technology and brands has multiple causes, many of which are not derived from government policy.

In terms of climate change and environmental preservation, the new government will also do a better job, because it will be probably more circumspect in extracting rent from the land and backed by an electorate which — according to polls — has a higher level of consciousness on these issues than the AK Parti cronies.

To the extent the new government will allocate fewer public resources to mega-projects in favor of social services, health and education, life expectancy, and quality of life indicators ought to advance, too, though countries like Turkey with still low female labor participation ratios (see Chapter 6 on Turkish Labor Market) will always have problem with longevity and striking the right balance between keeping the young healthy and devoting resources to the elderly.

8.4. The Tail Risk: External Shocks, Internal Fault Lines

The last scenario is selected from the leading Turkish fear about the country's future, namely Kurdish secessionism and its feasibility highlighted by the winter 2019 military campaign in North East Syria (Operation Pace Spring) to presumably eradicate the threat of PKK terror. However, it contains a spoonfull of all three major Turkish social divisions which have to date thwarted the advancement of consensual democracy and economic–social development. Its consequences appear largely negative at this juncture, but one cannot dismiss the possibility of a blessing in disguise.

To explain how Turkey's military involvement in Syrian civil war agitates and churns existing social divisions requires a lengthy intro because the issues are uniquely parochial and difficult for non-Turkish readers to intellectually penetrate.

a. *Turkey's Eternal Fault Lines*

Turkey's geographical location is a blessing and a curse. Because of its central location between the East and West, and cultural–economic links to both, the population has never quite decided in its heart and mind whether it is part of the "Western culture" or the Asiatic tradition. The majority of the Turks' Central Asian origins and adherence to the Sunni branch of the Islamic faith are main anchors pulling it East. On the other hand, the presence of a numerous urban and rich secular class, deeply seeped in the modernizing ideals of Kemalism, economically and culturally integrated into the West, supported by a broader number of citizenry still fond of 600 years of engagement with Europe during the Ottoman Era[24] have pulled the nation West. As a result, when East and West quarrel, Turkey's divided soul is one of the first to suffer.

The nation sits uneasily on top of three, age-long, and so far intractable fault lines, mostly as a result of its unique location and the historic journey that carried its population there.

Sunni versus Alevi: While almost 99% of Turkey's population is nominally Moslem, it is divided into two major sub-faiths, or denominations. The majority are Sunnis, following the traditional teachings of Quran and the four major *imams*. About 10–15% of the population adheres to the Alevi faith, which is a heterodox system of beliefs, incorporating elements from the Shia branch, Anatolian Sufi tradition as well as Turks' shamanists origins dating back to Central Asia. In general, Alevis tend to be more liberal, pro-Western, and secularist than the average Sunni citizen.[25] Regarding its sectarian composition, Turkey straddles the Shia and Sunni Moslem spheres, fitting in neither neatly.

Turk versus Kurd: Roughly 10–15% of the population is Kurdish (probably Indo-European) or has some Kurdish ancestry, which is a completely different ethnic group *vis-a-vis* the Ural–Altaic Turks. Kurds also live as minorities in Syria, Iran, and Iraq. Since 1980s, a bloody international strife between secessionist terror organization PKK and the military left over 45,000 dead, caused mass migration of Kurds to the rest of the country as well as an ever deepening resentment between two ethnic groups, with minority Kurds refusing to assimilate, being subject to discrimination and in some cases persecution. Kurds, as a result of rejection by large segments of the ethnic Turks, have sought and developed strong ties to European human rights and left-wing movements.

Islamists/conservative versus secular/laicist: This is the oldest ideological divide in Turkey, dating back to 18th century Ottoman era, when emperors and the elite had realized that to keep up with rival

---

[24] A very large number of the current population descends from Balkan refugees.

[25] For Alevis' minority status and violence against them, see De Atkine (2019).

Christian empires, a modernization drive is necessary. Since then, the traditionalists and progressives have quarreled incessantly, with Mustafa Kemal Atatürk delivering the progressives a final yet temporary victory by abolishing the Khalifate and introducing several reforms such as the Latin alphabet, modern law, and the dress code. Under the AK Parti administrations, the Islamists struck back, engaging in an ambitious plan to "re-Islamize" Turkey, which has invoked fear and backlash among the still numerous secularists.

Today, Islamists, conservatives, as well as some former left-wingers largely support the idea of a Turkey belonging to the Eastern tradition, while Alevis, most Kurds, most moderate secularists, and an increasing number of urban middle and upper classes are pro-Western. It is estimated that 30–35% of the nation can be classified as pro-Western secularist, with rest being of various degrees of "conservative-Islamist", though the meaning and practice of the latter term is much more nuanced than secularism.[26]

The Republican Era can in one sense be described as one of these groups trying to assimilate others or beating them into submission. These efforts have failed, with all social classes holding historic grudges against each other, as well as inheriting a culture of victors' avenging the vanquished.

Yet, focusing on the eternal divisions of the society may make one miss the strengths of the Republic of Turkey. It is a "nation", despite its disagreements on ideology, ethnicism, and sect, with a strong sense of identity and cohesion at times of external threats, which has belied prophecies of secession, evolving into a Sharia state, or one group completely assimilating others by force.

Turkey is rapidly evolving from a semi-rural to an urban society, which is gradually acting as a melting pot of ethnic, sectarian, and ideological differences. The youth is less inclined to adhere to the said divisions while the new urban bourgeois is more liberal and tolerant in their attitudes. These changes in the society mean that the right catalysts could reduce the eternal divides to mere polite disagreements posing lesser threats to development.

---

[26]There are for instance traditional conservatives, who are not necessarily Islamist.

Recently, the nation demonstrated unity crossing social divides in two major events. In the 2013 Gezi protests, secularists, Kurds, and Alevis stood side by side against the oppressive policies of the AK Parti. In July 2016, a coup inspired by Sunni pastor Fethullah Gülen was resisted by a coalition of conservative-Islamists and secularists.

Probably as important, even though both failed, the AK Parti has initiated several reform drives to voluntarily integrate Alevis and at least one major attempt to solve the Kurdish problem through the Peace Process,[27] which was sabotaged by the PKK, though opposition claims of the AK Parti baiting the PKK cannot be ruled out. Since currently there is no evidence that either initiative will be repeated, this scenario focuses on negative outcomes, however, AK Parti's survival is a testament to its flexibility and its alternative is more open to solving both the Alevi and Kurdish problems.

All this being said, the *status quo* among main social groupings is not sustainable from the perspective of development at a time when Turkey finds itself at the center of several global centrifugal forces led by another hegemonial struggle among the US, Russia,[28] and China, coupled with Islamophobia[29] gradually morphing into Huntington's *Clash of Civilizations*.[30] Turkey's long-term involvement in the Syrian War could turn out to be the cathartic event which could aggravate divisions (more likely scenario) already agitated by the processes mentioned previously, or heal them.

Now, let us move on to our external shock scenario.

b. *Turkey's Syria Entanglement: The Beginning of the End … of What?*

In October 2019, President Erdoğan ordered the Turkish military into North East Syria, a region named Rojova by its Kurdish population,[31] to

---

[27] For Turkey's battle against PKK, see International Crisis Group (2014).

[28] For Turkey's uneasy balancing act between the US and Russia, see "Turkey's juggling act with the US and Russia", Orton (2019).

[29] For Islamophobia in the West, see Gallup (2011).

[30] For a balanced review of the theoretical case and practical examples, see Cropsey and Halem (2018).

[31] There is a dispute about the demographic make-up of the region. Turkey claims the majority is Arab, with sprinkle of ancient Christian sects, while Kurds claim the opposite.

presumably end the terror threat from the reigning political–military entity YPG/PYD, which is closely affiliated with the PKK. To add some context, currently there are 3.6 million Syrian refugees in Turkey, which according to recent polls are becoming a major source of complaint for voters. The Turkish view is that these refugees would not wish to return to a post-war Syria governed by Bashar al-Assad, and an autonomous Kurdish state to the East of Euphrates run by an entity called SDF, or YPG–PYD, which has very strong links to its nemesis, the PKK terror organization. Therefore, Turkish military with the aid of assorted rebel Syrian militia staged several campaigns at the border, capturing Afrin, al Bab, and Azaz cantons (districts), as well as putting up a spirited defense of the Northern portion of the Idlib Province, including the refugee-swollen Idlib city.

Ankara plans to use these beachheads as bargaining tools at the peace table to force Assad into a form of governance giving rebel groups enough say and veto power over decision-making to defend the safety of refugees, when they go back.

The military objective in Operation Peace Spring is to carve out a "safe zone" stretching along a 440 km length of the Turkey–Syria border east of River Euphrates, at least 30 km deep, free of all YPG–PYD elements.

The safe zone will then be used:

- To resettle 1–2 million Syrian refugees in the new zone to be administered by Turkey, reinforcing the resistance to Assad.
- To resuscitate the dormant construction industry through the resettlement project, costed by Erdoğan at US$29 billion, thereby stimulating economic growth and creating jobs.
- To drive a wedge into the concealed partnership among pro-Kurdish Rights HDP and the official opposition alliance of CHP–IYIP–SP–DP.[32]

Since the Damascus government had never conducted a census, there are no official population figures to back either claim.

[32] The "concealed" or non-official member of the opposition alliance the HDP has pro-Kurdish rights which supports the opposition by voting for its candidates in districts where demographically it does not stand a chance. Its leadership has expressed deep frustration with CHP and IYIP which had backed Operation Peace Spring. On the other hand, some

- To cement Erdoğan's popularity among the nationalist voters of his partner Bahçeli's MHP party.
- Finally, to force Syrian President Bashar al-Assad into a peace agreement where the opposition would have a meaningful role and the 3.6 million refugees in Syria, a safe passage to return home.

The incursion stopped in its tracks after Turkish troops and its Syrian ally Syrian National Army (formerly called Free Syrian Army) captured an area of 120 km by 30 km from YPG, *as per* demarcation protocols signed with the US and Russia. However, even the brief hostilities elicited widespread condemnation from the EU, the Arab League, and the US, the last of which is threatening devastating sanctions through the Congress.

As this chapter is written, neither the military nor the eco-political dimension of the Operation Peace Spring is complete, which is one of the reasons why the external shock scenario could go either "bad" or "good" as time evolves.

Politically, President Donald Trump remains supportive of the military campaign. If Erdoğan loses Trump's patronage, Congress will go ahead with the said sanctions, which may be matched by some EU members such as Germany imposing loan restrictions, which could severely undermine economic activity, reducing support for the regime and taking Turkey back to Scenario II (see Section 8.3).

Erdoğan appears to rely on his close friendship with the Russian President Vladimir Putin to extend Turkey's footprint in North East Syria to expand the safe zone to accommodate enough Syrian refugees without clashing with the Syrian Army, which had rapidly moved into positions vacated by YPG–PYD. However, the closest ally of Damascus, Iran is steadfastly against Turkey's presence in Syria, because it is acutely aware that the safe zone interrupts the Shia Wall it intends to erect from Tehran to Lebanon. Thus, harassment by Assad's forces and the still present YPG–PKK guerillas to challenge the safe zone could change the so-far positive public opinion on the Operation Peace Spring, significantly raise the cost of defending it, or even weaken the alliance between Turkey, Iran, and Russia.

---

polls show conservative Kurds who traditionally vote for the AK Parti abandoning it, hence it is not clear which side won a net advantage from the said military incursion.

c. *How Would Such a Scenario Affect Turkey's Development?*

It is important to explore the political consequences of Turkey's Syrian involvement to make judgments about its impact on development.

Turkey has lost the trust of Pentagon and the Congress in the US and the EU by helping Iran–Assad and Russia laying claim to entire Syria, with ties reaching a point where they are becoming very difficult to repair without major political reform and policy alteration by Turkey. Either the regime adopts these policy changes, or it might be the subject of economic sanctions which would deal a blow to economic growth and potentially to the re-election prospects of Erdoğan and the AK Parti.

Turkey has gained the right to stay in Syria for the foreseeable future, probably for the reason of forcing Assad into a final peace agreement which would give the opposition enough voice to make sure Turkey's 3.6 million refugees can go home to a political and security structure which assures their safety. Thus, Assad and Iran are likely to hold a lasting grudge against Turkey for prolonging the war, which they may retaliate by provoking the ISIS–PKK terror and Alevite anger in the future.

Turkey once again got involved in a major regional conflict between the US and Russia, appeasing neither.[33] Lacking the delicacy to play one against each other at a time when relations between them is deteriorating may draw the wrath of one or the other, forcing Turkey to take sides, which would deepen the Islamist–Secularist divide at home.

If Turkey remains in Syria, the cost of administering a large territory with mostly hostile inhabitants and open to guerilla/terror attacks will be paid through higher taxes and/or lower state services at home, further increasing voter discontent.

Finally and most importantly, Turkey dealt a lethal blow to Syrian Kurds' aspirations of an autonomous homeland where they can live free of Assad's oppression, ISIS harassment, and Turkish military threats, dislocating an estimated 100,000–200,000 civilians from their homes. Most of these newly displaced have tribal or family links in Turkey, which spills the Kurdish anger at home. Additionally, Syrian Kurds are now

---

[33] The chapter makes ample reference to the conflicts between Turkey and the US. For the fragility of Turko-Russian relations, see Has (2019).

herded into a narrow piece of land between Ras-al-Ayn, Haseke, and the Iraqi border, still under the nominal influence of the PKK, which will find it easy to direct Kurdish anguish toward new terror campaigns in Turkey and justify its agenda of separatism. At home, two recent polls reveal the share of Kurds' voting for the AK Parti dropping visibly.

Going forward, it is important to make a guess about whether Erdoğan and the AK Parti will remain in power. This chapter operates under the assumption that the Syrian involvement will not change voter dynamics to the extent of deciding the next election, where the regime's ability to manipulate or buy public opinion will win the day. This assumption, takes the narrative back to Scenario I (see Section 8.2, Erdoğan remains in power for the foreseeable future, retarding Turkey's development) where the regime remains in power for the foreseeable future, with strongly negative results for development.

On the other hand, the lesser likely scenario must also be considered. A large number of conservative Kurdish votes could gravitate from AKP to HDP, which is nominally allied with the opposition block. Already retreating in polls, both Erdoğan and the AK Parti–MHP alliance could lose the next elections (Scenario II, Erdoğan goes back to pragmatism or is replaced by a centrists coalition employing orthodox policies, Section 8.3). Turkey may be ruled by a coalition of several parties representing different ideologies, which may be able to solve the Kurdish and Alevite problems, as it shall be a constellation of parties which favor the Kurdish equality cause (HDP, CHP) and Alevite rights (CHP).

While this scenario is speculative, it turns the external shock into an "upside risk", because the new administration may decide to grant Turkey's Kurds equal citizenship rights, at the same time befriending YPG–PYD in Syria, provided that it promises to sever all links with the PKK terror organization.[34] This is an optimal solution to Turkey's twin dilemmas of the Kurdish segregation and threats from Syria, because Ankara becomes the *de facto* protector of Kurds in the region, building a buffer state in Syria against terror and Assad's provocation, as well as making progress toward isolating PKK from the general Kurdish population. Finally, as Kurdish unrest eases and Syrian Kurds come under the umbrella of the Turkish trading zone, war expenses are replaced with rapid development of Kurdish regions and a "peace dividend".

---

[34] According to press sources in Turkey, such a solution has been put forth by the US, which also promised to help eradicate the PKK, but had been rejected by the Turkish government.

However, the chapter prefers to explore the implications of the current regime staying in power to remain consistent with the first two scenarios, wherein this possibility was ranked superior to a change in administration.

The regime intends preserving Turkey's dominions in Syria and relocating a large number of Syrian refugees there, which can be subject to sanctions by US and EU members. Sanctions of an economic nature, such as curtailment of trade credit guarantees, or syndicated loans, could deepen the current economic stagnation and raise the specter of another currency shock similar to the one experienced in August 2018. To recall, the said shock had caused a 30% depreciation of the TL vs the dollar, passing through rapidly to inflation for a period of 12 months and causing deep distress for the heavily FX indebted private sector, triggering a recession.

The current regime is likely to use the threat of terror as a pretext to delay political and judicial reforms, accelerating the decline of institutions and the exodus of liberal and well-educated members of the society. As discussed in Scenario I, brain drain and further hallowing out of fundamental institutions of democracy and free markets would retard growth and development, with consequences very similar to the said scenario.

Ethnic segregation is very likely to seep into the education system through bans of Kurdish language and persecution of politically active Kurds and (Alevi) dissidents, further reducing the quality of the curriculum and raising cohorts ill-suited for the job requirements of the 21st century.

Public health and average living age could deteriorate as a result of a higher share of budget revenues being dedicated to defense and security, as discrimination against minorities, emergence of sub-cultures being refused treatment (or receiving less than their fair share thereof), costly guerilla wars, and most importantly the inability to import costly Western medical equipment (because of potential sanctions or lack of Health Ministry funds).

Culturally, visa restrictions as a result of the internal strife and hostility in some nations with large Kurdish populations could retard Turkey's integration into the world community.

8.5. Conclusion: *Quo Vadis* Turkey?

Every good story deserves a conclusion, but this one makes a point of leaving the final scene to the imagination of the reader. The conclusion, if it can be called such, is that the prevailing majority views about Turkey's future must be questioned thoroughly from an impartial point of view with the audience being ready to discard "conventional wisdom" quickly, as events unfold over the winter of 2019–2020.

What is the prevailing view? By the end of 2019, pessimism about Turkey was the predominant episteme among scholars and the public. The most recent survey by Ada Surveying Agency found that 72% of the participants lost faith in the future. In the academic and scholarly debate, a majority held the opinion that by invading a portion of North East Syria, President Erdoğan managed to turn the tide of voter discontent and prolonged his shelf life.[35] In addition, the view that the initial "victory" in Syria became the harbinger of long-term turbulence was also frequently voiced.

These views seem to strengthen the path for Turkey discussed in Scenario I, i.e., the current regime staying in power for the foreseeable future, acting as a drag on the country's development. Yet, the dividend from Operation Peace Spring is ephemeral, while economic discontent is the direct result of the regime's polices of dismantling the democracy. Thus, the majority view about Turkey's future underestimates the very visible discontent of the population with the current regime and its habit of endlessly seeking adventures abroad while overstating its staying power.

At the end, it is too simplistic to write the story of Turkey from the perspective of President Erdoğan and his AK Parti, relegating other actors and the will of the people to mere side players. Turkey has a 70-year-love affair with democracy, as attested by voluntary voting rates of over 80%, frequent changes of governments, and a tradition of severely punishing fraudsters. At the end, it will not be external actors, or the whims of a man or party, which shall dictate Turkey's future. It will be *Vox Populi, Vox Dei.*

Populi has not spoken yet.

References

Acemoğlu, D., Naidu, S., Restrepo, P. and Robinson, J. A. (2019). "Democracy Does Cause Growth", *Journal of Political Economy*, Vol. 127, No. 1, pp. 47–100.

---

[35]Turkey's Syria incursion brightens Erdoğan's political horizon, see *Wall Street Journal* (2019).

Acemoğlu, D. and Robinson, J. (2012). *Why Nations Fail*, Crown Publishing Group.

Acemoğlu, D. and Üçer, M. (2015). "The Ups and Downs of Turkish Growth, 2002–2015: Political Dynamics, the European Union and the Institutional Slide", *The Search for Europe: Contrasting Approaches,* BBVA Open Mind Press.

Amnesty International (2013). "Gezi Park Protests, Brutal Denial of the Right to Peaceful Assembly in Turkey", Amnesty International Report.

Ayata, S. (2017). "Gençler AK Parti'den Niye Kopuyor?", https://t24.com.tr/yazarlar/sencer-ayata/gencler-akpden-neden-kopuyor,17824.

Aydıntaşbaş, A. (2019). "The Battle of Istanbul Will Shape Turkey's Future, European Council on Foreign Relations". https://www.ecfr.eu/article/commentary_the_battle_of_istanbul_will_shape_turkeys_future#.

Aydogus, O. (2017). "Sorunlu Milli Gelir Revizyonu ve Kuşkulu Büyüme", *İktisat ve Toplum Dergisi*, Vol. 78, pp. 4–9.

Bekdil, B. (2019). Turkish "Brain Drain", Middle East Forum. https://www.meforum.org/57577/turkish-brain-drain.

BIA News Desk (2019). "Turkey Ranks Worse in Rule of Law Index". http://bianet.org/english/law/206052-turkey-ranks-worse-in-rule-of-law-index.

Cropsey, S. and Harry, H. (2018). "Clash of Civilizations — Or Clash Within Civilizations? The American Interest". https://www.the-american-interest.com/2018/08/31/clash-of-civilizations-or-clash-within-civilizations/.

De Atkine, N. B. (2019). "The Alevis Dilemma — Turkey's Erdogan Sets a Religious Minority on a Collision Course with Erdogan's Turkey". https://limacharlienews.com/politics-society/alevis-dilemma/.

Gürcan, M. (2017). "Bir Daha Asla! Ama Nasıl? 15 Temmuz Sonrasında Ordu". https://t24.com.tr/yazarlar/metin-gurcan/bir-daha-asla-ama-nasil-15-temmuz-sonrasinda-ordu,17133.

International Crisis Group (2014). "Turkey and the PKK: Saving the Peace Process", *Europe Report*, No. 234.

Gallup (2011). "Islamophobia: Understanding Anti-Muslim Sentiment in the West". https://news.gallup.com/poll/157082/islamophobia-understanding-anti-muslim-sentiment-west.aspx.

Halis, M. (2019). "Babacan's Movement Creates Panic among Turkey's Ruling Party". https://middle-east-online.com/en/babacan%E2%80%99s-movement-creates-panic-among-turkey%E2%80%99s-ruling-party.

Has, K. (2019). "Türkiye-Rusya Ilişkilerinde Üç Risk, Bir Fırsat", KARAR Gazetesil. https://www.karar.com/gorusler/turkiye-rusya-iliskilerinde-uc-risk-bir-firsat-1388928.

International Crisis Group (2014). "Turkey, Syria and Saving the PKK Peace Process", ICG. https://www.crisisgroup.org/europe-central-asia/westerneuropemediterranean/turkey/turkey-syria-and-saving-pkk-peace-process.

Israel, S. (2018). "What is Development, Sid Security for International Development". https://www.sid-israel.org/en/Development-Issues/What-is-Development.

Malik, N. (2019). "The Spectre of Syria Silenced Arab Protest. But Now It's Finding Its Voice". https://www.theguardian.com/commentisfree/2019/oct/21/syria-arab-spring-egypt-sudan-syria.

Orton, K. (2019). "Turkey's Juggling Act with the US and Russia", Observer Research Foundation. https://www.orfonline.org/expert-speak/turkeys-juggling-act-with-the-us-and-russia-53243/.

Metropoll Survey (2019). "Metropoll: Babacan ve Davutoğlu'nun Seçime Etkisi ne Olur?", https://www.paraanaliz.com/2019/siyaset-ve-kamu-haberleri/metropoll-babacan-ve-davutoglunun-secime-etkisi-ne-olur-39855/.

Pitel, L. (2019). "Turkey: Old Friends Threaten Recep Tayyip Erdogan's Reign". https://www.ft.com/content/4514ad9c-dbd6-11e9-8f9b-77216ebe1f17.

Rodrik, D. (2011). "Ergenekon and Sledgehammer, Building or Undermining the Law", *Turkish Policy Quarterly*, Vol. 10, No. 1, pp. 99–109.

Rodrik, D. (n.d.), "Ergenekon and Sledgehammer: Building or Undermining the Rule of Law?", *Turkish Policy Quarterly*, Vol. 10, No. 1, pp. 99–109.

Schwerin, U. (2018). "The Gulen Movement and the Failed Coup in Turkey, Harmless is not the Word", *Qantara.de*.

Serchuk, V. (2018). "The Myth of Authoritarian Competence", *The Atlantic*.

Turkey, Trade and Investment Statistical Note (2017). "OECD International Trade, Foreign Direct Investment and Global Value Chains Reports".

Wall Street Journal (2019). "Turkey's Syria Incursion Brightens Erdogan's Political Horizon". https://ahvalnews.com/recep-tayyip-erdogan/turkeys-syria-incursion-brightens-erdogans-political-horizon-wsj.

World Bank (2018). "The Changing Wealth of Nations 2018", in Glenn-Marie Lange, Quentin Wodon, and Kevin Carey (eds.), *Building a Sustainable Future*, World Bank Group Publications.

Yeni Çağ Gazetesi (2019). "KONDA: AKP'nin Çekirdek Seçmeni Yüzde 38'den 27'ye Düştü". https://www.yenicaggazetesi.com.tr/konda-akpnin-cekirdek-secmeni-yuzde-38den-27ye-dustu-241950h.htm.

Yetkin, M. (2019). "Ankara'da Küçük Siyasi Yer Sarsıntılarına Hazır Olun", Yetkin blog. https://yetkinreport.com/2019/10/04/ankarada-kucuk-siyasi-yer-sarsintilarina-hazir-olun/.

Index

Printed in the United States
by Baker & Taylor Publisher Services